CW01198123

# ANGKOR
SPLENDORS OF THE KHMER CIVILIZATION

WHITE STAR PUBLISHERS

## Text by
*MARILIA ALBANESE*

### Editorial Project
*VALERIA MANFERTO DE FABIANIS*
*LAURA ACCOMAZZO*

### Editorial Coordination
*MARIA VALERIA URBANI GRECCHI*

### Graphic Design
*CLARA ZANOTTI*

### Translation
*A.B.A. - MILAN*

WHITE STAR PUBLISHERS

WS White Star Publishers® is a registered trademark
property of De Agostini Libri S.p.A.

© 2002, 2013 De Agostini Libri S.p.A.
Via G. da Verrazano, 15
28100 Novara, Italy
www.whitestar.it - www.deagostini.it

Revised Edition

All rights reserved. No part of this publication may be reproduced,
stored in a retrieval system or transmitted in any form or by any means,
electronic, mechanical, photocopying, recording or otherwise, without
written permission from the publisher.

ISBN 978-88-544-0751-0
1 2 3 4 5 6   17 16 15 14 13

Printed in China

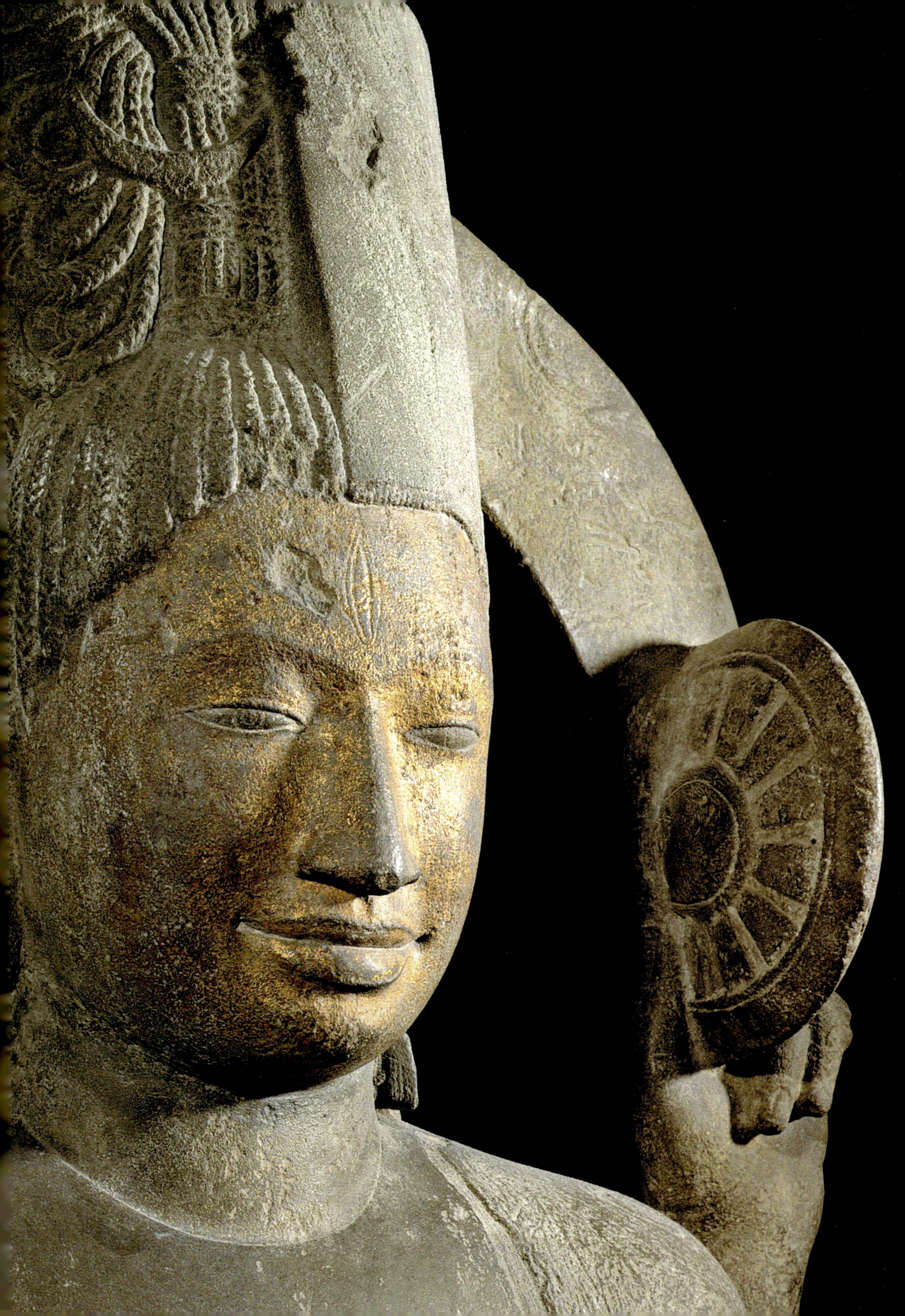

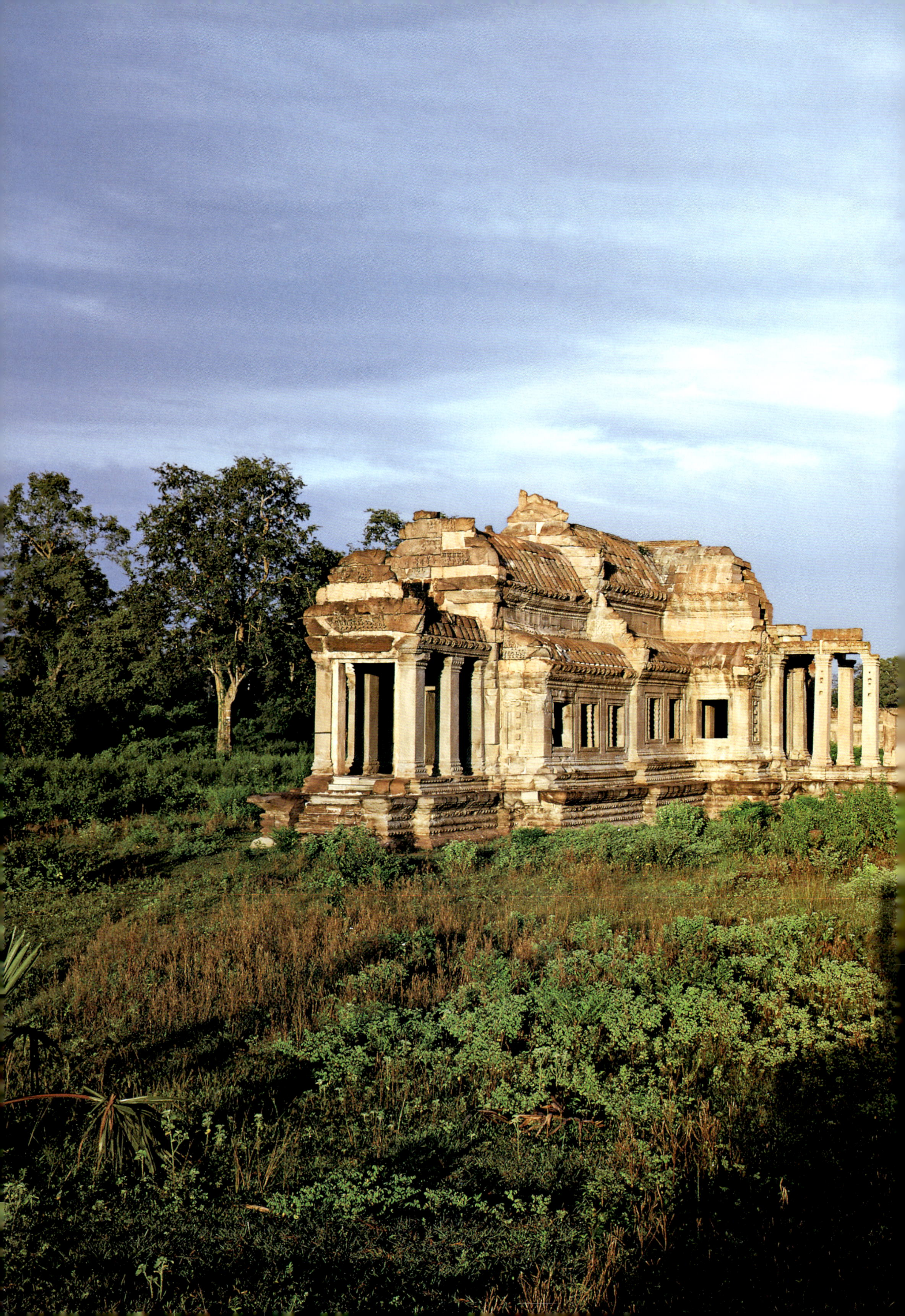

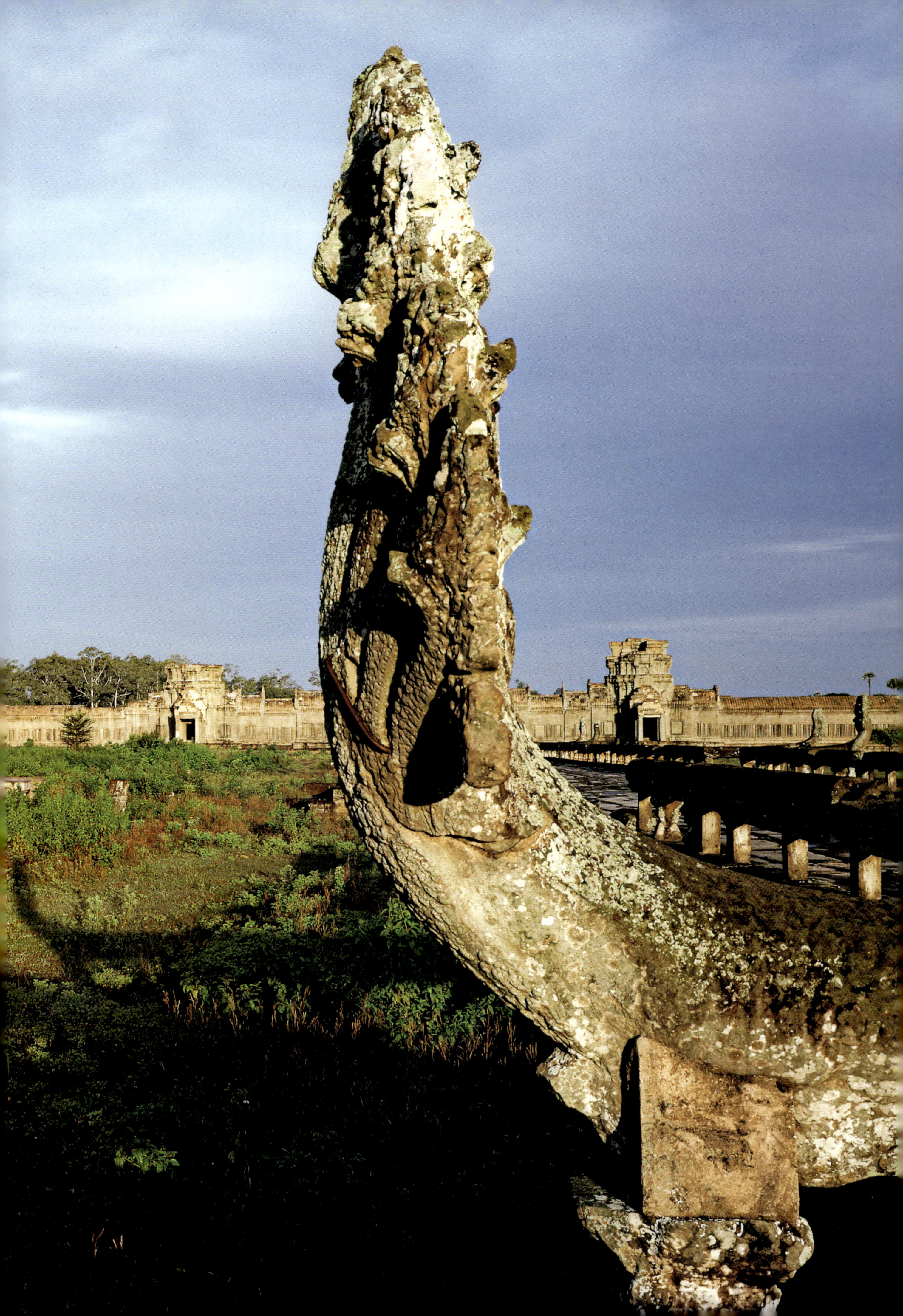

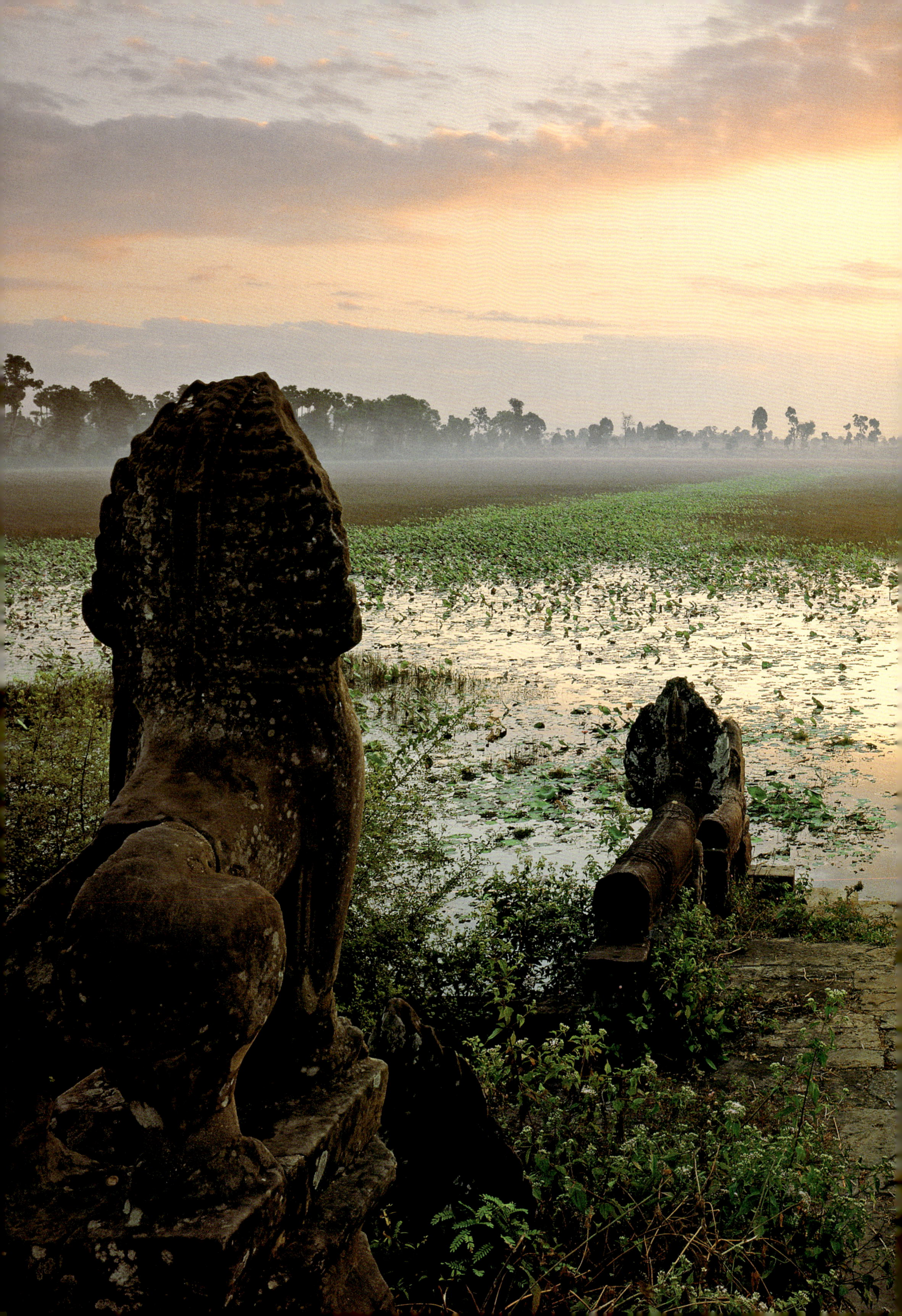

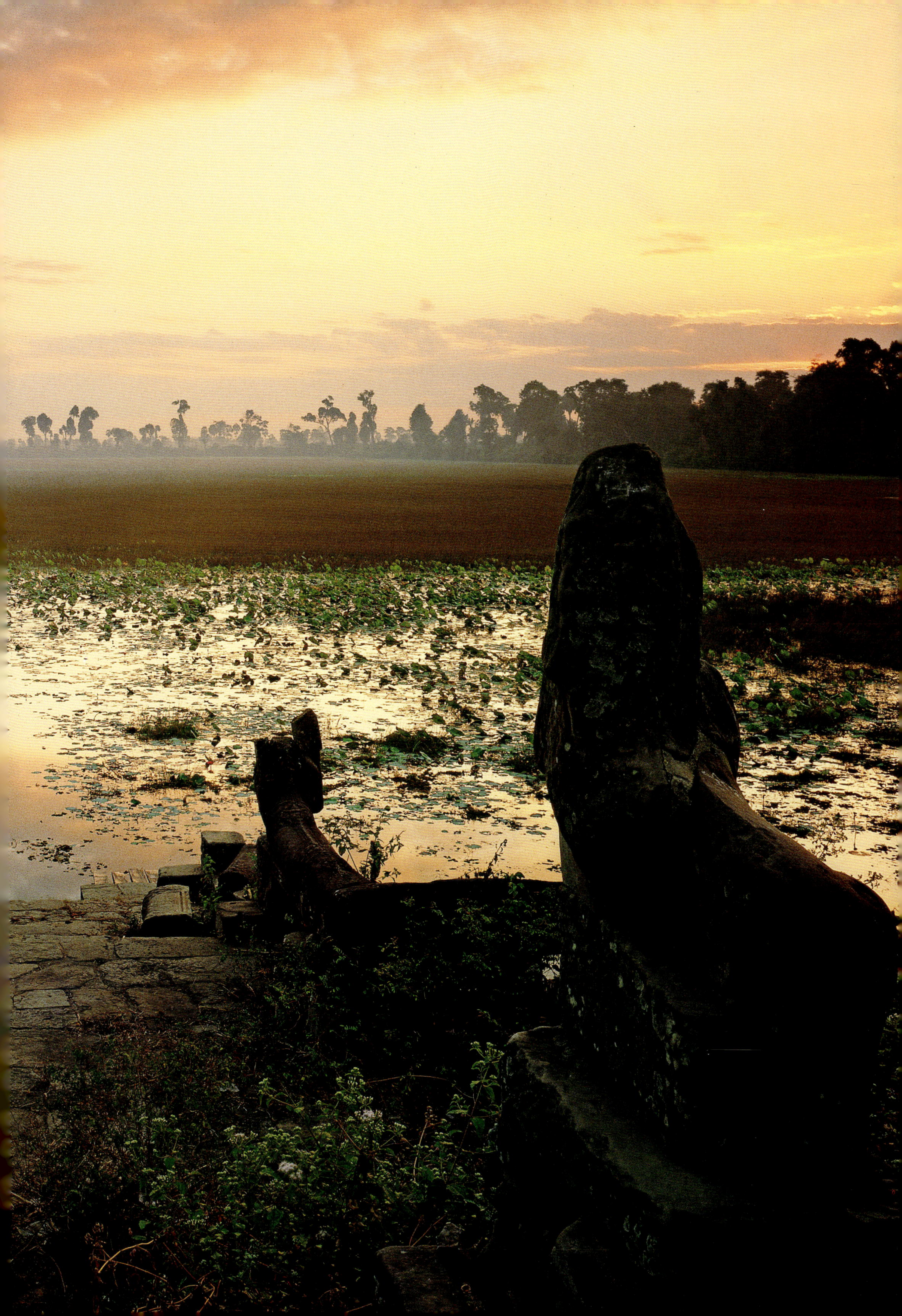

1 and 2  Between the ninth and thirteenth centuries, the Khmer produced some exquisite works of art in which attention was lavished on the smallest details. These two photos show details from the decoration of Phnom Chisor, dating to the eleventh century.

3  In this seventh-century Harihara, in the Phnom Da style, found at Angkor Borei and now in the Guimet Museum, in Paris, the gods Vishnu and Shiva merge, emphasizing the uniqueness of the Divine.

4-5  Although the history of Khmer civilization have been reconstructed from inscriptions, a great deal is still a mystery. One example is the "libraries," like this one at Angkor Wat, whose real purpose is still unknown.

6-7  One of the most important features of the Khmer empire was the irrigation system, which enabled three rice crops to be harvested every year. This complex network was based on reservoirs called baray, formed by constructing embankments. This photo shows Srah Srang, begun in the tenth century and renovated in the twelfth.

8  The mudra (positions of the fingers) are essential to understanding the spiritual message conveyed by statues. These bronze hands of Buddha in the Phnom Penh National Museum express a teaching attitude. The lotus on the palm is one of the characteristic signs of the Enlightened One.

9  The apsaras (bewitching nymphs) and devatas (female deities of sublime beauty), like this example from Angkor Wat at Angkor, are portrayals in stone of the celestial creatures that graced the palaces of the gods, which were reproduced in the Khmer temples.

# CONTENTS

| | |
|---|---|
| PREFACE | Page 10 |
| THE HISTORY FROM ITS ORIGINS TO THE FOURTEENTH CENTURY | Page 18 |
| CHRONOLOGY | Page 50 |
| KHMER COSMOLOGY AND EVERYDAY LIFE | Page 60 |
| REALMS OF IMMORTALITY: ARCHAEOLOGICAL ITINERARIES | Page 146 |
| GLOSSARY | Page 290 |
| INDEX | Page 291 |
| BIBLIOGRAPHY | Page 295 |
| PHOTOGRAPHIC CREDITS | Page 296 |

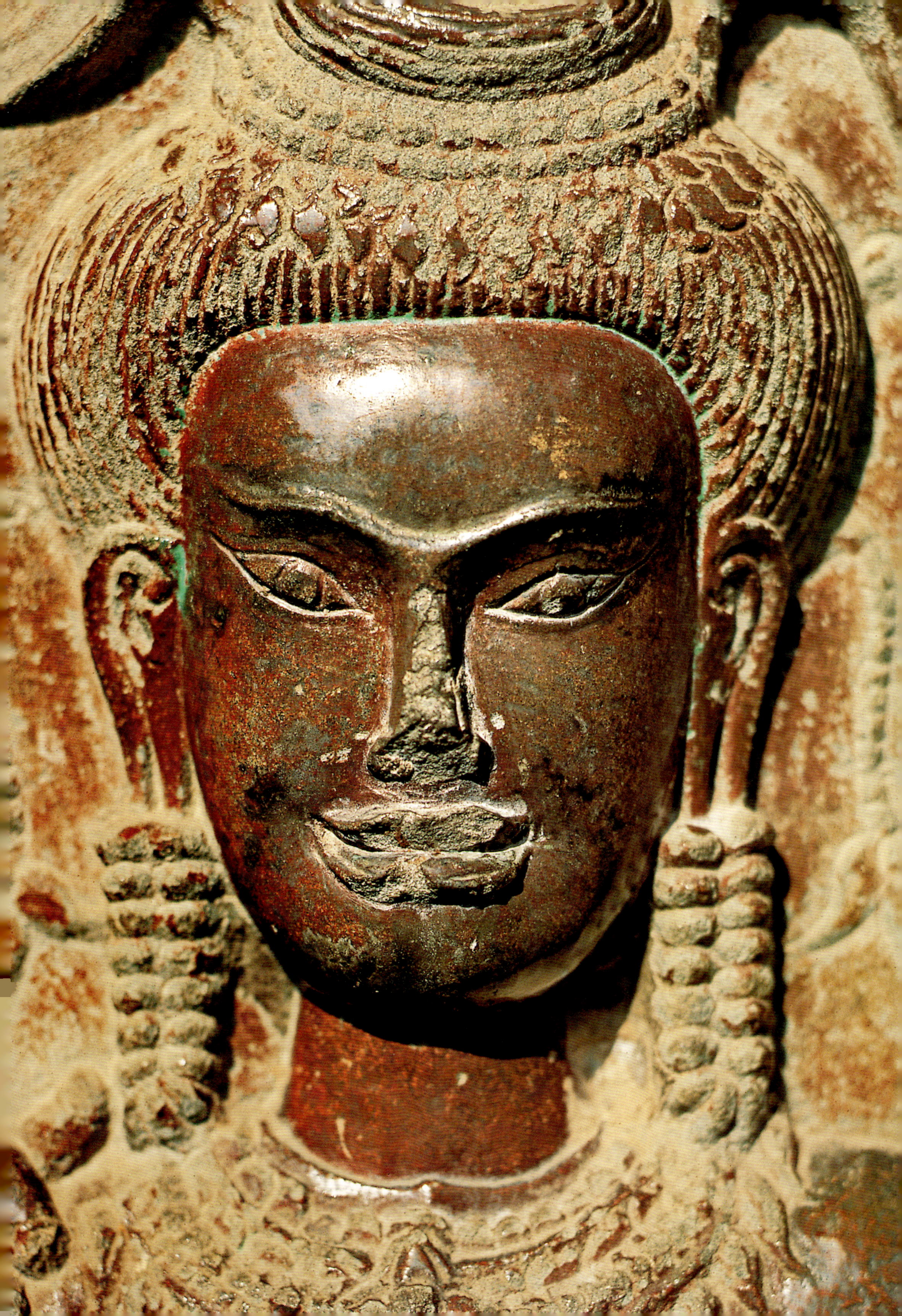

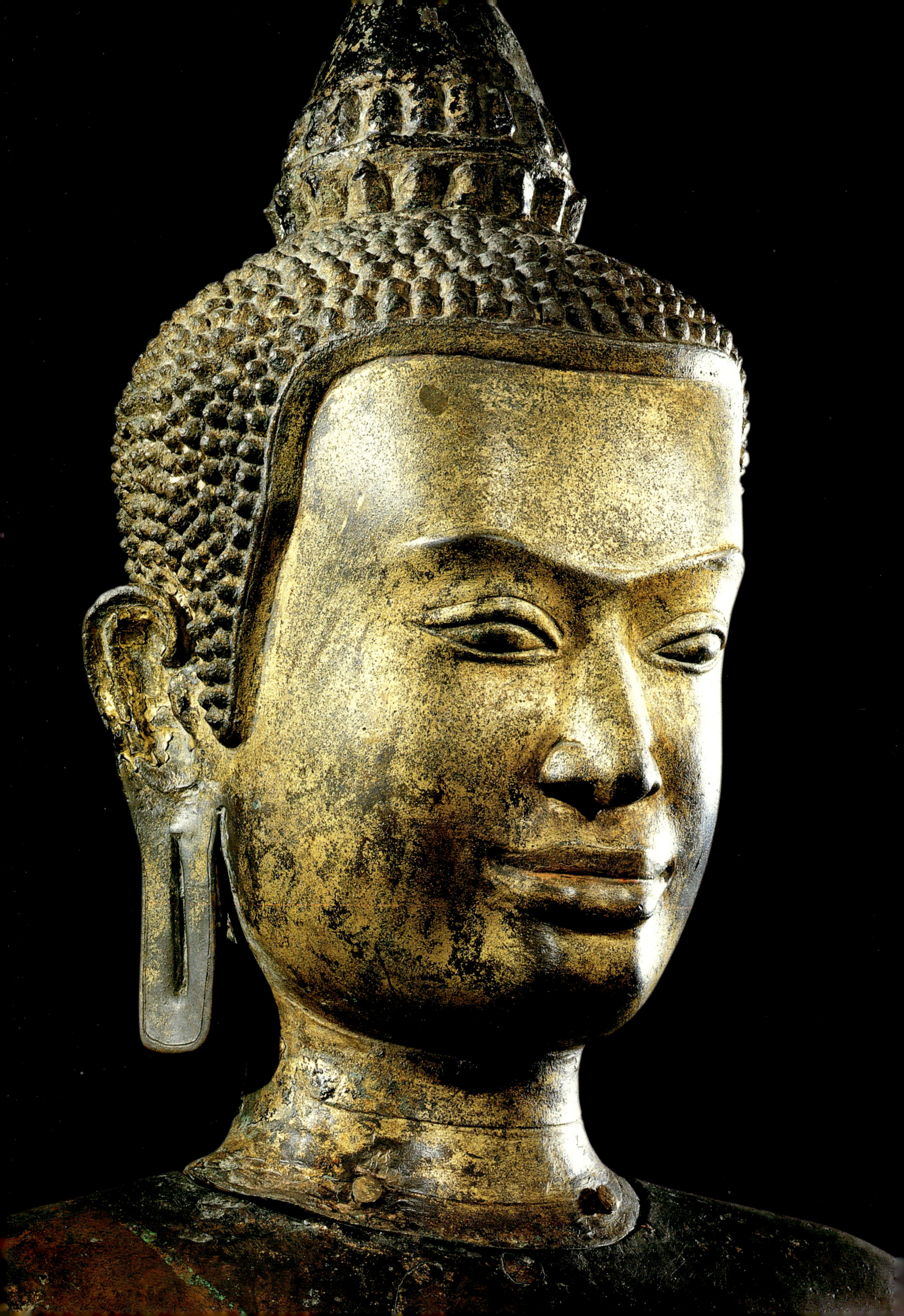

# PREFACE

*10 Hinduism and Buddhism were both present in the Khmer region. Until the twelfth century the official court religion was Hinduism, but later sovereigns converted to the message of Buddha. This gilded bronze Buddha, dating from the late thirteenth century, is housed in the Guimet Museum in Paris.*

Between the ninth and thirteenth centuries, Indochina witnessed the emergence of one of the most powerful and fascinating empires in the history of the Khmer empire. The extent and splendor of this civilization is demonstrated by the numerous buildings scattered over an area which included Laos and part of Thailand in addition to present-day Cambodia. Though influenced by India, the Khmer developed their own special culture, drawing on their ancestral heritage and adapting Hindu and Buddhist customs to their society. Their religious beliefs are magnificently reflected by the temples, the only structures to be made of durable materials (brick and stone) because they were the dwelling-places of the immortal Lords of Heaven.

In addition to their architectural, sculptural, and decorative beauty, the charm of the temples is increased by their location. Inspired by a cosmic symbolism designed to guarantee the fertility of the soil and the prosperity of the kingdom, the palaces of the gods were built in the middle of lakes of various sizes, connected to one another by a network of channels supplied with water by a complex hydraulic system. This water system made the Khmer Empire unique, and its center on the Angkor plain was transformed into the greatest rice-producing area in Indochina. This amazing feat was the result of a happy combination of symbolic conventions and practical needs, put into practice by brilliant warrior sovereigns inspired by the Indian concepts of absolute monarchy and the local cults of the genius loci and deified ancestors. The construction of the temples, in strict accordance with magical-symbolic criteria, conveyed divine forces to earth and turned the sovereign, who acted as their intermediary, into an incarnation of divinity.

Little or nothing would be known about Khmer history if the temples had not borne inscriptions that help reconstruct the lives of the country's sovereigns and the basic concepts that inspired their religious, political, and social beliefs. The inscriptions cast some light on the genealogies, feats, and beliefs of the kings and their courts, although they are always adapted to give them a legendary, or at least highly eulogistic, tone. However, the daily life of the population would have been wholly unknown without the bas-reliefs, codes illustrated on the stone of the temple walls, which show scenes from everyday life in the background.

The Customs of Cambodia, written by Chinese official Zhou Daguan, who stayed at Angkor from August 1296 to July 1297, are even more valuable in this respect. The huge patchwork of paddy fields, interspersed with lakes and studded with the pyramid-shaped mountain temples symbolizing Mount Meru, the hub of the universe, was crowded with exquisite wooden palaces, huts, markets, carts, canoes, animals, and people. The first part of Daguan's volume recounts the history of the country, while the second reconstructs the life of the Khmer as far as possible, from the Indianized courtiers to the workers in the paddy fields, describing the main religious concepts, the most widespread legends, and the social structure. Where Zhou Daguan's iconographical sources or accounts are

*12-13 Khmer decoration is based on repetitive patterns and their symmetrical, centered construction, as in this example from Angkor Wat in which floral scrolls are arranged around a praying figure. The very slight relief of the carving creates a tapestry motif.*

inadequate, observations of contemporary life in Cambodia have been drawn upon, which in many respects has changed little in a thousand years. This book has consequently described everyday scenes, dominated by the powerful figure of the sovereign, who acted as the link between heaven and earth, Lord of the Waters, and guarantor of his people's lives. The Khmer kings, convinced of their divinity, subordinated art and religion to their apotheosis, using the country's resources to build magnificent celestial dwellings in an architectural profusion that was ultimately to cause the collapse of Angkor civilization. The most important monuments of this unique, fascinating art with its romantic, intriguing charm are reconstructed in the third part of this book, which describes a number of archaeological itineraries in Cambodia and the neighboring countries.

Once again, the most striking factor to emerge from the petrified past, clasped in the tentacles of the jungle, is the personality of the kings, who were hungry for power but even more desirous of immortality. The most outstanding example is the last great Emperor of Angkor, Jayavarman VII, who at the height of his power guessed that the end was approaching and unconsciously sought in vain to avoid it with frenetic building activity. Jayavarman VII, ascetic and sensual, philanthropist and tyrant who, like all Buddhists, sought nirvana, the extinction of life, yet was profoundly convinced of his divine essence and consequently desirous of eternity, was the very incarnation of the twilight period that was to reign for two more centuries after his death. After that, a long night of oblivion fell over Angkor, and its splendors were not to be rediscovered by Europeans until the late nineteenth century.

Yet another period of darkness descended on Cambodia in the 1970s with the hideous genocide that weighs on the conscience of mankind and above all the countries of the West, which pretended to be unaware of it out of indifference, convenience, or shameful political choice. Now, Cambodia has finally come back to life, fully aware of its heritage and determined to preserve it.

This volume pays homage to Khmer civilization and expresses the heartfelt wish that the people of Cambodia may be able to walk in the bright light of morning once again.

*14-15 The sovereign was the center of the country's political and religious life, and his deification derived not so much from Indian influence as from Indochinese ancestor worship. The faces on the towers of Bayon, the central temple of Angkor Thom during the twelfth/ thirteenth century, have the features of Jayavarman VII, as shown in this picture.*

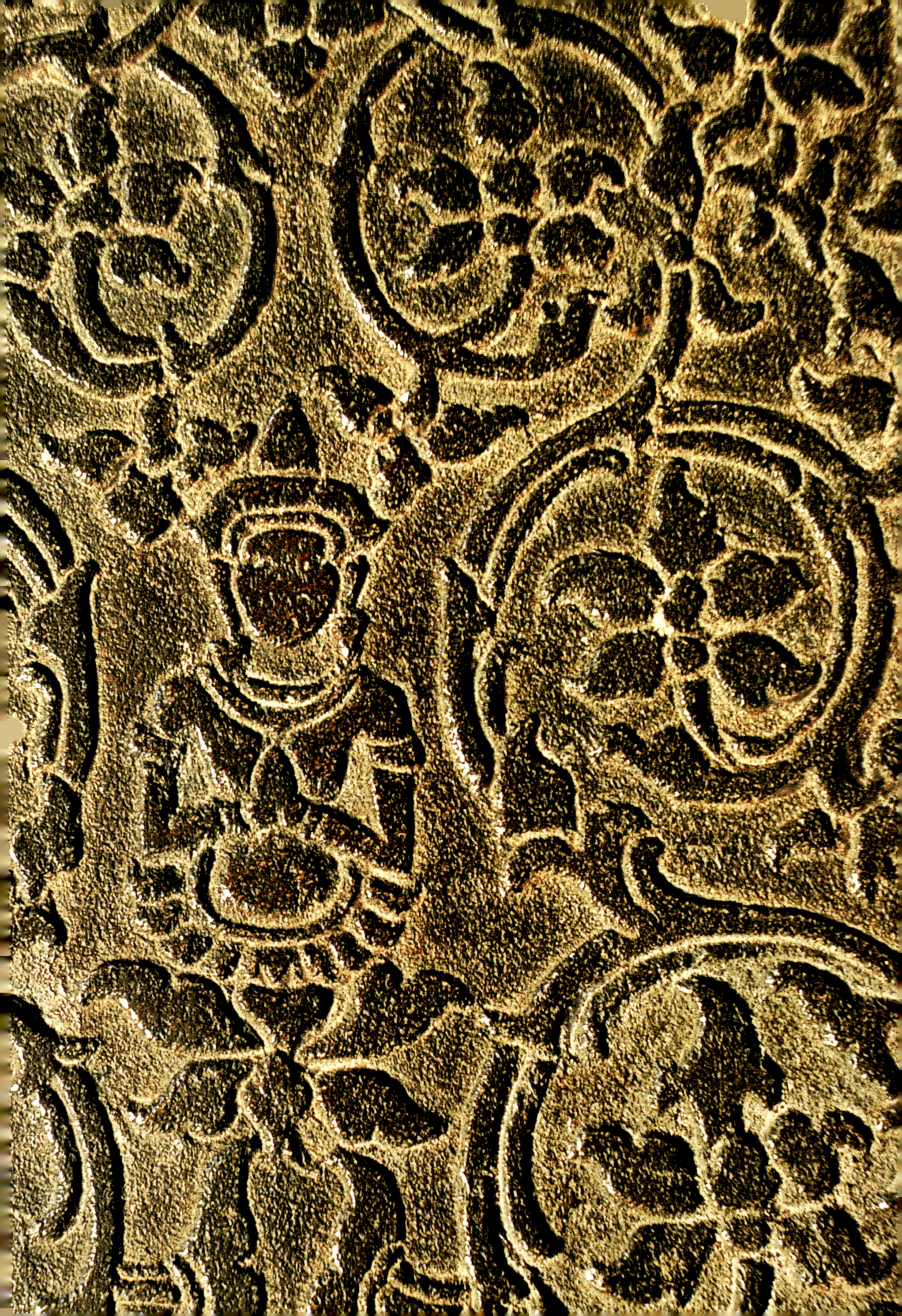

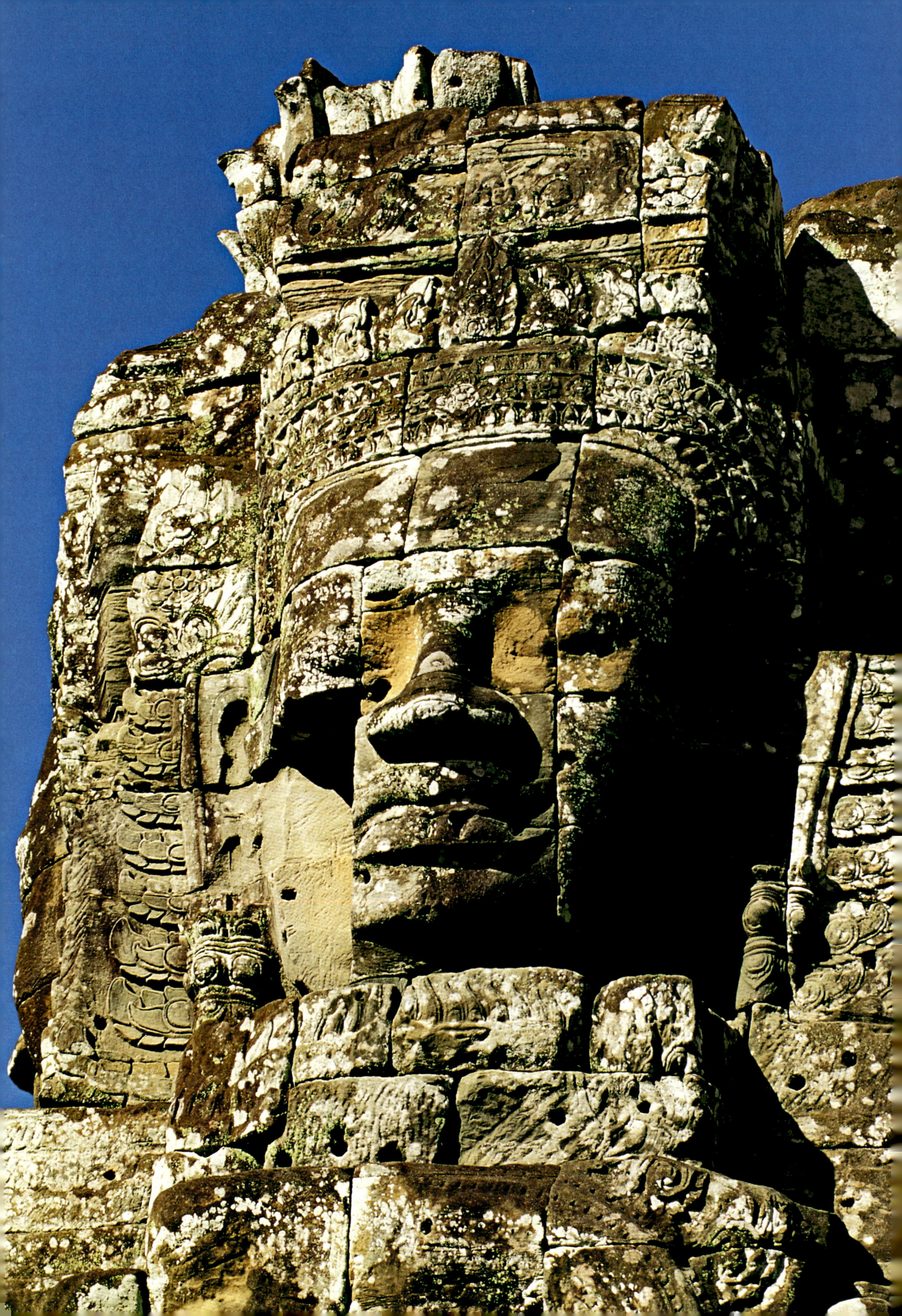

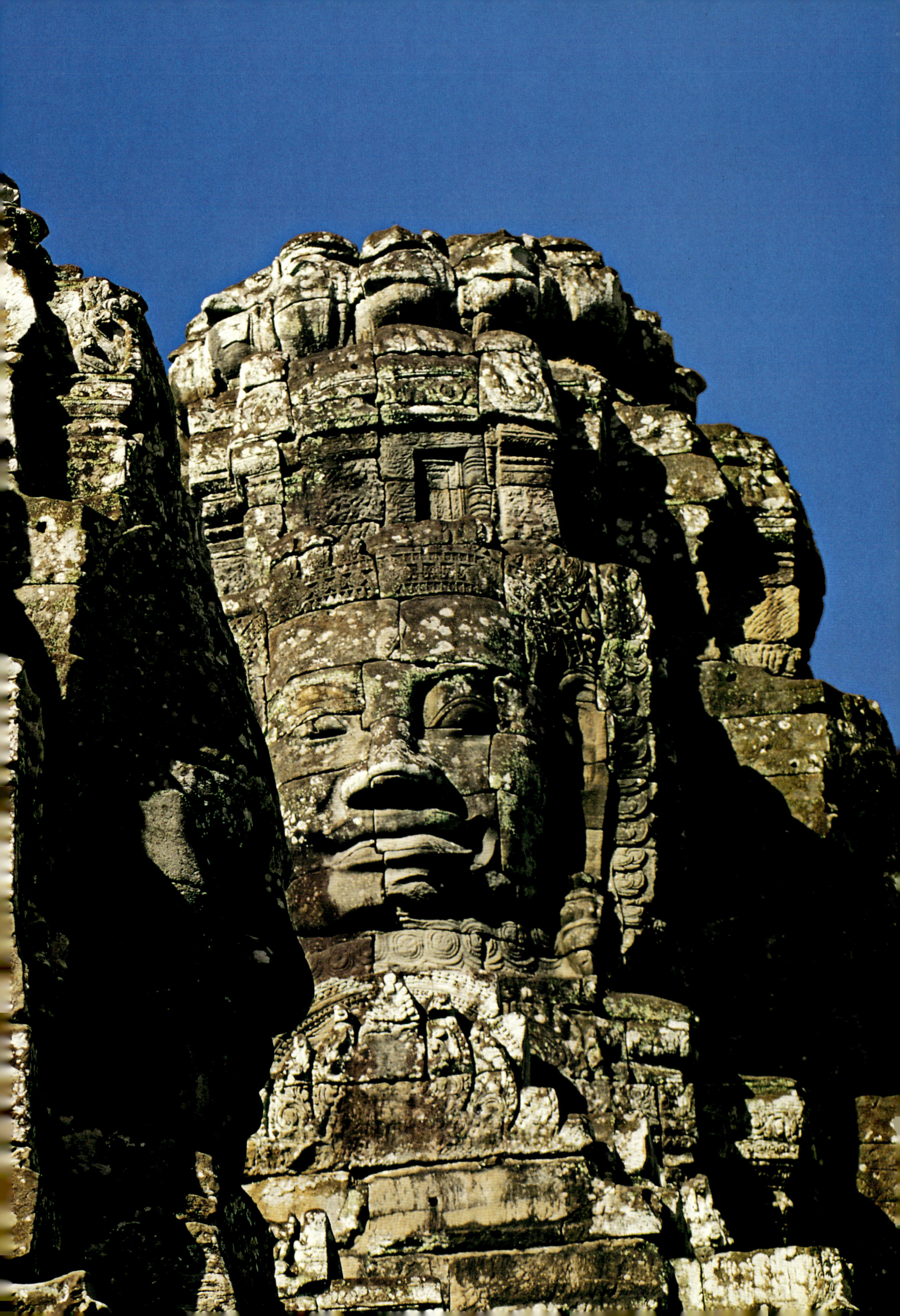

*16 These* dvarapala *(gatekeepers), depicted in the flower of their youth, guard the 10th-century Banteay Srei temple, armed with lances.*

|   | PLACE |
|---|---|
| 1 | DONG SON |
| 2 | HARIPUNJAYA |
| 3 | SUKHOTHAI |
| 4 | LOBPURI |
| 5 | AYUTHYA |
| 6 | PHIMAI |
| 7 | PHNOM RUNG |
| 8 | TA MUEN THOM |
| 9 | PREAH VIHEAR |
| 10 | VAT PHU |
| 11 | MI SON |
| 12 | BANTEAY CHMAR |
| 13 | KOH KER |
| 14 | SDOK KAK THOM |
| 15 | BANTEAY SREI |
| 16 | ANGKOR |
| 17 | BENG MEALEA |
| 18 | ROLUOS |
| 19 | SAMBOR PREI KUK |
| 20 | KOMPONG THOM (KOMPONG SVAY) |
| 21 | SAMBOR |
| 22 | SAMRONG SEN |
| 23 | PREI NOKOR |
| 24 | LOVEK |
| 25 | PREI VENG |
| 26 | ANGKOR BOREI |
| 27 | PHNOM CHISOR |
| 28 | OC-ÉO |
| 29 | TAMBRALINGA (LIGOR) |
| 30 | CHANTABURI |

✱ *Researchers have so far been unable to determine the borders of the ancient Indochinese kingdoms with certainty. Funan probably lay along the Gulf of Siam, between the lower Menam valley and the Mekong delta, incorporating southern Cambodia; at the height of its glory its influence extended to Burma and the Malay peninsula. Chenla must have included the lower Menam valley and the Mun valley in present-day Thailand, together with what is now southern Laos and part of northeastern Cambodia, possibly stretching as far as the Annamite coast. The Kingdom of Champa lay along the coasts of Annam and Cochin China in present-day Vietnam.*

CHINA

MYANMAR
(BURMA)

Gulf of
Tonkin

LAOS

Saluen River

THAILAND

Menam River

Mun River

1
2
3
4
5
6
7
8

Dangrek
Mountains

* CHENLA

9
10
11 *

CHAMPA

Kulen
Mountain

CAMBODIA

VIETNAM

12
13
14
15
16
17
18
19
20
21
22
23

Tonlé Sap
Lake

Tonlé Sap River

Mekong River

Andaman
Sea

30

24 25
26
27

Gulf of
Siam

28 * FUNAN

29

South China Sea

Strait of
Malacca

SUMATRA       MALAYSIA

# THE HISTORY

## FROM ITS ORIGINS TO THE FOURTEENTH CENTURY

~~~

*THE HISTORY OF KAMBUJA*
*Page 20*

*FUNAN AND THE MOUNTAIN KINGS*
*Page 22*

*CHENLA AND THE ADVENT OF THE KHMER*
*Page 28*

*ANGKOR, PLAIN OF CAPITALS*
*Page 32*

*AN EVER-EXPANDING EMPIRE*
*Page 36*

*BUDDHA, THE SUPREME LORD*
*Page 42*

*CHRONOLOGY*
*Page 50*

*ANGKOR, THE REDISCOVERY*
*Page 56*

*18-19 The battle fought at Kurukshetra, a field north of Delhi, between the armies of the Pandavas and the Kauravas, the mythical protagonists of the Mahabharata, is portrayed in the south wing of the west gallery of Angkor Wat and symbolizes the eternal clash between the forces of good and evil.*

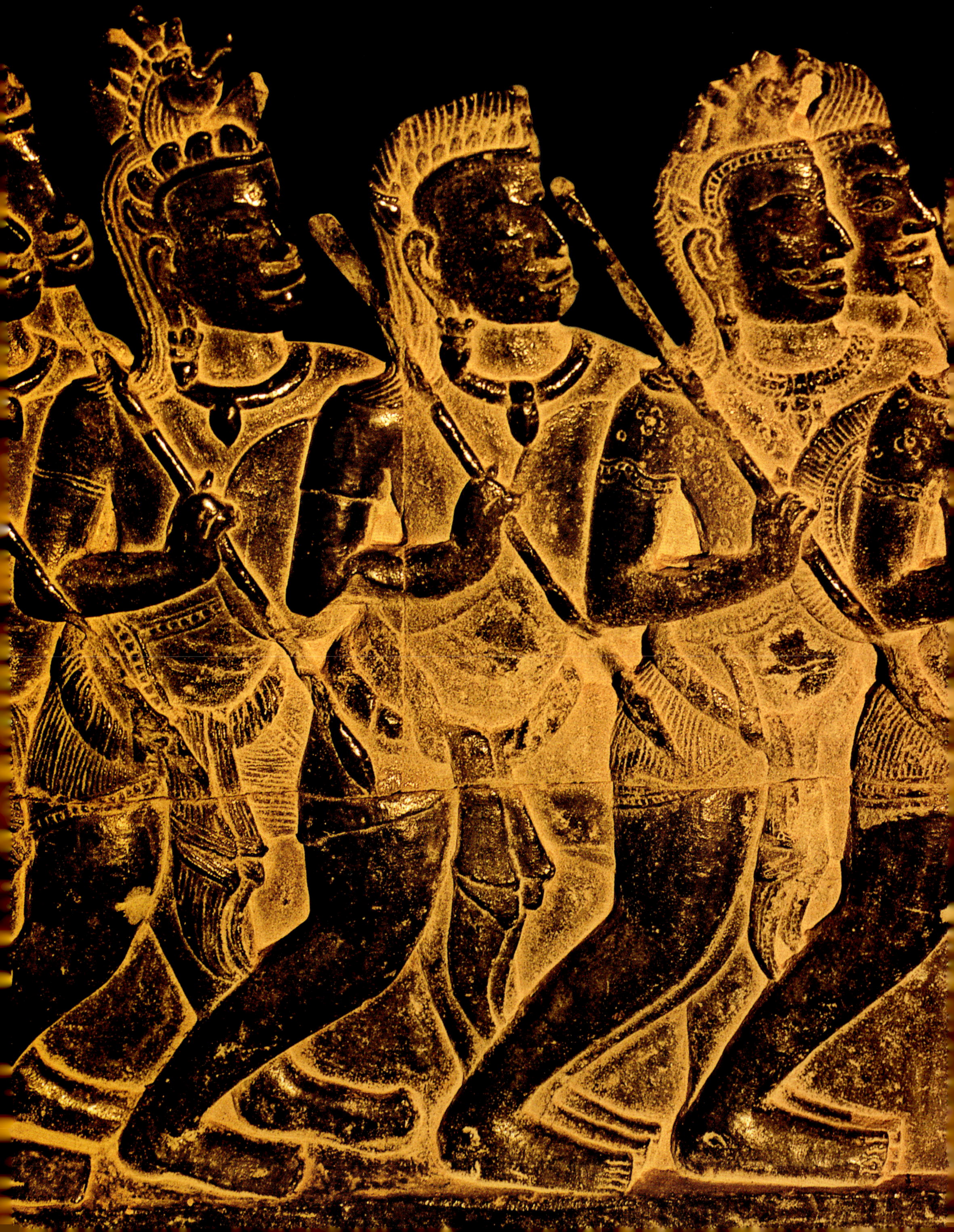

# The History of Kambuja

*21 Inscriptions constitute an invaluable source of information. These two specimens, on display in the Phnom Penh National Museum, are in ancient Khmer, while the one in the background, dating from the seventh/eighth century and originating from Tuol Neak Ta Bak Ka, shows the bull Nandin, mount of the god Shiva.*

The history of the Khmer Empire has been reconstructed on the basis of inscriptions, bas-reliefs, Chinese dynastic chronicles, and the invaluable Customs of Cambodia, written by Chinese official Zhou Daguan, who lived at Angkor from August 1296 to July 1297.

Some 1,200 inscriptions have been found, mainly carved in stone. They are written partly in Sanskrit, sometimes with Pali inserts, and partly in ancient Khmer. Nothing survives of the manuscripts written on chamois or deerskin dyed black on which the characters were written from left to right with sticks of a powder similar to chalk. The epigraphs, which begin in the fifth century A.D., are written in an alphabet known as Calukya-Pallava because it derives from the Pallava dynasty of southern India. Another kind of writing called Nagari, which was already used in Java and originated in northern India, was adopted during the reign of Yashovarman I in the ninth century. A specific feature of this period are the inscriptions which were written on the jamb of the main door to the temple, always in Sanskrit, but in two different alphabets: modified Pallava, known as Kamvujakshara, which means "writing of the descendents of Kambu" (i.e. the Khmer), and Nagari.

The Sanskrit inscriptions were first deciphered in 1879 by Dutchman Hendrik Kern, and his work was continued by Frenchmen Auguste Barthe and Abel Bergaigne, who published a first volume of inscriptions in 1885. Their fellow-countryman Étienne Aymonier, an expert in ancient Khmer who was appointed to draw up the first archaeological inventory in Cambodia, reproduced 350 inscriptions, which were published in three collections between 1900 and 1903. Some very important work was also done by Louis Finot and above all Georges Coedès, who published no less then eight volumes of inscriptions in Sanskrit and ancient Khmer that allowed the most important stages in Khmer history to be reconstructed and cast light on the political, social, and cultural policies of the Empire.

The inscriptions in Sanskrit, the sacred language of India, were inspired by the Indian *prashasti*, panegyrics written in ornate prose or *shloka* (verses of four octosyllables) that celebrate the greatness and feats of the sovereigns and the monuments erected by them. After the invocation to the gods, the genealogy of the sovereign or donor was recounted and his praises sung; the inscription concluded with details of the management of the donated site.

The dates are calculated in accordance with the Indian Shaka era, which began in A.D. 78/79, and are often expressed by convoluted phrases. For example, "in the year designated by the flavors, the Ashvins, and the arrows of love" is interpreted to mean that there were six flavors, the Ashvins were divine twins, and there were five arrows of love, so when the numbers are read backwards, as was customary, the date was 526 of the Shaka era, or A.D. 604.

The epigraphs in ancient Khmer which appeared for the first time during the reign of Ishanavarman (early seventh century to A.D. 628) are in prose and mostly contain lists of people, lands, and goods allocated to the various temples for their operation and the stipends of the priests and attendants. Although the beliefs and actions of the common people were not described in either case (in the Sanskrit or Khmer inscriptions), it is possible to read between the lines.

Information about everyday life is also provided by bas-reliefs, especially those carved on the walls of the Bayon temple at Angkor Thom, which show scenes from daily life together with military parades and battle scenes.

The Chinese dynastic chronicles refer to the Kingdom of Funan and the kingdoms of Land Chenla and Water Chenla, which included part of present-day Cambodia, and they continued to use the term Chenla when referring to the subsequent Khmer Empire. The legends and exaggerations designed to emphasize Chinese predominance over the neighboring countries include some information that is useful for the purpose of historical reconstructions.

The only surviving account of how the Khmer lived is contained in The Customs of Cambodia by Zhou Daguan, a Chinese official who was a member of the diplomatic mission sent by Timur Khan, grandson and successor of Kublai Khan, to the court of Shrindravarman III, the Khmer sovereign who ruled from 1295 to 1307. Zhou Daguan wrote the book upon his return to China, which was definitely completed by 1312. Although it only relates to the last glorious period of the Khmer Empire, the book offers an invaluable insight into everyday life in ancient Cambodia.

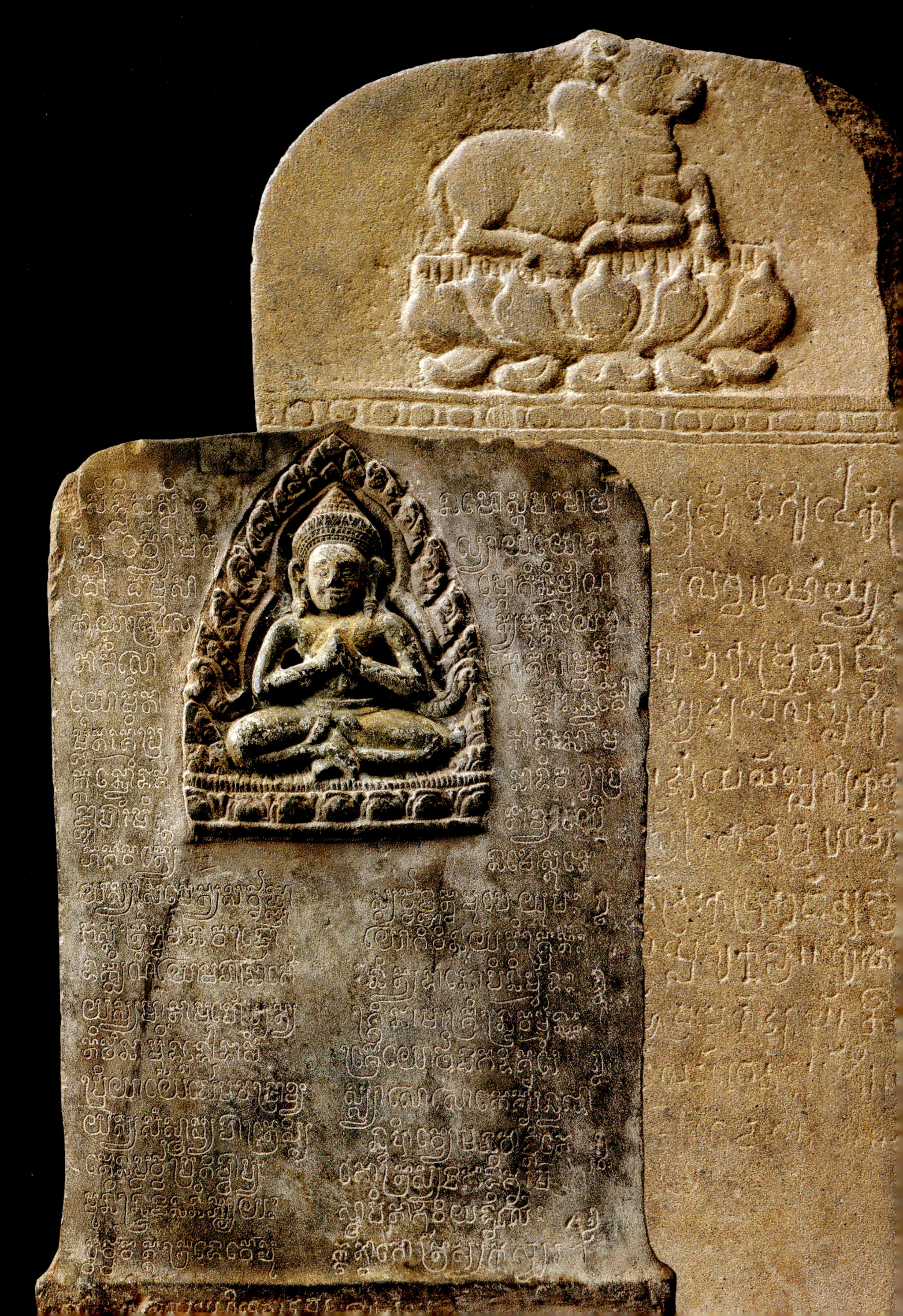

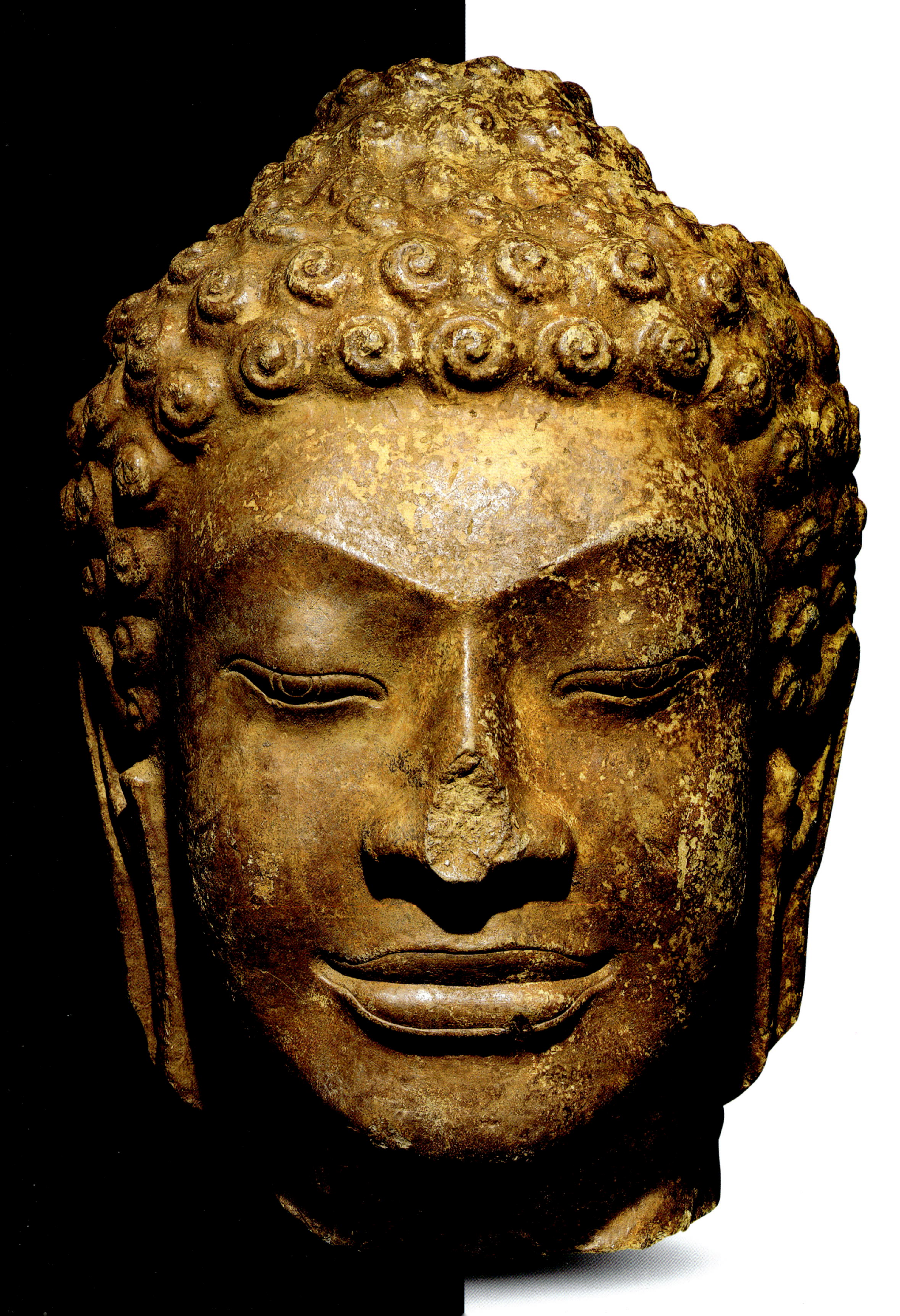

# Funan and the Mountain Kings

*22 Khmer civilization was influenced by its Indian counterpart. The portrayal of the facial features and hair in this seventh/eighth-century head of Buddha from the period of Dvaravati, a Buddhist kingdom in the Menam delta, is inspired by Gupta art, which flourished in India between the fourth and sixth centuries. Private collection.*

*23 This stela in the Prei Kmeng style, dating from the second half of the seventh century, is engraved with the symbols of the deities of the Hindu Trimurti or "Triple Form," adopted by the Divine to emanate, control, and dissolve the universe. The rosary, jug of water, and lotus blossom on the left are associated with Brahma, the trident in the center is the emblem of Shiva, and the shell, sunburst disc, and mace on the right characterize Vishnu. Guimet National Museum of Asian Arts, Paris.*

Human settlements in Cambodia date back to time immemorial, but the first traces of organized civilization date from the third millennium B.C. when a Neolithic culture with considerable lithic production had already developed. The most important settlement was Samrong Sen, on a tributary of the Tonlé Sap river, where pottery of excellent workmanship has been found. It was active until 500 B.C., when high quality bronze ware was made, mainly found in connection with megalithic tombs.

Megalithic civilization inaugurated a cult of stone that gradually increased over the centuries as a result of external (mainly Indian) influences and eventually acquired central importance in Khmer history. Menhirs were erected as funeral monuments, probably to commemorate the deceased and transfer his energy and charisma to his successor. The upward-pointing stones acted as an intermediary between heaven and earth and the emblem of a supernatural presence that controlled and fertilized the surrounding land. They consequently became a tangible symbol of the invisible genius loci, or local spirit. Ancestor worship and the cult of the chthonic powers thus merged in the menhirs, which at the same time acquired land survey functions, marking the ownership and boundaries of land.

In the centuries preceding the Christian era, the Khmer lived in homes on stilts and engaged in hunting, fishing, and agriculture, probably rice growing. Weaving and rearing domestic animals such as pigs were also known. Excavations have brought to light jewelry made of stone, bones, and shells, together with pottery, which was modeled without a wheel, fired in the open air, and featured geometrical and corded decorations. Bronze weapons, tools, and jewelry have also been found. The date when iron was introduced, perhaps imported from the Indian state of Orissa, is unknown.

The first great kingdom that developed at the start of the Christian era was situated on the Gulf of Siam, between the lower Menam basin and the Mekong delta, incorporating southern Cambodia. At the height of its glory its influence extended to the Malay peninsula and Burma. This information is obtained from the Chinese chronicles History of the Chin (265-419) and History of the Liang (502-556), which attributed to the kingdom the name of Funan. According to some experts, "Funan" was the Chinese form of the ancient Khmer word bnam (mountain), the meaning of which survives in the present-day Cambodian word phnom. However, Khmer inscriptions refer neither to Funan nor to Chenla, but mainly use the names of the capitals to describe territories and kingdoms.

The population of Funan seems to have consisted of two main races, the Paleoindonesian race, which overlapped with Australoid and Melanesian groups, and the Mon-Khmer. Their main activities were agriculture and trade; intensive trade had been conducted with India since the third century B.C., as demonstrated by relics and inscriptions. Indian customs had a major influence on Khmer civilization, which obtained practical and cultural teachings from India and adapted them to meet its own needs, thus producing its own original version.

There are various theories as to how Indian culture spread to the lands that came to constitute the Khmer Empire. The theory in vogue at the beginning of the twentieth century, namely that India had known a glorious period of colonization of Southeast Asia by an adventurous warrior aristocracy, has been disproved, and all the experts now agree that the Indian penetration of the area was peaceful.

*However, they disagree as to which social groups were responsible for spreading Indian culture. Some believe it was the traders who traveled far and wide, searching for gold in particular, and built numerous warehouses on the coast, promoting the circulation of Indian principles, rituals, and customs by their presence, and perhaps as a result of mixed marriages. However, this theory is belied by the fact that Indianization spread not along the coastlines, but in the interior of the country, where traders rarely ventured. They merely created a trading network and paved the way for penetration, but it was the* **Brahmans**, *the caste of priests, who were the messengers of Hindu culture.*

*The Brahmans were considered the repositories of the sacred and profane sciences (the boundary between the two was highly nebulous in a traditional civilization like India). They were surrounded by an aura of power and mystery, considered capable of propitiation, exorcism, and magic, and often had particular charisma. As a result, they were invited to court by various local sovereigns wishing to consolidate and expand their power. The complex Hindu royal ritual monopolized by the Brahmans appeared to be the most effective way of transforming rule obtained by force into a divine mandate.*

*The largest contingents of Brahmans came from the south of India, from the maritime kingdom of the Pallava and their capital Mahaballipuram. However, some also came from central and northern India, where the Gupta Empire, and subsequently the Pala Kingdom, flourished. Some ships set sail from the ports of Orissa and the Gulf of Bengal and hugged the coastline, while the boldest crossed the Gulf by way of the Nicobar Islands.*

*So it was that Hindu civilization arrived and merged with local elements, giving rise to a fascinating syncretism. The indigenous cult of the mountain (the rulers of Funan called themselves "king of the mountain") was strengthened by the sacredness that the Hindus attributed to the Himalayas, the seat of the god Shiva. He was the third member of the* **Trimurti**, *the "Triple Form" taken by the Absolute, whose three persons are Brahma, god of the origin, Vishnu, keeper of the world, and Shiva, who dissolves the universe to allow its rebirth.*

*The spread of the cult of powerful Hindu deity Shiva in the Khmer area and the concept of* **chakravartin**, *the universal sovereign who was "lord of the wheel," i.e. of the sacred order, paved the way for the deification of the monarch, which was officially introduced a few centuries later. And when architects began to use stone, they built temples inspired by the symbolism of the cosmic mountain, the axis and hub of the world, just as the king was the focal point of the organized social system.*

*Only the Brahmans could have introduced these concepts, and their presence is indirectly demonstrated by the Chinese chronicles which*

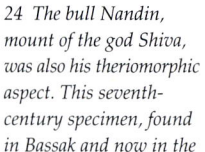

24 *The bull Nandin, mount of the god Shiva, was also his theriomorphic aspect. This seventh-century specimen, found in Bassak and now in the Phnom Penh National Museum, complies with the traditional Hindu criteria, which require it to be short-horned and crouching.*

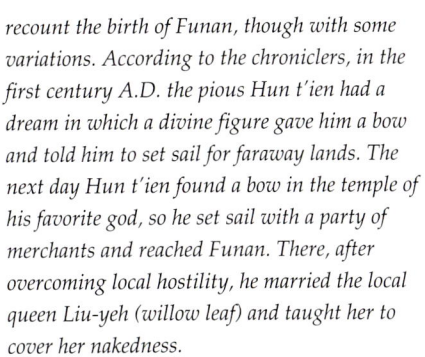

recount the birth of Funan, though with some variations. According to the chroniclers, in the first century A.D. the pious Hun t'ien had a dream in which a divine figure gave him a bow and told him to set sail for faraway lands. The next day Hun t'ien found a bow in the temple of his favorite god, so he set sail with a party of merchants and reached Funan. There, after overcoming local hostility, he married the local queen Liu-yeh (willow leaf) and taught her to cover her nakedness.

Some affinities with the Chinese version appear in a Sanskrit inscription dating from 658, found at Mi-son in Champa, now south Vietnam. Kaundinya (who according to linguists could have been known in Chinese as Hun t'ien) came to India as a result of a dream. On disembarking he threw the javelin he had received from the great Brahman Ashvatthaman to decide on the spot where he would build his capital.

25 top right and 25 bottom Ganesh, the elephant-headed god who was the son of Shiva and the goddess Parvati, was worshipped as he who removes obstacles and brings prosperity. This cross-legged specimen dating from the seventh/eighth century, found at Tuol Pheak Kin and now in the Phnom Penh National Museum, buries its trunk in a cup of sweets and holds a radish in its hand. The standing Ganesh, also in the Phnom Penh Museum, carries an elephant goad in his raised left hand in addition to the other two objects.

He then married Soma, a local princess belonging to the naga (mythical creatures who were part cobra, believed to be the ancestors of numerous Indian dynasties). Her father, the Nagaraja (king of the naga), who was also the dragon lord of the area, "drank" the waters so as to give the couple a huge dry area as a wedding present. The two versions are obviously based on a common source, which suggests reclamation work performed by an expert from India and his marriage to the daughter of the local lord, who was thus guaranteed the lasting loyalty and services of the Brahman expert. Soma and Kaundinya had a son who founded the first Funan dynasty of the Kaundinya, probably associated, on the basis of Pallavan influence, with the candravamsha (moon dynasty), which derived from Krishna, an incarnation of the god Vishnu. The Chinese chronicles contain details of the various rulers, the greatest of whom was Fan Shih-man (205-225), but the overall picture still remains vague. The same sources contain a more certain item of information, namely that a second Kaundinya came from India in the fifth century to restore the Indianized customs, which had been forgotten. Under King Kaundinya Jayavarman (478-514), the rulers of Funan acquired greater historical importance. The Chinese chronicles refer to two delegations sent by that King to their Emperor: one in 484, to ask for help against the neighbouring Kingdom of Champa, and the other to bring gifts. The first was led by Indian monk Nagasena, who gave a description of Funan in which he said that Buddhism prospered, but that Maheshvara (Shiva) was worshipped on Mount Mo-tan. Mo-tan is identified by some experts with Ba Phnom, from which the kings of Funan may have taken their title "lord of the mountain."

The story of Kaundinya and Soma became more widely known during the reign of Kaundinya Jayavarman, and the suffix "varman" was added to the name of all Khmer kings from that time onward. Varman means "breastplate" or "protection," so that Jayavarman, for example, means "he who is protected by victory (jaya)."

The chronicles describe the Funanese as negroid, and say that they lived in houses on stilts, created bronze images of the "spirits of the sky," rode elephants, and had boats with the bow and stern in the shape of a fish head and tail. The description of the way in which the king sat with his left leg dangling and right leg bent clearly shows an Indian influence, whereas the widespread freedom of behavior between the two sexes was definitely a local characteristic. The four types of funeral listed—consigning the body to the waters, burial, cremation, and exposure to birds of prey and wild animals—demonstrate that local customs survived alongside those imported from India.

The capital of Funan was Vyadhapura, whose location is uncertain (it may have been in the Prei Veng area, at the foot of Ba Phnom, or further south, at Angkor Borei), while the main port was Oc-èo, a huge trading center situated to the north of what is now Rach Gia in Vietnam, which even had contacts with Rome, as demonstrated by the Roman and Hellenistic relics found. The city was surrounded by successive rows of ramparts and moats, and intersected by canals; the houses were built on stilts. Excavations have brought to light a great deal of material, including tin plates and tableware, numerous jewels, mainly made of gold, what were probably silver coins, beads made of glass paste, seals, cameos, and earthenware decorations of brick structures betraying an evident Gupta influence.

In 514 Rudravarman, son of a concubine of Kaundinya Jayavarman, succeeded to the throne and chose as his capital Angkor Borei, where he probably lived until after 539. The first Khmer sculptures, in the style of Phnom Da, a sacred hill at Angkor Borei, are attributed to that period. Rudravarman sent delegations to China, like his predecessor, and it is known from inscriptions that he appointed as court doctors two brothers from a family of Brahmans from Adhyapura (now Ang Chumnik), which was to supply ministers to four generations of kings. From this time on, there was a close connection between the sovereigns and certain families of Brahmans, who came to play a key role in the history of the Khmer Empire.

*26 The numerous statues of Buddha dating from the Funan period demonstrate that Buddhism was widespread by the start of that period. This magnificent seventh-century statue, originating from Tuol Ta Hoy and now in Phnom Penh National Museum, radiates gentleness and spirituality.*

*27 These two bronzes housed in the Phnom Penh National Museum clearly betray the artistic influence exerted by the Buddhist kingdom of Dvaravati, founded by the Mon in the Menam delta in the sixth century. The statue in the background, found at Angkor Borei and dating from the seventh century, portrays Avalokiteshvara, a* bodhisattva *or "perfectly enlightened being." The one in the foreground is a seventh/eighth century Buddha originating from Angkor.*

# CHENLA
## and the Advent of the Khmer

Rudravarman seems to have been the last king of Funan. After his death the kingdom disintegrated, and in the fifth century a group of Khmer, who had perhaps been vassals of Funan, founded an independent principality to the north of Tonlé Sap, the great lake supplied with water by the river of the same name, which constitutes the heart of present-day Cambodia. The name Cambodia derives from the Sanskrit Kambujadesha, meaning "land of the descendents of Kambu." The Kambu in question was the legendary hermit Kambu Svayambhuva, to whom Shiva gave the nymph Mera as his bride. The name Kambujadesha, abbreviated to Kambuja, appears for the first time in 817, in an inscription at Po Nagar in Champa (present-day Nha-trang in Vietnam).

The Khmer came from the upper Menam valley. By following the Mun river valley they reached the Mekong, encountering and perhaps supplanting the Cham in the area of present-day Champassak. They probably acquired from the Cham the Hindu religion and the cult of Shiva Bhadreshvara, worshipped by the Cham on Mount Wat Phu in what is now southern Laos.

The history of the Khmer is closely entwined with that of the Cham. From their original settlement in the middle reaches of the Mekong, the Cham gradually moved east and south-east, reaching the coasts of Annam and Cochin China and founding the powerful maritime kingdom of Champa, which stretched to the Hill of Clouds. Champa, which was mentioned in Chinese sources as early as the second century A.D., was divided into numerous warring principalities, the main ones being Vijaya (now Binh Dinh), Khautara on the Nha Trang plain, and Panduranga on the Phan Rang plain, all of which are in present-day Vietnam. The first historic king of Champa, Bhadravarman, founded the temple of Shiva Bhadreshvara at My Son, to the south of Da Nang, in the fourth century A.D., and it was sacked by the Vietnamese in 605.

The first stages of the clashes between the Khmer and the Cham are unclear, and the account given in the Chronicles of Cambodia is unreliable. The Chronicles, reconstructed during the reign of King Ang Chan (1806-1834) on the basis of an earlier work destroyed in the wars of the eighteenth century, were revised during the reign of Norodom (1859-1904) and made to start from 1346. They state that a descendant of Kambu, Prince Preah Thong of Indraprashtha, the legendary Indian capital near Delhi, came to the country of Kok Thlok (the local name of Cambodia, after the thlok tree) and found it occupied by the Cham. He married the daughter of the Nagaraja, and drove out the Cham with the latter's help.

Kambuja appears for the first time in the Chinese Chronicles (always with the name Chenla) History of the Sui (589-618), in connection with a delegation sent to China from Chenla in 616/617. At the time of its greatest expansion, Chenla must have included the lower Menam valley and the Mun valley in what is now Thailand, together with southern Laos and part of northeast Cambodia, as far as the Annamite coast.

There were great differences between Funan and Chenla. Funan, which was mainly inhabited by populations of Indonesian origin, was a seagoing, cosmopolitan nation open to outside influences. Agriculture was practiced, and because of the excess water, the population was constantly busy drying and draining the delta. Chenla, which was populated solely by the Khmer, was situated on high ground, and in view of the scarcity of water, the farmers were only able to grow mountain rice by using captation systems to store water. They migrated south in search of better land, consequently becoming raiders and conquerors.

However, Funan and Chenla had a common denominator: the need for a highly centralized political apparatus capable of promoting and maintaining an efficient water system.

The first kings of Chenla, part historical and part legendary, were Shrutavarman and Shreshthavarman, whose capital Shreshthapura must have been in southern Laos, at the foot of the Wat Phu complex, a center of the Shivaite religion embraced by nearly all the kings of Chenla. In the tenth century a genealogy was created for these sovereigns which connected them to the mythical couple Kambu and Mera and to the suryavamsha (sun dynasty) descended from Rama, another incarnation of the god Vishnu.

However, Chenla was not a united kingdom but was divided into numerous principalities in a precarious political balance. One of them, situated in the area of what is now Kratié in east Cambodia, was ruled by Viravarman, who had at least two sons, Citrasena and Bhavavarman. Citrasena, who was chosen by his father as his successor, extended his domains northwards and made incursions as far as present-day Khon Kaen, in the heart of Thailand. The second son, Bhavavarman, married Kambujarajalakshmi, a descendent of Shreshthavarman, who therefore belonged to the oldest dynasty in Chenla. This marriage was lauded by later Khmer genealogists as Kambujarajalakshmi belonged to the sun dynasty and Bhavavarman was a nephew of Rudravarman on his mother's side and therefore related to the moon dynasty. His Funanese origins gained him the services of the famous Brahmans of Adhyapura, who continued to serve the later kings as ministers too.

Bhavavarman took up residence at Bhavapura, whose most likely location seems to

29 Harihara, a divine form incorporating Shiva and Vishnu, was redesigned by the Khmer in a brilliant, independent style during this period. This eighth-century specimen, originating from Trapang Phong and now in the Phnom Penh National Museum, shows Shiva on the right, recognizable by the trident in his raised hand and his hair twisted into a chignon, and Vishnu on the left, with half of his head covered by a miter.

be the Sambor Prei Kuk area, near the present-day Kompong Thom, and commenced a series of campaigns against Funan. He died shortly after 598 and his kingdom was inherited by his brother Citrasena, who succeeded to the throne of Bhavapura under the name Mahendravarman.

Citrasena continued the conquest of Funan, which was completed by his son Ishanavarman, crowned between 611 and 616. Ishanavarman chose as his capital Sambor Prei Kuk, which was named Ishanapura (city of Ishana) after him. During his reign Chenla reached its largest size: its westernmost point was at Chantaburi on the Gulf of Siam, huge territories in western Thailand and southern Laos were added to the northern territories, and nearly the whole of present-day Cambodia was ruled by Ishanavarman. The King maintained good relations with the Champa and gave his daughter to a Cham prince.

628 is the last known date of his kingdom, from which many inscriptions survive, including the first stele in Khmer, dating from 612, found at Angkor Borei (historian Lawrence Palmer Briggs also mentions another found at Ak Yum, which possibly dates from 609). The main court religion continued to be Shivaism but not in an absolute form. The worship of Harihara, a divine form incorporating both Shiva and Vishnu, became widespread during this period. The Brahmans of Adhyapura continued to hold the most important spiritual offices, a particularly distinguished member of the family being Simhavira, minister to Ishanavarman. On the death of Ishanavarman in 628 there seem to have been problems with the succession, a frequent event in Khmer history.

The new king, Bhavavarman II, whose only certain date is 644, may not have been a direct descendent of Ishanavarman; this theory is borne out by the fact that he was not served by the Brahmans of Adhyapura like his predecessors.

*30 right The form of Buddhism called Mahayana, meaning "great vehicle (of salvation)," in which* **bodhisattvas** *(compassionate guides of mankind) play a very important role, became widespread during this period. This eighth-century bronze from Phnom Ta Kream, now in the Phnom Penh National Museum, portrays Avalokiteshvara.*

In any event, the king declared himself to be a descendent of the moon dynasty and was the first to be designated a posthumous name: Shivaloka. Nearly all the subsequent kings followed his example. The name of the deity with which they identified was included in their posthumous name, followed by the Sanskrit term loka (paradise-world). Shivaloka therefore means "he who has gone to the paradise of Shiva."

Buddhist images inspired by the second version of Buddhism, known as Mahayana, meaning "great vehicle (of salvation)," became widespread during this period.

Under Bhavavarman II, much of Chenla again split into small, independent states, and his successor Jayavarman I, who came to power in 657, attempted to unify the country. Jayavarman was the son of a niece of Ishanavarman, and one of his ministers was Simhadatta, son of Simhavira, of the Adhyapura Brahmans. The location of his capital Purandarapura is uncertain, although some experts consider it to have been located around the mountain temple of Ak Yum in the Angkor region. Jayavarman I regained most of the territories ruled by Ishanavarman, but on his death the kingdom disintegrated once more. Although the last known inscription dates from 691, Jayavarman I probably lived until 700. He took the posthumous name of Shivapura (he who has gone to the citadel of Shiva).

Jayadevi, one of the wives of Jayavarman I (although researcher Claude Jacques believes that she was his daughter and married to Nripaditya, who held power for a very short time), who is referred to as queen in an inscription dating from 713, attempted in vain to keep the kingdom united on her husband's death. One of the first secessionist kingdoms was Aninditapura, founded by Baladitya in the seventh century, which seems to have controlled the lower Mekong valley as far as the delta. The last two kings, Nripatindravarman and his successor Pushkaraksha, were contemporaries of Jayavarman I and Jayadevi. Pushkaraksha is

*30 left Maitreya, the Buddha of the future, portrayed in this eighth-century bronze housed in the Guimet Museum in Paris, is easily recognizable by the symbol at the base of his tall top-knot, a* **stupa**, *the monument-reliquary with multiple meanings. The beauty of the statue demonstrates the skill of the bronze casters.*

*31 left Shiva's wife is represented here in the form of Durga, the warrior goddess who conquered Mahisha, the buffalo-demon whose head appears on the base. The seventh/eighth-century statue, found at Tuol Kamnap and now in the Phnom Penh National Museum, celebrates the beauty of a young woman.*

*31 right This magnificent seventh-century statue in the Sambor Prei Kuk style, originating from Koh Krieng and now in the Phnom Penh National Museum, portrays Devi, another aspect of Shiva's wife. Her features are those of a mature woman of restrained opulence, radiating serene authority.*

mentioned in an inscription dating from 716 found in the Kratié region as the King of Shambhupura, also known as Sambor on the Mekong (not to be confused with Sambor Prei Kuk, i.e. Ishanapura), another kingdom which had regained its independence on the death of Jayavarman I. Whether he seized power by force or married the crown princess, Pushkaraksha challenged the dynasty of Jayavarman I and proclaimed himself king of all Kambuja. Later genealogists included him in the line of Kings of Funan from the moon dynasty and praised his marriage with a princess of the sun dynasty.

References to the sun dynasty only appear after the eighth century (a period when only the moon dynasty is mentioned in inscriptions), and they were probably invented by the court Brahmans, anxious to find a famous ancestor for their masters of humble origin. The inclusion of some sovereigns and the exclusion of others from the genealogical lists makes it possible to guess the most probable origin of the king in power, especially if he was a usurper, and which monarchs of the past he intended to emulate.

In relation to the obscure, early part of the eighth century, the Chinese chronicles refer to the existence of a "Land Chenla" and a "Water Chenla." Land Chenla was apparently united and centered in the ancient territories of Chenla, while Water Chenla was fragmented into numerous small states in the area that once constituted Funan. The main states of Water Chenla were Shambhupura, Vyadhapura, south of Prei Veng, and Bhavapura, which was centered in Sambor Prei Kuk. Their affairs are described in ninth century inscriptions, but it is not known how historically accurate they are or whether they were more concerned with genealogies.

The inscriptions state that Shambhuvarman, the son or successor of Pushkaraksha, married a princess from Vyadhapura and thus came to control much of Water Chenla and the Mekong delta. The son of the couple, Rajendravarman I, therefore descended from the three great dynasties: Aninditapura-Shambhupura, Bhavapura, and Vyadhapura. His son Mahipativarman is said to have traced his ancestry back to one of the great kings of Angkor, Yashovarman I, who reigned in the ninth and tenth centuries.

The Chinese chronicles refer to four delegations sent to China between 717 and 799 by Land Chenla linking their foreign policy with that of China, who was busy dealing with invasions by Thais from the Kingdom of Nan Chao (present-day Yunnan) on the southeastern borders of the Empire. There is no reference to delegations being sent from Water Chenla.

The situation in the southern part of Kambuja was influenced by raids by the Malays and above all the advent of two great empires, the Shrivijaya Empire, which already controlled the straits from Sumatra in the seventh century, and the Shailendra Empire in Java, whose power rapidly increased from the eighth century onwards. Many of the principalities in Water Chenla must have acknowledged the sovereignty of Java, and an account published in 916 by Abu Zayd Hasan attributed to the merchant Sulayman, who appears to have sailed in the area in 851, is very interesting in this respect. An impetuous young Khmer king verbally challenged the King of Java, who made a rapid punitive expedition to the Khmer kingdom and beheaded the culprit. According to Briggs, the victim may actually have been Mahipativarman. Nonetheless, the story clearly demonstrates the subjection of much of Kambuja to Java.

# Angkor, Plain of Capitals

The historical situation becomes clearer in the early ninth century with the appearance of Jayavarman II. Although there are no inscriptions relating directly to him, he is described in detail on the stela of Sdok Kak Thom dating from 1052, found 16 miles from Sisophon. It states that King Jayavarman II, having thrown off the yoke of Java, founded four capitals and unified Kambuja, celebrating a magnificent coronation rite in 802. Khmer genealogists associate him with Nripatindravarman of Aninditapura. However it may be, Jayavarman II came to Kambuja from Java (although the identification of the island is not absolutely certain), where he had lived either as a prisoner or as a hostage.

Jayavarman became king around 790 after conquering the kingdoms of Vyadhapura and Shambhupura (although he may have inherited them). He founded four capitals: Indrapura in the middle Mekong area (some believe it was located at Kompong Cham, and others at Banteay Prei Nokor); Hariharalaya (now Roluos) on the Angkor plain, which was to become the heart of the Khmer Empire; Amarendrapura, possibly centered around the mountain temple of Ak Yum, a settlement which existed as early as the sixth century and is now partly covered by the west baray, one of the great Angkor reservoirs; and Mahendrapura on Mount Mahendraparvata, now Phnom Kulen.

Shivakaivalya, a member of a family of Brahmans from Aninditapura, celebrated Janapada, the magnificent consecration rite of Jayavarman, on this mountain, which had been sacred since time immemorial, under the guidance of Hiranyadama, another well-known Brahman from an unknown location. On this occasion a linga, the phallic stone symbolizing the god Shiva, was erected, and the cult of the devaraja (god-king), the celestial counterpart of the earthly sovereign, was inaugurated. Just as Shiva was the absolute lord among the gods and therefore the ruler of the universe, so the Khmer king dominated all the other monarchs and was the sole ruler of the kingdom. The dynasty of performers of the devaraja rites was inaugurated by Shivakaivalya, to whom the king gave the village of Kuti near the present temple of Banteay Kdei. Members of the dynasty also performed purohita tasks, acting as spiritual masters and advisers to the king. Jayavarman II returned to Hariharalaya, where he died in 850. He received the posthumous name of Parameshvara.

His son Jayavarman III was one of the few kings who worshipped the god Vishnu, as demonstrated by his posthumous name Vishnuloka. The inscriptions state that his spiritual master was Shivakaivalya's maternal grandson Sukshmavindu, who also officiated over the cult of the devaraja for Jayavarman's successor Indravarman, who became king in 877, possibly after an interregnum, as the latest definite date for Jayavarman III is 860.

The numerous inscriptions relating to Indravarman demonstrate that he fulfilled the main tasks of a Khmer king: the foundation of a capital and performance of public works for the good of his subjects, the building and maintenance of shrines to the ancestors, and the erection of a temple for the devaraja, which was destined to become the mausoleum of the king himself.

In order to transform and develop Hariharalaya, Indravarman built at Lolei the Indratataka, a reservoir 12,500 feet long and 2,600 feet wide which exploited the waters of the River Roluos and guaranteed a regular water supply for the city and the paddy fields. This was the first example of hydraulic architecture based on barays, reservoirs that were not excavated but enclosed between embankments, which assured the fortune of Angkor by combining practicality and propitiatory symbolism. The management of the waters by the sovereign guaranteed life on earth and confirmed the divinity of the king, who was identified with the Indra, warrior chief of the Hindu gods and lord of the rain.

Indravarman built the temple of Preah Ko at Hariharalaya in honor of the ancestors in 879, establishing the cult of the deified sovereigns. This cult, probably of Javanese inspiration, combined the ancestor worship typical of the indigenous Khmer culture with propitiation of the custodian spirits of the land, also based on local animist tradition. Two years later, in 881, the Bakhong mountain temple was consecrated to house the royal linga, symbol of the devaraja and of Indravarman himself.

The association with the Brahmans continued under this king, not only with the descendants of Shivakaivalya, but also with other families of priests; the inscriptions refer to Shivasoma, a chaplain of royal lineage, who founded the Shivashrama, which was to become the most important monastery in supplying Brahman high officials to the court. By the time of Indravarman's death in 889, his realm stretched to the north as far as Ubon in Thailand, the lower Mun valley having been reconquered, and south as far as Phom Bayang, at the southernmost tip of Kambuja. His posthumous name was Ishvaraloka.

Yashovarman, who came to the throne in a not entirely peaceful manner in 889, built Lolei temple in the middle of Indratataka in 893 as the first act of his reign, in memory of his father Indravarman and his royal ancestors. Descended on the side of his mother, Indradevi, from Mahipativarman, and therefore having ancient Funanese origins, he was guided by an outstanding spiritual master, Vamashiva, and succeeded in retaining all his father's possessions. Wishing to found his own capital and requiring a reliable water supply which enabled the cultivated areas to be expanded, Yashovarman emulated his father and built a new reservoir, Yashodharatataka, known as the East Baray. It was 23,000 feet long and 5,900 feet wide, and was supplied by the Siem Reap river, which was partly transformed into a canal to form the eastern moat of the new capital built by the King: Yashodharapura. The huge city, which measured two and a half miles square, was centered on a natural hill where the royal temple, Phnom Bakheng, was built to house the linga Yashodhareshvara, meaning the "lord of Yashodhara." The King also built other mountain temples, including Phnom Krom and Phnom Bok on two hills near Angkor, and numerous hermitages and monasteries, thus assuring himself of the loyalty of powerful, prestigious religious centers. On his death in 910, Yashovarman received the posthumous name of Paramashivaloka.

*33 Koh Ker, about 56 miles from Angkor, was the short-lived capital of the Empire from 921 to 944. These hands carrying a staff, which probably belonged to a* dvarapala *(gatekeeper), a majestic figure responsible for guarding the temple entrance, were found there. The club, mace, and scepter, crowned with lotus petals, symbolize authority and power.*

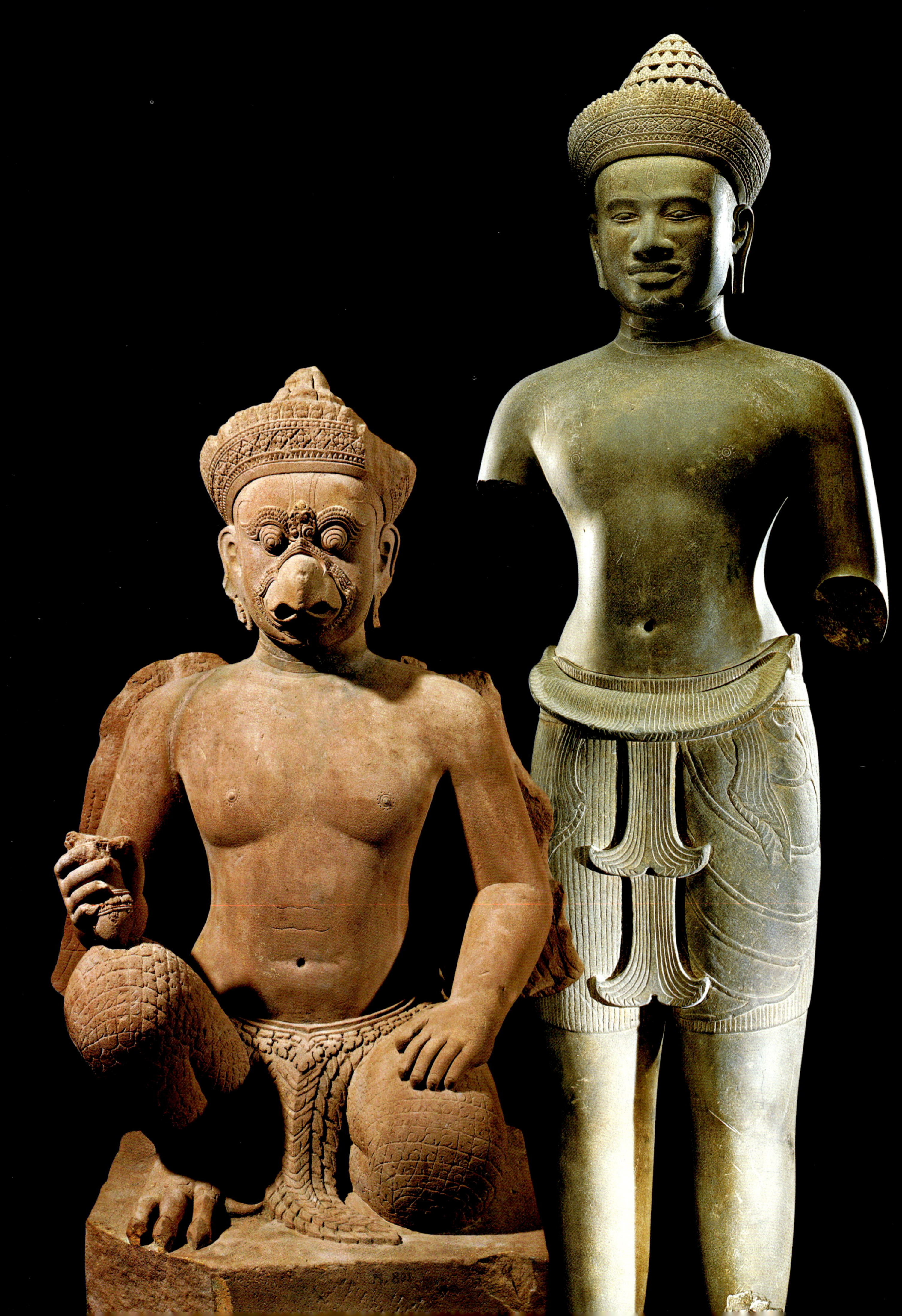

*34 left The power obtained by the Brahmans, priests of Indian descent, is demonstrated by some of the temples they erected, such as the temple of Banteay Srei, built by order of Yajnavaraha in 967. This gatekeeper, now in the Phnom Penh Museum, whose predatory features recall the mythical bird Garuda, Vishnu's mount, was found there.*

*34 right Shiva, lord of the mountain, who came to be considered the king of the gods in the Khmer area too, was the tutelary deity of the empire. He was consequently portrayed in many statues, like this tenth/eleventh century specimen in the Khleang style, now in the Guimet Museum, in which the majesty of the god is emphasized by his mukuta (conical crown).*

He was succeeded by his son Harshavarman I, whose reign was short but turbulent. In 921 one of his maternal uncles, the lord of a fief whose capital was Koh Ker, about 56 miles northeast of Angkor, rebelled and had himself crowned in his city with the name of Jayavarman IV. Koh Ker acted as rival capital to Yashodharapura, and Jayavarman IV had a baray called the Rahal built by exploiting a depression in the terrain and a nearby river.

In the meantime, Harshavarman had died at Yashodharapura in 923, receiving the posthumous name of Rudraloka. He was succeeded by his brother Ishanavarman II, whose reign was short-lived; he died in 928 and was given the name of Paramarudraloka. Jayavarman IV of Koh Ker then became the legitimate heir to the Khmer throne because his chief wife, Queen Jayadevi, was Yashovarman's sister. The area over which Jayavarman IV ruled had become smaller, including only the Koh Ker area and southern Kambuja.

When Jayavarman IV died in 941, he was deified with the name of Parameshvarapada or Paramashivapada. His son Harshavarman II, known by the posthumous name of Brahmaloka, governed Koh Ker until 944, when his cousin Rajendravarman II, son of a sister of Yashovarman I and a prince of Bhavapura (Sambor Prei Kuk), returned to reign at Angkor. The inscription at Baksei Chamkrong temple describes the genealogy of the king, connecting him on his father's side to the sun dynasty, mentioned here for the first time along with the legend of Kambu and Mera, and on his mother's side to the moon dynasty.

Wishing to continue the ancient traditions and inspired by his spiritual guide Shivacarya, Rajendravarman built the Mebon, the mountain temple dedicated to the ancestors and the linga Rajendreshvara, in the middle of the East Baray in 953. He built his capital to the south of the same baray, and in 961 erected another mountain temple, Pre Rup, dedicated to the linga Rajendrabhadreshvara. He was probably responsible for the construction of the Preah Vihar, a shrine in honor of Shiva on the spurs of the Dangrek mountains. Having inherited the policy of religious tolerance from his predecessors, Rajendravarman also promoted Buddhist foundations, like that of Bat Chum in the capital. In order to establish his authority firmly, Rajendravarman reduced the vassal kingdoms included in the Khmer Empire to the status of vishaya (provinces), creating considerable discontent among the sovereigns thus deprived of their titles. He then turned his attention to his natural enemy, the neighboring kingdom of Champa, conducted a series of raids between 945 and 946, and looted a golden image of the goddess Bhagavati from the temple of Po Nagar (present-day Nha-trang). By his death in 967, when he was deified with the posthumous name of Shivaloka, his authority extended as far as the Annamite chain in the east, the Saluen River in Burma to the west, and Grahi, now the Nakhon Si Thammarat area on the Gulf of Siam, to the south.

The Brahmans continued to play an important role during the reign of Rajendravarman. In addition to the historic Shivakaivalya family from Aninditapura and the descendents of Pranavatman, who had also served Jayavarman II, the most powerful families of priests, which owned fiefs and received large stipends, included the Saptadevakula and Haripura families. The frequent marriages between members of the royal family and Brahmans had created numerous Brahmanic lines of noble blood. Thus a line of prestigious spiritual masters was descended from Jayavarman II's queen, Hyang Pavitra. Prana, the wife of Rajendravarman II, praised in the inscriptions for her learning, came from the Saptadevakula family.

Shivacarya, the influential spiritual master of Rajendravarman, descended from the three main Brahmanic families: the Shivakaivalya family, which supplied the purohita (spiritual advisers) and managed the rites of the devaraja, the Pravatman family, which provided the hotar (performers of the most complex liturgical sacrifices), and the family descended from Queen Hyang Pavitra.

The magnificent temple of Banteay Srei, built by Yajnavaraha in 967, testifies to the independence, power, and wealth accumulated by the families of priests. Yajnavaraha, a Brahman of royal blood because he was the grandson of Harshavarman I, was the purohita of Rajendravarman and tutor to his son, the future King Jayavarman V, and was awarded the prestigious title of vrah guru (holy spiritual master) by the latter. Another famous Brahman of the period was Divakarabhatta, who came from India and married Jayavarman V's sister Indralakshmi. Divakarabhatta was responsible for the construction of a number of temples and probably for the elegant Sanskrit compositions carved on the East Mebon and Pre Rup temples.

Jayavarman V succeeded his father Rajendravarman in 968 at a very early age and probably owed his survival to the protection of Yajnavaraha. Following in his father's footsteps, he continued hostilities with the Champa, who apparently paid tribute to him. His capital, Jayendranagari, appears to have been situated on the west side of the East Baray, while the two mountain temples of the period, Phimeanakas and Ta Keo, have not yet been attributed with certainty. Although little is known of the policies of Jayavarman V, the inscriptions testify to a high level of culture and education and important positions held by women, who were sophisticated, elegant companions, such as Indralakshmi, and Yajnavaraha's sister Jahnavi, who was also involved in the foundation of Banteay Srei.

Jayavarman V died without an heir and was deified as Paramashivaloka. He was succeeded in 1001 by his nephew Udayadityavarman I, all trace of whom disappeared a year later, when Jayaviravarman took the throne. He was challenged by Suryavarman, the son of a prince of Tambralinga, in the area of present-day Ligor on the Malaccan peninsula, and attempted to protect his capital by building a city wall, the first of its kind in the history of Khmer architecture. The last inscription by Jayaviravarman at Yashodharapura dates from 1006.

Danish researcher F.D.K. Bosch sustains an interesting theory, namely that Udayadityavarman and Jayaviravarman may have been brothers who grew up in Java, where their mother had taken refuge after fleeing from the Khmer court. He postulates that Udayadityavarman married a local princess and became King of Bali under the name Udayana, later returning to Kambuja to claim the throne. On obtaining power he ceded it to his brother Narapativiravarman, who took the name of Jayaviravarman. Jayaviravarman was defeated in battle by Suryavarman and returned to Java, where he took back the name Narapativiravarman, which became Norottama in Javanese.

# An Empire
## ever-expanding

*However it may be, Suryavarman, who probably came from the eastern region of Kambuja, namely Shambhupura, which was under his control, settled in Yashodharapura in 1010 and was crowned king in 1012. The oath of loyalty pronounced by the royal officials, immortalized on the pillars of the east entrance to the royal palace, described what was to be his policy of centralization. To limit the power of the Brahman families the King made some drastic changes; in particular he abolished the hereditary appointment of the Shivakaivalya family as custodians of the rites of the* devaraja. *This does not mean that he dispensed with the services of the Brahmans altogether. His guru, Yogishvarapandita, was a descendent of Jayavarman II, and Suryavarman gave him his daughter's hand in marriage.*

*As Suryavarman was a usurper, the genealogists endeavored to find a suitable ancestry for him. Thus, he was recorded as descending on his mother's side from the maternal line of Indravarman and the Saptadevakula family. An energetic military leader, he conquered nearly all of Kambuja and annexed or levied tribute from the south of Thailand, including the Kingdom of Lavo, now Lobpuri, and part of southern Laos.*

*He initiated the construction of the gigantic West Baray at Yashodharapura, which was 26,200 feet long and 7,200 feet wide, and installed his court in the area now known as the Royal Palace.*

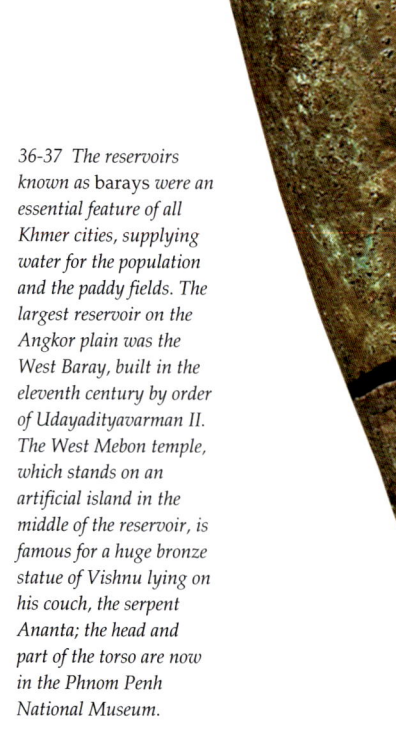

*36-37 The reservoirs known as* barays *were an essential feature of all Khmer cities, supplying water for the population and the paddy fields. The largest reservoir on the Angkor plain was the West Baray, built in the eleventh century by order of Udayadityavarman II. The West Mebon temple, which stands on an artificial island in the middle of the reservoir, is famous for a huge bronze statue of Vishnu lying on his couch, the serpent Ananta; the head and part of the torso are now in the Phnom Penh National Museum.*

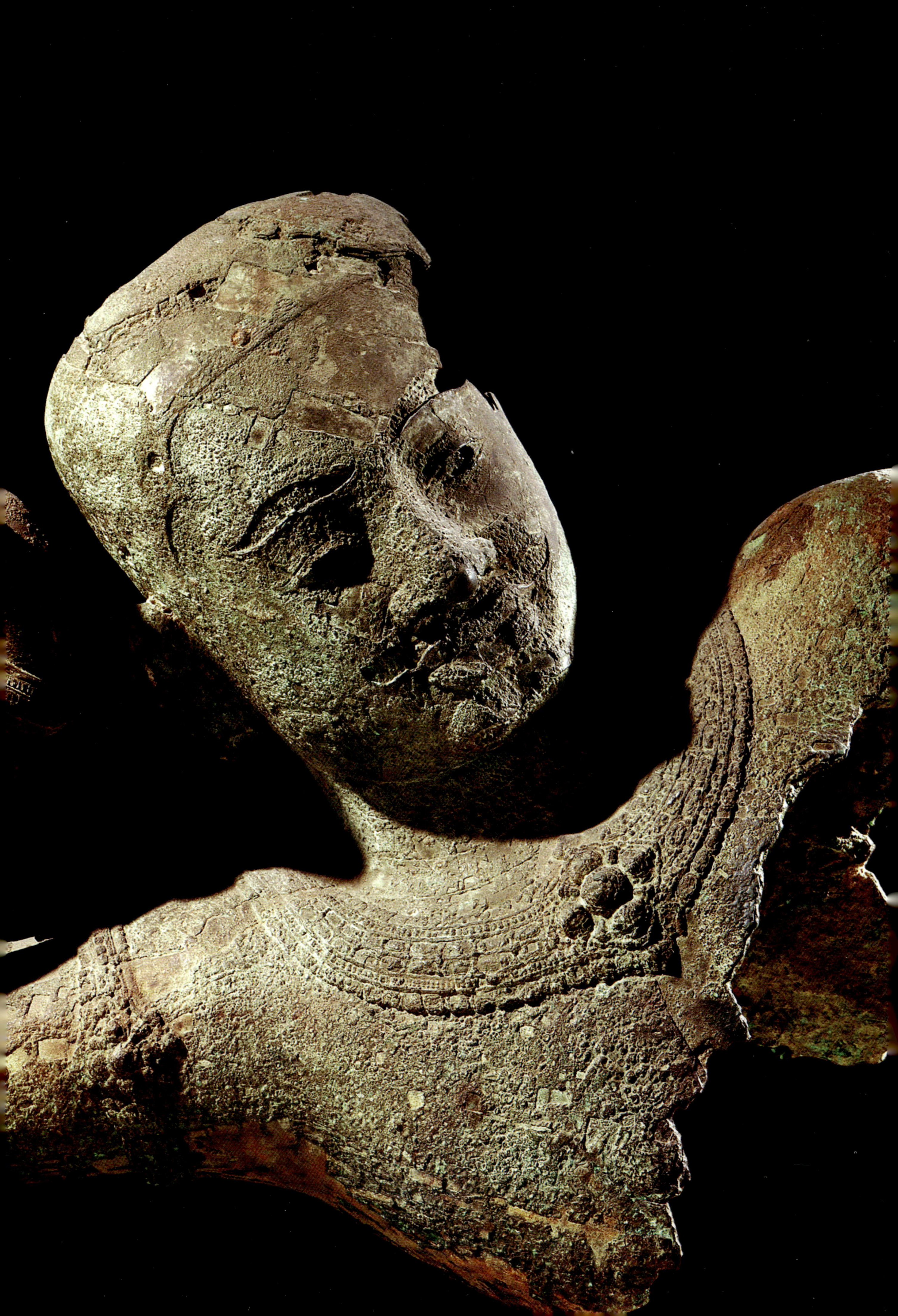

*38 The iconography of the* naga *(many-headed cobra) includes the features of the dragon, which was the genius loci according to indigenous Khmer tradition. This twelfth/thirteenth century specimen in the Bayon style, now in the Guimet Museum, originates from the Preah Khan at Angkor.*

*39 The cult of Vishnu became very important in the twelfth century. The image of a four-armed Vishnu is reproduced 1,020 times on the sides of the monument shown here, found in the Preah Khan at Kompong Svay and now in the Guimet Museum.*

It is not clear whether Phimeanakas was actually built by Suryavarman or whether it was begun by another king and completed or restored by him. He built new sanctuaries in the provinces, including Wat Ek, Wat Baset, and Phnom Chisor, and modified or enlarged some ancient complexes like Preah Vihar.

Although he supported Shivaism as the state religion, Suryavarman preferred Mahayana Buddhism, the iconographic themes of which reappeared in Khmer art. The king's preference for the doctrine of the Enlightened One may confirm the theory of his Malay origin, as Tambralinga, like the entire Malacca area, was strongly influenced by the great neighboring Buddhist kingdom of Dvaravati in the Menam delta. Apart from his personal inclinations, Suryavarman may have attempted to counterbalance the power of the Brahmans by supporting the Buddhist monks. The posthumous name of Nirvanapada that he received on his death in 1049 clearly alludes to nirvana, the ineffable state of extinction of painful existence which is the supreme goal of Buddhists.

His son or close relation Udayadityavarman II, who was only a child when he was crowned King in 1050, had the good fortune to have a loyal vrah guru, Jayendrapandita, and an excellent general, Sangrama, who kept the kingdom united despite numerous provincial revolts. Jayendrapandita is mentioned in the famous inscription of Sdok Kak Thom, the swansong of the Shivakaivalya to which he belonged. In 1051 Sangrama regained the city of Shambhupura and the Panduranga area, now Phan Rang in south Vietnam, both of which had been sacked by the Cham and had come under the control of Aravindhahrada, who was perhaps of Cham descent. In 1065 the same gallant general put down the rebellion led by one Kamvau in an area to the north-west of Angkor.

Despite its domestic problems, the Khmer Empire expanded further, especially to the west, and new temples were built. The capital of Udayadityavarman II was situated around the gigantic mountain temple of Baphuon, seat of the devaraja, whose rites were celebrated by Shankarapandita of the Saptadevakula Brahmans, and Jayendrapandita of the Shivakaivalya family was appointed rajapurohita (royal chaplain).

The new city of Angkor commissioned by Udayadityavarman II was supplied with water by the West Baray, which was completed by that king, although the plans and the start of the work were probably commissioned by Suryavarman I. In the middle of the reservoir stood the West Mebon temple, famous for a large bronze statue of Vishnu lying on his couch, the serpent Ananta, the remains of which have been found.

On the death in 1066 of Udayadityavarman II, whose posthumous name is unknown, he was succeeded by his brother Harshavarman III. The new king was repeatedly forced to fight the Cham, who made a devastating raid on the ancient capital of Shambupura (now Sambor) on the Mekong. According to Chinese sources, in 1076 the emperor, who considered both the Khmer and the Cham as his vassals, ordered them to help in the campaign against the Dai Viet, which turned out to be a failure. However, there is no mention of this event in the Khmer epigraphs.

On the death of Harshavarman III, who received the posthumous name of Sadashivapada, a sovereign of different ancestry conquered the throne of Angkor in 1080. Jayavarman VI came from the principality of Mahidharapura, possibly in northeast Thailand, and was legitimized by Divakarapandita, vrah guru of the previous king, who presumably changed sides. Jayavarman VI only reigned over northern Kambuja, while an unknown king, probably a direct descendent of Harshavarman III, ruled in the south.

Jayavarman VI made numerous donations to existing religious centers, but his name is not associated with any new monuments; as a result, some experts suggest that he did not live at Angkor.

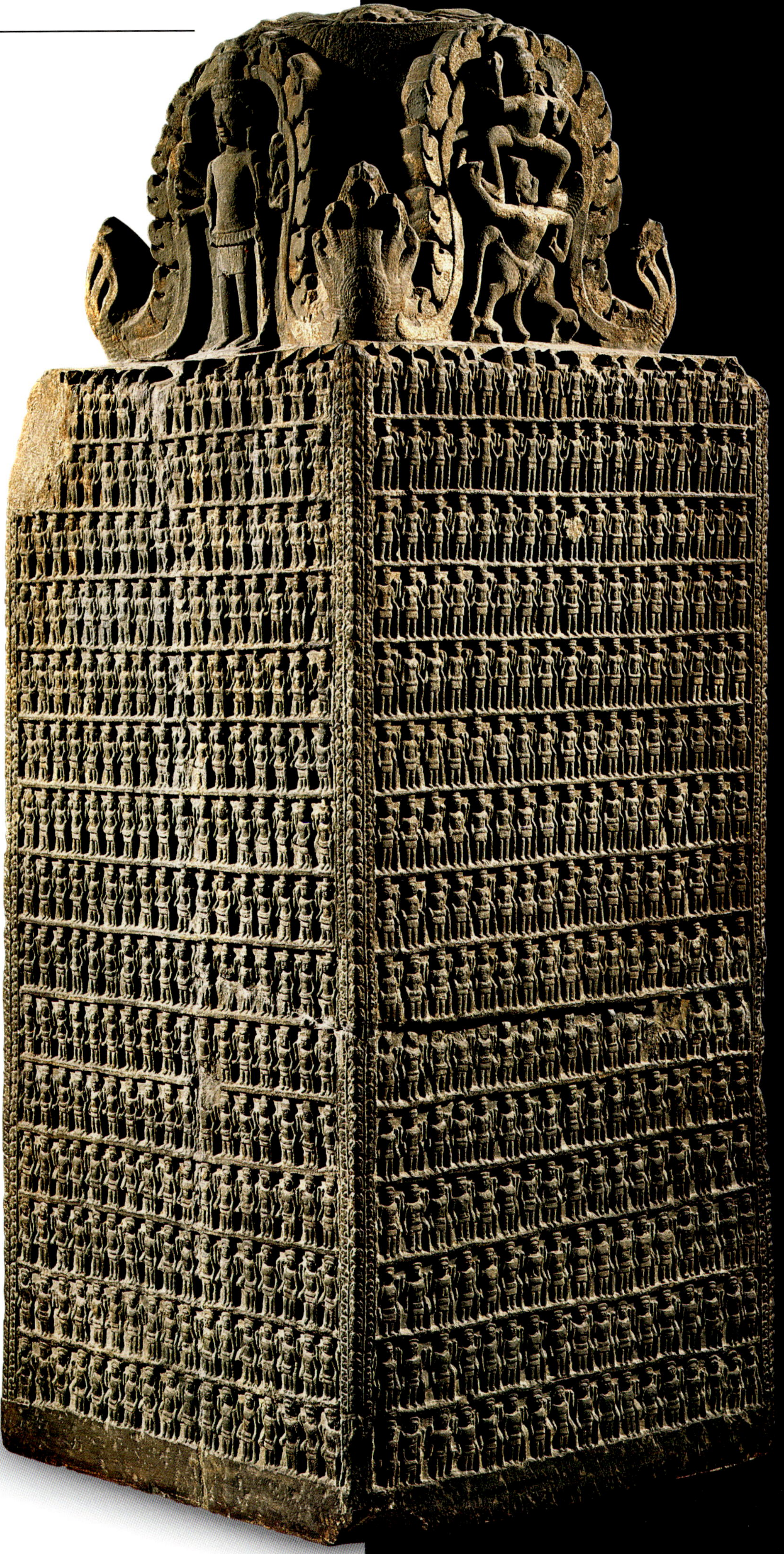

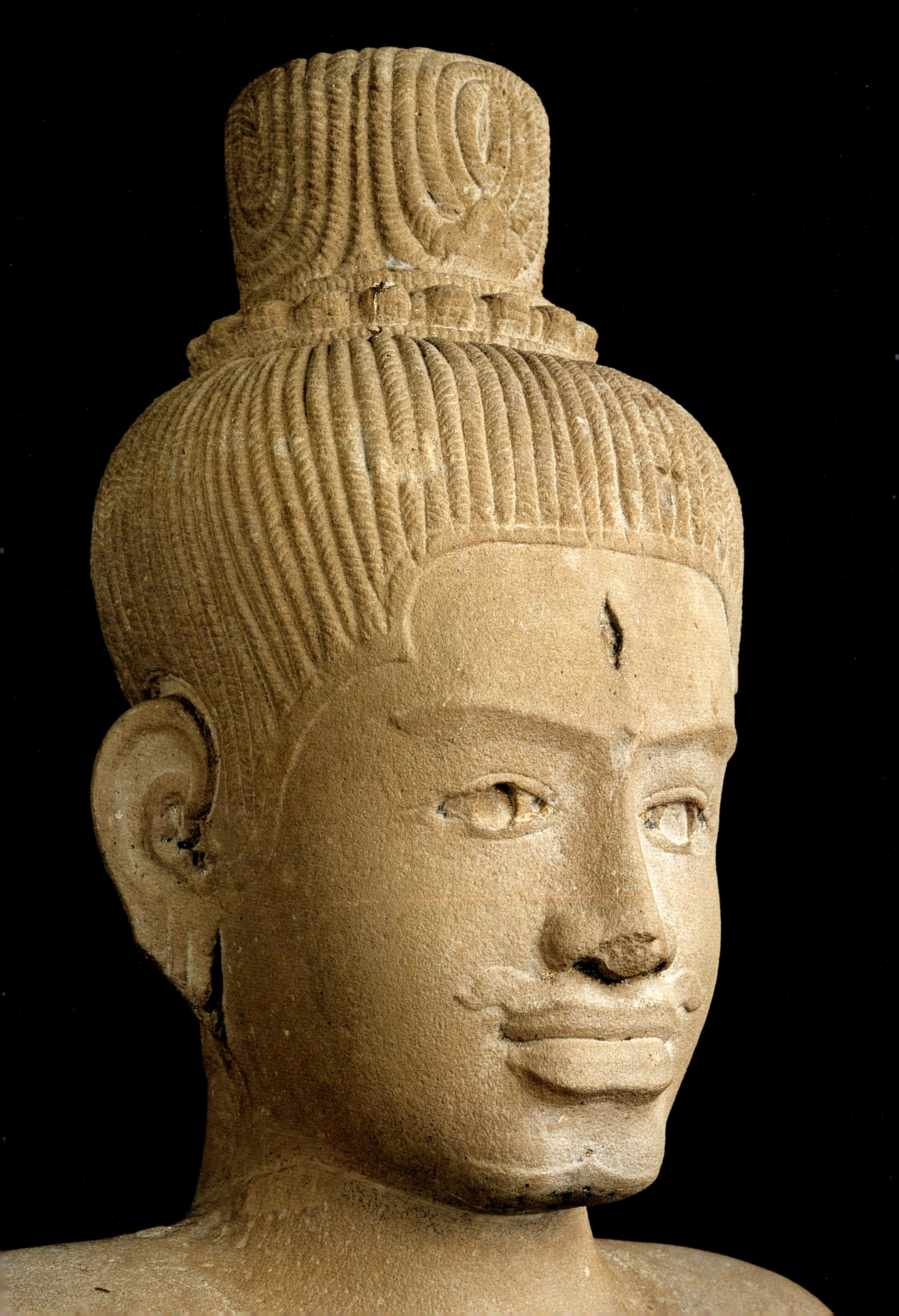

40 The Khmer kings identified with Shiva, obtaining their legitimization from the cult of the devaraja (god-king); just as Shiva ruled over all the deities, so the monarch ruled over all the princes. This beautiful eleventh-century head of Shiva in the Baphuon style, found at Basak Romduol and now in the Phnom Penh National Museum, was illuminated by inserts of precious materials in the pupil sockets and the third eye on the forehead.

However, the temple of Phimai, in what is now Thailand, was built during this period, and it seems likely that it was commissioned by Jayavarman, because his birthplace Mahidharapura is believed to have been in the same area. During the reign of Jayavarman VI, women were distinguished by their educational accomplishments, and one woman, Tilaka, the mother of Subhadra, another famous court Brahman, was even associated with the goddess Vagishvari Bhagavati. On his death in 1107, Jayavarman VI was given the posthumous name of Paramakaivalyapada.

Because of the premature death of the heir to the throne, a brother of Jayavarman's who died before 1092, his elder brother was obliged to leave the monastery to which he had retired and take the throne as Dharanindravarman I. The dead brother's wife Vijayendralakshmi first married Jayavarman and then Dharanindravarman I, which demonstrates the importance of women in legitimizing the succession. When Dharanindravarman was crowned, Buddhism made its official entry to court.

In the meantime another king had appeared on the political scene, probably a direct descendent of Harshavarman III and possibly identifiable with Nripatindravarman. However, it was not this king who deposed Dharanindravarman, but the latter's great-nephew Suryavarman, who eliminated him in 1112. Dharanindravarman received the posthumous name of Paramanishkalapada.

Suryavarman II was consecrated by the now elderly Divakarapandita in 1113 and crowned in 1119. He was a warrior king, and after unifying Kambuja attempted on several occasions to invade Annam, where the Dai Viet had been freed from Chinese rule in 939. The inscriptions from this period are few, incomplete, or clearly biased, so that the facts cannot be reconstructed with certainty. Moreover, both the Cham and the Dai Viet were divided into various principalities, and the confused and changing alliances may have involved some of them. However it may be, Suryavarman, defeated by the Dai Viet in 1128, appears to have struck up an alliance with the Cham in 1132 and invaded the Annamite territories, but was again repulsed.

In 1136 the Cham made peace with the Viet and Suryavarman was forced to give up his designs on Annam. In order to take his revenge, he conducted a series of raids against Champa in 1138 and occupied the country in 1144. The deposed king and a few loyal followers took refuge in Panduranga. From there, Jaya Harivarman I, who succeeded his father in 1147 and was destined to become one of the greatest Cham kings, challenged Suryavarman. Suryavarman sent an army from Vijaya, the capital of Champa (now Binh Dinh), but it was defeated. In 1149 Jaya Harivarman I retook Vijaya and killed Harideva, Suryavarman's brother-in-law who ruled there, and took his place. After shaking off the Khmer yoke, Jaya proclaimed himself "supreme lord of the Cham kings," and prepared to take his revenge.

In the meantime, to the west, the Mon of Haripunjaya, a kingdom situated around Lamphun in what is now northwest Thailand, had attacked the Khmer possession of Lavo (now Lobpuri, also in Thailand), and were pursued to their capital. However, Suryavarman does not seem to have conquered that area. More information is given by Chinese sources: in 1116, Kambuja resumed relations with China, and the chronicles speak of the Khmer sovereign with great respect. According to these chronicles, Suryavarman's dominions stretched west as far as the borders of the Burmese kingdom of Pagan and east to the sea; to the north they bordered on Champa, and to the south on the Kingdom of Grahi, in the heart of the Malay peninsula. The Chinese accounts, though approximate, cannot have been very far from the truth.

Despite the continual wars, Suryavarman built numerous magnificent monuments that reflected his power and expressed the grandeur of the age. The most important is the famous Angkor Wat, in which the court was probably established. The King was a Vishnuite, as indicated by his posthumous name Paramavishnuloka, and the cult of the devaraja may no longer have been celebrated at this time. The last inscription referring to Suryavarman dates from 1145, but he is believed to have died in 1150 after a disastrous expedition to Annam.

He was succeeded in 1150 by his cousin Dharanindravarman II, a Buddhist, although Jacques advocates the theory that Dharanindravarman may not have exercised absolute power but only ruled over a limited area. Whether he was the supreme ruler or not, he is known to have engaged in a military campaign against the Cham, led by his son Jayavarman. After Dharanindravarman's death in 1160 he received the posthumous name of Paramanishkalapada, and a new character, Yashovarman II, came onto the scene. His origins are obscure, but Jacques suggests that he may have replaced Dharanindravarman as Lord of Angkor as early as 1150.

Equally nebulous is the story told in the inscription on the temple of Banteay Chmar, which refers to a palace revolt during the reign of Yashovarman II fomented by Bharata Rahu (it is not known whether this refers to one man or two). Briggs believes that this may have been a class rebellion. The situation was saved by the intervention of a prince who, according to Briggs, may have been Indrakumara, son of the future King Jayavarman VII. If this is the case, Yashovarman must have been related in some way to the family of Dharanindravarman and Jayavarman, namely the Mahidharapura dynasty.

Yashovarman was assassinated in 1165 by one of his ministers, who had himself crowned with the name of Tribhuvanadityavarman. Dharanindravarman's son, Prince Jayavarman, rushed back from Champa, but not in time to intervene, and withdrew, possibly to the Preah Khan of Kompong Thom, waiting for the tide to turn. In the meantime a palace revolt had also taken place in Champa, and the throne had been conquered by Jaya Indravarman IV, an energetic leader who had not forgotten the Khmer incursions into his territory. He saw the opportunity to take his revenge, and in 1177 sailed up the Mekong, the Tonlé Sap, and perhaps the Siem Reap, disembarked at Yashodharapura, sacked the city, killed Tribhuvanadityavarman, and took up residence in the Angkor area.

# BUDDHA
## The Supreme Lord

*42 Hinduism was supplanted by Buddhism during the last Khmer period. The Mahayana school was originally predominant but the ancient Theravada school (Doctrine of the Elders) was later revived. The influence of Singhalese iconography is demonstrated by the flame of illumination on the cranial protuberance of this fourteenth-century bronze Buddha, housed in the Phnom Penh National Museum.*

*43 The protagonist of the magnificent twilight of the Khmer Empire was Jayavarman VII, a complex, fascinating character under whom the empire reached the height of its glory. The King was probably in his fifties when he was crowned in 1181, and was still alive in 1219. Some statues, like this one from Angkor Thom, now in the Phnom Penh National Museum, show his features, which were also attributed to some images of Buddha.*

The events that followed the sack of Angkor are unclear. However, there is no doubt that Jayavarman waged a great naval battle against the Cham on the Tonlé Sap (the huge lake to the south of the Angkor plain into which the Tonlé Sap river flowed) and won. Fighting continued on dry land and in the heart of Yashodharapura, and according to an ambiguous passage in an inscription, the Cham king seems to have been killed in a bloody clash near the royal palace. Having driven the Cham out the Angkor area, Jayavarman had to subdue the numerous Khmer princes who had proclaimed their independence following the disaster in the capital and probably even earlier, during the reign of Dharanindravarman. Now the ruler of unified Kambuja, he was crowned in 1181 as Jayavarman VII.

The date of birth of Jayavarman VII, the best-known Khmer emperor, is unknown, but is believed to have been between 1125 and 1130. This would mean that he was over fifty at the time of his coronation. It is known from the epigraphs that he was the son of Jayarajacudamani, a daughter of Harshavarman III ( Jacques believes that the latter was not King of Angkor, but a minor sovereign from Banteay Chmar), and married Jayarajadevi, a cultured, energetic princess who inspired and supported him until her death, which threw the king into despair. Indradevi, Jayarajadevi's cultured older sister and the King's second wife, sang the praises of the dead queen in the inscriptions, emphasizing her love for her husband and Buddhist piety. Jayavarman was also a Buddhist and filled the country with religious foundations, but this did not prevent him from being a great conqueror.

In 1182 a revolt broke out at Malyang, a dependent kingdom in the present-day province of Battambang, and the King sent a young Cham commander, Vidyanandana, to put it down. When Vidyanandana returned victorious, he was nominated crown prince. Jayavarman evidently placed far more trust in Vidyanandana than his Khmer generals and sent him to subjugate the Champa in 1190, having long meditated and prepared his revenge. Vidyanandana conquered Vijaya, the capital of Champa, and sent the Cham king to Angkor as a prisoner. According to some inscriptions, the Cham king was still Jaya Indravarman IV, in which case he was obviously not killed in the skirmish at the royal palace of Yashodharapura. A new Cham sovereign, Suryavarmadeva, the brother-in-law of Jayavarman VII, was installed on the throne of Vijaya, and Vidyanandana took for himself a fief in Panduranga, now Phan Rang.

However, when Vijaya rebelled and deposed Suryavarmadeva, Vidyanandana seized his opportunity, took the city by storm, and annexed its territories to Panduranga. Jayavarman then freed the deposed Cham King who was held hostage at the Khmer court and sent him with a large army against Vidyanandana, but without success. Other attempts also seem to have failed, and it was not until 1203 that Vidyanandana was driven out by a relative in the pay of Jayavarman VII, who was thus able to annex Champa once more.

*44 left One of the masterpieces housed in the Phnom Penh Museum is this head of Jayavarman VII, found in the Preah Khan at Kompong Svay. The artist has skillfully captured the essence of the King, who was younger here than in the previous statue, wearing no ornaments, meditating yet radiating charismatic power.*

*44 right Jayavarman VII, who was identified with Lokeshvara, the bodhisattva of compassion, and with Buddha, as in this head, now in the Guimet Museum, was deified during his lifetime. According to the inscriptions, the king's conduct was inspired by the loving care of the enlightened followers of Buddhism.*

With the annexation of Champa, the Khmer Empire reached its greatest size. Jayavarman had to deal with new incursions in the west by the Burmese of Haripunjaya in Lavo, but he eventually forced them to pay tribute to him. The same fate befell Annam to the north-east; it had actually been invaded with little success in 1216 and 1218, but preferred to declare itself at least nominally the vassal of Angkor. To the north, where the Korat plateau and the entire Menam valley were now firmly in Khmer hands, Jayavarman's armies marched as far as northern Laos, reaching what is now Vientiane and the borders of the Thai kingdom of Nan Chao (now Yunnan). To the south the armies reached southern Malaysia, conquering the kingdoms of Dvaravati, Grahi and Tambralinga, and Java also appears to have recognized the suzerainty of Jayavarman.

Within the Empire, and especially on the Angkor plain, Jayavarman conducted a frenetic building program, during which a myriad of new buildings were erected and others demolished. The road system was reorganized, and according to the inscription on the Preah Khan and the report by Zhou Daguan, 121 "fire houses" were built. These seem to have been a kind of rest area, although researchers are unsure of their real purpose. Some consider that they were **dharmashala** (resting places for travelers), while others point out that **dharmashala**, which are still used in Indochina today, must have been made of perishable materials like the houses in the villages. Jayavarman's buildings, however, were made of stone, and may have been shrines, with travelers' huts made of wood and straw built alongside them.

45 Images of the "decorated Buddha," ornamented with jewels and wearing a precious belt to close his gown, emphasize the fact that Enlightened One, holder of spiritual supremacy, was identified with the chakravartin, the universal sovereign who held supreme temporal power. This gilded bronze figure, now in the Guimet Museum, dates from the late thirteenth century.

The Preah Khan inscription states that the King built or reopened 102 hospitals and includes a very interesting list of the personnel and supplies with which they were endowed. Jayavarman improved the water system; he extended the Srah Srang reservoir and built a new baray called Jayatataka, 11,500 feet long and 3,000 feet wide, to which 13 smaller reservoirs were connected.

Continuing the tradition of building shrines to the ancestors, the King dedicated the Ta Prohm to his mother in 1186 and the Preah Khan to his father in 1191. These were veritable religious citadels with a huge allocation of personnel and goods. Other important buildings commissioned by the King were the Ta Som, Ta Nei, Banteay Kdei, and Neak Pean. However, his name is mainly associated with his capital Jayashri (fortunate city of victory), now known as Angkor Thom (great city). Surrounded by walls and centered exactly on the Bayon mountain temple, Jayashri was built in accordance with defensive criteria and above all had a precise symbolic layout, which was believed to provide magical protection for the city against attacks and evil influences.

The Bayon, with its towers consisting of four faces looking out towards the cardinal points, is the most astonishing expression of Jayavarman's personality. A Buddhist, the king no longer recognized the authority of Shiva-devaraja, although he continued to use the services of the Brahmans at court, as stated by the inscriptions that refer to some of them, such as Jaya Mangalartha, who hailed from an up-and-coming family. Although no Hindu monuments were built during this period, generous donations were still made to the existing ones.

Jayavarman replaced the ancient image of the devaraja (king of the gods) with that of the Buddharaja (lord of the universe). The faces on the Bayon temple are those of Lokeshvara, the bodhisattva of compassion. In Mahayana Buddhism, the bodhisattva is one who, despite having achieved spiritual enlightenment and the

46 This twelfth/thirteenth-century goddess Lakshmi in the Bayon style, originally in the Preah Ko complex and now housed in the Phnom Penh National Museum, is identifiable by the lotus buds in her hands. She probably has the delicate features of Jayarajadevi, beloved wife of Jayavarman VII.

*ability to leave the painful world of life, chooses to remain among men to help them find the way to salvation.*

*This figure is the incarnation of compassion, and represented the ideal model for Jayavarman, who liked to think of himself as a merciful lord. To him, the Bayon temple expressed the synthesis between the social aspect of the King, who was identified as Lokeshvara, and therefore as the solicitous protector of his subjects' welfare, and his most intimate essence, that of Buddha, from which the* bodhisattvas *emanated. The incredible mountain temple of Jayashri thus became the shrine of the* Buddharaja, *whose features were those of the Emperor.*

*Almost as if he was afraid of impermanence (hardly a Buddhist trait, because Buddha proclaimed the transience of all phenomena and the desirability of their extinction in* nirvana), *Jayavarman erected statues of himself all over the country, some of which have survived to the present day. His features reveal the powerful, complex personality of the man. His high forehead indicates great intelligence, and his strong-willed expression is barely muted by his contemplative attitude. His half-closed eyes conceal his gaze, intent on inner contemplation, but his mouth, with its large, fleshy lips, reveals the formidable appetites of this king, who exuded spirituality and sensuality, humility and pride with equal intensity.*

*In his desire for immortality, revealed by his frenzied building campaign, Jayavarman identified his mother with the goddess Prajnaparamita, the mistress of supreme Buddhist knowledge, and his father with the bodhisattva Lokeshvara, of whom the Emperor considered himself the incarnation. However, it was not only the royal family who sought immortality; as if they had had a presentiment of the end, princes, dignitaries, and officials filled the temples with their statues, hoping in this way to cheat time as Angkor began its ineluctable decline.*

The last dated inscription relating to Jayavarman was written in 1206, but he is thought to have died in 1219/1220. If this is true, either he was nearly 100 years old at his death or his date of birth must have been 1140. The posthumous name attributed to him was Paramasaugata or Mahaparamasaugata.

Two years after the presumed death of Jayavarman, the Khmer evacuated Champa and the throne passed to the legitimate Cham heir Ansaraja, who was crowned as Jaya Parmeshvara IV and had to fight the Annamites. In the meantime the Thais, called Syam by their neighbors and Hsien by the Chinese, were threatening the borders of Kambuja. After being driven out of the Yangtze Kiang basin by the Chinese, they had settled in Yunnan in the seventh century A.D., founding the kingdom of Nan Chao, and from there had descended on the rich lands of Indochina.

In the meantime, King Indravarman II, perhaps a son of Jayavarman VII, had been consecrated at Jayashri, the designated heir, Prince Indrakumara, and other brothers of his having died during their father's lifetime. The Brahman families, penalized but by no means annihilated by Jayavarman, fomented a strong Shivaite reaction against the spread of Buddhism, demonstrated by the destruction and profanation of the Buddhist temples, many of which had been converted to Shivaite shrines. Secessions became increasingly frequent in the outlying parts of the Khmer Empire, and Tambralinga became independent by 1230, as did Lavo.

When Indravarman died in 1243 he was succeeded by Jayavarman VIII, and pressure from the neighboring countries became stronger. When Kublai Khan, founder of the Mongol dynasty, came to power in China in 1260, a series of offensives began at the expense of the Burmese and Thai kingdoms, as well as the Champa and Annam, whose capitals, Vijaya and Hanoi, were taken by storm. The Mongol hordes reached Malaysia, where some small states were subjugated, but their the expedition against Java was a failure. Kambuja seems to have been spared the raids of Kublai Khan, and although it sent diplomatic missions to China in 1285 and 1292, it did not accept Chinese supremacy.

This was the political situation in 1296 when the new Chinese emperor, Timur Khan, sent a mission to Kambuja. One of its members was Zhou Daguan, who recounts that in 1295 Jayavarman VIII was forced to abdicate in favor of his son-in-law Shrindravarman, having been betrayed by his own daughter, who had delivered the sacred palladian sword of the kingdom to her husband. During the reign of Jayavarman VIII, who received the posthumous name of Parameshvarapada, the first great Thai state, Sukhothai, had been formed under the leadership of the powerful Rama Kamheng, who occupied numerous western and northern territories of the Khmer Empire. According to Zhou Daguan, the Thais had also devastated Kambuja.

Nonetheless, Zhou Daguan's descriptions of the kingdom of Shrindravarman do not seem to portray a country that had been brought to its knees; the capital was still flourishing. In any event, a major change had certainly taken place, as demonstrated by the first inscription in Pali by Shrindravarman, which appeared in 1309, two years after he, too, had abdicated, leaving the throne to a relative. The use of the Pali language confirms the spread of Hinayana Buddhism, which had infiltrated even the court. In fact, the King may have abdicated as a result of his conversion. The Buddhist monks, who had been spreading the message of Buddha among the population since ancient times, were much closer to the ordinary people than the Hindu priests. Hinayana, which means the "the small vehicle (of salvation)," is a very simple, basic, and more ancient form of Buddhism. It had been introduced by the Khmerized Mon of Lavo, and soon obtained a huge following. When places of worship were built to receive the congregations and monks, they were no longer huge, expensive creations which the common people were partly prohibited from entering, but modest wooden or brick buildings that were democratically open to all. Thus the religion of the Enlightened One eventually ousted Hinduism and became the official religion, in which 88 percent of the Cambodian population still believe. However, under Shrindrajayavarman, Shrindravarman's heir who reigned between 1307 and 1327, Hinduism by no means disappeared. The Brahmans continued to hold important posts at court and to act as spiritual masters, as stated by the inscriptions, and their power and wealth were still considerable. In fact, the last temple of Angkor, called the Mangalartha, was built by the Mangalartha family of priests.

The last king of Angkor, Jayavarman Parameshvara or Jayavarman IX, is known to have sent two delegations, one to China and the other to Annam. The last inscription in Sanskrit, found in the moat of Angkor Wat, dates from his coronation in 1327. From that date until 1432, generally considered to be the date when Angkor was abandoned, the situation is highly unclear.

However, the Khmer Empire was still powerful enough to support the formation of a new neighboring kingdom. Following clashes between Thai chieftains, the lord of a principality situated in what is now northern Laos had been forced to take refuge at the Angkor court. His son Fa Ngun grew up there, married a Khmer princess, and was given military aid to win back his native land. Fa Ngun, who reigned between 1353 and 1373, thus founded the Kingdom of Lan Xang, which included the Khorat plateau in present-day Thailand and what is now central and northern Laos, incorporating a huge, though sparsely populated territory. Fa Ngun converted to Hinayana Buddhism, the religion of his wife and the Khmer court, and received as a gift a venerated golden image of Buddha, the Pha Bang (holy image). The image became the palladium of the Kingdom of Laos, hence the name of the city in which it is still kept, Liang Phabang, which means "(city of) the great Pha Bang."

In the meantime, more upheavals had taken place among the Thai kingdoms. In 1347 Ramadhipati had founded Ayuthya (now Ayutthaya in southern Thailand), which had subjugated Sukhothai. The experts disagree about the probable raids made from Ayuthya against the Khmer capital, the most devastating of which is believed to have taken place in 1353. The Chinese chronicles make no mention of them, although Khmer delegations are recorded between 1371 and 1403. In 1430 the Thai King of Ayuthya, Paramaraja or Boromaraja II, invaded the Angkor plain and laid siege to the capital. He took it after seven months, apparently helped by the defection of a number of commanders and monks.

However, the end of Angkor cannot be attributed to the Thai invasion, but to a series of causes that began to emerge during the reign of Jayavarman VII. His building frenzy depleted the empire's resources and exhausted the population, which no longer participated in the incomprehensible projects of its god-kings with its former enthusiasm. Labor became scarce, and the maintenance of the complex water system gradually deteriorated. The power of Angkor depended on the paddy fields, and rice depended on water. B.P. Groslier suggests that the irrigation network bears the signs of a catastrophe, and folk tradition talks of a flood. Whether this was the decisive factor or the system was already at the point of collapse is unknown. What is certain is that without the formidable system of barays and canals, and without an absolute monarch capable of managing it, the god-king's capital could not survive.

The court moved elsewhere, and nature reclaimed its own. The now stagnant reservoirs became breeding grounds for malaria, and Angkor was depopulated. However, contrary to common belief in the West, it was never forgotten or totally abandoned.

49 This twelfth/thirteenth-century image in the Bayon style, illuminated by an inner light, originates from the Preah Khan at Kompong Svay and is now in the Guimet Museum. It portrays Buddha protected by Mucilinda, King of the Naga, only two of whose five heads have survived intact. The cobra has many meanings, associated with a very ancient chthonian religious creed: symbol of the genius loci, repository of wisdom, and bringer of rain, because it is identified with the rainbow. Here, it pays homage to Buddha by acting as a canopy.

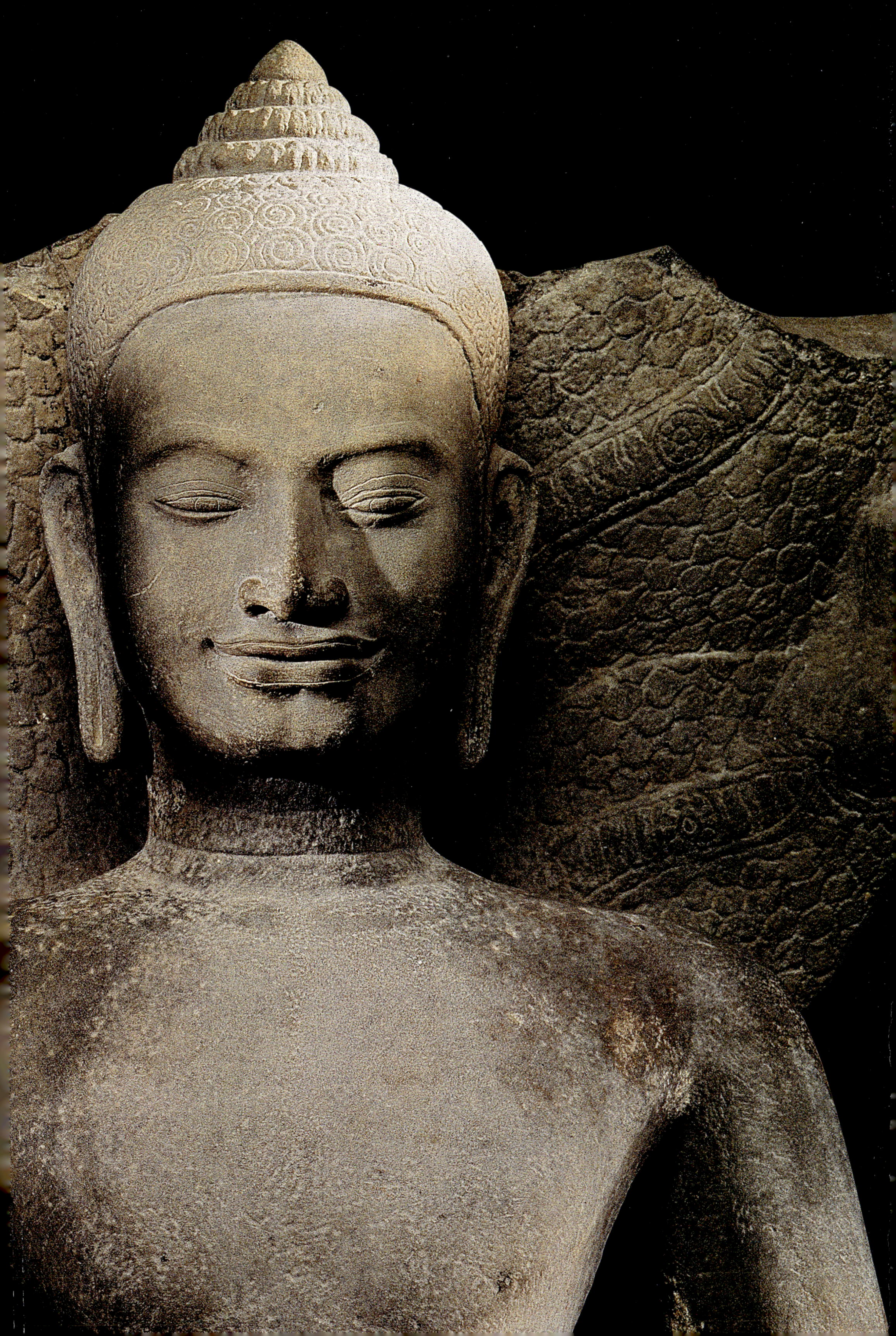

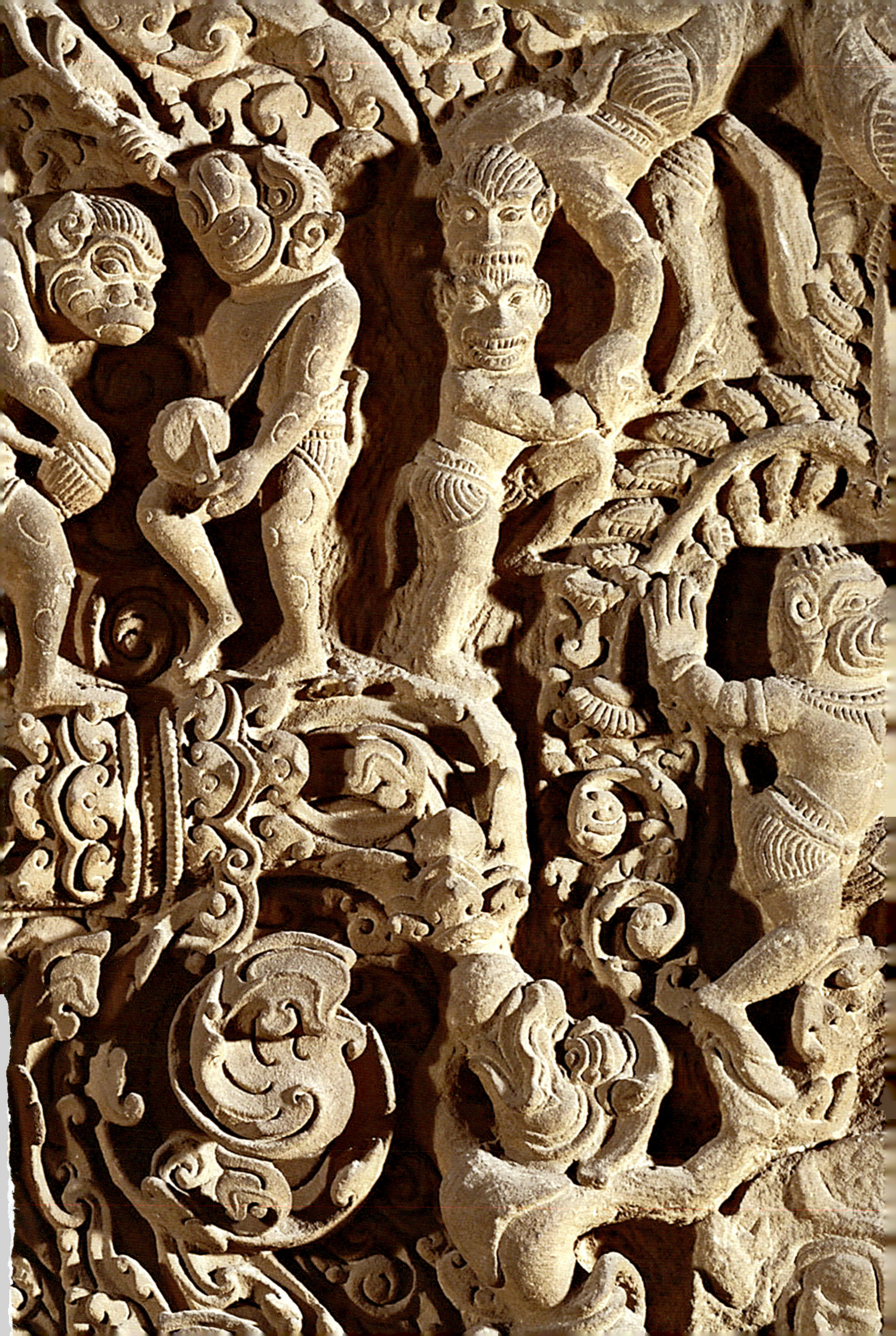

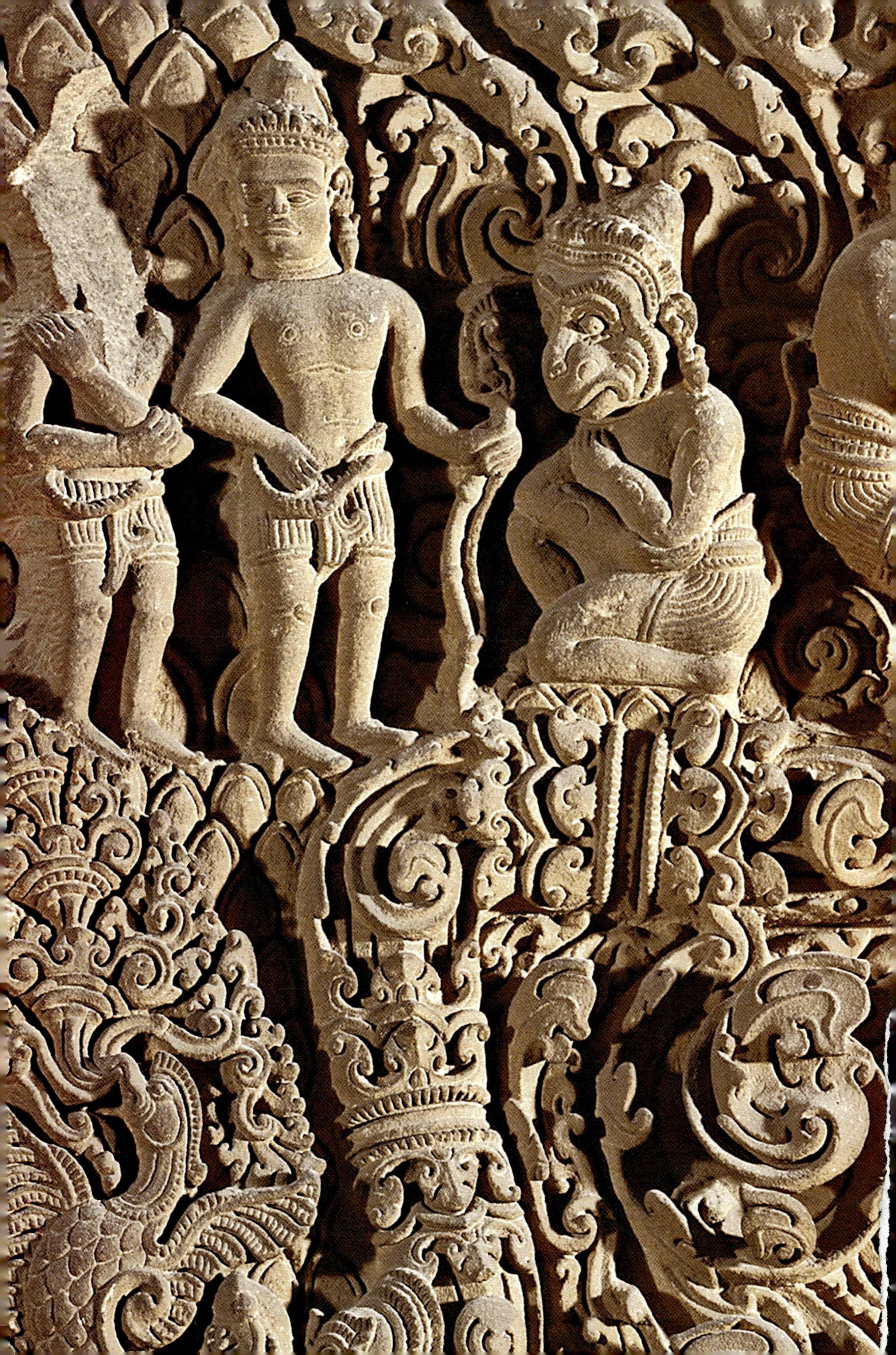

# CHRONOLOGY

## FUNAN AND THE MOUNTAIN KINGS

Cambodia, or rather Kambuja (land of the descendents of Kambu), has been inhabited since the third millennium B.C., and its first great kingdom developed along the Gulf of Siam at the start of the Christian era. The Chinese chronicles call it Funan, a name that derives from the Khmer word bnam (mountain), and a strong Indian influence is evident from the surviving relics. Funan seems to have been founded by one Kaundinya who, after a dream, traveled there from India and married Soma, a local princess who belonged to the naga people, mythical beings who were part cobra. The son of Soma and Kaundinya was to be the founder of the first Funanese Kaundinya dynasty. In the fifth century a second Kaundinya arrived from India to revive the Indianized customs which had been lost, and from the time of King Kaundinya Jayavarman (A.D. 478-514) the rulers of Funan acquired greater historical importance. Their capital was Vyadhapura, and Oc-èo, north of the present-day Rach Gia in Vietnam, was the kingdom's main port. In 514 Rudravarman became king and elected as his capital Angkor Borei, where he may have lived until after 539.

*Phnom Da style, 540-600*

50 The characters with clasped hands who often appear in bas-reliefs, like this one at Phnom Bakheng, are in the anjali position, which indicates greeting, respect, and veneration.

51-54 The architraves use a "freeze-frame" sequence to illustrate their story. This ninth/tenth-century architrave at Wat Baset shows the alliance between Rama and Sugriva, deposed king of the monkeys, on the left, the combat between these allies and the usurper Valin in the center, and the death of the rival Valin, mourned by his wives and followers, on the right.

## CHENLA AND THE ADVENT OF THE KHMER

The Khmer came from the upper reaches of the Menam river and followed the Mon valley to the Mekong. Their first independent principality was founded in the fifth century to the north of Tonlé Sap. The Chinese chronicles use the name Chenla to describe the Khmer territories, and the first kings mentioned are Shrutavarman and Shreshthavarman, whose capital Shreshthapura must have been in southern Laos. Chenla was divided into a number of kingdoms, one of the main ones being Bhavapura, in the Sambor Prei Kuk area near present-day Kompong Thom. The most important king was Ishanavarman, who completed the conquest of Funan between 612 and 628 and chose as his capital Sambor Prei Kuk, which he renamed Ishanapura. Chenla split up into independent states but was reunified by Jayavarman I in 657. When he died sometime after 700 his wife Jayadevi tried in vain to keep the kingdom united. Among the principalities which subsequently formed was Shambhupura, now Sambor on the Mekong, whose king Pushkaraksha proclaimed himself king of all Kambuja in 716. According to the Chinese chronicles, in the early eighth century there was a "Land Chenla" and a "Water Chenla," the former united and centering on the ancient territories of Chenla, and the latter divided into numerous fiefs in the area that once constituted Funan. Pushkaraksha's son Shambhuvarman and the latter's heir Rajendravarman I managed to keep control of much of Water Chenla until the late eighth century, when the Malays and Javanese imposed their rule on many Khmer principalities.

*Sambor Prei Kuk style, 600-650*
*Prei Kmeng style, 635-700*
*Prasat Andet style, seventh-eighth century*
*Kompong Preah style, 706-800*

# KAMBUJA
## through the Centuries

### ANGKOR, PLAIN OF CAPITALS

The consecration rite of Jayavarman II on Mount Julen in 802 freed Kambuja from the rule of Java and inaugurated the cult of the devaraja (god-king), the heavenly counterpart of the earthly king. The newly-founded Hariharalaya was the first settlement of the Angkor Empire. The hydraulic architecture based on barays (water reservoirs), which was to assure the fortune of Angkor, was inaugurated by Indravarman, who built the Indratataka reservoir at Lolei in 877. By the time of Indravarman's death in 889, the Khmer Empire held control as far as Ubon in Thailand in the north and Phom Bayang in the south, at the southernmost tip of Kambuja. His successor Yashovarman retained his father's possessions and built the East Baray to supply water to the new capital Yashodharapura. The capital was moved to Koh Ker, about 56 miles northeast of Angkor, under the usurper Jayavarman IV between 921 and 944. Rajendravarman II returned to Angkor in 944, and after battles with the Champa kingdom, extended his rule as far as the Annamite chain in the east, Burma in the west, and the Gulf of Siam in the south.

**Jayavarman II (790-850)** *founds Hariharalaya. Krus Preah Aram Rong Chen on the Phnom Kulen. Phnom Kulen style, 825-875*
**Jayavarman III (850-877)** *builds the Prei Monti at Hariharalaya.*
**Indravarman I (877-889)** *builds the Lolei baray, the Preah Ko and the Bakong.*
*Preah Ko style*
**Yashovarman (889-910)** *builds Yashodharapura, the East Baray, Phnom Bakheng, Phnom Krom, and Phnom Bok.*
*Bakheng style, 889-925*
**Harshavarman I (910-923)** *builds Baksei Chamkrong and Prasat Kravan.*
**Ishanavarman II (923-928)**
**Jayavarman IV (928-941)** *moves to Koh Ker.*
*Koh Ker style, 921-944*
**Harshavarman II (941-944)** *at Koh Ker.*
**Rajendravarman (944-968)** *returns to Angkor and builds Pre Rup, East Mebon, Bat Chum, and Srah Srang; the Brahman Yajnavaraha builds Banteay Srei.*
*Pre Rup style, 944-968.*
*Banteay Srey style, 960-1000*
**Jayavarman V (968-1001)** *founds Jayendranagari and builds Ta Keo.*

### AN EVER-EXPANDING EMPIRE

During the first decade of the eleventh century a powerful king, Suryavarman I, came to the throne. He unified almost the whole of Kambuja and levied tribute from southern Thailand and part of southern Laos. He began work on the gigantic West Baray and it was completed by his son Udayadityavarman II, who kept his father's kingdom united despite revolts. He was succeeded by his brother, Harshavarman III, who had to fight the Cham. On Harshavarman's death in 1080 the throne of Angkor passed to Jayavarman VI, a prince from Mahidharapura, a fief possibly located in northeast Thailand. Following the reigns of a few unimportant kings, Suryavarman II conquered the throne and was crowned in 1119. This warrior king reunited Kambuja, attempted to invade Annam on several occasions, and occupied Champa in 1144. His dominions stretched to the borders of the Burmese Kingdom of Pagan in the west, to the sea in the east, and to the heart of the Malay peninsula in the south. In 1165 the usurper Tribhuvanadityavarman assassinated the legitimate king Yashovarman II. Seizing the opportunity, the King of Champa, Jaya Indravarman IV, sailed to Yashodharapura in 1177, sacked the city, killed Tribhuvanadityavarman, and settled in the area.

**Udayadityavarman I (1001-1002)**
**Jayaviravarman (1002-1006)** *builds the north Khleang.*
**Suryavarman I (1010-1050)** *begins the West Baray and builds the Phimeanakas in the Royal Palace, Phnom Chisor, and parts of the Preah Khan of Kompong Svay, Preah Vihear, and Wat Phu.*
*Khleang style, 1010-1050*
**Udayadityavarman II (1050-1066)** *builds the Baphuon and West Mebon.*
*Baphuon style, 1050-1066*
**Harshavarman III (1066-1080)**
**Jayavarman VI (1080-1107)** *builds Phimai.*
**Dharanindravarman I (1107-1112)**
**Suryavarman II (1113-1150)** *builds the Thommanon, Chau Say Tevoda, Angkor Wat, Beng Mealea, Preah Pithu, Banteay Samré, some buildings of the Preah Khan of Kompong Svay, and Phnom Rung.*
*Angkor Wat style, 1100-1175*
**Dharanindravarman II (1150-1160)**
**Yashovarman II (1150-1165)**
**Tribhuvanadityavarman (1165-1177)**
*The Cham sack the capital.*

### BUDDHA, THE SUPREME LORD

Jayavarman VII, who was crowned in 1181 at over fifty years old, drove out the Cham and reunified Kambuja. He was a fervent Buddhist and replaced the cult of Shiva-devaraja with that of the Buddharaja, lord of the universe. During his reign the Khmer Empire reached its largest size, growing to include the Korat plain, the entire Menam valley, and part of southern Malaysia. Champa and northern Laos were also annexed, and tribute was levied on the Burmese kingdom of Haripunjaya, Annam, and apparently from Java too. Two years after the presumed death of Jayavarman in 1219/20 the Khmer evacuated Champa, meanwhile secessions became more frequent in the outlying parts of the Empire and the Thai threatened the borders. The Brahmanic families fomented a strong Shivaite reaction against the spread of Buddhism, but Hinayana, the "small vehicle [of salvation]," the simplest and oldest form of Buddhism, eventually prevailed. In 1296 the Chinese Emperor Timur Khan sent a mission to Kambuja, and some invaluable accounts of the country were written by one of its members, Zhou Daguan. The first great Thai state, Sukhothai, which had been formed during the reign of Jayavarman VIII, occupied numerous western and northern territories of the Empire. In 1430 a Thai King, Paramaraja II of Ayuthya, invaded the Angkor plain and laid siege on the capital, which he took after seven months. From that moment on, the evacuation and decline of Angkor began.

**Jayavarman VII (1181-1219/20)** *builds the Preah Khan of Kompong Svay, Ta Prohm, the Preah Khan of Angkor, Neak Pean, Banteay Kdei, Ta Som, Ta Nei, Srah Srang, Angkor Thom, the Bayon, the Elephant Terrace, the Terrace of the Leper King, and the reservoirs of the Royal Palace, Banteay Chmar, and south Khleang. Bayon style, 1181-1219/20*
**Indravarman II (1218-1243)** *builds Prasat Suor Prat.*
**Jayavarman VIII (1243-1295)** *builds the Mangalartha.*
**Shrindravarman (1295-1307)**
**Shrindrajayavarman (1307-1327)**
**Jayavarman Parameshvara (1327-?)**

# Angkor
## The Rediscovery

Despite the vicissitudes of history and the transfer of the capital elsewhere, contrary to common belief Angkor Wat was never completely forgotten, but rather was turned into a Buddhist monastery and continued to be a place of worship. In a letter dated 1668, French missionary Father Chevreul described it as being a popular place of pilgrimage. In any event, the ruins of the ancient Khmer Empire had been known to Portuguese and Spanish missionaries and adventurers since the previous century.

The first significant descriptions of Angkor were written by the Portuguese Diogo do Couto in a 1614 manuscript. They probably do not relate to a journey made by do Couto himself but were based on accounts provided by Capuchin friar Antonio da Magdalena, who visited Angkor between 1585 and 1558. The Portuguese visitors, who were numerous in the early seventeenth century, nearly all agreed that the great Khmer city must have been constructed by non-local builders, hypotheses ranging from Trajan to Chinese Jews!

The oldest map of Angkor Wat was drawn between 1623 and 1636 by a Japanese pilgrim convinced that he had reached Jetavana, a venerable monastery situated in the Magadha region of India, where Buddha is believed to have spent much of his life. The map, which was copied in 1715, was not recognized as being a plan of the Khmer masterpiece until the early nineteenth century.

However, it was not until the nineteenth century, the century of adventurous explorers and amateur archaeologists, that Angkor was really "rediscovered." The first to devote a short essay to it was a French missionary, Father Charles Émile Bouillevaux, who stayed there for two days in 1850. The essay was published in 1858, and that same year naturalist Henri Mouhot spent all he had on a voyage to Indochina, where he traveled until his death in Laos in 1861. His letters and notebooks were published posthumously in English and French, and his book "Travels in Siam, Cambodia, Laos, and other Central Parts of Indochina" was published in French in 1863.

Europeans now began to take an interest in Angkor and in Khmer civilization. German ethnographer Adolf Bastian guessed that it had links to Indian culture. Scottish photographer

# KAMBUJA
## through the Centuries

### ANGKOR, PLAIN OF CAPITALS

*The consecration rite of Jayavarman II on Mount Julen in 802 freed Kambuja from the rule of Java and inaugurated the cult of the* devaraja *(godking), the heavenly counterpart of the earthly king. The newly-founded Hariharalaya was the first settlement of the Angkor Empire. The hydraulic architecture based on barays (water reservoirs), which was to assure the fortune of Angkor, was inaugurated by Indravarman, who built the Indratataka reservoir at Lolei in 877. By the time of Indravarman's death in 889, the Khmer Empire held control as far as Ubon in Thailand in the north and Phom Bayang in the south, at the southernmost tip of Kambuja. His successor Yashovarman retained his father's possessions and built the East Baray to supply water to the new capital Yashodharapura. The capital was moved to Koh Ker, about 56 miles northeast of Angkor, under the usurper Jayavarman IV between 921 and 944. Rajendravarman II returned to Angkor in 944, and after battles with the Champa kingdom, extended his rule as far as the Annamite chain in the east, Burma in the west, and the Gulf of Siam in the south.*

**Jayavarman II (790-850)** *founds Hariharalaya. Krus Preah Aram Rong Chen on the Phnom Kulen. Phnom Kulen style, 825-875*
**Jayavarman III (850-877)** *builds the Prei Monti at Hariharalaya.*
**Indravarman I (877-889)** *builds the Lolei baray, the Preah Ko and the Bakong.*
*Preah Ko style*
**Yashovarman (889-910)** *builds Yashodharapura, the East Baray, Phnom Bakheng, Phnom Krom, and Phnom Bok.*
*Bakheng style, 889-925*
**Harshavarman I (910-923)** *builds Baksei Chamkrong and Prasat Kravan.*
**Ishanavarman II (923-928)**
**Jayavarman IV (928-941)** *moves to Koh Ker.*
*Koh Ker style, 921-944*
**Harshavarman II (941-944)** *at Koh Ker.*
**Rajendravarman (944-968)** *returns to Angkor and builds Pre Rup, East Mebon, Bat Chum, and Srah Srang; the Brahman Yajnavaraha builds Banteay Srei.*
*Pre Rup style, 944-968.*
*Banteay Srey style, 960-1000*
**Jayavarman V (968-1001)** *founds Jayendranagari and builds Ta Keo.*

### AN EVER-EXPANDING EMPIRE

*During the first decade of the eleventh century a powerful king, Suryavarman I, came to the throne. He unified almost the whole of Kambuja and levied tribute from southern Thailand and part of southern Laos. He began work on the gigantic West Baray and it was completed by his son Udayadityavarman II, who kept his father's kingdom united despite revolts. He was succeeded by his brother, Harshavarman III, who had to fight the Cham. On Harshavarman's death in 1080 the throne of Angkor passed to Jayavarman VI, a prince from Mahidharapura, a fief possibly located in northeast Thailand. Following the reigns of a few unimportant kings, Suryavarman II conquered the throne and was crowned in 1119. This warrior king reunited Kambuja, attempted to invade Annam on several occasions, and occupied Champa in 1144. His dominions stretched to the borders of the Burmese Kingdom of Pagan in the west, to the sea in the east, and to the heart of the Malay peninsula in the south. In 1165 the usurper Tribhuvanadityavarman assassinated the legitimate king Yashovarman II. Seizing the opportunity, the King of Champa, Jaya Indravarman IV, sailed to Yashodharapura in 1177, sacked the city, killed Tribhuvanadityavarman, and settled in the area.*

**Udayadityavarman I (1001-1002)**
**Jayaviravarman (1002-1006)** *builds the north Khleang.*
**Suryavarman I (1010-1050)** *begins the West Baray and builds the Phimeanakas in the Royal Palace, Phnom Chisor, and parts of the Preah Khan of Kompong Svay, Preah Vihear, and Wat Phu.*
*Khleang style, 1010-1050*
**Udayadityavarman II (1050-1066)** *builds the Baphuon and West Mebon.*
*Baphuon style, 1050-1066*
**Harshavarman III (1066-1080)**
**Jayavarman VI (1080-1107)** *builds Phimai.*
**Dharanindravarman I (1107-1112)**
**Suryavarman II (1113-1150)** *builds the Thommanon, Chau Say Tevoda, Angkor Wat, Beng Mealea, Preah Pithu, Banteay Samré, some buildings of the Preah Khan of Kompong Svay, and Phnom Rung.*
*Angkor Wat style, 1100-1175*
**Dharanindravarman II (1150-1160)**
**Yashovarman II (1150-1165)**
**Tribhuvanadityavarman (1165-1177)**
*The Cham sack the capital.*

### BUDDHA, THE SUPREME LORD

*Jayavarman VII, who was crowned in 1181 at over fifty years old, drove out the Cham and reunified Kambuja. He was a fervent Buddhist and replaced the cult of Shiva-*devaraja *with that of the Buddharaja, lord of the universe. During his reign the Khmer Empire reached its largest size, growing to include the Korat plain, the entire Menam valley, and part of southern Malaysia. Champa and northern Laos were also annexed, and tribute was levied on the Burmese kingdom of Haripunjaya, Annam, and apparently from Java too. Two years after the presumed death of Jayavarman in 1219/20 the Khmer evacuated Champa, meanwhile secessions became more frequent in the outlying parts of the Empire and the Thai threatened the borders. The Brahmanic families fomented a strong Shivaite reaction against the spread of Buddhism, but Hinayana, the "small vehicle [of salvation]," the simplest and oldest form of Buddhism, eventually prevailed. In 1296 the Chinese Emperor Timur Khan sent a mission to Kambuja, and some invaluable accounts of the country were written by one of its members, Zhou Daguan. The first great Thai state, Sukhothai, which had been formed during the reign of Jayavarman VIII, occupied numerous western and northern territories of the Empire. In 1430 a Thai King, Paramaraja II of Ayuthya, invaded the Angkor plain and laid siege on the capital, which he took after seven months. From that moment on, the evacuation and decline of Angkor began.*

**Jayavarman VII (1181-1219/20)** *builds the Preah Khan of Kompong Svay, Ta Prohm, the Preah Khan of Angkor, Neak Pean, Banteay Kdei, Ta Som, Ta Nei, Srah Srang, Angkor Thom, the Bayon, the Elephant Terrace, the Terrace of the Leper King, and the reservoirs of the Royal Palace, Banteay Chmar, and south Khleang. Bayon style, 1181-1219/20*
**Indravarman II (1218-1243)** *builds Prasat Suor Prat.*
**Jayavarman VIII (1243-1295)** *builds the Mangalartha.*
**Shrindravarman (1295-1307)**
**Shrindrajayavarman (1307-1327)**
**Jayavarman Parameshvara (1327-?)**

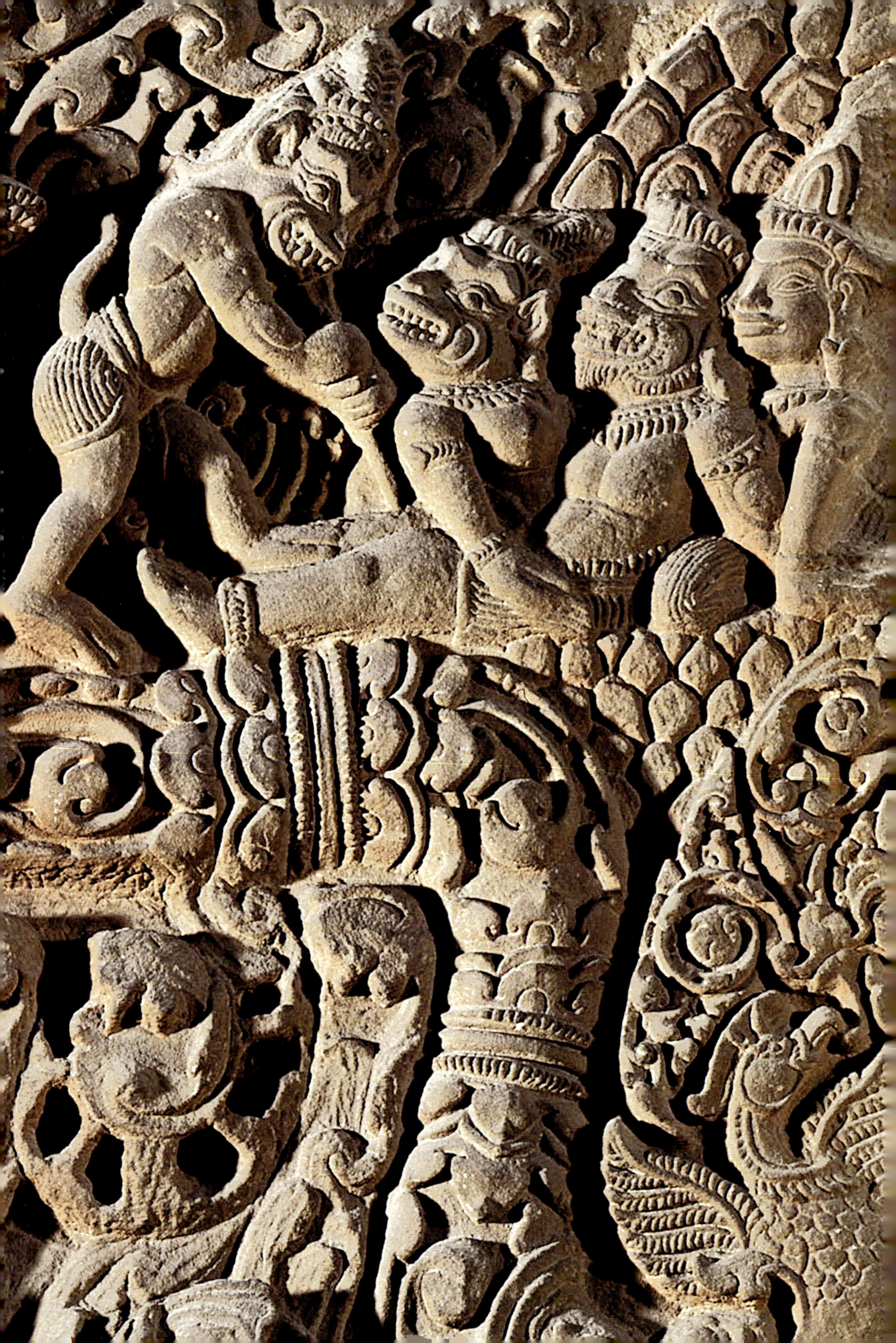

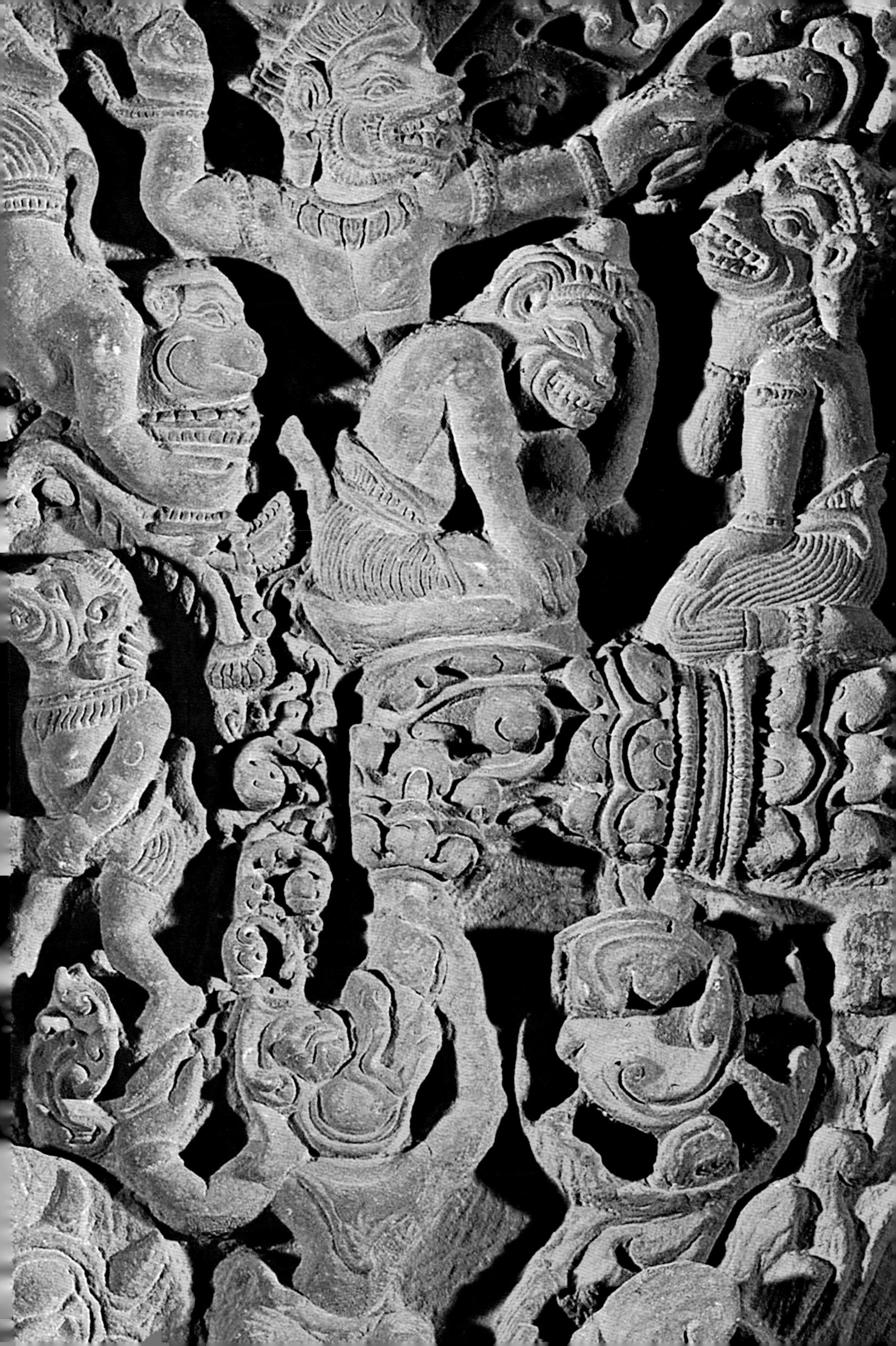

# Angkor
## The Rediscovery

*Despite the vicissitudes of history and the transfer of the capital elsewhere, contrary to common belief Angkor Wat was never completely forgotten, but rather was turned into a Buddhist monastery and continued to be a place of worship. In a letter dated 1668, French missionary Father Chevreul described it as being a popular place of pilgrimage. In any event, the ruins of the ancient Khmer Empire had been known to Portuguese and Spanish missionaries and adventurers since the previous century.*

*The first significant descriptions of Angkor were written by the Portuguese Diogo do Couto in a 1614 manuscript. They probably do not relate to a journey made by do Couto himself but were based on accounts provided by Capuchin friar Antonio da Magdalena, who visited Angkor between 1585 and 1558. The Portuguese visitors, who were numerous in the early seventeenth century, nearly all agreed that the great Khmer city must have been constructed by non-local builders, hypotheses ranging from Trajan to Chinese Jews!*

*The oldest map of Angkor Wat was drawn between 1623 and 1636 by a Japanese pilgrim convinced that he had reached Jetavana, a venerable monastery situated in the Magadha region of India, where Buddha is believed to have spent much of his life. The map, which was copied in 1715, was not recognized as being a plan of the Khmer masterpiece until the early nineteenth century.*

*However, it was not until the nineteenth century, the century of adventurous explorers and amateur archaeologists, that Angkor was really "rediscovered." The first to devote a short essay to it was a French missionary, Father Charles Émile Bouillevaux, who stayed there for two days in 1850. The essay was published in 1858, and that same year naturalist Henri Mouhot spent all he had on a voyage to Indochina, where he traveled until his death in Laos in 1861. His letters and notebooks were published posthumously in English and French, and his book "Travels in Siam, Cambodia, Laos, and other Central Parts of Indochina" was published in French in 1863.*

*Europeans now began to take an interest in Angkor and in Khmer civilization. German ethnographer Adolf Bastian guessed that it had links to Indian culture. Scottish photographer*

*56-57 Louis Delaporte made the first, somewhat imaginative, exotic reconstructions of Angkor Wat, like this one, and of other Khmer sites. They were published in the "Album Pittoresque annexed to Voyage d'exploration en Indochine," published in 1873.*

John Thomson recognized a cosmological symbolism in the temples and his wealth of documentation impressed art historian James Ferguson, who included the Khmer temples in his "History of Universal Architecture" published in 1867.

In the meantime, Cambodia had become a French protectorate, and although the Angkor area was included among the possessions of the Kingdom of Siam (now Thailand), the French organized an expedition in 1866 to investigate the navigability of the Mekong River as a way of entering China and restoring the borders of ancient Cambodia. This task was entrusted to naval officer Ernest Doudart de Lagrée, France's representative in Cambodia. After a stopover at Angkor, he journeyed as far as southern Laos, visiting and describing numerous Khmer monuments. The members of the expedition included Francis Garnier, Doudart de Lagrée's second-in-command, diplomat Louis de Carné, two navy doctors, Clovis Thorel and Eugène Joubert, and artist Louis Delaporte. Delaporte drew the somewhat fanciful pictures collected in the "Album Pittoresque" annexed to the two volumes of "Voyage d'exploration en Indochine," the account of the expedition which was published in 1873. Delaporte fell in love with Khmer art and brought numerous items back to Paris, where he founded the Indochinese Museum at the Trocadero a few years later. The material and drawings presented at the Paris Universal Exposition in 1878 attracted the interest of the leading architects of the day, and one of them, Lucien Fournereau, visited Angkor between 1887 and 1888 and brought back photos, sketches, plans, plaster casts, and numerous relics.

By the early twentieth century Cambodia had become a popular tourist venue. The École Française d'Extrême Orient (French Far Eastern School), known as EFEO, was founded in 1898, and the age of organized archaeology began. Siam returned Angkor and the neighboring provinces to Cambodia in 1907, and the Conservation des Monuments d'Angkor (Angkor Monument Conservation Bureau) was set up in 1908. The first curators of Angkor led an adventurous, dangerous life in a pioneering, almost heroic archaeological era. Angkor, like the Egyptian pyramids, seemed to be cursed. The first curator, Jean Commaille, was murdered by bandits in an ambush in 1916. Georges Alexandre Trouvé, who conducted the excavations of the main Bayon well and discovered the huge Buddha housed there, died in an accident in 1935, at the age of 33. Maurice Glaze, who worked in Angkor from 1936 to 1945, also suffered many trials and tribulations.

In the meantime, surveying work in Cambodia had become increasingly careful and scientific. Naval officer Étienne Aymonier began the first archaeological inventory in 1879; he collected 350 reproductions of epigraphs and published three books about his work between 1900 and 1903. The cataloguing of the Khmer monuments was completed by another military man, colonial infantry officer Lunet de Lajonquière, who wrote the seminal "Archaeological and Descriptive Inventory of the Monuments of Cambodia," published between 1902 and 1911, which records 910 monuments along with some listed as secondary. Henri Parmentier, head of the EFEO's archaeology department, and Erik Seidenfaden added the Khmer monuments located in Thai provinces in 1922. The Angkor Archaeological Park was founded in 1925 and Philippe Stern, art historian of the Guimet Museum in Paris, reviewed and redefined the Khmer chronology two years later on the basis of inscriptions, without visiting the area. His work was completed in 1929 by EFEO's director George Coedès, who finally established the chronological progression of the Khmer civilization and its styles in light of the surviving epigraphs.

Some personalities of great stature and interest gravitated in and around EFEO, including architect Henri Parmentier, head of the archaeology department, and Russian nobleman Victor Goloubeff, who used the recently invented means of air transport to take aerial photographs of the Angkor monuments, discovering in 1931 that Phnom Bakheng had been the focal point of the first Angkor. Painter George Groslier, who fell in love with Cambodian dancing, instituted the Cambodian School of Arts to revive the country's traditions and crafts, and founded the first nucleus of the Phnom Penh Archaeology Museum. His son, Bernard-Philippe, became its curator in the 1960s.

Men of letters also took an interest in the intriguing ruins in the depths of the jungle. Pierre Loti spent three days at Angkor in November 1901 and expressed his amazement that in the 1912 novel A Pilgrim in Angkor Paul Claudel had described his unfavorable impression of the Khmer capital, where he perceived an aura of death. André Malreaux traveled in Cambodia with the intention of finding statues and bas-reliefs to sell to collectors. After being sentenced for art theft in 1924, he told his story in the autobiographical novel Life of Kings in 1930.

Interest in Khmer civilization grew to such an extent that Angkor Wat was reproduced at the 1931 Colonial Exhibition by father and son architects Charles and Gabriel Blanche, who took six years to draw up the plans, and was decorated by sculptor Auberlet. The reconstruction cost the astronomical sum of 12,400,000 francs, and the electricity used for lighting during the exhibition was enough to serve a city of 100,000 inhabitants.

While 1931 was the year of reproductive folly in Europe, it became memorable in Cambodia for quite a different reason. Dutch archaeologist van Stein-Callenfels of the Dutch East Indies Archaeology Department had visited Angkor in 1929 and suggested to the curator, Henri Marchal, that the anastylosis technique, which had already been used successfully in Indonesia, should be applied to the restoration of the Khmer monuments. The process, which is still used today, involves completely dismantling the building, numbering each piece and at the same time recovering all those that have fallen to the ground, and reassembling it in accordance with a meticulous plan of reconstruction and consolidation. The missing pieces are replaced with others that blend in harmoniously but are easily recognizable as new by their special markings. The anastylosis technique, perfected by Bernard-Philippe Groslier, was used for the first time in 1931 at the temple of Banteay Srei. Henri Marchal, the curator from 1920 to 1933, was asked back to the Conservation Bureau from 1947 to 1953 and spent the rest of his days in Cambodia, until his death in 1970.

After the terrible genocide of the 1970s, Cambodia came back to life. Angkor was declared a world heritage site, and in 1989 came under the protection of UNESCO, which is currently restoring many works, aided first by Indian and now by Japanese archaeologists, under the supervision of Phnom Penh University's Fine Arts Department. However, threats have not been eliminated yet; unscrupulous raiders of statues for collectors, careless tourists, and the encroaching jungle continue to menace one of the most fascinating, magnificent artistic complexes in the world.

58 This drawing by Delaporte portrays the Bayon, the temple built by Jayavarman VII as the center of his capital, Angkor Thom. Delaporte's blend of reality and fantasy matched the expectations of late nineteenth-century explorers and travelers in search of adventure, mystery, and excitement.

58-59 This reconstruction of one of the city gates of Angkor Thom, also in the "Album Pittoresque," reveals all the elements that appeared on it, though with some artist's license: the three-headed elephant of the god Indra, the many-headed cobras, and the faces of Jayavarman/Lokeshvara among worshipping deities.

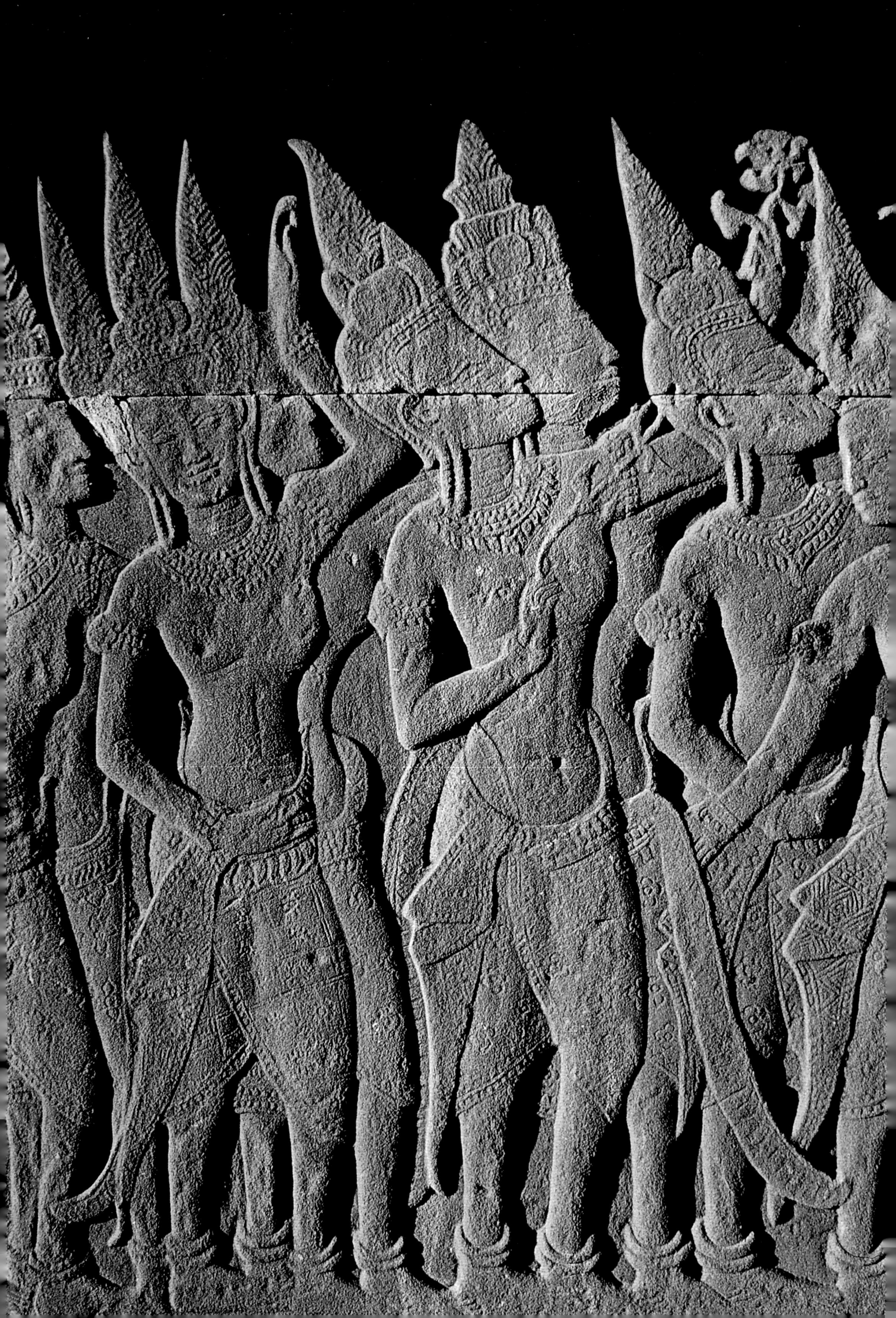

# Khmer Cosmology and Everyday Life

*THE RELIGIOUS WORLD*
Page 62

*THE GREAT MYTHS*
Page 74

*THE PATHS OF THE ENLIGHTENED ONE*
Page 80

*THE KING AND SOCIETY*
Page 92

*THE HYDRAULIC CITY*
Page 102

*EVERYDAY LIFE*
Page 104

*CLOTHING*
Page 112

*SCULPTURE*
Page 118

*CELESTIAL DWELLINGS*
Page 136

*60-61 Bas-reliefs represent an invaluable source of information about the everyday life of the Khmer, although in some cases such as this panel in one of the corner pavilions of the third gallery of Angkor Wat, the clothing and hairstyles, being those of deities, are ceremonial or even imaginary.*

# The Religious World

*62 This seventh-century image, now in a private collection, portrays Vishnu, the providential aspect of the Divine and ruler of human destinies, who comes down to earth at intervals to combat evil. His* kirita-mukuta, *a crown in the shape of a tiara or miter, emphasizes his majesty.*

*63 The distinctive feature of Shiva, shown here in a tenth-century sculpture from Phnom Bok, now in the Guimet Museum in Paris, was a third vertical eye in the middle of the forehead, symbolizing the unified consciousness that transcends the duality represented by the left and right eyes.*

The surviving artistic and epigraphic evidence indicates that the Khmer kings and aristocracy mainly followed the principal Hindu teachings related to the formation and evolution of the universe, the destiny of man, and the afterlife. The most notable exception was Jayavarman VII, who embraced Buddhism.

The Brahmans of Indian descent, who were the custodians of Hindu culture, knew its main texts: the two great epic poems, the Mahabharata and the Ramayana; the legal codes, which were the source of inspiration for the conduct of government and the regulation of interaction between the various social groups; the doctrinal literature, which expressed various schools of thought; and the Purana (Ancient Tales), composite works containing religious and philosophical concepts, moral and political precepts, social and cultural rules, and mythological and historical traditions.

The Purana, which belonged to the epic genre and were composed in shloka (epic verses) with occasional interpolations of prose, were probably written in India from the fifth century A.D. on, and are attributed to the same author as the Mahabharata, the legendary Vyasa. This attribution gives these works the same status of divine revelation as the Mahabharata. The great mass of texts contributed to the formation of religious beliefs at the highest levels of Khmer society.

The Khmer, like the Indians, believed that the universe had been formed by the evolution of primordial matter (prakriti) into the various forms of being, which had gradually degenerated from their original perfection. The cyclical concept of time was expressed in the myth of the four cosmic eras (yuga), each of which was named after a particular throw of the dice, which in India was not merely a game but a projection of the clash between conflicting forces within the individual and in the scheme of destiny. The winning throw of the dice was the one which gave a number divisible by four with no remainder. Less fortunate throws produced a remainder of three or two, while a throw with a remainder of one was considered the worst.

During the first yuga, called Krita, all beings lived at peace with themselves, in total, spontaneous obedience to the dharma, a complex, polysemantic term that expresses the concept of the rule that informs every aspect of the manifestation, conforms its relationships and transforms its procedures, and in man takes the form of an intimate vocational essence, an ethical code, and the possibility of salvation. Sanctity was inherent in this first era, and there was no need for any religious structure to awaken it. The Kritayuga reigned on earth for 1,728,000 years, a period corresponding to 4000 celestial years, plus 400 years of divine dawn and 400 years of twilight.

When natural obedience to the dharma began to fade, the Tretayuga (Triad Era) appeared. This period lasted for 1,296,000 human years, corresponding to 3000 divine years, 300 years of dawn, and 300 years of twilight. During this period, observance of the rules was no longer innate and had to be learned. Because there was no spontaneous communion with the divine world, a religious structure began to take shape.

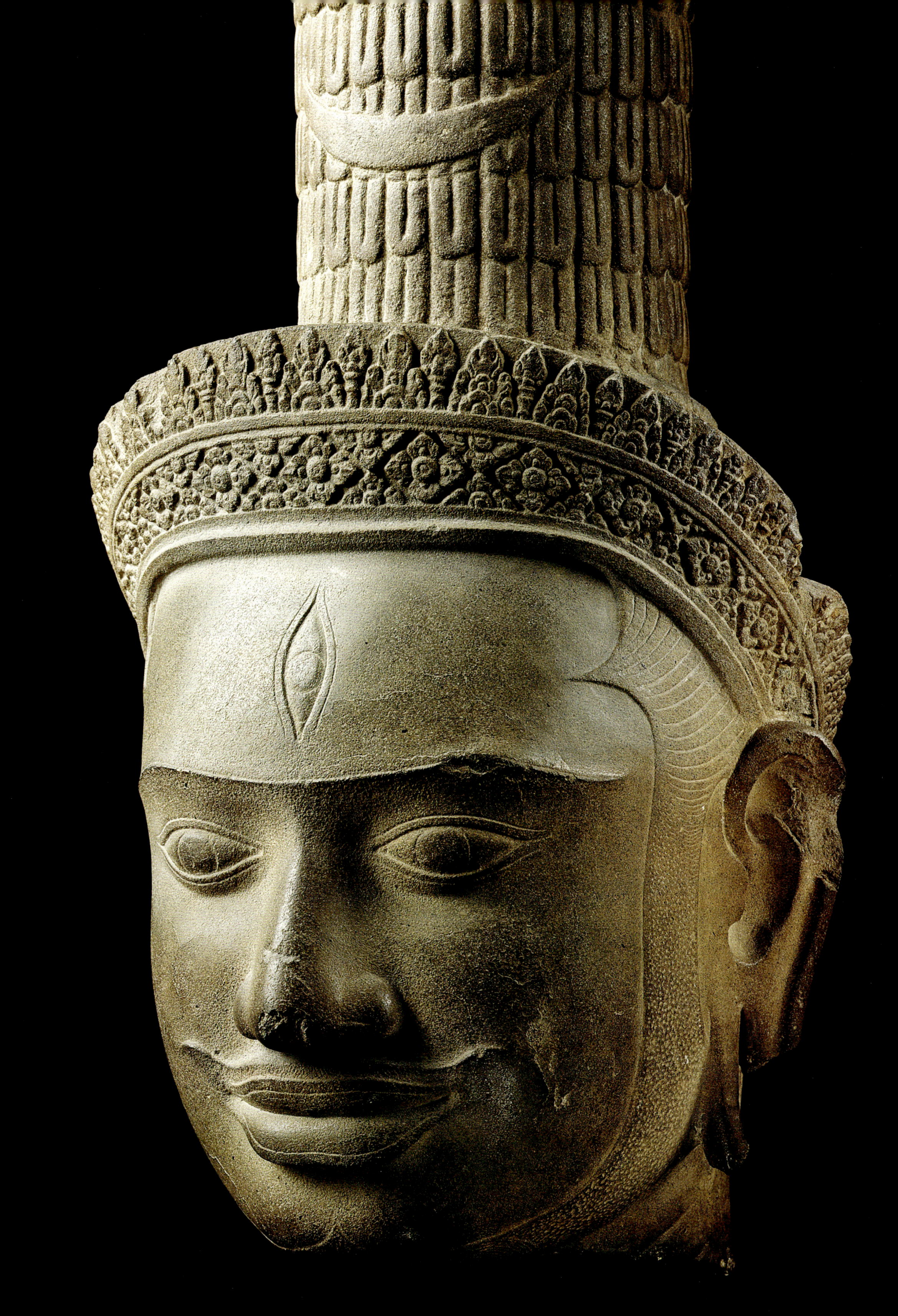

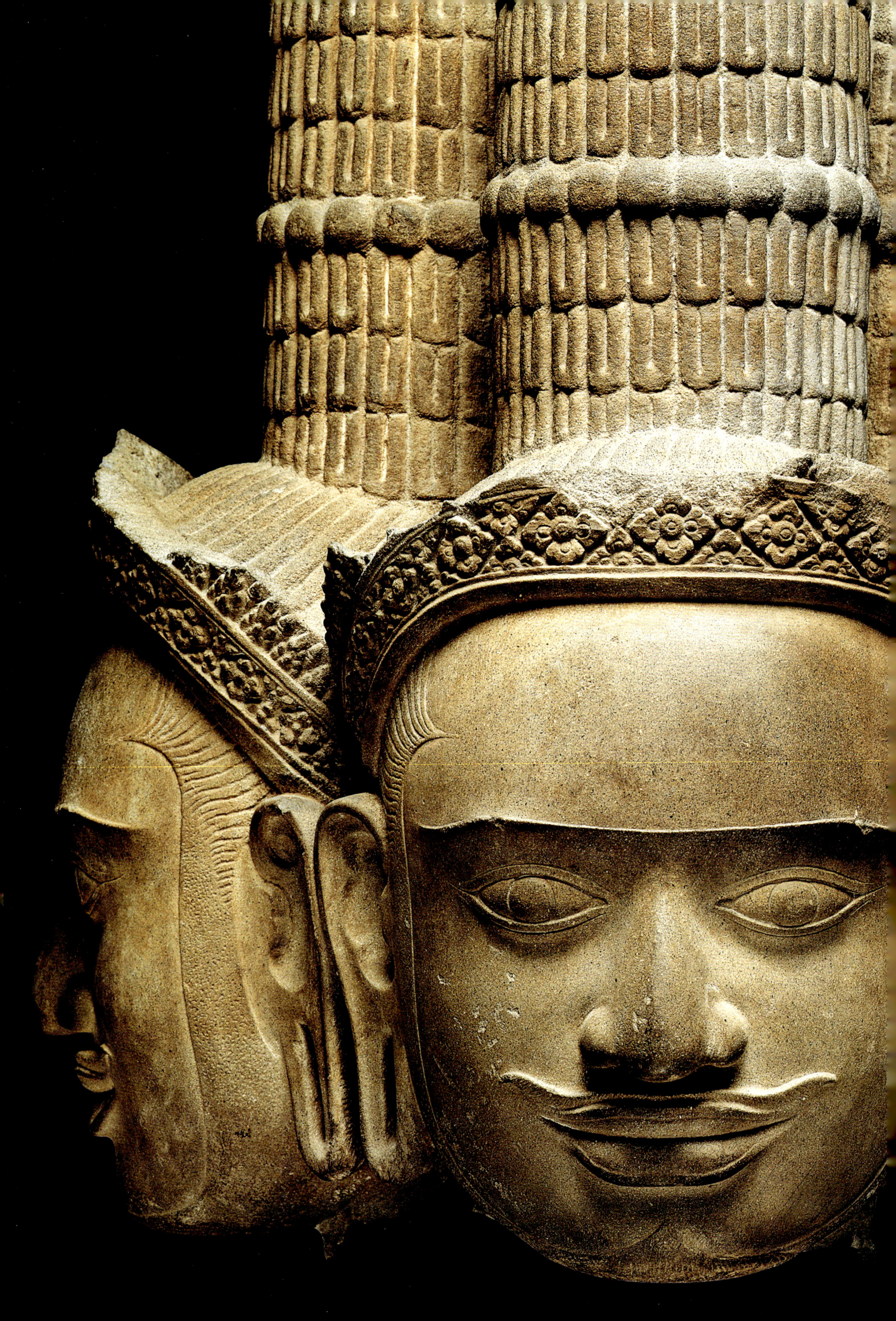

*64-65 The first appearance taken on by the Absolute in the* Trimurti, *the "triple form" of the Divine, is Brahma, the demiurge whose task was to emanate the universe. The four faces of the god allude to the spatial expansion of the cosmos, and they face towards the four points of the compass. The crowns of pearls that clasp the tall topknots in the middle are a specific characteristic of Brahma, shown here in a ninth/tenth-century statue from Phnom Bok, now in the Guimet Museum.*

The degeneration continued during the Dvaparayuga (Dyad era), when obedience to the dharma became increasingly rare. The sacred science endeavored to compensate for the decline of truth but instead lost its unity and conflicts emerged within it. Illness became widespread and natural disasters befell the earth for 864,000 human years, corresponding to 2000 divine years plus 200 years of dawn and 200 years of twilight, until February 18, 3102 B.C. when the universe entered the terrible, dark Kaliyuga era. This last cosmic period of discord and depravation will last for 432,000 years, corresponding to 1000 divine years, 100 years of dawn, and 100 years of twilight. Then, purifying fire will destroy the putrefied world and bury its ashes under a liquid cloak of cosmic night. According to this concept, the Ramayana was composed in the second period and the compilation of the Mahabharata marked the end of the third and the beginning of the fourth era.

A mahayuga *(great cosmic cycle)* consists of 4,320,000 human years, corresponding to 12,000 divine years. The samsara *(wheel of life)*, which imprisons the universe and all beings in the space-time dimension while tied to a continual return to life, pain, and death by their actions (karman), will come to a standstill at the end of the mahayuga.

Although a mahayuga represents a very long time for earth and its creatures, it is nothing by comparison with the life of the divine beings. Brahma, the deity who presides over the origin of every new universe, lives for a hundred years of which one of his days is equal to 1000 mahayuga, or 4,320 million human years. At the end of every day Brahma falls asleep; the universe then undergoes a kind of process of fusion and plunges into cosmic night, waiting to reappear when the god opens his eyes again at dawn. At the end of his 100 years, Brahma will be absorbed into the total dissolution of the void, and an eon will thus come to an end.

The three fundamental stages of the universe – emanation, conservation, and dissolution – are controlled by three deities who are not separate entities but aspects of the one, ineffable, fathomless Absolute. This Trimurti (Triple Form) is constituted by Brahma, Vishnu, and Shiva.

Brahma, the result of speculation by Hindu priests, was the least important figure; his function is to issue the world, and this act is seen as a great liturgical operation. The god's four heads and his arms allude to the process of expansion in which earthly space unfolds towards the four cardinal points, indicated by the sun, which in turn determines the temporal dimension. Time and space are the two coordinates or measurements within which the cosmic drama is played out and its protagonist, mankind, acts.

The custody and control of life are the responsibility of the second person of the Trimurti, Vishnu, Lord of Providence. He comes down to earth in various saving forms known as avatars, two of which, Rama and Krishna, become crucial figures in the devotional process.

When the time is ripe for the universe to be absorbed into cosmic night, the third member of the Trimurti, the god Shiva, dissolves it in order to allow the dawning of another world.

Shiva, worshipped by the Khmer under numerous names (Tumburu, Bhadreshvara, Sadesha, etc.), is the most important deity and has numerous functions and attributes. Being immanent, he reverberates in every aspect of the universe but never loses his unity, just like the light that shines in particles of water yet always remains one. All beings emanate from him, and in the guise of Sadashiva he is represented with five heads, associated with earth, water, fire, air, and ethereal space, the five elements constituting the cosmos, and with the points of the compass including the zenith. The generating power of the god is symbolized by his aniconic shape, the linga, a phallic stone with numerous meanings such as the axis and center of the universe, and the origin and end of manifestation. In the Khmer belief system, this essential symbol merged with the stones that represented the genius loci and were therefore bringers of fertility.

Brahma, who was of minor importance in India, also occupied a secondary place in Kambuja, while Vishnu and Shiva shared the favors of kings and the populace. However, the two deities never came into conflict with one another; in fact they merge in Harihara, the syncretistic form of Hari (Vishnu) and Hara (Shiva), as demonstrated by the numerous statues sculpted between the sixth and tenth centuries. The Harihara iconography confirms the oneness of the Divine which underlies its multiple manifestations.

Each of the deities in the Trimurti is accompanied by a spouse who often reflects his characteristics. Brahma's consort is Sarasvati, goddess of the Indian river of the same name, now dry. She is also known as Vac (the Word, or divine Verb) because, by uttering the name of the world, she brings it into existence.

Vishnu's spouse is Lakshmi, the beautiful goddess of fertility and abundance, also known as Shri (Prosperity), who accompanies Vishnu in his numerous descents to earth in various guises.

Shiva's wife embodies the ambivalence of the primordial Great Goddess more than any other female deity. She is the sweet, devoted wife Parvati who protects the crops, but also Durga, female warrior and exterminator of demons, and Kali, the "Black" manifestation of devouring time and indomitable nature.

*66 left Each Hindu deity has a* vahana *(mount). The mount of Vishnu, shown here in a twelfth-century bronze, now in the Guimet Museum, was Garuda, a creature that was part human, part bird of prey. The* vahana *constitute the theriomorphic aspect of the Divine.*

*66 right The Brahmanic triad with Vishnu in the middle, Shiva on his left, and the Goddess Devi on his right, are shown here in a twelfth/thirteenth-century gilded bronze in the Bayon style, now in the Phnom Penh National Museum. This triad unites the main deities of the Khmer Hindu world, where Brahma, unlike the Goddess, was not widely worshipped.*

*67 This tenth-century image from Banteay Srei, known as Umamaheshvara, now in the Phnom Penh Museum, portrays Shiva Maheshvara (the great god) with his spouse Uma, one of the many names of the consort Goddess. Each Hindu deity is accompanied by its* shakti, *the female projection that symbolizes its creative energy.*

The other main Hindu deities worshipped by the Khmer were Ganesh, the elephant-headed god, son of Parvati, and Hanuman, the monkey god, devoted to Rama. The attendants, minor deities, semi-divine beings, asura (evil powers divided into various categories), and vahana (the "vehicles" of the gods) were also of Indian origin. Brahma and Sarasvati rode the hamsa, the goose with a striped neck; Vishnu and Lakshmi flew on Garuda, the vulture with human features; Shiva and Parvati rode the bull Nandi; and Ganesh is associated with the mouse, in a symbolic paradox in which the greatest and the smallest converge in the Divine. The sacredness of animals, a remnant from very ancient times, inspired the feral appearance sometimes taken by the gods themselves; for example, Vishnu sometimes manifested as a boar (Varaha) or a lion-man (Narasimha).

Other important figures in Khmer iconography were some Vedic deities, namely gods referred to in the Vedas, the most ancient sacred Hindu texts, in which cosmic phenomena and functions acquired a divine dimension. The gods, divided into three main categories, perennially fought the asura to ensure the cosmic balance and protect mankind. The most important earthly deities included Agni, god of fire, and Indra, king of the gods and prototype of the warrior who dominated the atmosphere, while Varuna controlled the actions of human beings from the heavens, where the sun was his eye.

68 left This twelfth/thirteenth century bronze Ganesh from Phnom Penh Museum holds one of his tusks, which he broke off to use as a pen to write the "Mahabharata" epic, in his raised right hand, and in his raised left hand a serpent, alluding to his father Shiva, who is also ornamented with a cobra. He holds a sweet in his lowered left hand, and there was once a mobile attribute in the right.

*68 right This tenth-century Vajimukha (horse-head image), now in the Guimet Museum, may portray two aspects of Vishnu: Hayagriva, the form he adopted to recover the sacred texts of the Veda which had been stolen by two demons, or Kalkin, the last avatar or descent of the god to earth to conclude its present cosmic cycle.*

*69 This tenth-century temple gatekeeper from Banteay Srei, now in the Phnom Penh Museum, may be the monkey god Hanuman, son of the Wind and faithful companion of Rama, another avatar of Vishnu, celebrated with him in the epic poem "Ramayana."*

To propitiate the gods and avert their anger, the Khmer celebrated complex rituals which included offerings and sacrifices of animals, recitation of formulas and praises, donations, codified gestures, and other ceremonies. Only the brahmana (the priest) could officiate at the great celebrations and turn the mysterious energies that pervaded the cosmos to the benefit of man. The rite was not performed solely to obtain earthly benefits (health, wealth, victory, and heirs) but was considered to be the fundamental means of restoring vigor to the divine forces themselves. In addition, belief in the subtle identity between man/microcosm and the universe/macrocosm gave the sacrifice magical and symbolic overtones and turned it into a portrayal of the grandiose rite of existence. According to some Hindu legends, the multiple universe, with its burden of pain and imperfection, originated when a gigantic being was dismembered. Thus it was believed that if the One had been divided into the many, a sacrifice could symbolically restore his perfect, blessed unity.

One of the favorite sacrificial victims of the Khmer was the buffalo. On the other hand, Zhou Daguan recounts that in bygone days the king of the Champa offered the gods thousands of gall bladders removed treacherously from the people. Although this report seems very unlikely, it may allude to ancient human sacrifices connected with the worship of Shiva or with indigenous Indochinese traditions, of which nothing is known.

Despite the importance of sacrifices and the proliferation of divine figures, the most enlightened (those aware that the religious structure was merely a way of promoting final liberation from the samsara, the world of limitations and pain) embraced the Indian concept that all the gods were none other than aspects of the faceless, ineffable, unmanifested One, the **Brahman** or "Absolute One," who incorporated and transcended every form. The atman *(soul)*, *enclosed in the bodily shell and led astray by* maya *(the most common meaning of this word was "illusion" but, as it also derives from a root that means "to measure," it was also interpreted in the sense of "incorrect evaluation"), reaches out to Him, the ultimate Mystery. The world has a relative value precisely because it is measured, and if man attributes an absolute value to it, he makes a mistake and remains a prisoner of the material dimension. Nescience is the fundamental reason why mankind goes astray; only by rending the veil of maya can man perceive the path that leads to the Divine, indefinable and immeasurable.*

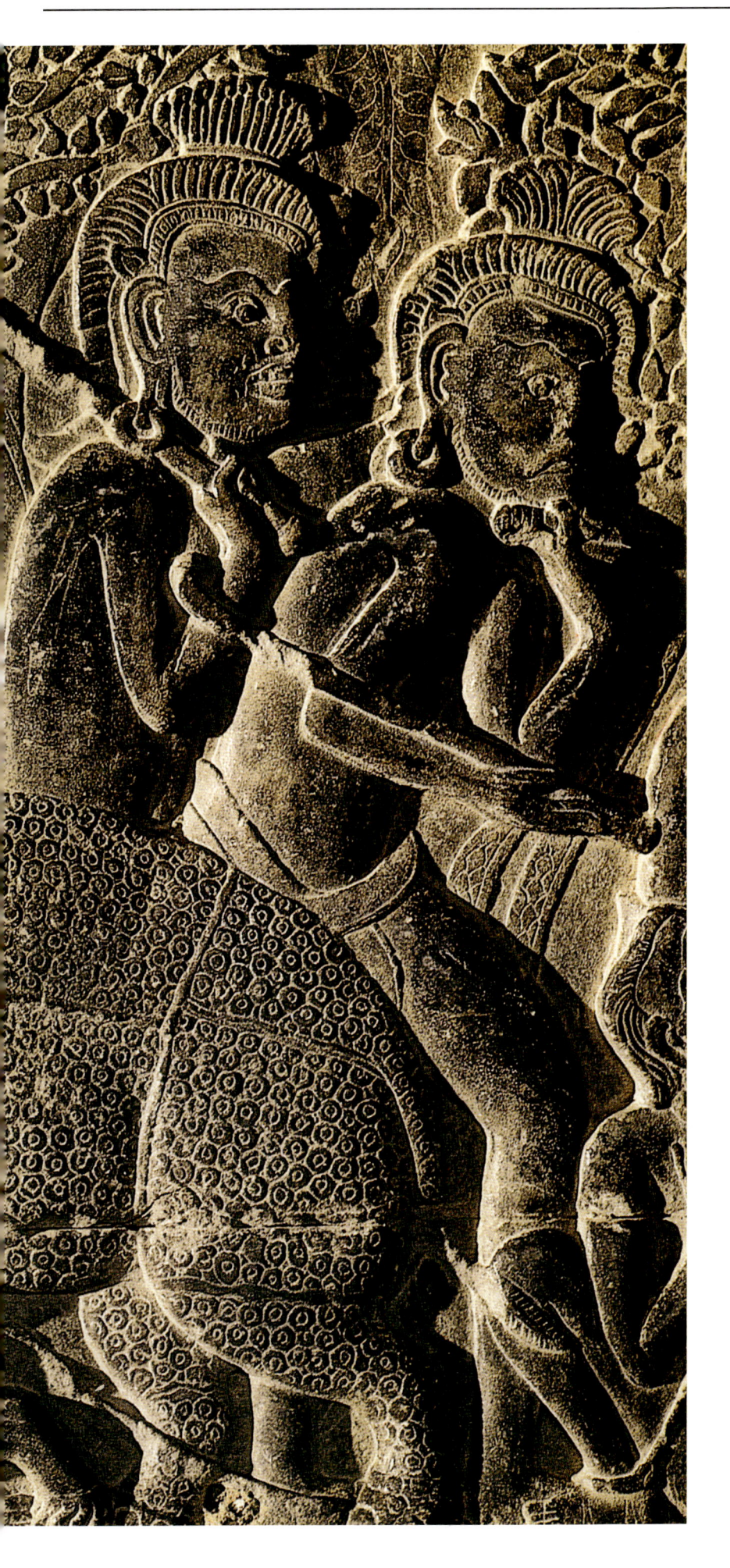

*According to the traditional Hindu view, the destiny of man was determined by the actions he committed (*karman*), whose effects, far from ending with the current existence, led to consequent reincarnations in different manifestations. These could range from plant life to divine form, which were also considered transient aspects of existence. Reincarnation was not considered desirable but implied a repetition of limitation, suffering, and death, in which the soul was tied to matter. Therefore, many attempted to neutralize the effects of action in order to inhibit the* karman *mechanism. As total inaction is impossible, an attempt was made to change the significance of action in a conscious process, controlled by ritual, inspired by devotion, and enlightened by knowledge, to transform life and achieve* moksha *– liberation from material ties and the painful, incessant cycle of lives and deaths. Until this happened, between one incarnation and the next the soul remained in heavens and hells, and projections of worldly joys and earthly torments, which were evocatively portrayed in the bas-reliefs of Angkor Wat.*

*70 The Khmer offered bloodthirsty sacrifices to propitiate the gods. Their favorite sacrificial animal was the buffalo, shown here in one of the twelfth/thirteenth-century bas-reliefs in the east gallery on the south side of the Bayon temple.*

*70-71 The afterlife is portrayed in the twelfth-century bas-relief in the south gallery of the east wing of Angkor Wat, which shows heaven and hell. The creatures seen in this detail are demons, recognizable by their round eyes and fangs.*

*72 The cruel torments inflicted on sinners in the afterlife probably reflect the actual punishments used at the time.*

*72-73 Yama, Lord of the Afterworld, judged the dead seated on a buffalo. In this portrayal in the south gallery of the east wing of Angkor Wat he is identified with King Suryavarman II, who built the monument.*

However, in addition to the Hindu vision proclaimed by the Brahman caste of priests and embraced by the Khmer aristocracy, the common people must have had a simpler and more immediate animist faith, a form of religion which is still widely practiced in Indochina. In light of the strength of tradition and its ability to survive practically intact for centuries, it can be assumed that the present faith of the ordinary Khmer people does not differ greatly from that of ancient times. Mountains, hills, springs, trees, and fields are inhabited by a myriad of spirits that govern the earth, which are called neak-ta *in modern Cambodian. Vishnu himself has become a* neak-ta, *specifically a* neak-ta-moha-reach *(Great King of the Spirits). The powerful but capricious spirits must be propitiated daily, and there are few everyday operations in which they are not involved in some way. The* Arak, *spirits of disease, are dangerous, as are the* Khmorch chhav *(the "raw dead"), those who come to a bad end, whose life cycle was interrupted prematurely by murder, drowning, suicide, pregnancy, or childbirth. Unhusked, uncooked rice is offered to them, whereas the other spirits always receive cooked rice.*

Those who come to a bad end are buried instead of being cremated, and this was probably the case at the time of the Khmer Empire too. Little or nothing is known about the funeral rites of that time. Zhou Daguan states that the funeral cortège which escorted the body, carried on a litter covered with draperies, was accompanied by music, flags, and scattering of grilled rice along the way. The deceased, whose sons shaved their heads as a sign of mourning whereas their daughters cut their hair, were taken to a place outside the town and left for dogs and wild animals to devour. If the body was entirely eaten by animals it was considered a sign that the deceased was blameless; if not, he still had something to atone for.

Noblemen and kings were probably cremated and their ashes placed in urns. Zhou Daguan referred to royal burials but admitted that he did not know whether the whole bodies of the dead were buried, or only their ashes. Some experts suggest that the sarcophagi found in the temple enclosure served to dry the bodies of the king and the members of the royal family before cremation.

The present-day rites reserved for the kings of Cambodia are probably based on ancient rituals. The body of the deceased, in the fetal position (a clear allusion to rebirth) is enclosed in a golden urn placed under a mên, a canopy of wood or stone with four slender columns. After the population has paid its last respects over the stipulated period, the body is cremated in a sandalwood urn. The outline of a body is made with the ashes and it is turned from east to west in the pre rup (body-turning) ceremony, after which a temple at Angkor is named.

During excavations at Srah Srang, Philippe Groslier brought to light a series of small brick chambers containing cinerary urns. Because there were few cemeteries, the Khmer may sometimes have consigned the ashes to water. While the rich could afford cremation, the poor had to be satisfied with exposing their dead to the elements, as they were unable to pay for the wood needed for the funeral pyre.

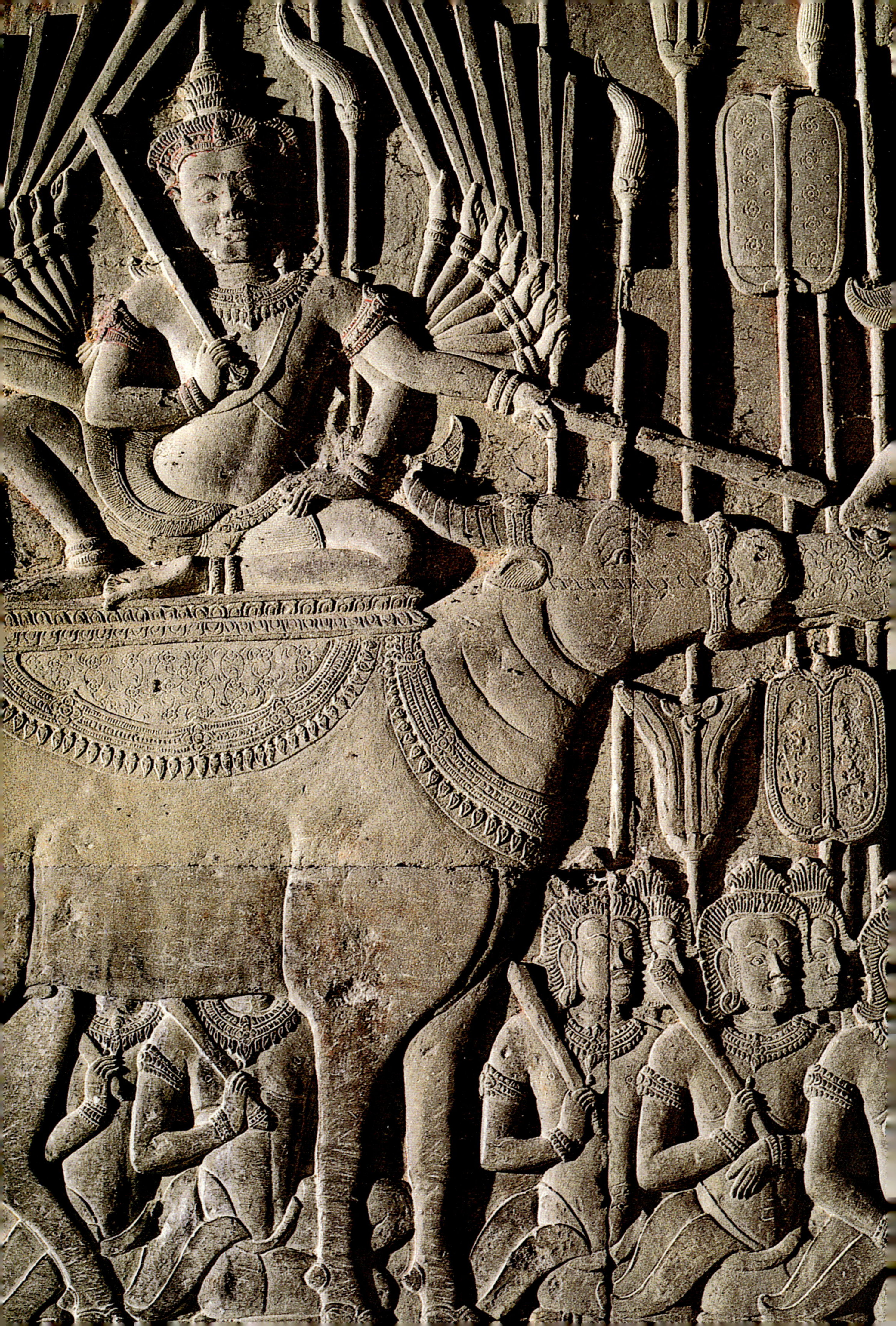

74

# THE GREAT MYTHS

The mythical events portrayed on bas-reliefs and the deities represented in sculptures belong to the Hindu religious world and, apart from some local variations, were reproduced in accordance with Indian models. The two great Indian epic poems, the "Mahabharata" and the "Ramayama," were known to the Khmer, as were many Puranic legends, namely those collected in the "Purana" (Ancient Tales), which are invaluable sources of information about the gods, their deeds, rituals, and places of worship.

The "Mahabharata," composed between the fourth century B.C. and the fourth century A.D., represents the supreme compendium of the Hindu religious and social structure. The poem, consisting of over 100,000 verses, incorporates various ambits and periods of Indian civilization. Although it is attributed to the legendary compiler Vyasa, it contains compositions of various origins, mainly by squire-bards of the time and wandering ballad singers. This profane material, which had great impact because of the heroic and erotic content of the chivalrous feats it recounts, appears to have been reworked by the Brahmans, the caste of priests who were the repositories of religion and knowledge, as a means of disseminating their beliefs. Vyasa was a Brahman, and it is significant that he was the common ancestor of the two rival groups of cousins who are the protagonists of the work: the Pandava brothers and the Kaurava brothers. His direct participation in the events gives the "Mahabharata" credibility so that it is not simply an arbitrary artistic creation but a chronicle of supernatural events.

The conflicting forces described in the work are the ancestral forces of the gods, the deva, lords of light and guardians of order, and the asura, demon lords of darkness and bringers of disorder. Although the main geographical locations are the cities of Hastinapura, capital of the Pandava brothers, Indraprastha, capital of the Kaurava brothers, and Kurukshetra, near Thanesar, to the north of present-day Delhi, where the great final battle was fought, the location is actually the cosmic battlefield of polar forces and the individual battlefield of the conscience. Even though the poem may have been based on actual battles between the various Aryan tribes, groups of nomads believed to have migrated to India from the Afghan areas in the second millennium B.C., its atmosphere is essentially legendary.

The earth, weighed down by the presence of too many demons embodied in the princely families, calls for help from heaven. The gods come down to earth in partial or total incarnations or by procreating children to fight the demons and restore moral and social order. Most heroes are therefore the forces of good and evil in disguise, antagonists in the bloody conflict that closed the third of the four cosmic eras in which the existence of the universe unfolds. In this work, which translates metaphysics into epic language, the dramatic clash between gods and demons, transferred to the world of men, is enriched by an inexhaustible range of human feelings. Faith causes man to glimpse the designs of providence in war and blind, destroying destiny, the terrible sacrifice of blood purifies the land and transforms slaughter into holocaust, until finally the new race will emerge, though scarred by the degeneration of the times, and guarantee peace and justice.

Despite its myriad of deities, the "Mahabharata" reveals a powerful monotheistic core whose culminating moment is the great theophany of the "Bhagavad-Gita" (Song of the Blessed Lord), which occupies 18 chapters of the sixth book. The "Bhagavad-Gita," an exaltation of the bhaktimarga (the path of salvation constituted by mystical abandonment to God), advocates acting in accordance with the dharma, the rule inherent in every aspect of being, without expecting anything in return for one's actions, dedicating them to God in an depersonalized offering.

*74-75 The scene portrayed on the architrave of the western entrance to the main temple of Banteay Srei, dating from the tenth century, shows the abduction of Sita, spouse of Prince Rama, the incarnation of the god Vishnu, by the demon Ravana, Lord of the island of Lanka. This event is narrated in the "Ramayana," the great Hindu epic poem composed between the second century B.C. and the first century A.D.*

76 In the Battle of Lanka, portrayed in the north wing of the west gallery of Angkor Wat, the adversaries of the monkeys who were allied with Rama were the rakshasa, *the demon hordes of Ravana, who can be distinguished from the other warriors by their features: frowning, with wide-open round eyes, and tusks at the sides of the mouth.*

The highly composite nature of the "Mahabharata" makes it the most complete account of the Indian view of the world. The compelling narrative is divided into numerous parallel stories. Vyasa, the future compiler of the "Mahabharata," was the son of Satyavati and an ascetic. Satyavati later married King Shantanu and had two sons, both of whom died childless. The Queen then ordered Vyasa to marry the two widowed princesses, to ensure the continuity of the royal line. Vyasa had two sons by the princesses: Dhritarashtra, who fathered the 100 Kaurava brothers, and Pandu, the father of the five Pandava brothers. The Pandava brothers were in reality the children of gods because Pandu had been forbidden by a curse to have intercourse with his two wives, and therefore asked one of them, Kunti, to use a magic formula she knew to induce the gods to have children by the queens.

Despite the curse, Pandu made love to his younger wife. He died and she was immolated on his funeral pyre. The surviving queen, Kunti, took the children to the court of her brother-in-law Dhritarashtra, where the five Pandava brothers grew up with their cousins. The young men were divided by bitter rivalry and the Pandavas, who several times escaped ambushes set by the Kauravas, were eventually tricked into a fraudulent game of dice in which they lost all their possessions and even their shared wife Draupadi. Forced into exile, they returned 12 years later to claim their kingdom, and when the Kauravas refused, war broke out. Krishna, who was related to both groups, offered himself or his soldiers. The Kauravas chose the army and the Pandavas chose Krishna who, as the incarnation of Vishnu, Lord of Providence, guided and protected them. The terrible massacre ended with the victory of the Pandavas, who ascended to heaven with their wife Draupadi after a long and prosperous reign.

The Khmer knew the "Mahabharata" as demonstrated by the fact that the great battle of Kurukshetra is portrayed in the bas-reliefs in the east gallery of Angkor Wat.

The second major Indian source that inspired Khmer artists in their iconographic representations was the "Ramayana," which was better known than the "Mahabharata," perhaps because it is shorter (24,000 verses) and more systematically organized. The period when the "Ramayana" was composed is the subject of controversy but it is thought to have been between the second century B.C. and the second century A.D. Its author, the ascetic Valmiki, recounted the feats of Rama, another incarnation of the god Vishnu, in an ornate style, organizing the set of legends into a compact collection. Valmiki, like Vyasa in the "Mahabharata," took part in the events narrated in the poem himself; he is the hermit who welcomes Sita, the repudiated wife of Rama, to his hermitage.

The story goes as follows: after a palace plot by one of the queen mothers, Rama, the designated heir to the throne, is sent into exile in the forest. Sita, the beautiful wife conquered by the prince during a tournament, decides to follow her husband, and they are joined by Lakshmana, Rama's younger brother.

In the forest the two young men fight the asura who are disturbing the ascetic practices of the hermits. They eventually encounter the demoness Surpanaka, who endeavors to seduce first Rama, then Lakshmana. Lakshmana angrily cuts off her ears and nose. To take her revenge, Surpanaka goes to her brother Ravana, lord of the island of Lanka and an invincible thousand-headed asura, and urges him to kill Rama, who has already exterminated too many demons. Surpanaka also plants the idea of abducting Sita into her brother's mind, by cleverly and subtly praising her divine beauty.

Ravana goes secretly to the forest where Sita lives with her husband and brother-in-law, and is dazzled by the princess. He gets Rama and Lakshmana out of the way by a stratagem (a gazelle with a golden coat suddenly appears in the forest, and the two young men dash off after it), approaches Sita in the guise of an old, wandering ascetic, and kidnaps her. Rama and Lakshmana desperately search for the princess, and in the meantime strike up an alliance with Sugriva, the monkey king, and his army. Among these heroic animals is Hanuman, son of the god of wind, who is able to fly. He discovers that Sita is being held prisoner on the island of Lanka where Ravana tries in vain to induce her to yield to his desires. The princess always bravely refuses, and the demon cannot take her against her will because he once raped a celestial nymph and was cursed by her husband to die if he ever took another woman by force.

77 The symbols of Vishnu, shown here in a twelfth-century bronze housed in Phnom Penh Museum, are the shell, which recalls the generation of life from the primeval waters; the chakra, a sharp ring used as a weapon against demons, which alludes to the samsara, the cycle of human destinies governed by Vishnu; the mace/scepter which symbolizes the King's function as guide and judge; and the ball of earth, which represents the world.

When Hanuman returns to Rama with the news that he has found Sita, the monkeys build a bridge between the mainland and the island of Lanka, and the allied armies march on the enemy city. After days of bloody fighting, Rama and Ravana confront one another and the demon is killed. Rama returns in triumph to his capital Ayodhya and is crowned king, but Sita has to undergo ordeal by fire to prove her purity because she has lived under another man's roof. Agni, the fire god, emerges from the flames of the pyre, proclaims Sita's chastity, and restores her to her husband. But shortly afterwards the populace begins to murmur against the Queen once more, and Rama is forced to repudiate her. She takes refuge in the hermitage of the sage Valmiki and gives birth to twins. A few years later the children encounter their royal father by chance; he recognizes them as his sons and takes them to his court. Rama agrees to take Sita back provided that she submits to another ordeal. Sita invokes the goddess Earth to testify to her chastity, but the earth opens and swallows up the unfortunate Queen.

The sources of the "Ramayana," which is considered as sacred as the "Mahabharata," are a controversial subject and scholars oscillate between two extreme hypotheses. Some experts consider that the poem contains echoes of the historical conflict between the oldest populations of India, the indigenous Dravidians and the Aryan invaders from the northwest. Others see it as the transposition of a cosmogonic myth: Sita, born from a furrow, is the goddess Earth fertilized by the god of rain, who is identified with Rama.

*78 and 78-79 An important role is played in the "Ramayana" by the monkey population, called the Vanara, whose king, Sugriva, was one of Rama's allies against Ravana, and who appointed Hanuman the monkey god as commander of his troops. In these two views of the Battle of Lanka, portrayed in the north wing of the west gallery of Angkor Wat, the monkeys can be distinguished from the throng of soldiers by their cruel features and sharp teeth.*

In any event, the work is based on a Dravidian nucleus of myths featuring the hero Rama, and these popular tales were reworked as a means of spreading the ideology of the Brahmans, who promoted Rama to the role of incarnation of the god Vishnu and Sita to that of his divine consort, Lakshmi.

What clearly emerges from the poem is the sacredness of the monarchy: Rama is the prototype of the perfect sovereign and Sita symbolizes the kingdom as the place where he chooses to exercise his sovereignty. It is this aspect that impressed the Khmer kings, leading their artists to portray more frequently some episodes rather than others. For example, Sita's ordeal by fire is not often portrayed, and her second repudiation by Rama seems to be unknown. This may indicate that women played a more important role in Khmer society, or it may be due to local circulation of versions of the "Ramayana" which were incomplete or differed from the official Hindu version. These were the texts which inspired the "Reamker," the Cambodian version of the feats of Ream or Rama, compiled in the seventeenth century.

The contest in which Rama won Sita at the tournament held to find a husband for the princess is depicted differently in the Khmer bas-reliefs. Instead of bending and snapping Shiva's heavy bow as recounted in the Indian "Ramayana," Rama hits a bird by shooting an arrow through a turning wheel. The extermination of the asuras is often portrayed: Rama and his brother Lakshmana kill Viradha (who had attempted to devour Sita), the demoness Tataka, the demon Marica, and Kabandha, a monstrous headless creature with a face on its stomach. Another popular subject is the battle between the deposed Sugriva, king of the monkeys, and the usurper Valin, and the latter's death. However, the masterpiece of the bas-reliefs inspired by the "Ramayana" is the Battle of Lanka, portrayed in the west gallery of Angkor Wat.

Another important legend, portrayed in the east gallery of Angkor Wat, deeply influenced the religious, social, economic, and artistic life of the Khmer: the churning of the sea of milk, recounted in the "Mahabharata" and some of the "Puranas," including the "Bhagavata."

Before the world began, the devas were

kaustabha *(the jewel that ornamented Vishnu's breast)*, the parijata *tree that grants wishes, and so on. However a poisonous miasma had also been released, and Shiva promptly swallowed it to save the universe. The poison dyed his throat blue, which is how he earned the name of Nilakantha, "the blue-throated one."*

*The last to emerge was Dhanvantari, the doctor of the gods, holding the vessel of ambrosia. The danavas called loudly for their share, but Vishnu, in the guise of the beautiful girl Mohini, bewitched them with his charms and distributed the ambrosia to the gods who, invigorated, defeated the* danavas *and became lords of the universe.*

*This legend has numerous symbolic meanings. Life, trapped in potential form in the sea of milk, symbolizes fertile chaos and requires motion to come into being. The joint operation performed by the* devas *and the* danavas *signifies that the dynamism of life requires the involvement of opposing forces. Its development is not due to chance but to the fact that it is structured by providence around a cosmic axis, Mount Mandara, whose base is divine, namely Vishnu in the guise of a turtle. Vasuki, the many-headed cobra, represents the potential of nature, and the opening of his coils symbolizes the activation of nature's manifestation.*

*Poison, representing negativity, is part of the cycle of life but it is neutralized by the gods. This is confirmed by the intervention of Shiva, and more importantly that of Vishnu in the form of Mohini who awards the prize to the deva because the powers of light are charged with governing the cosmos. The character of Mohini has two attributes: for the gods she is providential, but for the demons she represents the fatal attraction that distracts them from their goal. Beauty can mean initiation and salvation or confusion and damnation; it is spiritual maturity that makes the difference. Thus ambrosia, called amrita (immortality) in Sanskrit, is not the elixir of long life but the supreme knowledge that turns those who drink it into gods.*

*continually threatened by the* danavas, *a kind of demonic antigod. They called on Vishnu, Lord of Providence, for help, and he advised them to obtain ambrosia, which would make them immortal. The prodigious nectar lay at the bottom of the sea of milk. In order to obtain it the gods needed the help of the demons and promised them part of the ambrosia. The bargain was struck, and the cosmic mountain (in this case Mount Mandara) was placed in the ocean with the serpent Vasuki tied round it to form a churn. The two groups began to pull the snake, the gods by the tail and the demons by the head, causing the mountain to turn like a whisk, but it began to sink, so Vishnu turned himself into a turtle and swam down into the ocean to act as a base for Mount Mandara.*

*Marvelous creatures and objects emerged during the churning including the beautiful goddess Lakshmi, who became Vishnu's bride, the apsaras (celestial nymphs), Surabhi, the cow of plenty, the white horse, the moon, the*

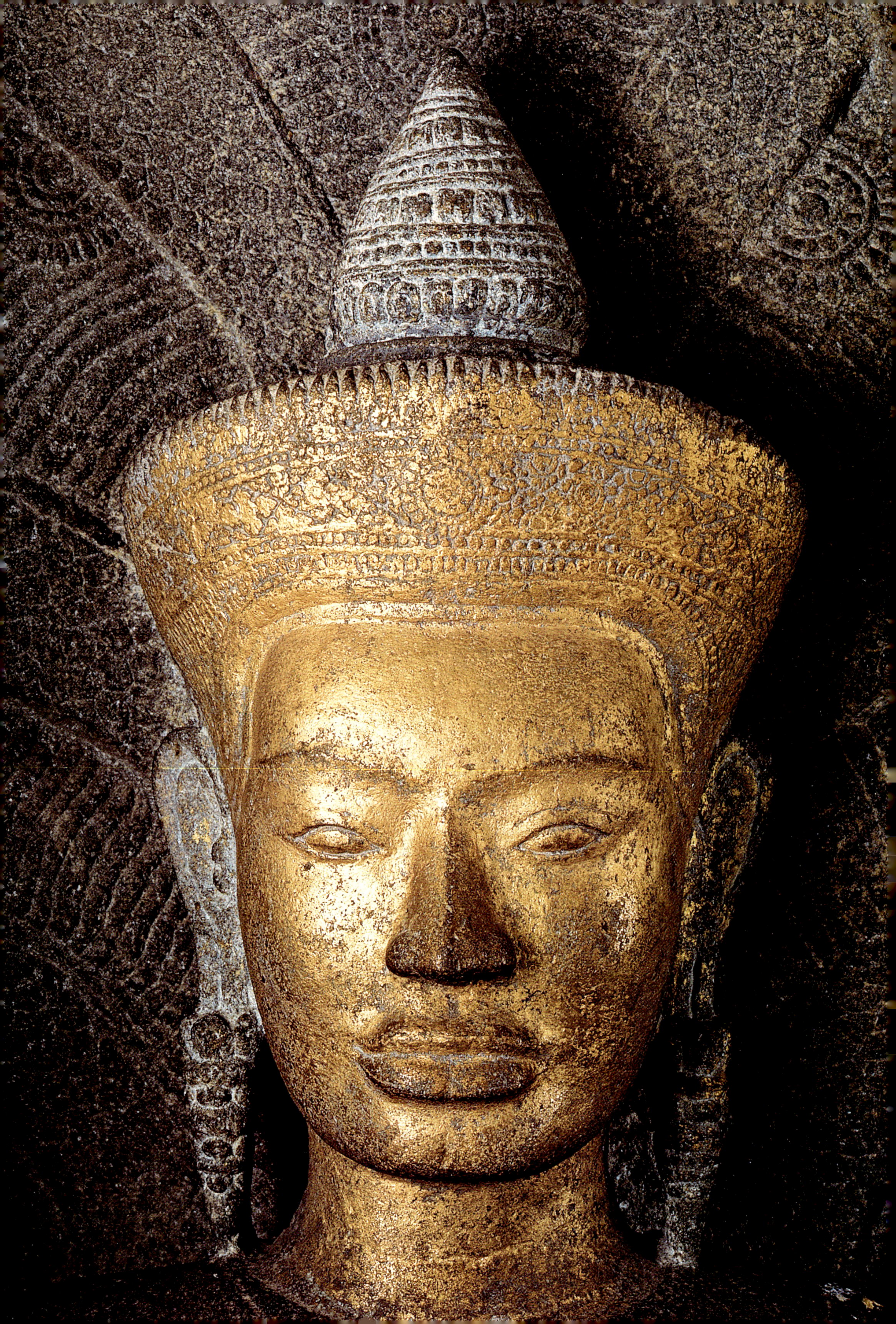

*80 When the worship of the* devaraja *(the god-king), or Shiva, was replaced by the cult of the* Buddharaja, *images of Buddha were given regal symbols such as the diadem and crown, as in this thirteenth-century specimen from Wat Na Phra Men, now in the Bangkok National Museum.*

*81 This group, on display in Phnom Penh Museum, forms a stela that marked the boundaries of a monastery. The Buddha seated at the foot of the figure on the cobra may be Bhaishajyaguru (the master of remedies), because in one hand he is holding an ampulla, symbolizing the spiritual "treatment" offered by the Enlightened One.*

# The Paths of the Enlightened One

Buddhism began to spread in Kambuja in the early centuries of the Christian era, but only became predominant during the reign of Jayavarman VII, who converted to Buddhism and promoted the message of Buddha.

This fundamental view of life, imported from India, was originated by Siddhartha Gautama, born of a princely family from the warrior clan of the Shakya, in the Lumbini woods near Kapilavastu, in present-day Nepal, towards the middle of the sixth century B.C. He was married at 16 and fathered a son, but soon realized the futility of the luxury and pleasure in which he had grown up. After four emblematic encounters—with an old man, a sick man, a dead man, and an ascetic—he decided to leave the luxury of the court to seek an antidote to the pain of life. He embarked on an itinerant life, and when he found no answer to his thirst for truth in philosophical speculations or arduous ascetic practices, he immersed himself in profound meditation. He came out of it "awoken" to perfect truth, which is why the name "Buddha" (the past participle of the verb root budh, which means "to become aware")

was attributed to him. As the path of his inner search unfolded through the shadows of the unconscious during a long night to find the light, the other term used to describe Buddha was "the Enlightened One."

He began preaching and attracted a large number of disciples. Shortly after his passing away in 480 B.C., the community divided into various schools of thought, which led to the formation of three main versions of Buddhism. The oldest was the Hinayana school, meaning "small vehicle," as it was described by the later *followers of the Mahayana, meaning "large vehicle," school, convinced that they were the upholders of the true saving message, which they described as "large" because it included esoteric aspects which, according to the Mahayanans, were not understood by followers of the "small vehicle." From the first to the fourth century the two schools flourished simultaneously in India, but Mahayana predominated from the fourth to the seventh century. Vajrayana, meaning "diamond vehicle," an esoteric and ritually complex version of Buddhism, mainly developed in the Himalayan countries and Tibet. It was known to be present in Kambuja from 953 on, and gained popularity in the twelfth and thirteenth centuries, as demonstrated by a number of inscriptions and magnificent bronzes, but was never particularly widespread.*

*In Kambuja as elsewhere, Buddhism was based on the "four noble truths" announced by Buddha: the fact that suffering is universal, because everything in the world is impermanent, painful and senseless; that suffering originates in thirst for life, which means attachment and desire; that this insatiable thirst which makes men cling to life can be extinguished; and that the way to suppress this thirst and gain salvation is the eightfold path of right view, right resolve, right speech, right action, right livelihood, right effort, right mindfulness, and right concentration.*

*Buddha's lucid, acute analysis lays bare the inanity of life. The universe is overwhelmed by a perennial cycle of becoming in which every phenomenon is momentary formation, generated by the aggregation and breakdown of constituting principles, the "minimums" of physical and mental order, beyond which it is impossible to penetrate. The individual as a substantial entity and psychophysical unit does not exist; what is called "man" is a phenomenal personality in continual development, an aggregate of material and mental factors (skandhas), connected by the fictitious concept of "ego." On the dissolution of the five skandhas that form the appearance of individuality (form, sensation, conception, predisposition, and consciousness), they are replaced by a new set of compounds, in which the karman accumulated in the previous life acts as the catalyst and determinant.*

*Human life is therefore no more than a concatenation of mental and physical states which are influenced by those that preceded them, and in turn influence the subsequent ones, in the karmic cycle that imprisons man in the world and condemns him to pain. The origin of suffering is illustrated by a sequence of 12 interconnected factors triggered by the ignorance that governs the mental world, causing the accumulation of karman and structuring the consciousness accordingly. The consciousness is expressed through the individual personality, a psychophysical entity that operates and is consolidated in the activity of the senses, whose contact with the objects of the material world generates sensations. These sensations give rise to the desire that leads to attachment, which in turn produces life, divided into a continuous succession of births and deaths. There is no place in this context for the concept of atman, the permanent, immutable soul which is reincarnated, or that of Brahman, the Absolute, a Being beyond becoming, which are crucial concepts in the Hindu world.*

*Hinayana Buddhism, also known as Theravada (Doctrine of the Elders), which preserves the concise original message of Buddha who preferred moral teachings and the monastic life to metaphysical speculation and mystical realizations, was the first to spread through the Khmer area, brought by missionary monks who followed in the footsteps of the merchants.*

*To the Buddhist world, the samsara (cycle of existence) is like a great fire continually fed by passions, which burn all beings in the flames of suffering. The purpose of Theravada is to put out that fire, namely to annihilate empirical existence and its fictitious consciousness. The term "nirvana" alludes to this difficult process.*

Nirvana literally means "blowing out a flame," and alludes to the concept that the fire of existence is extinguished if the fuel of desire is lacking. However, it also alludes to the traditional Indian concept of fire according to which the flame is not annihilated when it goes out, but rather returns to its true dimension of being, beyond conditioning and manifestation.

Nirvana basically designates the opposite state to the human condition and is quite impossible to define. At most, it can only be expressed by negative propositions: nirvana is not pain, not impermanence, and so on. In the view of the Theravada school, nirvana can only be achieved by monks, whose life is austere but never excessively hard, in accordance with the teachings of Buddha, who indicated that the right course of behavior was a happy medium between total laxity and extreme asceticism. This is achieved in a solitary path that involves moral conduct, concentration, and the clear vision that everything is transient, painful, and lacking in intrinsic sense. By following this way of life, which dissipates ignorance and dissolves attachment, the monk achieves enlightenment and becomes arhat, a "saint" who has liberated himself. Theravada laymen can also accumulate merit by cultivating the virtues of faith, morality, and generosity, and thus ensure that future births will lead them to the monastic life.

*82  A very common image during the reign of Jayavarman VII was the triad constituted by Buddha seated on the coils of the serpent Mucilinda, the bodhisattva Lokeshvara or Avalokiteshvara on his right, and the goddess Prajnaparamita on his left, as in this specimen from a private collection.*

*83  The doctrinal transformations which Buddhism underwent over the centuries are reflected in its iconography, a local version of which was produced in Kambuja. A good example is the "decorated Buddha," which contrasts with the choice of poverty made in reality by Buddha, a wandering ascetic. The fact that temporal power was attributed to him by the Khmer sovereigns led to this iconographic development. This twelfth/thirteenth-century bronze specimen is housed in a private collection.*

*84 Buddhism was introduced in the early centuries of the Christian era by monks from India, and the oldest images of Buddha, like this seventh-century image from Angkor Borei, now in Phnom Penh Museum, were influenced by Indian aesthetics.*

The first statues of Buddha, dating from the sixth and seventh centuries, were inspired by Theravada Buddhism and mainly portray the Enlightened One standing. He wears a floor-length gown consisting of the **antaravasaka** *(a cloth wound round the hips)* and the **uttarasanga**, *a kind of ample cloak that covered one or both shoulders, ensured the stability of the statue, and enabled the supporting arch used in Hindu statues to be eliminated.*

Of the 32 signs which distinguish Buddha according to the various texts, those most often represented in Khmer art are the **ushnisha**, *the cranial protuberance portrayed as a chignon, the symbol of* **nirvana**, *and earlobes elongated by heavy earrings worn before he renounced the world of princes. The* **mudra** *(gestures of the hands) "seal" the inner states and attitudes of the Enlightened One. The most common* **mudra** *are the* **abhayamudra**, *the gesture of reassurance, in which the palm of the raised right hand is shown; the* **vitarkamudra**, *the teaching attitude expressed by the fingers forming a ring; and the* **dhyanamudra**, *with the back of the right hand on the palm of the left, indicating the state of meditation.*

Some sculptures and epigraphs indicate that Mahayana Buddhism was already practiced in Kambuja in addition to Theravada by the seventh and eighth centuries. The Mahayana school, which was less intransigent in interpreting the disciplinary rules, viewed salvation not as the sole right of monks but as the entitlement of all beings. The school was therefore called the "Great Vehicle" because it received and fulfilled speculative and mystic aspirations not permitted by Theravada.

Mahayana also teaches that the ego is illusory, a negative concept fed by the "three poisons" (greed, hatred, and ignorance), and that every phenomenon which is empty and devoid of a spiritual basis is transient. The concepts **shunya** *(empty)* and **shunyata** *(emptiness)* allude to the only true essence of all phenomena, the absolute Reality that incorporates and transcends opposites beyond all definition, and that can only be achieved through a process of enlightened intuition. In this context, **samsara** *(conditioned, painful existence)* and **nirvana** *(its extinction)* are no longer irreconcilably antagonistic opposites but two interdependent aspects of the same inner reality, that of consciousness, both a stormy sea under the impulse of desire, and a calm mirror that reflects its own vacuity.

*85 The pre-eminence of Buddha over other men is demonstrated by 32 special signs on his body. One of them is the* **ushnisha**, *a cranial protuberance depicted as a chignon, as seen in this eleventh-century specimen from the Guimet Museum.*

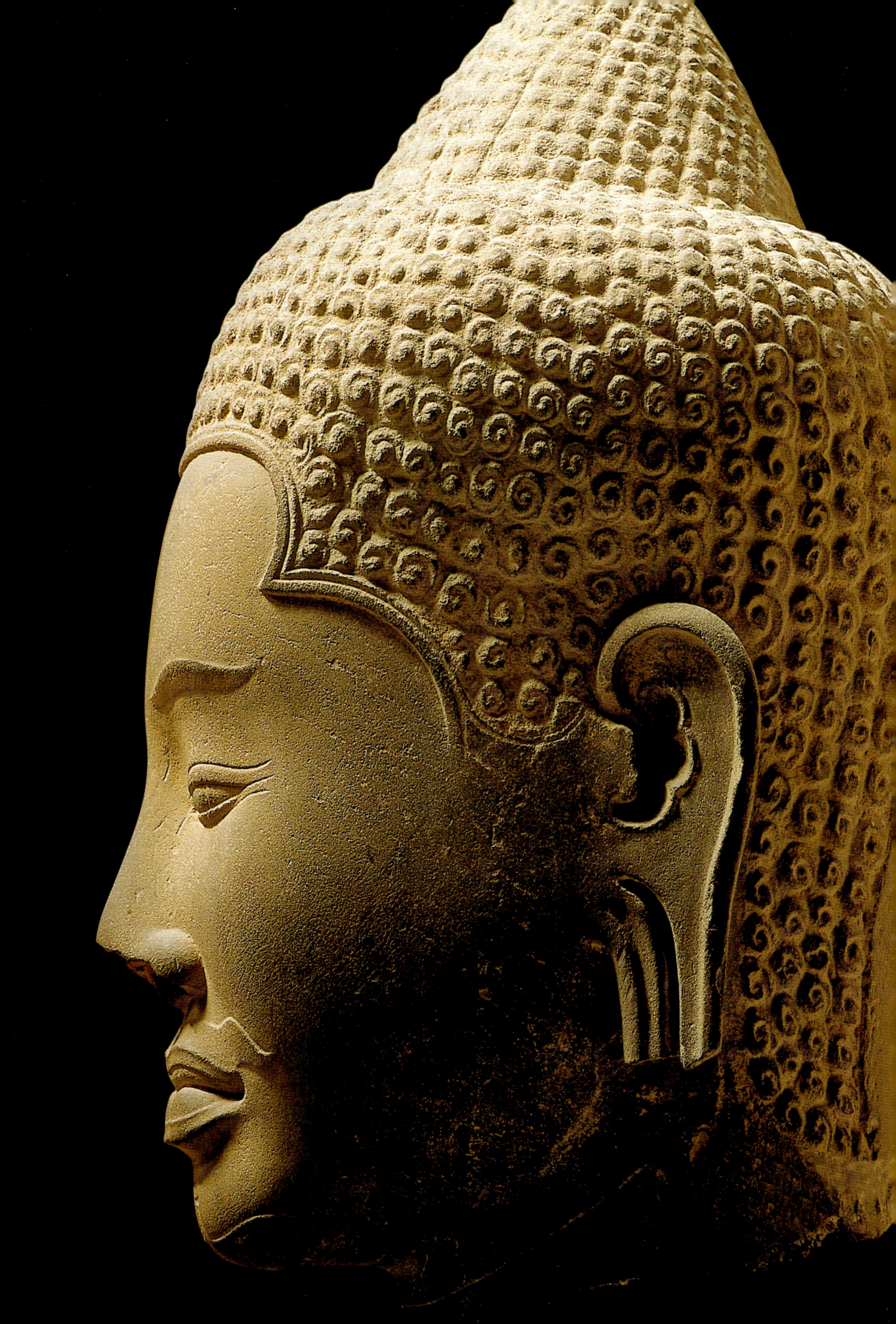

*86-87 The bodhisattvas are emanations of particular Buddhas. Lokeshvara, shown here in a twelfth/thirteenth-century specimen from a private collection, features an image of the Buddha Amitabha, from whom he emanates, in a medallion at the base of the chignon. The symbols of Lokeshvara are the rosary and a tablet of a sacred text held in his raised hands and a lotus bud and an vessel of the nectar of immortality in his lowered hands.*

*In the mystic sphere, Mahayana radically alters the prospects of laymen as it proclaims the right of every being to enlightenment. Everyone can achieve "buddhahood," aided by the* bodhisattva, *which literally means "he whose essence is* bodhi *(illumination)." Although the* bodhisattva *is enlightened and therefore ready to achieve* nirvana, *he renounces his own immediate liberation to show others the way of salvation as the perfect embodiment of benevolence and compassion, the cardinal virtues of Mahayana Buddhism.*

*The figure of the* bodhissattva *falls into a wider religious context in which the historical and human contours of Siddhartha Gautama, who became Buddha, are increasingly hazy, and the spiritual master is transfigured into the ineffable Absolute.*

*The new doctrine which constituted the core of the religious structure of Mahayana Buddhism postulated that Buddha had three bodies: the fictitious appearance of the noble Siddhartha, which is the transformation body perceptible by men; the enjoyment body, from which issue forth infinite divine forms enjoyed by the* bodhisattva *in the celestial domain as a result of their faith, and the body of* Dharma *(the Doctrine), which symbolizes the ultimate Reality beyond all manifestation, the Absolute only knowable by Buddhas. There is no longer only one Buddha, but countless Buddhas assisted by countless* bodhisattva, *in an iconographical expansion that betrays a Hindu influence.*

*One of the most famous* bodhisattva *was Avalokiteshvara, meaning "he who looks down," the representation of the supreme compassion emanated by the Buddha Amitabha, whose image is always included in the medallion that decorates the* jatamukuta, *the crown-shaped topknot of Avalokiteshvara. Better known in the Khmer world as Lokeshvara (Lord of the World), he usually holds a rosary in his right hand and a jug of water in his left; when he is portrayed with four arms, he also holds a book and a lotus bud.*

*Another Bodhisattva often portrayed was Maitreya, who was exceptionally venerated in Theravada Buddhism as well, and frequently represented in pre-Angkor statues. He is the Buddha of the future, and the base of his* jatamukuta *reproduces a* stupa, *the most important Buddhist monument, which is both a reliquary, a symbol of the universe, and an allusion to the omnipresence of the Enlightened One.*

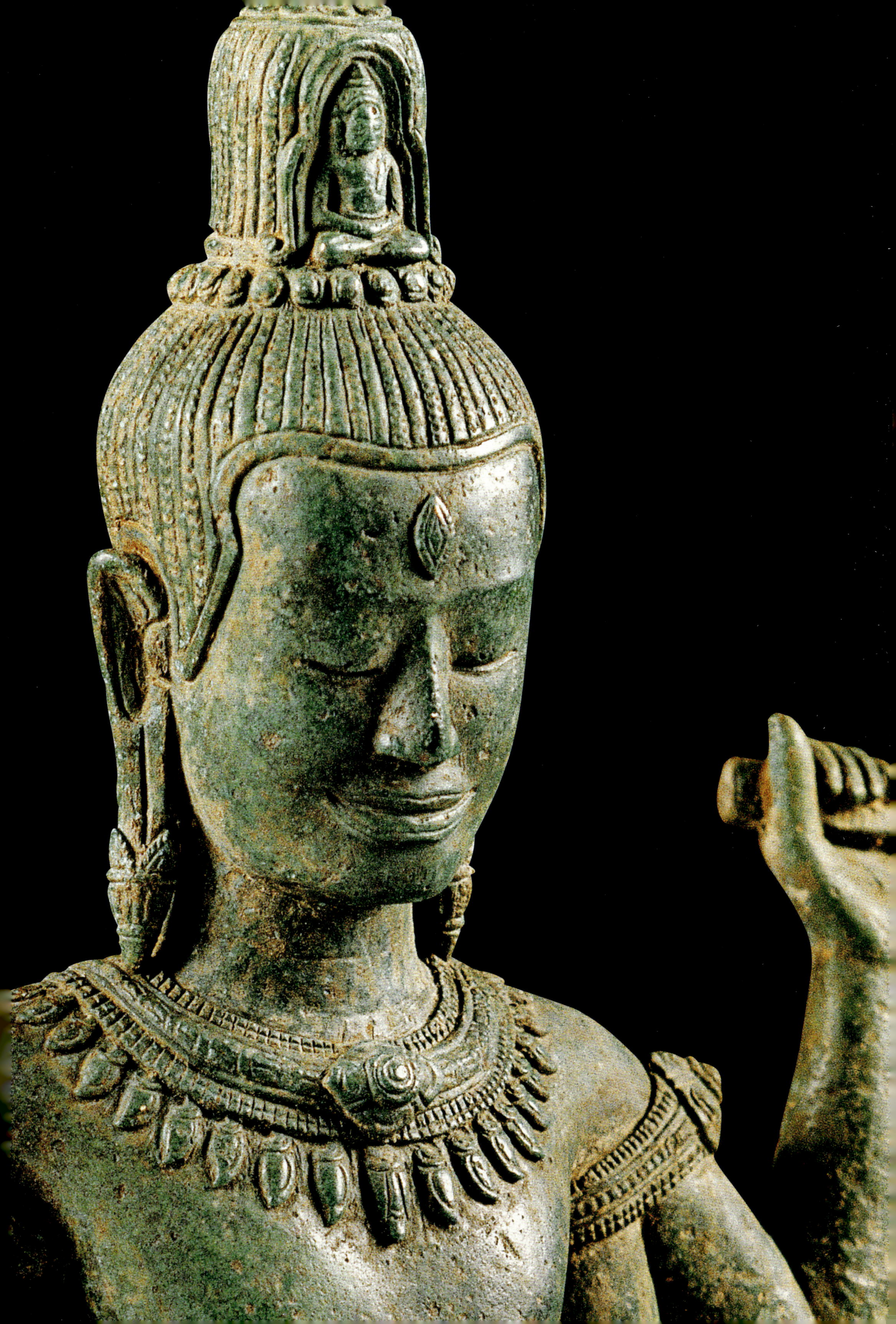

88 *A typical image of Khmer Buddhism is that of the Enlightened One seated on the coils of Mucilinda, seven-headed king of the cobras, who emerged from the depths of the earth to protect him from the rain. The serpent has numerous symbolic implications, including that of portraying the forces of the unconscious recognized and tamed by Buddha. This twelfth-century bronze in the Angkor Wat style is housed in Phnom Penh Museum.*

A portrayal typical of Kambuja, and to some extent the emblem of Khmer Mahayana, shows Buddha seated on the serpent Mucilinda, king of the naga (cobras), who emerged from the roots of the tree under which Buddha sat in meditation to protect him against a shower of rain. The animal symbolizes both the earlier chthonic religion illuminated by the doctrine of Buddha and the dangerous primordial energy dominated and spiritualized by Buddha. Mucilinda's three coils serves as the throne for the Enlightened One, sitting in the meditation posture, and his multi-headed hood opens to act as a canopy. The cobra's hood alludes to the bodhi tree (tree of illumination), and the three rings formed by its coils may symbolize either the tri-fold world (earth, atmosphere, and sky) in which Buddha triumphs, or the triple jewel (Buddha, his Doctrine, and the community).

A more esoteric interpretation of Indian origin views the rearing-up serpent as representative of the ascent of the kundalini, the dangerous potential energy latent in the sacro-coccygeal area of man, portrayed in the form of a female deity who is part woman, part snake: the goddess Kundalini. This view belongs to Tantrism, the complex philosophical and ritual movement that profoundly influenced Indian civilization between the fourth and fifteenth centuries and involved arduous mental and physical practices, designed to give power and able to cause radical transformations of consciousness. Hathayoga, a particular version of Yoga (the spiritual path that uses the body as the means to salvation) based on mystic/symbolic physiology, which includes the seven chakras (centers situated at various levels of the spinal

89 The Mahayana describes the concept of the three bodies of Buddha: the historical body of Siddhartha Gautama which was visible to men, the "enjoyment body" perceived by the bodhisattva, and the "truth body" perceived by the Buddhas. Decorated Buddhas, like this twelfth-century specimen now housed in the Guimet Museum, show an aspect of the enjoyment body.

column and the crown of the head which diffuse the energy of Kundalini) belongs to the Tantra movement. These levels are precisely what the seven heads of Mucilinda's hood allude to.

Mahayana Buddhism also produced the "decorated Buddha," ornamented with jewels, an image developed between the ninth and tenth centuries in the Indian monastery of Nalanda, which spread more widely in Indochina than in India. The incongruous addition of jewelry (Buddha took a vow of poverty, and therefore wore no ornaments) is explained by the desire to emphasize the pre-eminence of the Enlightened One who, having achieved spiritual supremacy, is identified with the chakravartin (universal sovereign) and, like him, is adorned with the most magnificent jewels.

Researcher Paul Mus considers the image of Buddha adorned with precious gems to be a manifestation of the sambhogakaya (the enjoyment body), while the image in which he is seated on Mucilinda portrays the dharmakaya (the Doctrinal body) and the nirmanakaya (fictitious body) alludes to the monastic image of the Enlightened One.

The appearance of female deities such as the goddess Prajna or Prajnaparamita, the representation of the prajna (intuitive wisdom or perfect knowledge) resulting from the state of enlightenment, testifies to the last transformation of Buddhism: Vajrayana ("the diamond vehicle"). In the oldest stage of Hinduism, the term vajra referred to the attribute of Indra the rain god, and meant "thunderbolt." Later, by extension, it symbolized enlightenment and the indestructible nature of Buddhist message, and came to mean "diamond," the element which can scratch everything, but can be scratched by nothing.

*The* vajra, *which symbolizes the spiritual force that destroys the three poisons, is the diamond scepter that ensures liberation. It was a very important Khmer ceremonial object, cast in bronze, and always exquisitely crafted. The handle symbolizes the nucleus from which everything originated and its workmanship alludes to the spiral energy that led to the manifestation of the cosmos. The two ends of the* vajra *symbolize the poles which generate the current of life and its four tips allude to the cardinal points. The fifth tip in the center, which is often missing, evokes the zenith.*

*The* vajra *possesses a penetrating force, and is perceived as male. It also alludes to the* upaya, *the ideal means of achieving* prajna *(perfect knowledge), which is constituted by compassion and love of all beings. These are the two cardinal virtues that lead to enlightenment, which is the union of* prajna *and* upaya, *the end and the means, and the synthesis of intellect and heart.*

*While the* vajra *symbolizes the means in the rituals, the bronze* ghanta *(bell) symbolizes the* prajna, *and its shape alludes to the cosmic womb. The ringing of the bell evokes the primordial sound, the vibration that gave rise to life.*

*The deities of Vajrayana Buddhism include Hevajra, who embodies the immediate enlightenment obtained by an arduous process of inner battles. The beautiful bronzes portraying him are imbued with esoteric meanings. Hevajra has four legs and feet with ten toes each, and eight heads on different levels. The three heads on the first level allude to the Vajrayana triad, namely Buddha and the two* bodhisattvas *Lokeshvara and Vajrapani (lord of the* vajra*). The four heads on the second level and the one on the third allude to the five cosmic buddhas (Vairocana, Akshobhya, Ratnasambhava, Amitabha, and Amoghasiddhi) from whom the various pentads of the Vajrayana derive, such as the five cosmic elements (earth, water, fire, air, and ethereal space), the five colors (white, blue, yellow, red, and green), the five* bodhisattvas *(Samantabhadra, Vajrapani, Ratnapani, Avalokiteshvara, and Vishvapani), etc. The figure on which Hevajra dances symbolizes attachment to the material world, which must be destroyed.*

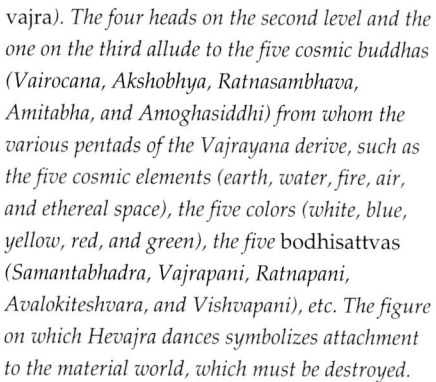

*When Jayavarman VII, the last great Khmer Emperor, ascended to the throne, Mahayana Buddhism became the state religion and the king's actions were motivated by compassion. In his inscriptions, Jayavarman VII states that "public pain constitutes the pain of the king, not his own suffering," therefore the task of the enlightened monarch is "to perform eminent and meritorious actions in favor of all beings." The foundation of hospices for travelers and hospitals provides tangible proof of the benevolence and compassion of Jayavarman, who proclaimed himself the incarnation of Lokeshava, the pious "Lord who looks down," namely down on the world, to save it. Jayavarman's favorite wife, Jayarajadevi, was identified with the goddess Prajna or, according to another version, the goddess Tara, Lady of Compassion. Other relatives of the Emperor were also identified after their deaths with figures from the Buddhist pantheon.*

*However, although Jayavarman claimed to be a compassionate ruler, his building frenzy and anxiety to become immortal forced the population to make extreme sacrifices. As a result, it was not the Mahayana version of Buddhism that survived in the Khmer area. On the death of the megalomaniac Jayavarman, his exhausted kingdom, its resources depleted, abandoned the "Great Vehicle" and turned to the more basic Theravada Buddhism, which was still being practiced with great simplicity by a few monks and part of the population.*

90 *The last transformation of Buddhism is the Vajrayana (diamond vehicle), an esoteric path peopled with deities of terrifying appearance like this eleventh-century Hevajra, lord of the* vajra *(diamond scepter) after which the Vajrayana school is named. Originally from Banteay Kdei, it is now housed in the Guimet Museum.*

91 *The scepter, mace, and club are symbols of power, held by the temple gatekeepers and the deities. This huge fragment of a hand, resting on the knob of a club, belonged to a tenth-century Shiva from Koh Ker, now in the Guimet Museum.*

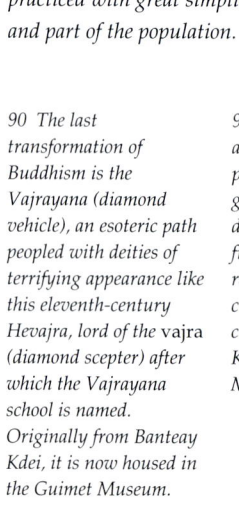

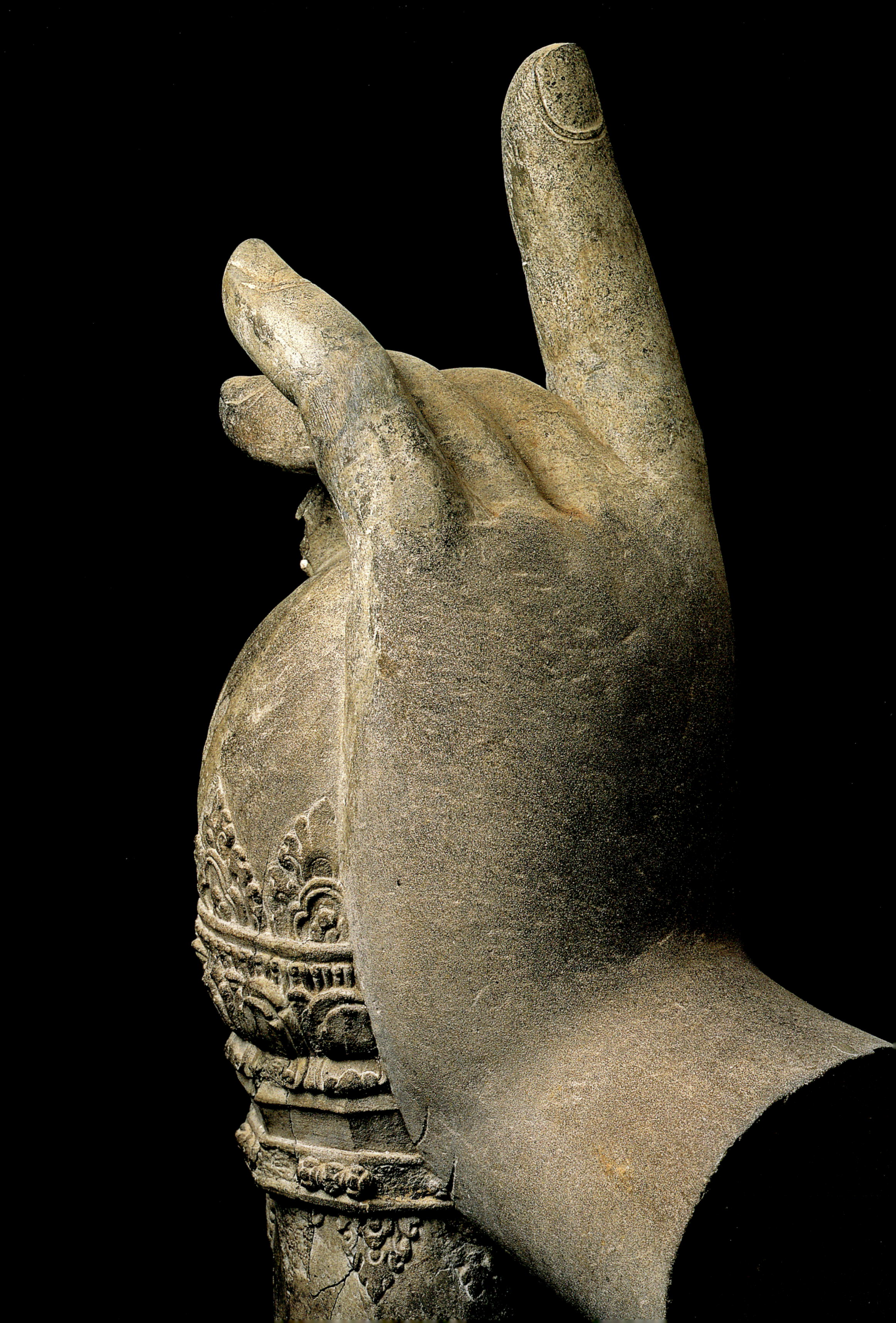

# THE KING AND SOCIETY

Hindu cultural influence was undoubtedly felt in social and political fields in Kambuja. However, Khmer society does not seem to have been divided into castes like Indian society, but into classes. Even when the term varna (which in Sanskrit means both "caste" and "color," with obvious racial implications) appears in inscriptions, it usually refers to groups of people who perform the same function or job. Although jobs tended to be passed down from father to son, they do not appear to have been hereditary, and civil service and military appointments certainly were not as the king granted and terminated them at his pleasure.

The only group who expressly constituted a caste were the Brahmans of Indian descent. Being the repositories of the sacred science and performers of the complex royal rituals, they enjoyed great prestige. They were organized in matrilineal clans, did not comply with the rigid Indian endogamous rules, and often married members of the warrior aristocracy.

The names, jobs, and feats of the various Brahmanic clans are known from inscriptions. The most eminent family was the one descended from Shivakaivalya, which was given responsibility for the cult of the Devaraja (god-king) in 802. The appointment held by Shivakaivalya and his descendents involved the custody and performance of the rites of the Devaraja and the job of spiritual adviser to the king and tutor to the Crown Prince. The extension of the ceremonial court apparatus, as a result of which the rites became more complex, led to a gradual increase in the appointments held by the Brahmans. The inscriptions refer mainly to the hotar (officiating priest), the purohita (royal tutor), and the vrah guru (the first spiritual master and performer of the rites of the Devaraja). In particular, an inscription at the Banteay Srei temple which celebrates its founder Yajnavaraha, vrah guru to King Jayavarman V during the tenth century, goes into great detail about the vrah gurus and their tasks. There are still numerous doubts about the institution of the Devaraja and its exact scope. The only precise reference to it appears on the stela of Sdok

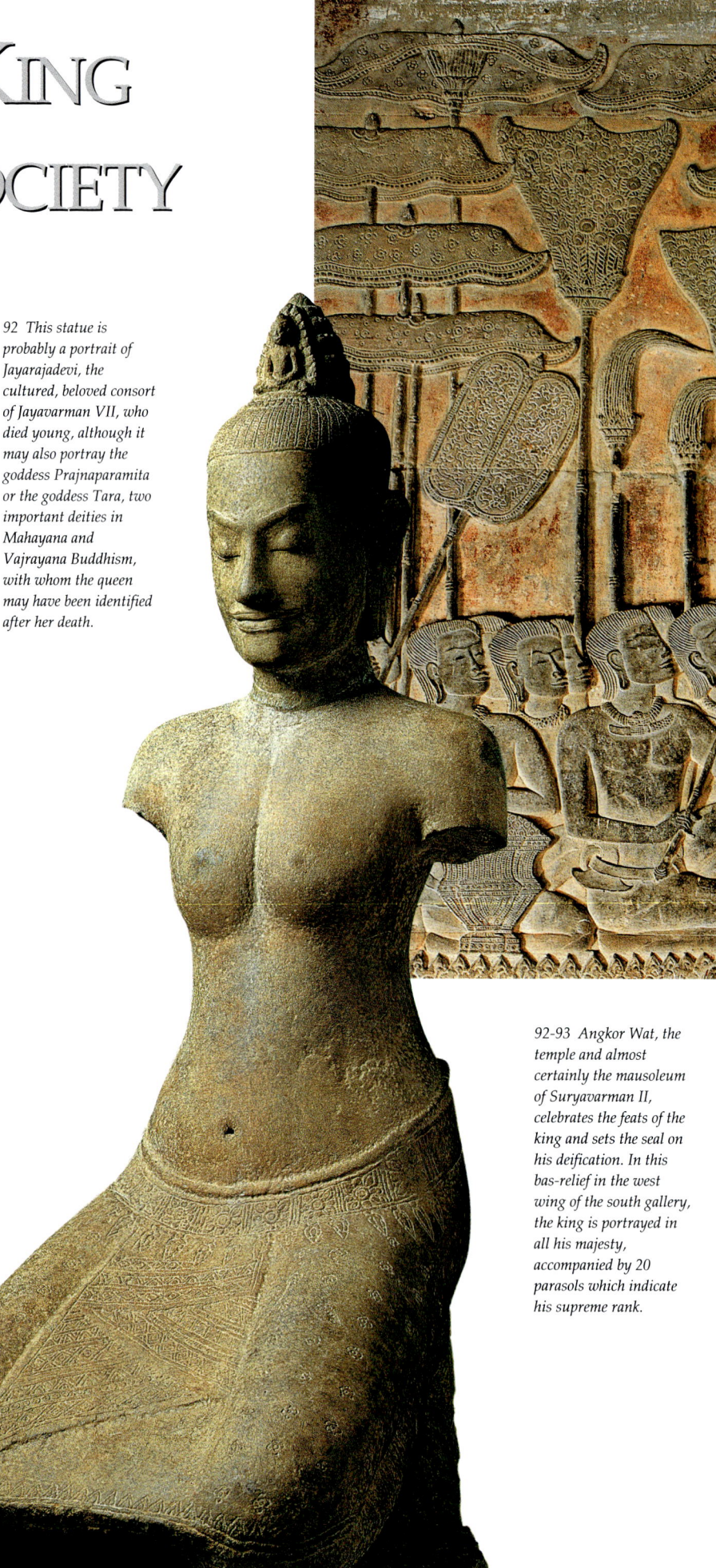

92 This statue is probably a portrait of Jayarajadevi, the cultured, beloved consort of Jayavarman VII, who died young, although it may also portray the goddess Prajnaparamita or the goddess Tara, two important deities in Mahayana and Vajrayana Buddhism, with whom the queen may have been identified after her death.

92-93 Angkor Wat, the temple and almost certainly the mausoleum of Suryavarman II, celebrates the feats of the king and sets the seal on his deification. In this bas-relief in the west wing of the south gallery, the king is portrayed in all his majesty, accompanied by 20 parasols which indicate his supreme rank.

Kak Thom, dated 1052, which was written by a descendent of Shivakaivalya. It states that after a period of anarchy and probable Javanese domination, King Jayavarman II threw off the Javanese yoke and unified the country in the ninth century, founding four capitals in the future Angkor area: Indrapura, Hariharalaya, Amarendrapura, and Mahendrapura.

To consecrate his sovereignty, Jayavarman II, who did not leave any inscriptions himself, had a great Brahmanic rite celebrated in 802 on Mount Mahendraparvata (Mountain of the Great God Indra), now known as Phnom Kulen, an ancient place of worship situated some 25 miles from what was to become Angkor. The officiator was the Brahman Hiranyadama from Janapada, an unidentified place somewhere in Kambuja, not in India. He erected a linga, the phallic stone symbolizing Shiva. Tradition has it that the god himself gave it to the king as the emblem of his investiture as chakravartin (universal sovereign) and of the divine mandate of sovereignty.

The Hindu model of the chakravartin, the universal monarch who was the guarantor of social order and custodian of the dharma (the sacred rule that permeated every aspect of life), was fully accepted by the Khmer sovereigns. The chakravratin, the metaphorical fulcrum of Indian society, freed mankind with his firm, enlightened rule from the "fish condition" (the savage law of the jungle in which the strongest destroyed the weakest) and guided them with compassionate justice.

To make the consecration of Jayavarman II even more effective, Hiranyadama instituted the cult of the Devaraja, appointing as its custodian Shivakaivalya, who handed it down to his matrilineal descendents. Hiranyadama also dictated four Tantric texts, of those belonging to the school of Tantrism, an esoteric ritual movement which was very widespread in India between the fourth and fifteenth centuries: the "Vinashikha," on which the coronation rite was based, the "Sammoha," the "Nayottara," and the "Siraccheda." All that remains of these works is a mention in a Nepalese document, and their content is unknown. The inscription at Sdok Kak Thom states that they were emitted by the four mouths of Shiva who, in his four-headed version, was identified with Tumburu, chief of the gandharva (celestial musicians). The texts were probably intended to be recited in correlation with the four cardinal points, thus emphasizing that the chakravartin ruled over the four corners of the universe.

The focal point of the ceremony conducted on Mount Mahendraparvata seems to have been the erection of the linga, but what the ritual involved for the Devaraja is controversial. Philippe Stern believes it was a kind of close alliance between Shiva and the king, affirmed in the consecration ceremony and confirmed by the cult of the linga. The phallic stone was given the name of the king followed by the word Ishvara (Lord). For example, the linga Rajendreshvara, installed by King Rajendravarman in the East Mebon temple in 953, represented the "Lord of Rajendra," confirming Shiva's protection of that king. According to Indian expert Bhattacharya, the linga erection ceremony transformed the king into a part of Shiva, so that although there is no explicit declaration to that effect in the epigraphs, the king was considered an incarnation of the god. This theory was advocated in the second century B.C. by the great Indian legislator Manu in his "Manavadharmashastra" (Doctrinal Exposition of the Dharma of Manu), which said that the king was made of divine particles.

The Sanskrit expression devaraja and its Khmer counterpart Kamrateng jagat ta rajya, which seems to allude to a "divine sovereignty" associated with Shiva, appear in ninth-century inscriptions. However, the situation is clarified by the Sdok Kak Thom inscription, which dates from two centuries later: the ancient Khmer phrase Kamrateng jagat ta raja, meaning "the Lord of the universe who is king," was used for the first time to proclaim the supremacy of Shiva over the other deities. As stated by expert Chiara Silvi Antonini, rajya (royalty) was replaced with raja (king), alluding not to a concept but to a person, in this case a deity, Shiva Devaraja. Just as the earthly chakravartin ruled over the other kings, so the Devaraja predominated in the Khmer pantheon, which was also crowded with indigenous deities, especially the various genii loci.

The linga thus came to be an emblem of absolute sovereignty shared by the god and the king. However, according to the inscriptions found so far, the cult of the Devaraja was not followed by all the Khmer sovereigns, only by some of them, most of whom were usurpers and therefore in need of legitimization. The invocation of the Devaraja

94-95 Harihara (tenth century, Bakheng style, Guimet Museum) was Shiva on the right-hand side, identified by the halved third eye and the crescent moon in his chignon, and Vishnu on the left, wearing the four-tiered, octagonal, pagoda-shaped crown which replaced the mukuta (miter) from the ninth century onwards. The crown and the diadem, tied with a lace at the back of the neck, were the fundamental symbols of royalty.

constituted the ideal solution in times of political instability. Nonetheless, new archaeological discoveries may yet cast more light on the question in future.

The Hindu concept of chakravartin was adapted to suit a local context in which ancestor worship and the cult of the genius loci and the sacred mountain were firmly established. All these factors combined to form a sovereignty in which the earthly sovereign and the god Shiva formed two opposing poles, which met at the mountain. The king, the central hub of the organized social system, occupied in the microcosm the place held by Mont Meru, center and axis of the universe, in the macrocosm. The modern ceremony of investiture of the King of Cambodia, derived from the ancient rajasuya (royal anointing rite), includes abhisheka, the anointing of the king by the Brahmans, which is still performed under a canopy constructed on a platform with nine stories, the same number as Mount Meru. During the abhisheka, the king is identified with the cosmic mountain. The symbolism is repeated in the throne room where the throne, on a raised dais, is flanked by a nine-tiered golden parasol, which in this case alludes to the worlds that rotate around the axis mundi, namely the chakravartin.

If the ancient kings of Funan were the kings of the mountain, according to the Chinese chronicles, Shiva was the Lord of the Himalayas, and the name of his bride Parvati was derived from the Sanskrit parvat (mountain). Thus the mountain became the place of convergence of the two sovereigns, earthly and heavenly, and on it the two became one. The temple built on a hill, constructed as if it were a mountain, represented the crux of the religious system of the Devaraja. Each king had a personal temple built during his reign and placed a linga in it that bore his name, symbolizing his sovereignty and divine nature. On his death, the king took a posthumous name that testified to his apotheosis. The name usually consisted of the name of a god and the Sanskrit term loka (world). Together, they formed a compound word which indicated that the earthly sovereign returned after his death to the paradise of the god whose incarnation he had been on earth.

96

Thus, for example, Suryavarman II, the builder of Angkor Wat, took the posthumous name of Paramavishnuloka, meaning "[the king who has gone to] the world of the Supreme Vishnu." The personal temple of the dead king thus became his mausoleum, while his successor built a new temple for his own linga, and at the same time cultivated the worship of his deified predecessors. It is likely, though not certain, that the kings' ashes were placed in the base of statues of the deities with which they identified, which constituted the main image of the temple.

The last great Khmer sovereign, Jayavarman VII, was a Buddhist, and replaced the linga with the image of Buddha, considering himself to be the incarnation of Lokeshara, the bodhisattva of compassion. The Devaraja thus became the Buddharaja, but in practice all that changed was the name, not the concept. The king thus exercised absolute power by divine mandate; his kingdom stretched in all directions, and numerous factors emphasized this universal claim. There were five royal consorts. The first wife, companion in the rituals and (at least in theory) mother of the heir to the throne, symbolized the zenith and therefore occupied the central pavilion in the women's quarters, while the other four wives were associated with the four cardinal points and housed accordingly.

The modern coronation ceremony, which certainly derives from the ancient Khmer ceremony of taking possession of the universe, involves a royal march towards the four cardinal points, moving in a clockwise direction, as in the case of the traditional pradakshina, the rite of perambulation, which was performed by turning in a circle to one's right. At each stop the king changes his headdress and mount. The starting point is the east (the Royal Palace), from which the king is carried out in a litter, wearing his crown. The first stop is to the south, where he puts on a different, five-pointed crown and boards a chariot pulled by six horses. The next stop is to the west, where he mounts a horse and puts on a wide-brimmed felt hat. At the north stop, he dons a hemispherical gold and silk helmet, and rides an elephant back to the palace. The procession from one station to another indicates taking possession and domination of the kingdom, symbolically considered universal, while the changes of vehicle and headgear, in addition to more recent associations, allude to the Lokapala (the Hindu protectors of space) and the Buddhist guardians of the four directions.

Although the king designated his successor, the yuvaraja (crown prince), the succession to the throne was hardly ever peaceful because in addition to the princes there were also the sons of the king's numerous concubines. Some researchers believe that matrilineal succession was adhered to, but others think that in the event of usurpation, power was legitimized by marrying the widow or daughter of the previous king.

The importance of women in legitimizing the title to the throne is confirmed by the account of Zhou Daguan, who reports that there was a golden tower in the palace where the king made love every evening to a deity who was part woman, part snake, the Nagini of Indian tradition. Many royal dynasties in India claimed to derive from the union of a prince with a Nagini, or traced their ancestry to the moon dynasty originated by Krishna, the incarnation of the god Vishnu, or the sun dynasty, descended from Rama, another descendant of the same god.

The Khmer kings gradually adopted these beliefs too; the first Funan dynasty traced its origins to the Indian Brahman Kaundinya and the Nagini Soma, daughter of the king of the nagas, who in the Khmer tradition was the dragon genius loci. To maintain his power and ensure the fertility of his kingdom, the king had to propitiate the genius loci, and this operation is symbolized by union with his daughter, the many-headed serpentine Nagini referred to by Zhou Daguan.

In addition to the more ancient lineage deriving from Kaundinya and Soma, another genealogical myth emerged which involved Kambu, another Indian Brahman, and the celestial nymph Mera. The two families traced their ancestry to the moon and sun dynasties respectively, and marriages between their members were considered highly auspicious.

*96-97 Courtiers and noblemen traveled in litters. This panel in the west wing of the south gallery of Angkor Wat shows a princess being carried on a litter, and demonstrates how it is made: a mat on which the passenger sat, shaded by a canopy from which curtains could be hung, hangs on elaborate hooks from an arched rod with the ends in the shape of many-headed nagas.*

*98 top  The Cham, the sworn enemies of the Khmer, sacked Angkor in 1177 and settled in the area. In this scene from the south wing of the outer east gallery of the Bayon temple, the Cham warriors are identified by the helmet with a gorget and the jerkin.*

*98 bottom  The bow and arrow were part of the infantry's equipment together with lances and shields. These bronze specimens are on display in the Guimet Museum.*

*98-99  The panels of Angkor Wat show war chariots, although they were actually not used by the Khmer army because they were ill-suited to the uneven terrain. They only appear in mythical scenes, like this portrayal of the Battle of Kurukshetra in the south wing of the west gallery of Angkor Wat. These warriors wear jewels, diadems, and flowered breastplates, which real infantrymen did not.*

However, power and force prevailed over any other consideration in the end. Once the sovereign had gained the throne, in accordance with the dictates of the Hindu codes he had to perform seven tasks: guarantee security by eliminating probable rivals; protect and enlarge the kingdom; form a body of devoted ministers able to provide good administrative services; govern the capital, which was the center of the universe and mirror of his power; increase the treasury; create an unbeatable army; and seek allies.

War was the main task of the king, who used it to increased his prestige and his revenues. The troops, led by the king and princes, consisted of conscripted contingents, mercenary units (in the Bayon bas-reliefs, Siamese troops are recognizable by their particular clothing with pineapple-shaped crests, the Cham by their helmets with gorgets which resembled upside-down flowers, and the Vietnamese by their breastplates, possibly made of rhinoceros hide or wooden scales), and slaves forced to fight. The officers belonged to the warrior aristocracy and are distinguished in the bas-reliefs by their taller stature, parasols, insignia, and mounts, which were usually elephants, and in some cases, horses.

The Khmer army was divided into four corps, like the Indian army, but their composition was different; the infantry, cavalry, and elephants were retained, but chariots were replaced by the fleet. Chariots are actually portrayed in the bas-reliefs, but only in the mythical, not the historical scenes; in fact, the chariot was unsuited to the morphology of the Khmer terrain. The infantry were equipped with bows and arrows, lances, and various kinds of shields, and in some cases protected by breastplates or reinforced tunics. The elephant was accompanied by four infantrymen who protected its legs, and guided by the mahout, who sat on its neck armed with the traditional ankusha (goad). There was room in the palanquin on the elephant's back for one to three warriors armed with bows and arrows; javelin throwers could also be carried in a kind of basket hanging from its sides. Elephants were also used to break through enemy lines; they were enraged by various methods, and then launched against the enemy infantry. The cavalrymen rode without saddle or stirrups, sitting on a saddlecloth, and guided the horse with bit and reins.

The civil service and army were maintained out of tax revenues, which were paid in kind. The king was the sole owner of the land and gave it in usufruct at his pleasure, although in practice the farmers could hand it down to their descendants. Numerous stelae marking the boundaries of the properties assigned testify to the use of usufruct. They were engraved with details of the royal concession and the order that they should not be moved.

The kingdom was divided into provinces, sometimes called paraman, and sometimes vishaya. They were governed by princes or other dignitaries and could be further sub-divided into districts, which were composed of a variable number of villages, called sruk or grama. Officials of various ranks were responsible for collecting taxes and managing the land. They were distinguished by the type of litter and the number of parasols they used. Zhou Daguan says that high officials used litters with golden carrying poles and parasols made of red and green cloth woven with gold thread, with gold handles. The task of holding parasols, flyswatters, and fans, which are known to have been made of twigs, feathers, and cloth, was an important one, and those who performed it belonged to a high social class.

The temples were not only exempt from paying taxes, but also endowed with prebends. They often belonged to important families who worshipped their ancestors in addition to the main deity to which the temple was dedicated. The stelae state that contingents of khnum were allocated to the temples; the term is difficult to interpret, but implies the concept of service rather than slavery. The khnum was perhaps "dedicated" in the sense that he was obliged to perform certain services or give certain produce to the temple in the context of religious servitude, in which the community supplied the gods with personnel, free labor, and goods. This may not have been considered a burden, at least in the early days of the Khmer Empire. It probably reflected a deep faith, and may have been considered a meritorious act.

Slaves certainly existed: they were mainly prisoners of war, debtors (although this is not certain), and savages captured on specific expeditions. Zhou Daguan states that some savages had integrated into Khmer society and "spoke the language," while others lived a free, semi-nomadic life in the forests or inaccessible areas, and engaged in slash-and-burn subsistence farming. The slaves were not given the opportunity of buying their freedom and their children were born into slavery. Marriage between a free man and a slave woman was considered totally improper.

Law was administered in the capital by the king, who appeared at a gold-framed palace window once or twice a day, offering the darshana (view of himself), with the sacred sword of the kingdom in his hand and the primary queen at his side. His judgments were based on the Indian codes, the advice of the vrah guru (high priest) and other learned Brahmans, and local customs. Local courts operated in the various provinces. A stela at Lolei describes the system of fines, the amount of which depended on the social group to which the offender belonged: princes, ministers, high officials, heads of guilds, worshippers of Vishnu and Shiva, or the ordinary people.

In conclusion, it is hard to establish the exact distribution of this society. Some experts believe that independent groups were constituted by the royal family and all its branches, the Brahmans of Indian descent, the royal officials, the army and its officers, and the civil population, namely farmers, fishermen, manual workers, and craftsmen, organized in guilds. Trade was conducted by women, who enjoyed considerable respect and consideration in Khmer society, and the Chinese. However, the most significant division seems to have been between those who performed a task by royal appointment and those who did not.

100-101 The bas-reliefs in the Bayon temple, built by Jayavarman VII between the twelfth and thirteenth centuries, are far more useful than those of Angkor Wat in reconstructing the everyday life of the Khmer because they portray the battle in which Jayavarman conquered the Cham, a historical rather than a mythological event. Infantry, a cavalryman, probably their leader, and two war elephants appear in this scene from the south wing of the south gallery. Note the parasols and standards in the background, important elements in determining the rank of the officers.

# The Idraulic City

One of the most distinctive features of the Khmer Empire was the irrigation system. When it was in full-scale operation, three annual rice harvests could be obtained, producing 3 tons of paddy or 2 tons of dehusked rice a year. A complex network of reservoirs, ditches, and canals provided a constant supply of water, independent of the unreliable monsoon rains, by exploiting some particular features of the Angkor plain.

To the south of the plain lay the Tonlé Sap (Great Lake), connected to the Mekong by the Tonlé Sap River. From mid-May to early October the level of the Mekong rose due to the rains and the thaw in Tibet, where the river originates. The Mekong becomes so swollen that the waters of its tributary, the Tonlé Sap, can no longer flow into it, and are pushed back in a north-west direction. The current of the Tonlé Sap river is consequently reversed, and it flows into the Great Lake, whose level rises from its usual seven to 53 feet, while its area increases from 1,000 to 4,000 square miles. In the dry season the level of the Mekong falls and the Tonlé Sap river flows into it once again, emptying the lake and leaving behind huge tracts of fertile silt.

During the first few centuries A.D., a network of straight, intercommunicating canals connected to the Mekong or Menan Rivers was developed in Funan, probably as a result of Indian influence, to convey the flood waters of the rivers into the Gulf of Siam and wash the soil, which was impregnated with sea salt when the tide rose up the estuaries. The water was retained in the various plots by small earthen dykes and then made to flow into those at a lower level until it reached a drainage channel that returned the surplus water to the river. However irrigation was dependent on the monsoons, the rains that fell from June to September after a long, hot, dry period. This meant only one rice harvest, followed by the cultivation of other crops. On the other hand, experimental, terraced paddy fields had been constructed in Chenla in an attempt to take advantage of its mountainous terrain, but even here the water supply was bound to the rainy season.

The solution to the problem of seasonal limitations was found by Jayavarman II. He had lived at the court of Shailandra in Java where he probably learned the hydraulic techniques which, after being inaugurated by him and improved by his successors, turned the Angkor plain into the largest rice-growing area in Indochina. The area is a huge alluvial plain crossed by three perennial rivers, which flow into the Great Lake. The special feature of the Angkor plain is its slight downward slope from north-north-east to south-south-west. This characteristic was exploited by the Khmer emperors to channel the river water into false canals (canals made not by excavation but by building dykes or embankments so that the water was at a higher level than the plain) with a gentler minimum slope than the terrain, thus producing a natural down-flow. At the same time they built the barays, huge reservoirs which held rainwater and the overflow water from the rivers. Once again, they were not excavated from the ground but were made by building embankments above ground level. The perimeter of the baray was marked by two parallel canals, the backfill from which was used to build the dyke in the middle. The outer canal served for drainage and collection of overflow water.

The baray stored the water at a higher level than the plain so that it could be tapped off as required through a system of locks, with no need for pumps, by exploiting the difference in height. Between 877 and 889 Indravarman built the first great baray, the Indratataka, at Lolei, present-day

*102-103 This tenth-century architrave in the Banteay Srei style, now in the Phnom Penh National Museum, shows Vishnu riding Garuda, in the middle of the scene. Garuda appears again at the ends of the festoon, spewing forth many-headed nagas. The lush floral decoration alludes to the precious waters showered from the sky by the gods and distributed on earth by the king.*

Roluos. It was 12,500 feet long and 2,625 feet wide, and could hold 212 million cubic feet of water. The reservoir, whose length was four times its width, was built perpendicular to the river and the natural slope of the plain, and was supplied with water by the river Roluos. This situation was exploited so that the channels downstream of the baray distributed water to the paddy fields and supplied the moats of the Preah Ko temple, Bakong, and the royal palace, which was probably located near what is now Prei Monti. The water was then channeled across other paddy fields and flowed into the lake. Indravarman's work at Roluos constituted a shining example to be followed in the future, and Yashovarman, who moved north in search of new living space, used it between 889 and 900 when he used the Siem Reap river to create the East Baray. The baray, known as Yashodharatataka, was 23,000 feet long and 5,900 feet wide; it could hold one billion cubic feet of water, enough to satisfy the new capital Yashodharapura. An even larger reservoir, which may have been commenced shortly before 1050 by King Suryavarman II, was built by Udayadityavarman II. The West Baray, supplied by the O Klok river, was 26,000 feet long and 7,200 feet wide, and could hold 1,400,000,000 cubic feet of water.

The vast hydraulic resources at Angkor and intelligent use of the land in an area covering almost 300,000 acres led to unrivaled intensive rice production, and this made the existence one of the highest population densities in Indochina possible. According to some experts, the population of the Angkor area reached a million inhabitants in the twelfth century, 70 percent of whom were engaged in agriculture.

Only a strong central power could guarantee the operation of the hydraulic system, and above all its maintenance, because the barays silted up and needed continual work. In this closely interconnected system, the weakness of one link led to the collapse of the whole structure, and the excessive building and continual wars during the last period of the Khmer Empire depleted its resources, leading to the decline of Angkor.

# Everyday Life

*Periodic flooding, damp, heat, and wild animals, many of which were dangerous, led the Khmer to build their homes on stilts right from the outset, and this architectural solution is still used today. The houses shown in the Bayon bas-reliefs are identical to those seen in the rural landscape today. Although there is no surviving written information about building techniques, the use of the various rooms, the prescribed rituals, and the observances which were customary at the time of the Khmer Empire, it is likely that the present-day building methods have ancient origins and represent a tradition that has been maintained practically unchanged over the centuries.*

*The Khmer houses were rectangular, built on stilts, and supported by pillars made of hard wood resistant to termites, rodents, and rot. There could be between eight and 20 pillars but 12 are common nowadays, and this was probably also the case in ancient times in view of the connection between the number 12 and the signs of the zodiac.*

*Then, as now, the walls were made of light wood or cane while the roof was made of straw, palm leaves, or matting. Tiled roofs were reserved for the homes of noblemen. The most common type of roof had two tall, steeply-pitched symmetrical sides. By lowering the gables and reducing their pitch, partial extensions of the roof could be inserted, serving on one side as a kitchen roof, and at the front, back, or on either of the sides to shelter the entrance and provide covered areas for tools, above all the pedal-operated rice mill. Inside, the rooms were separated by light partitions, matting, and curtains.*

*The furniture was minimal: low tables, chairs, stools, four-legged beds with no headboard, chests, and baskets. The fireplace was made from three stones, and in the wealthier homes consisted of a kind of earthenware or bronze tripod containing the fire over which the cooking pot was placed. The tableware was simple and basic; peasants made many vessels, including ladles, from coconuts, and used bamboo segments as containers. The baskets with conical lids shown in the bas-reliefs are still used to protect rice, and the nets and lobster pots shown in the fishing scenes have also remained unchanged.*

*Building a house undoubtedly required a number of geomantic procedures and rituals similar to those in use today. Analysis of the lie of the land was essential, and the best site in the Angkor period, as now, was probably one with a river to the south-east. It was vital not to build the house on the home of the local spirit. The entrance had to face east, never west, which was considered to be the province of the dead. Assuming that the layout was similar to that used today, the kitchen would have been situated to the north of the main building. However, the granary could not be positioned in that direction but had to face south-west. The southern part of present-day homes is open to strangers while the northern part is reserved for the family, and a spatial division no doubt existed in ancient times too.*

*Even if the best time to start work was indeed considered to be March whereas February was inauspicious, as it is believed today, it is impossible to be sure. Nonetheless, the choice and cutting of wood for the pillars was accompanied by expiatory and propitiatory rituals. When the building work was finished, the astrologer established the most auspicious time to enter the home (Zhou Daguan says that two days of the week were considered particularly propitious, two particularly inauspicious, and three neutral), and apotropaic rituals were performed*

104-105 The market scene portrayed in this bas-relief in the outer south gallery of the east wing of the Bayon shows goods being weighed and a cleaned fish being prepared by a woman under a pavilion. Trade seems to have been the responsibility of women. The men amused themselves by watching combat between animals, in this case a cockfight.

105 Khmer terracotta ware demonstrates a high degree of sophistication in terms of both shape and decoration, as demonstrated by the jar on the left. The celadon ceramics in animal shapes, like the elephant vase on the right, are particularly attractive. A glazed enamel coating was made by covering the vase with an iron oxide-based layer and firing it in a low-oxygen chamber.

*by the achar, a term which derives from the Sanskrit acaryam (spiritual master), but here meant one who knew the rites. Among other things he drew a yantra (an esoteric diagram of exorcism and propitiation) on red or white fabric and placed it at the entrance of the house, in the middle of the main beam. It is still believed today that the "Lady of the Home," a protective deity originating from the trees, lives in the main beam, and clothes and ornaments are offered to her by hanging them from it or from the main pillar.*

The homes of the aristocracy, and above all the royal palace, were surrounded by walls. They consisted of wooden pavilions standing on tall stone bases with axial staircases and balustrades, which in a way replaced stilts and performed the same protective function. The pavilions were used for various purposes and were reserved for the various members of the family and the court, while the service buildings housed stables, granaries, pantries, armories, treasuries, and kitchens. The quarters of the servants, court craftsmen, and the army were separate from those of the king and his wives. There was always a place of worship, even though the king celebrated the rites connected with his sovereignty in the stone temple inside in the palace enclosure, as in the case of Phimeanakas, or in the temple that marked the city center. Nonetheless, there was probably a sanctuary of the ancestors and a shrine to the tutelary deity of the family at court and in noblemen's homes, made of wood like the rest of the house.

The most important pavilions were cross-shaped, surrounded by verandas, and connected to one another by long hypostyle galleries. The pillars were carved and covered with precious metals, while the walls were covered with tapestry-like decorations and frescoed with mythical scenes. Carved frames surrounded the doors and windows, which were surmounted by elaborate pediments, and the rooms were screened by shutters.

106 Architraves and pediments supply invaluable information about everyday life. This tenth-century pediment, on the west door of the second enclosure of Banteay Srei, depicts an episode from the "Mahabharata:" the battle between Bhima, one of the Pandavas, and Duryodhana, chief of the Kauravas.

In light of the temple architecture, it is believed that the windows had gratings and turned columns, and that venetian blinds were hung from them to shade the rooms.

The roofs, covered with colored earthenware tiles, had various slopes placed one inside another to give a telescopic effect. Those which were pitched most gently covered the verandas. The triangular gables were carved with mythical scenes and plant decorations, while stylized nagas (many-headed cobras) and garudas (the vulture which was the mount of Vishnu) projected from the ridges and the edges of the roofs. The place where the roofs of the cross-shaped pavilions met was emphasized by a kind of slender pinnacled drum.

According to Zhou Daguan, the floors were covered with mats and hides and the furniture consisted of low couches with naga-shaped legs, used as sofas and beds, small tables, chairs, and stools. The magnificent lotus-shaped incense burners, elaborate oil lamps, glazed pottery in animal shapes, jugs, and mirrors which have survived to the present day demonstrate the elegance of luxury goods in the Khmer empire.

*106-107 The civil architecture of the Khmer Empire has been totally lost but can be reconstructed with the aid of the bas-reliefs, like this one at the Bayon. Multi-story buildings can be seen with verandas screened by curtains, shown here partly closed and knotted, and "telescopic" roofs, built in diminishing tiers. The ridge is decorated with pinnacles and the sloping roofs are tiled and ornamented with acroteria.*

*108-109 The Khmer soldiers that throng the bas-reliefs of the Bayon are preparing to eat under a large tent. On the right, a pig is ready for the cooking pot and a pile of skewers stands nearby, while on the left, rice is being cooked, ready to be taken to the troops in individual containers.*

The basic diet of the population was rice, but other crops were also grown, including millet, pumpkins, eggplants, broad beans, leeks, onions, and mustard, and various kinds of fruit including watermelons, bananas, guava, pomegranates, and pineapples. The flowers and roots of the lotus were eaten. Extensive use was made of spices, especially pepper, which grew plentifully. There was no lack of meat, as the Khmer raised cattle, buffaloes, zebus, goats, pigs, and poultry. However, meat was probably used mostly for religious reasons and the Khmer definitely did not eat beef, in accordance with the Brahman tradition. In the past, as in recent times, animals may have been butchered by the Chinese. The Bayon bas-reliefs include a scene

109 *The homes of the common people were simple huts with few furnishings, and present-day homes in rural parts of Cambodia are very similar. The baskets shown in the details of the Bayon bas-reliefs are still used today.*

that seems to depict the sale of meat kebabs, and hunting scenes are portrayed in numerous temples. Hunting, which was probably a pastime for the rich and a necessity for the poor, if indeed they were allowed to hunt, must have been widely practiced.

Fish, caught with baskets and nets, was the other important element of the Khmer diet, considering the abundance of water. The annual catch seems to have been around 20,000 tons. In view of the use made of it nowadays, fish was probably sometimes eaten in the form of fermented paste and liquid sauce. Fish stock must have been considered an excellent condiment then, as now. The Khmer used both sea salt and rock salt; as sweeteners they used palm sugar (obtained by cooking the juice, leaving it to crystallize, and then pulverizing it), treacle, and honey. Bees were kept for honey and wax. As in India, milk and curds must have been widely used, especially for desserts. Butter, possibly clarified like the Indian ghee, was not only used for cooking but also for ritual purposes.

Water and coconut milk were drunk and there were also alcoholic drinks using alcohol made from raw or cooked rice, honey fermented with special spices and dissolved in water, or the juice obtained from the flowers of the thnôt (palmyra palm), which was so dangerous to extract that its collector was exempt from paying taxes. The bas-reliefs show scenes in which people drink directly out of jars using a kind of pipette.

Tableware, cups, and spoons were made of leaves and thrown away after use. A vessel of water was always provided to clean the agglutinated rice cooked in bamboo canes from the fingers; the container would be made of leaves, earthenware, or metal, depending on the rank of the guests. The Khmer only ate with the right hand, as the left was used for bodily hygiene. They were meticulous about cleanliness and bathed frequently in the reservoirs and canals. In view of the climate and the abundance of water, there was no need for roofed bath houses. The teeth were cleaned by rubbing them with sticks of nim (Azadirachta indica).

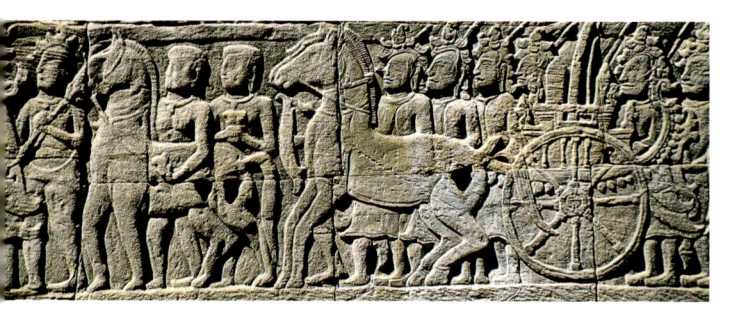

*According to Zhou Daguan, the Khmer used the barter system for small purchases and paid in lengths of cloth; precious metals were only used for more important transactions. The bas-reliefs demonstrate the use of the steelyard.*

*The peasants traveled on foot, carrying weights on their heads or hanging from a yoke on their shoulders. The most common vehicle was the large-wheeled cart, which was light and very elastic because it was slotted together without the use of nails and could be floated with the aid of a few inflated bladders in the event of flooding. A double transverse yoke, shaped like a naga, was attached to the raised helm so that two animals, oxen or zebus, could be harnessed to it. Skids were attached to the hubs of the two wheels to steer the vehicle over rough ground or ruts. A moveable hood protected the cart in bad weather.*

*Litters, described in detail by Zhou Daguan, were used for the shorter and less difficult journeys. They consisted of a single, slightly concave pole with two hooks, about a foot from each end. The passenger reclined in a large piece of folded fabric hung from the hooks on ropes. There must also have been a light canopy to protect the head. The tips of the litters and the hooks were made of metal and beautifully crafted, often in the shape of a* naga *or* garuda, *as demonstrated by the surviving specimens. Some bas-reliefs also show a sedan, consisting of two poles surmounted by an elaborate chair. However, sedan chairs are believed to have been used only during ritual parades and royal ceremonies.*

*Horses were used by the nobility for short journeys, processions, and battle. The usual means of transport over long distances was the elephant, which was vital to the economy, the administration, and the art of war: elephants carried supplies, officials, and army officers. The white elephant was considered sacred, and housed with honors in the royal stables. The seat placed on the animal was protected by tall sides and shaded by canopies when necessary. It was made of exquisitely crafted wood and ornamented with inlays of costly materials.*

*At the height of its splendor, the Khmer Empire had seven major roads, two of which ran as far as Phimai in present-day Thailand and Wat Phu in Laos. They were very wide, paved with laterite, and built on tall embankments. A number of bridges still survive from the Khmer period, such as the Spean Praptos bridge over the Siem Reap river. Stone buildings 13 to 16 feet metres wide and 46 to 49 feet long were built along the roads at intervals of about seven to nine miles. At the time of Jayavarman VII, there seem to have been 120 of these rest stations, known as "fire houses." The same king had more than 100 hospitals built, perhaps by restoring existing ones; they were wooden structures built around a small stone shrine.*

*The busiest communication routes were the waterways, and the most common vehicle was the dugout canoe, a tree trunk hollowed out with fire and axe. The canoe was caulked with a resin-based bitumen and its hull was waterproofed with fish grease and lime. The Bayon bas-reliefs show war canoes with bridges and 15 oarsmen* on each side. The prow was carved in the form of the head of a garuda or a makara (a mythical, composite aquatic animal), and the stern in the shape of a serpent. The rudder consisted of a single oar fixed in the stern and was used an anchor. Apparently, sailing ships that could hold up to 200 passengers cruised the sea. They had 20 oarsmen on each side and were fitted with a deck and two long oars in the stern that acted as rudders.

The most popular entertainments included fighting between animals (cocks, black pigs, and mastiffs), tumbling, and wrestling. The noblemen hunted and probably played a kind of polo or pall-mall.

There were numerous festivals: the new year, celebrated with the erection of scaffolding for fireworks, which were propelled by bat guano mixed with ash and sulfur; the procession and anointing of statues; the end of the rainy season and the festival of the waters, with ritual canoe racing; festivals associated with the rice-growing cycle; and royal parades with elephant fights. All were accompanied by music and dancing.

110 The bas-reliefs of the Bayon show horses, used for short journeys, and elephants, which were preferred because they were better suited to the uneven terrain. That is why the Khmer army had no cavalry, but rather contingents mounted on elephants.

110-111 The troops were accompanied by their families. This very detailed scene on two registers of the outer east gallery in the south wing of the Bayon temple shows carts with the traditional steering skids added to the wheels, which are still used today.

# CLOTHING

*112 left  The torso and arms of this Lokeshvara, portrayed in the Bayon style (Guimet Museum, twelfth/thirteenth century), are entirely covered with images of Buddha which exude from every pore. The short* sampot *is typical of the period.*

Information about Khmer clothing has been obtained not only from sculptures and bas-reliefs but also from the report by Zhou Daguan, who says that men and women wore a small piece of fabric round the waist at home and a longer one tied over it when they went out, but were always naked from the waist up. The fabrics used were cotton and kapok spun by hand (the winder was unknown to them) and they were worn draped over the body. The Khmer did not sew and embroidered fabrics were imported from the Thai kingdoms and Champa. All the tailors were Thais, who jealously protected the secrets of their trade. According to Zhou Daguan, the choice of embroidery was not determined by personal preferences but by membership in a given social class. Fabrics were colored with vegetable dyes: black was obtained from the bread tree; red from bixin, a pigment extracted from the substance that covers annatto seeds, and from the molucca bean; yellow from gardenia, mangrove, and the saffron crocus; and blue from indigo. Vermilion and the red dye made from the cochineal insect were purchased from China.

In addition to cotton and kapok, an unknown fiber called luoma, perhaps a climbing plant or liana, was woven and fabrics also seem to have been made from goat hair. Silk, which was highly prized, was imported from China and the Thai kingdoms and worn by the king and the aristocracy.

*112 right  One edge of the* sampot, *which was not sewn, could be folded over the belt, as in the case of this eleventh-century bronze Shiva in the British Museum, London, which is wearing an elaborate diadem and a* mukuta *(conical crown). The Khmer wore anklets, but no shoes.*

*113  As shown in this seventh-century example of the Dvaravati style, Buddha wore the traditional monk's habit, the* antaravasaka, *an ankle-length cloth wound round the waist, and the* uttarasanga, *a cloak draped to form a tunic which could cover one or both shoulders.*

*115 The detailed bas-reliefs of Angkor Wat and the statues of the devata peeping out from niches show the elegant embroidered fabrics of the sarongs and the patterns on the free edges that trailed from the belt. The sets of jewelry and jeweled belts carved on the images give some idea of how skilled the goldsmiths of the period must have been. The complicated hairstyles of the deities, with a profusion of rosettes and pinnacles, perhaps in filigree work, towering above the diadem, were probably only worn by the dancers who took part in temple ceremonies.*

*114 The women went bare-breasted and wound a long cloth called a* sarong *round their hips, fastening it in various ways. One of the simplest was to fold the free edge into a pocket and tuck it into the waist, as shown in this eighth-century image of Devi, originally at Popel and now in the Guimet Museum. Their hair was put up in ringlets, sometimes depicted in such a stylized way that they resemble a tiara.*

The materials used to make clothing and jewelry revealed the social and economic class of the wearer. The actual shape of the clothing was very simple. The men wore a piece of cloth of varying lengths wound round the waist with one corner passed between the legs, now called the sampot. The women wore an ankle-length drape, held in place by folding it at the front or side, now known by the Indonesian name of sarong. The way in which the sampot or sarong was fastened, and the resulting pattern of pleats and drapes, is invaluable in dating statues.

Depending on the period, the sampot was knee-length or mid-thigh length, and wound above or below the navel; the height of the waistline at the back varied. The bodhisattvas wore an ankle-length sampot.
In the tenth century the upper border became thicker and tended to stand out from the hips, giving a sort of "starched" effect. Whether plain or pleated, the sampot was fastened with knots at the side and center with a single or double loop and a complicated arrangement of the free edges. The last portion of the fabric was sometimes folded to form a pocket, tucked into the waist and left to fall in a soft drape, or could form a single or double anchor shape at the center in front. The pocket eventually became a fan of stylized pleats with more or less rounded edges, fastened at the left thigh, and the anchors became rigid ornamental motifs.

The sarong, a long drape wound round the hips which sometimes left the navel bare, was worn with or without folds, and kept in place by tucking it in at the waist. It was fastened with bows and/or belts; it was sometimes tight at the hips and then opened out in a slight flare, emphasized by groups of side pleats, and sometimes had rigid, compact drapes. The front drape consisted of a central band of pleats and clever use of the free edges, which were folded into a fishtail or shark's tail shape, draped in triangular panels folded over one another, or trailed from the belt. The upper edge was folded at the waist into a fan shape or a large yoke that stretched from one hip to the other. The sarong was originally plain, then pleated; from the twelfth century onwards it was decorated with embroidery, tiny flowers, and ornate hems, and the fishtail band was ornamented with elaborate patterns.

The bas-reliefs of Angkor Wat and Bayon (twelfth/thirteenth century) reveal other clothing details. In the scenes portrayed at Angkor Wat, King Suryavarman and the major dignitaries wore sampots embroidered with flowers with highly elaborate edges and trailing corners. In the battle scenes inspired by the epic poems, some warriors are pictured wearing jerkins with floral or sun patterns and embroidered along the hems and necks. However, these garments may actually have been leather breastplates.

In the scenes portrayed at Bayon, some people wear a kind of short-sleeved "shirt," which was open at the front, with a rounded hem. Various types of breastplate are depicted in the battle scenes, from a short one that protected only the chest to one worn by the crews of Khmer ships, which reached below the hips. The Cham warriors, their sworn enemies, wore a protective tunic made of leather or perhaps rhinoceros skin, and were immediately identifiable by their characteristic helmets in the shape of upside-down leaves with a gorget. Chinese warriors were recognizable by their clothing and flowing beards, demonstrating that mercenary contingents fought in the Khmer army.

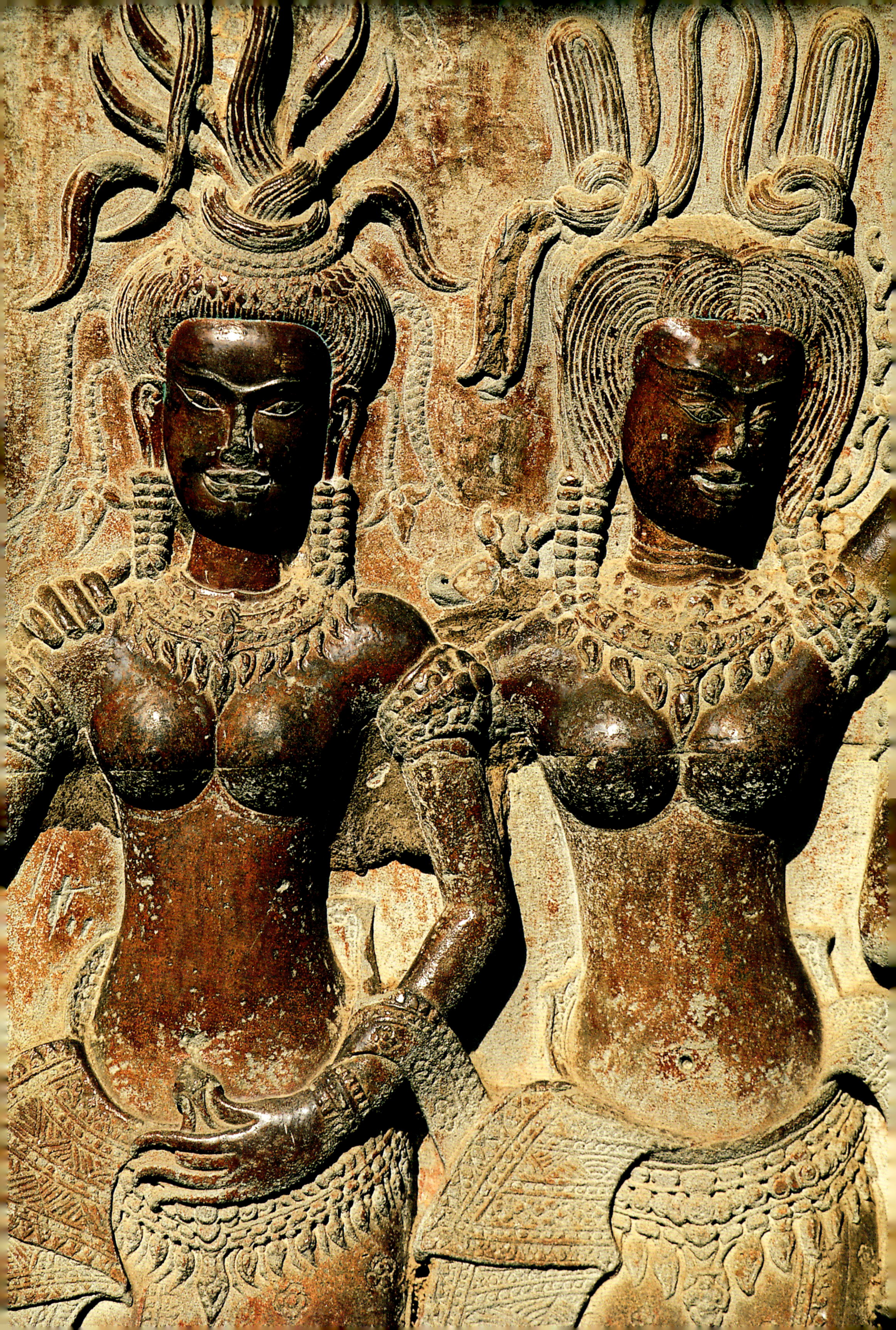

Few gold articles have been found. Judging from the statues and bas-reliefs, they included tiaras of various shapes, extended into two bands at the sides of the ears, decorated with complex geometrical and floral patterns or even in the shape of an octagonal pagoda, as in the case of the god Vishnu. Diadems were tied at the back of the neck, and the earlobes were elongated by heavy earrings. Necklaces of varying degrees of complexity, bracelets, rings, and ankle bracelets completed the range of jewelry worn. The belt, originally a simple band of fabric, was transformed over the centuries into an elegant jewel adorned with chains and pendants, fastened with laces at the front and bows at the back.

Sandals are not shown in the bas-reliefs or sculptures, so it is presumed that the Khmer went barefoot.

Both men and women wore their hair tied in chignons. The women tied their hair in thick plaits before putting it up at certain periods, and the chignon was sometimes fastened with a chain or flowers. The Brahmans wore their hair twisted into voluminous topknots and had flowing beards, as did the ascetics. The importance of the moustache and beard varied at different periods.

The women went about bare-breasted and used skin-bleaching cosmetics possibly based on sandalwood, which was the component of many perfumes, together with musk. A pale complexion was highly prized and set women of high lineage apart from ordinary women, who were forced to expose their skin to the sun. Some women shaved their hairlines and stained the sides of the temples and the parting red, a practice typical of married Indian women. Women also dyed their hands and feet vermilion; according to Zhou Daguan, the only man to follow this practice was the king, who used red dye on the palms of his hands and the soles of his feet.

116 Garlands of flowers, crowns, and pendants adorned the tresses of the devata of Angkor Wat, who wore their hair plaited in a variety of ways. Their elaborate chain belts and pendants imitate the motifs of the necklaces lying on their breasts, which were high and close together in accordance with the standards of beauty imported from India. The figure on the left holds an object which may have been a perfume holder.

117 left Men also put their hair up; the gods concealed theirs under miters, tiaras, and chignon caps. In the case of Buddha, the chignon cap highlights the presence of the ushnisha (cranial protuberance), as shown in this example of the Bayon style (twelfth/thirteenth century, Renzo Freschi Oriental Art).

117 right Portrayals of an undulating moustache and a thin beard, which surrounded the entire face and ended in a point on the chin, became popular towards the end of the ninth century, and their use continued in later periods, as demonstrated by this specimen (Renzo Freschi Oriental Art).

*118 Bronze articles were very elegant, as demonstrated by this chariot consisting of a* garuda *(a creature that was part human and part bird of prey) and* nagas *(cobras). Their enmity alludes to the contrast between heaven and earth, but snakes and birds are both included in the iconography of Vishnu and constitute particular aspects of it.*

# SCULPTURE

A Chinese text, the "Chronicles of the Liang," compiled in the first half of the seventh century, states that bronze images with multiple faces and arms portraying the "spirits of the sky" were made in Funan. This is the oldest reference to Khmer iconography and undoubtedly refers to statues that reproduced Brahmanic deities, inspired by Indian tradition.

The great bronze statues in the temples have nearly all been lost. All that remains to testify to their excellent workmanship is a portion of a huge figure of Vishnu lying on the serpent Ananta, which probably stood in the West Mebon temple and was over seven feet long. The smaller statues and ornaments found reveal a high level of technical and artistic skill. They were made by the lost wax technique and some parts were often cast separately and then riveted together. The statues, which were mostly gilded, were sometimes decorated with inserts of precious metals, glass paste, and filigree work, and encrusted with stones. Sadly, none of the articles made of gold, silver, or alloys of precious metals referred to in the Khmer inscriptions, known as samrit, have survived, apart from the magnificent Nandin, the bull ridden by Shiva. This statue, found at Tuol Kuhea and attributed to the seventh century, is made of an alloy containing a large proportion of silver.

*119 left  Hevajra, an esoteric deity of Vajrayana Buddhism with eight heads and 16 arms, dances among the* yogini, *female figures with initiatory functions who were repositories of knowledge and exceptional powers. This bronze statue from the Art Gallery of New South Wales in Sydney dates from the twelfth/thirteenth century and is in the Bayon style.*

*119 right  This bronze ferrule with a decorated Buddha protected by the many-headed cobra Mucilinda, which dates from the twelfth/thirteenth century and is on display in the Phnom Penh National Museum, was possibly used on the carrying poles of litters as the tip of a rudder or as an ornament. It was designed to be held and has a row of rampant lions and a* kala *on the handle.*

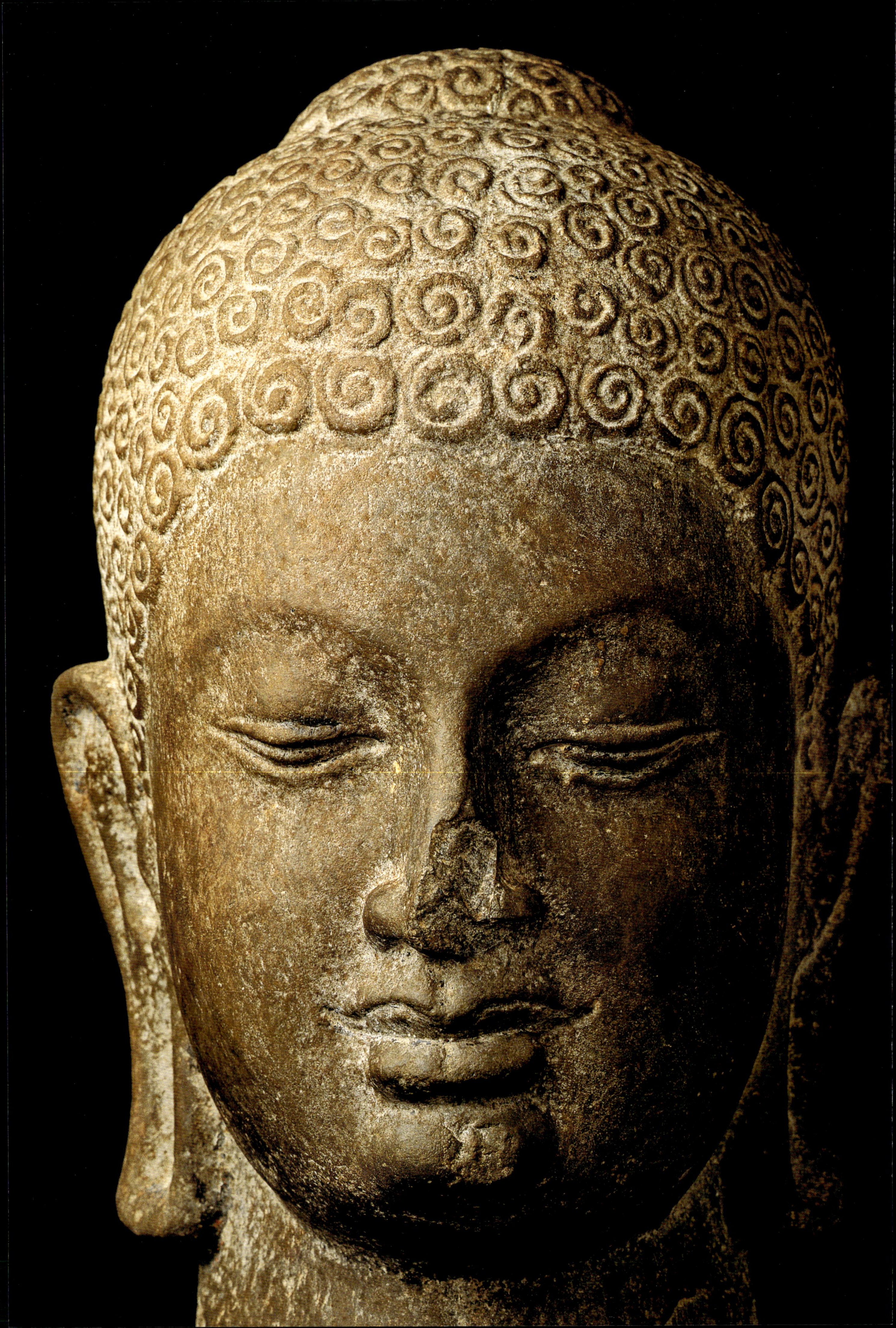

*India also inspired the creation of stone statues and its influence is particularly strong in the older examples. One of the most significant specimens in this respect is the sixth or seventh-century Krishna Govardhana which reproduced the most important* avatar *(descent) of the god Vishnu, portrayed as he lifts Mount Govardhana to protect the local shepherds from a terrible hurricane. The sinuous posture of the body reproduces the tribhanga, the traditional "triple bend" of Indian statues, based on a more or less accentuated movement of the hips. The loincloth he wears is the typical Indian* dhoti.

*The Krishna Govardhana rests on a supporting stela in accordance with the Indian tradition, which never developed in-the-round statues, preferring to sculpt them in very high relief and rest them on a support. This was also the case in the Khmer area until about the ninth century; the figures rest on a supporting arch (which in itself was an attempt to depart from the Indian stela by retaining only the outline of the arch), and the space between the ankles was sometimes not cut out in order to provide further support. In the case of divinities with several extremities, the arms were often connected to the head or the supporting arch with crosspieces. However, the artists gradually gained confidence with their materials, mostly sandstone, and departed from the Indian influence to produce three-dimensional statues.*

*One of the essential features of Khmer statues is their hieratic power; their impassable faces, illuminated by a faint interior smile, emphasize how mysterious and remote are the ineffable lords of the heavens.*

*The Khmer gods, being aspects of the one and only Prince who incorporates and transcends all, do not have any particular facial characteristics to define and distinguish them. The anthropomorphic shape they take is merely a way of helping men to focus their worship, giving them the opportunity to come into contact with the Divine through an* eidolon, *a visible, tangible image.*

*The artistic perfection of the statue does not fulfill aesthetic so much as canonical and ritual requirements because manufacture in accordance with the rules induces the Deity to descend into the stone and animate it with his presence, while the beauty of its form attracts worshippers and gives them aesthetic pleasure, the first emotion that prepares them for the encounter with the sacred. The deeper the spirituality of he who contemplates, the greater his ability to go beyond the formal aspect of that specific deity, perceiving behind it the ineffable presence of that which has no form and no name. The Khmer gods are consequently differentiated and their function emphasized by the symbolic objects they hold. However, if the upper limbs are missing it may be difficult to identify them, although their hairstyles and ornaments may help.*

*120 This face of Buddha, originally at Angkor Borei and now in the Phnom Penh National Museum, dates from the pre-Angkor period and still shows the influence of Indian aesthetic criteria. The half-closed petal-shaped eyes express the state of meditation, while the elongated earlobes recall the heavy earrings worn by Prince Siddhartha before he became Buddha.*

*121 The seventh-century Harihara from Angkor Borei, now in the Guimet Museum, is one of the masterpieces of pre-Angkor sculpture. It still has the supporting arch for the arms and attributes deriving from the supporting stela of Indian statues. Two centuries later, Khmer artists abandoned them to produce spatially free sculptures.*

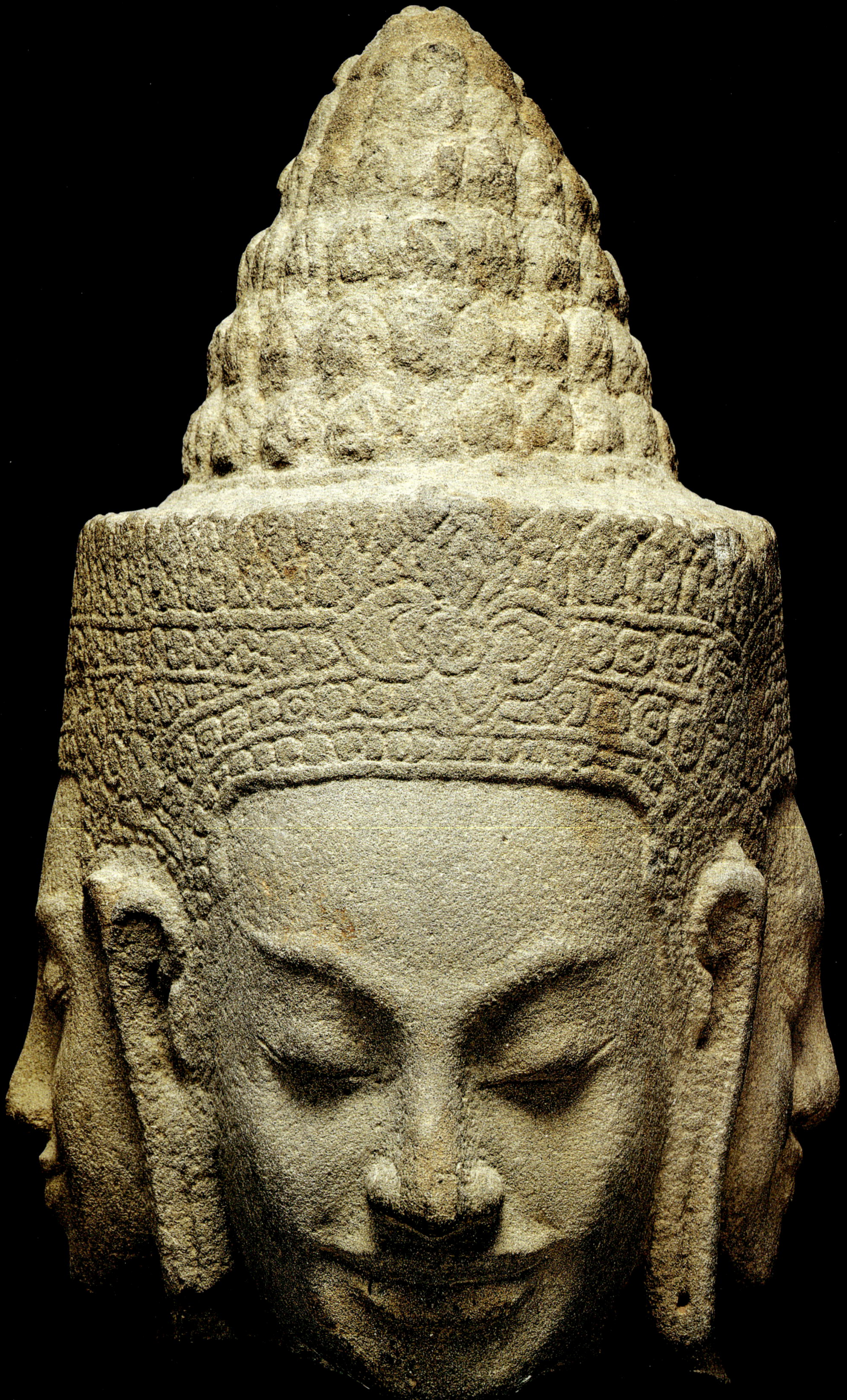

122 *The portrayal of the eyes varied according to the period. During the Bayon period in the twelfth/thirteenth centuries, to which this three-headed sculpture, now in the Guimet Museum, is attributed, the eyes of statues were mainly closed, symbolizing detachment from the world and a state of inner contemplation. The piercing or eye-opening ceremony was performed to bring the statue to "life."*

123 *The sculptures belonging to the Angkor Wat period (in the twelfth century) emphasize the frontal view and hieratic appearance and look rather squat, especially in the portrayal of the legs and feet, as can be seen in this Vishnu, now in the Phnom Penh National Museum. The pocket motif of the* sampot *is highly stylized, and the double anchor falls rigidly in the center.*

The god Brahma, the first member of the Trimurti (the Triple Form of the Divine), is portrayed with four faces because he is the lord of the origin and therefore governs the expansion of space towards the four cardinal points, and also because the Vedas (the most ancient, sacred Hindu texts) issue from his mouths. In addition to the number of heads, one of the distinctive features of this deity is the circle of pearls that clasps his chignon a third of the way down.

Vishnu is portrayed with four arms, alluding to the cosmic dimension of the god, who encircles the universe in a providential embrace. The symbols he holds in his four hands exemplify his task: the conch symbolizes life generated and nourished in the depths of the primordial sea; the chakra, a sharp ring used by the god as a boomerang against the demons, symbolizes the samsara (the cycle of human rebirths and destinies governed by Vishnu); the mace he holds is both a scepter and a club, emphasizing his function as guide and judge, typical of a king; and the globe, which replaced the lotus flower of Indian tradition in the Khmer area, represents the earth. His head is crowned by a mukuta (miter), whose shape varied over the centuries.

Shiva is distinguished by the trident, a weapon that alludes to the numerous triads of the Hindu world including the three gods of the Trimurti, the three levels of the universe (earth, atmosphere, and sky), the three dimensions of time, etc. The third eye in the middle of his forehead symbolizes the omniscience that transcends the duality represented by the other two eyes. His hair is twisted into the jatamukuta, the tall topknot worn by ascetics, decorated by a crescent moon. To escape the curse that condemned it to disappear, the moon took refuge on Shiva's head, obtaining in exchange the power to regenerate itself at intervals. In addition to his anthropomorphic form, Shiva was often portrayed in his aniconic and phallic aspect, the linga, a very basic image inspired by the ancient stones of the Khmer animist religion. The linga were placed in the fields as emblems of the local spirit who governed the earth and guaranteed its fertility and acted as channels of communication between heaven and earth, between the world of the ancestors and the world of the living. The axial, phallic, regal Hindu symbolism of the linga was consequently familiar in the indigenous context. The linga, which was often divided into three parts (square, octagonal, and circular), symbolized the three deities of the Trimurti. The snanadroni, the round base in which it was inserted terminating in a spout, also symbolized the yoni (the female matrix) and therefore alluded to the Goddess. The function of the snanadroni was also to hold and drain off the ablutions performed on the linga.

Another very common image in the Khmer Empire was that of Harihara, a syncretistic image incorporating both Vishnu and Shiva by portraying the features and attributes of the former on the right-hand side and the latter on the left-hand side.

124 During the Kulen period in the ninth century, Vishnu's two upper arms rested on a portion of a supporting arch and a column, as in this specimen from the Guimet Museum, in which the base of the arch survives, while the lower arms rested on the mace.

125 The numerous registers of the thirteenth-century bas-reliefs on the Terrace of the Leper King at Angkor Thom show the deities of the underworld. However, there is nothing terrifying about the goddess shown here, who is smiling in the gentle, thoughtful way typical of the Bayon style.

The female figures, unlike their Indian counterparts, were never excessively provocative, and despite the opulence of their bodies, were demure and almost virginal. The highly erotic tone of Hindu iconography is almost absent from Khmer art.

The most important operation in sacred statuary was the opening of the eyes, an act performed by engraving or perforating the pupils to make the image come alive and turn it into the tabernacle of Divinity.

In view of the present state of the surviving statues, it is impossible to tell whether they were colored, and if so which colors were used. Some seem to have been covered with a sort of patina while others appear to have been treated with a process similar to polishing. It is certain that during some periods of Khmer civilization the deities were decorated with jewels and mobile attributes and sometimes clothes.

Hardly anything has survived of the wooden statues produced earlier than the thirteenth and fourteenth centuries, but relics found in the post-Angkor period suggest that the older statues were mainly monoxylous (carved from a single piece of wood), while at a later period some parts, such as the forearms, were added separately and held together with small wooden pegs and glued with shellac. The joints were concealed by a thick layer of pliable black lacquer on which a second, thinner layer of red lacquer was spread and then gilded. During a later era inserts of semi-precious stones, mother-of-pearl, glass paste, and vitrified lead colored blue, turquoise, green, and gold were used to highlight the eyes and nails and depict decorations and jewelry.

The largest statues and bronzes were destined for the temples, the Brahman caste, and the warrior class. The common people must have owned much simpler idols, perhaps fetishes, or rather in their worship of the spirits they may have recognized them in particular environments and natural objects, thus having no need to portray them.

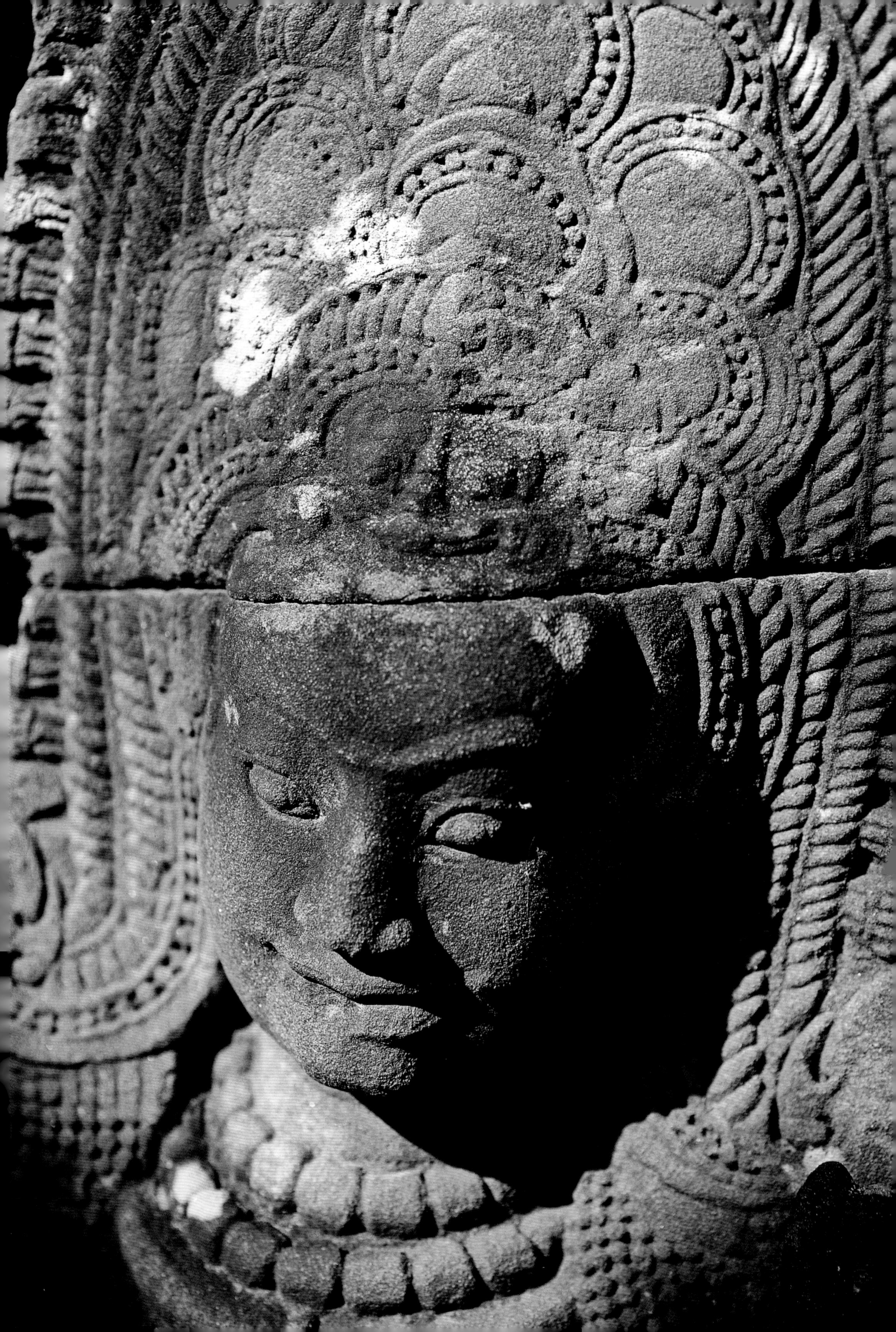

Khmer statues are distributed over a series of periods named after the temples in which they stood or the places where the main in-the-round specimens were found. The chronological subdivision has long been debated; the most widely accepted version now divides them into 15 styles, some of which partly overlap with others.

The oldest period, during the sixth and seventh centuries, described as the pre-Angkor period, features an anatomical realism which was later lost in the classical period, and which was aesthetically superior to it. The Phnom Da style (540-600) developed in the south of the country at Angkor Borei, constitutes the oldest stage of Brahmanic art in Kambuja. This was followed by the Sambor Prei Kuk style (600-650), named after a site in the northern part of central Cambodia, which overlaps with the style of Prei Kmeng, a temple in the southwestern corner of the West Baray (635-700), and Prasat Andet, near present-day Kompong Thom from the seventh or eighth century). The pre-Angkor period concludes with the style of Kompong Preah, near Pursat (706-800). The statues in the Phnom Da style, which were made of schist or sandstone, mainly portray Vishnu and characters associated with him, because Vishnuism appears to have been the religion of kings. However, Shivaism is also attested to by numerous lingas, and the first portrayals of Harihara began to appear. Their faces are wide, with arched eyebrows set close together, and their ringlets are surmounted by a tiara. Holes in their muscular bodies demonstrate the use of changeable sets of jewelry. The sampots passed between the legs are unpleated or have faintly drawn radiating pleats, and are knotted at the hip and at the center so that the free edges form an anchor shape. The bow and fillets supporting the head and arms demonstrate that the sculptor had little faith in the stability of the statue.

The statues in the Sambor Prei Kuk style realistically portray some anatomical details. The male figures have slender bodies and full faces illuminated by a faint smile, and wear sampots with a double pocket at the hip. Images of buxom women appear for the first time, wearing plain sarongs fastened below the navel with or without a central fan of pleats. The hair of the goddesses was arranged on the top of the head in a tall topknot (jata), which fell in soft ringlets at the side and back and later in front as well, forming a cylindrical crown (jatamukuta). Representations of Durga, wife of the god Shiva who was considered by the Khmer to be Vishnu's sister, were very common.

The Prei Kmeng style featured smaller figures and numerous female statues. The sampots are closed at the side and a lateral edge falls freely in the center. The sarongs are higher waisted, fastened with a bow, and sometimes have a belt. The first images of Brahma and the bodhisattvas appear, and the use of moveable attributes made of metal, designed to be placed in the hands of the gods, becomes widespread.

In the Prasat Andet style, the features of the previous periods come to maturity; the bodies are designed with great attention to anatomy, and the men wear thin moustaches. The sampot is short, sometimes merely engraved, and has a large side pocket and an anchor fastening along with a belt. The women's sarongs are slightly flared in a bell shape at the sides. The miter tends to cover the whole head and frames the ears, forming a sort of nape guard. Vishnu, Harihara, and Devi, the Goddess, were the most common images.

During the subsequent Kompong Preah period, during which sculptors attempted to produce in-the-round statues without supporting arches, the aesthetic quality of the pieces began to decline; the limbs become heavy, and the faces colder.

126 This sixth/seventh-century Vishnu from Phnom Da, now in the Phnom Penh National Museum, is nearly ten feet tall and is one of the oldest surviving examples of sculpture. Portrayed with eight arms to celebrate his universal majesty, Vishnu is wearing a diaphanous sampot wound tightly around his waist in a very realistic way.

127 This seventh-century portrayal of Durga from Sambor Prei Kuk, now in the Phnom Penh National Museum, shows the goddess about to kill Mahisha the buffalo demon, and the action is brilliantly suggested by the slightly twisted knee and the way in which the sarong fans out into pleats.

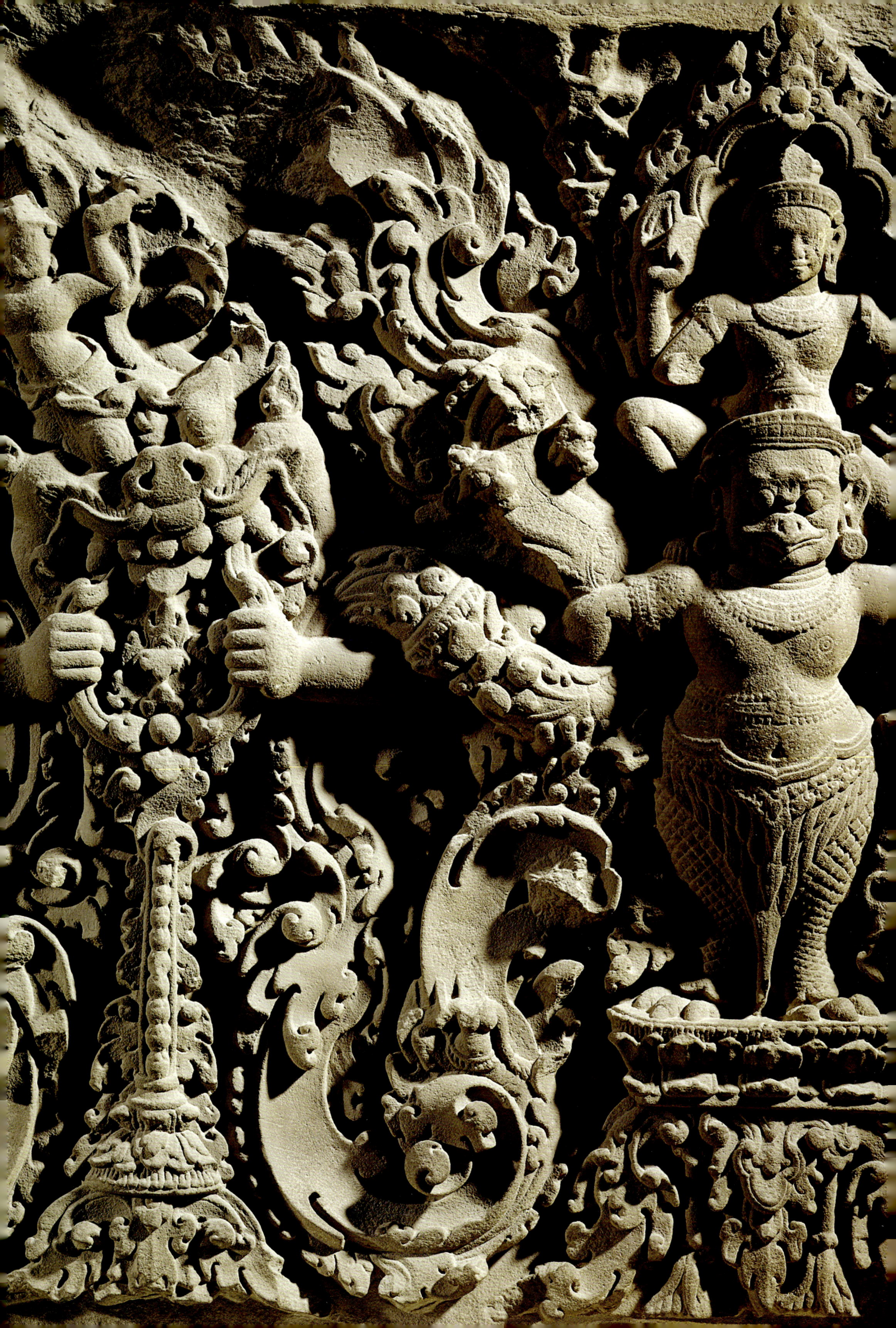

*128 This detail of a ninth-century architrave from Preah Ko, now in the Guimet Museum, shows Vishnu seated in a striking pose on his mount Garuda, with a* kala, *a monstrous creature that spews out complex garlands in a profusion of foliage, on the left.*

*129 left This ninth/tenth-century head of Vishnu from Phnom Bok, now in the Guimet Museum, has joined eyebrows in the typical Bakheng style. The cold smile, accentuated by the tips of the moustache, and the wide-open eyes give the god a remote expression.*

*129 right In the square face of this ninth-century Vishnu from Phnom Kulen, now in the Phnom Penh National Museum, the eyebrows, eyes, and lips are highlighted by thin contours. The statue does not wear sculpted jewelry because it was adorned with real jewels, as demonstrated by the holes in the earlobes.*

Angkor art began in the ninth century. It was produced almost entirely in the huge Angkor area, with the sole exception of the statues from Koh Ker, a town 53 miles from Angkor.

In the Kulen style (825-875) the supporting arch disappeared, but the statues, which were always male, were more solid. In some cases the eyebrows meet, giving the statue a fixed expression. The upper edge of the sampot tends to be thicker; the garment is knee-length and fastened by a ribbon belt with a knot hanging from the right hip. The pocket is turned into a fan of stylized pleats with rounded edges, fastened at the left thigh, and the free edge falls in elaborate anchor-shaped pleats. The first diadems appear.

The following development, namely the Preah Ko style, which coincided with the reign of Indravarman I (877-889), features more movement, although the heaviness of the limbs remains. The "collar" beard and moustache are common, and the faces are broad and expressionless. The sarong and sampot are unpleated, and the upper edge, which is even thicker than before, stands out from the body. The sarong is secured by folding it in the middle in a cascade of right-facing pleats folded over at the waist in a fan shape, while the other edge, also pleated, falls from the left hip in a triangle. The chignon becomes a cylinder with stylized tiers, and the tiara lengthens to form two bands at the sides of the ears. The tiara is decorated with complex patterns, and in the case of the god Vishnu, becomes a kind of octagonal pagoda. The diadem tied at the back of the neck was introduced. A particularly important feature was the appearance of bas-reliefs, the first examples of which are to be found in the Bakong temple.

In the Bakheng style (889-925), the facial features are even more marked and rigid: a double line emphasizes the eyes and mouth, while the sharp continuous line of the eyebrow arch is in relief. The beard and moustache are pointed and the overall impression is one of formal, abstract hieraticism. The pleated garments, with the edges folded over at the waist, fall with symmetrical rigidity from the hips, which have broadened. The detachment of the upper edge from the hips is accentuated and the patterns formed by the free edges of the sampot become more complex, forming a single or double anchor shape. The sarong is worn wound round the hips without overlapping, with the free edge folded over to form a wide yoke on the belt, which was embellished with pendants during this period.

When the capital moved to Koh Ker between 921 and 944, an unusual, innovative dynamism was introduced into the statues, which became monumental, their faces softened by a faint smile. The sculptors, who were far more confident by now, attempted large shapes and above all departed from the frontal view to portray movement. The two wrestlers found at the west gopura of Prasat Thom are among the most successful examples of this genre. The carved jewels that replace the mobile sets suggest that less wealth was available.

The Pre Rup style, which coincided with the reign of Rajendravarman (944-968), returned to smaller sizes and hieratic staticism. Belts multiplied, and hairstyles became more complex.

*130 left One of the characteristics of the tenth-century Koh Ker statues is their dynamism, as demonstrated by this dancing deity from the Guimet Museum, whose hair is unusually twisted into horizontal plaits.*

*130 right Voluptuous limbs were an important part of women's beauty according to the canons of the period, and they were emphasized by the folds on the abdomen and neck, as in this eleventh-century deity (Renzo Freschi Oriental Art).*

*131 This rare burnished portrayal of Varuna in the Pre Rup style dates from the tenth century and is now in the Phnom Penh National Museum. Varuna, an ancient deity who was the guardian of moral order, later became lord of the sea and above all dikpala (guardian) of the western quarter. His vahana (mount) was sometimes the hamsa (goose with a striped head), as in this photo.*

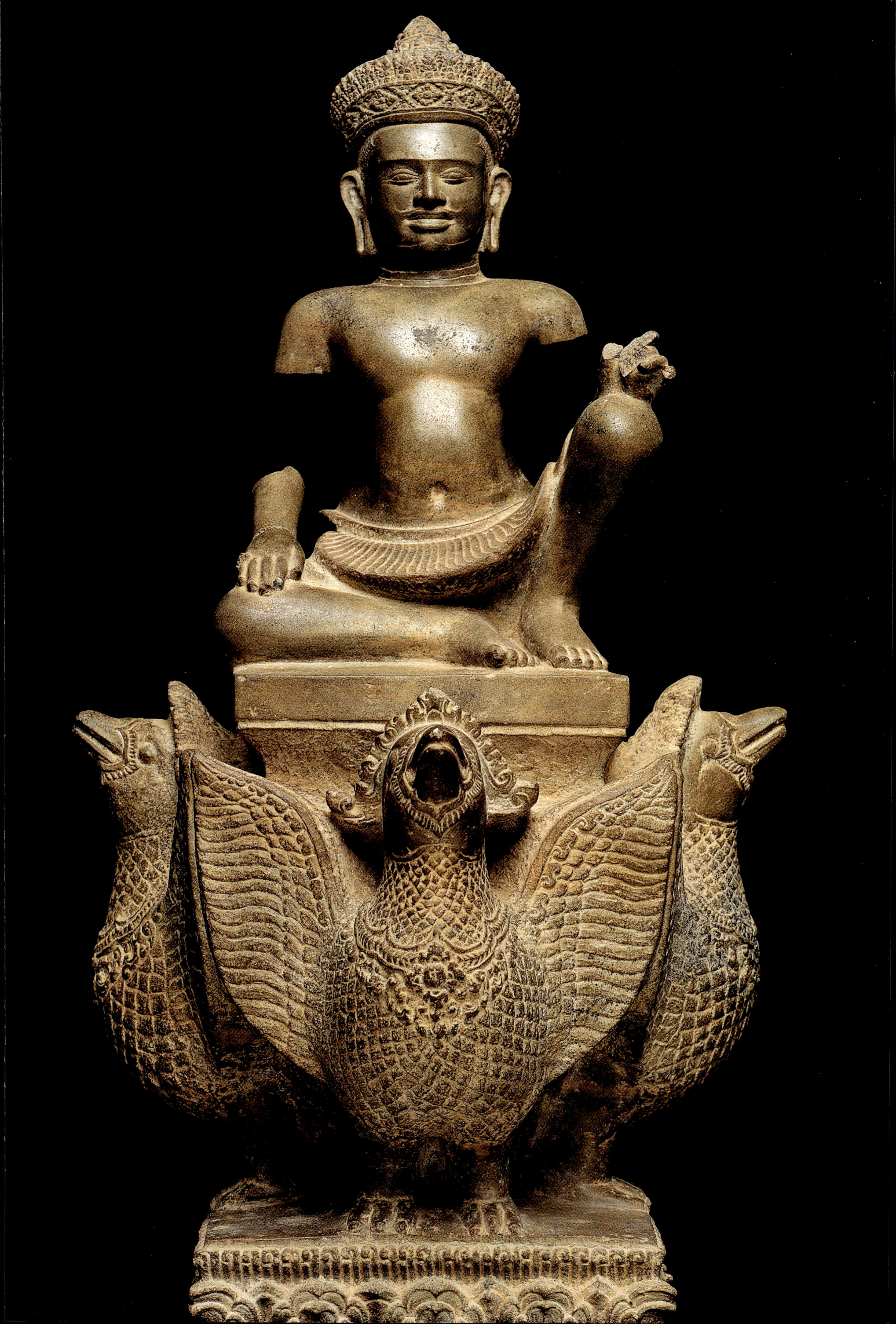

*132 top left The tenth-century archaic sculptures of Banteay Srei are among the most beautiful in Khmer art. This detail shows the perfect portrayal of the hand of a* dvarapala *(gatekeeper) holding a flower.*

*132 top right The decorations of Banteay Srei, created with great detail by chisellers, depict some delightful scenes amid tangles of flowers and* kala *monsters, like this scene of a dancer accompanied by two tambourine players.*

*132 bottom The typical feature of the eleventh-century Baphuon style, to which this Buddha on a* naga *(now in the Phnom Penh National Museum) belongs, is a gentle, dreamy smile, which gives the statue a touching spirituality.*

*132-133 The decoration of the architraves is symmetrical; the motifs start and end at the central one, which in this case at Banteay Srei, is the elephant Airavata, mount of Indra, king of the gods, between two* garudas.

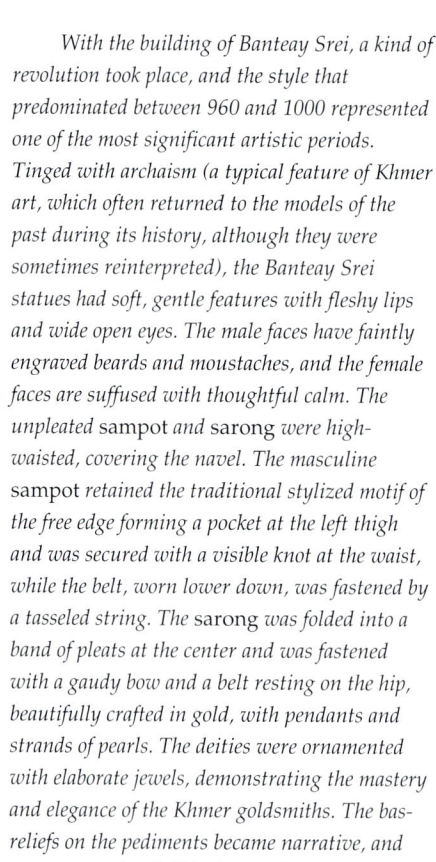

With the building of Banteay Srei, a kind of revolution took place, and the style that predominated between 960 and 1000 represented one of the most significant artistic periods. Tinged with archaism (a typical feature of Khmer art, which often returned to the models of the past during its history, although they were sometimes reinterpreted), the Banteay Srei statues had soft, gentle features with fleshy lips and wide open eyes. The male faces have faintly engraved beards and moustaches, and the female faces are suffused with thoughtful calm. The unpleated sampot and sarong were high-waisted, covering the navel. The masculine sampot retained the traditional stylized motif of the free edge forming a pocket at the left thigh and was secured with a visible knot at the waist, while the belt, worn lower down, was fastened by a tasseled string. The sarong was folded into a band of pleats at the center and was fastened with a gaudy bow and a belt resting on the hip, beautifully crafted in gold, with pendants and strands of pearls. The deities were ornamented with elaborate jewels, demonstrating the mastery and elegance of the Khmer goldsmiths. The bas-reliefs on the pediments became narrative, and consisted of highly plastic statuary groups.

Spiritual faces, faint smiles, and fine hair plaiting also continued to appear in the Khleang style, which partly coincided with the reign of Suryavarman I (1010-1050), whereas the height of grace and gentleness was reached in Baphuon art, which culminated during the reign of Udayadityavarman II (1050-1066). The smaller images have slender shapes, sometimes almost too much so compared with the size of the head, and the thinner legs are made possible by the presence of buttresses behind the heels. Great attention was paid to detail. The lips are taut and the eyes engraved, and were once perhaps ornamented with semi-precious stones, and the beard comes to a point on the chin, which has a characteristic dimple. The pleated sampot, which is tied with a single or double-loop knot, is shorter. The hemline rises slightly towards the center, the top edge is folded over several times at the waist to bare the navel, and the waistline is higher at the back, where it is fastened in a bow. The sarong was also higher-waisted at the back and lower at the front, and secured by folding it over several times in a central fishtail drape. It was secured with a bow, and completed by a pendant belt fastened by laces. The hair was styled in a small plaited jatamukuta, held in place by a string of pearls.

Contrary to general expectation, the sculptural style of Angkor Wat (1100-1175), despite its architectural perfection, appears somewhat stereotyped. Following the grace and gentleness of the Baphuon style, there was a return to frontal views and hieraticism. The figures have square shoulders, swollen chests, and awkward legs and feet. In the mainly hairless faces the eyebrows still meet, and the eyes, emphasized by an incision, are elongated in a mannerist fashion. The female figures are more characterized and their faces are more expressive than those of the male figures.

In the highly stylized sampot, the pocket motif starts at the right hip and ends at the left thigh, while the double anchor falls rigidly in the middle, fastened by a bow above the flat belt. The sarong is worn by folding the upper edge into a yoke that stretches from one hip to the other, secured with a central fishtail drape. This band is ornamented with elaborate motifs, and the edges of the sarong are also beautifully embroidered; they fall from the pendant belt in long swathes or triangular panels folded over one another. The complexity of the clothes is matched by that of the hairstyles, often supported by a framework. Some devatas have their hair tied in a chignon with a dangling lock but most have exquisite diadems with daring, imaginative constructions under which the hair falls into ringlets and plaits. The jewelry is mostly of floral inspiration and profusely covers the deities.

The portrayal of Buddha sitting in meditation on the coils of the many-headed cobra Mucilinda, king of the naga, first appeared at this time. It was destined to become very popular in the subsequent period and eventually to become one of the emblems of Khmer statuary.

133

*134 top The inscriptions state that there were 25 images of Jayabuddhamahanatha (Buddha the great victorious Lord) in the main temples of the empire in the twelfth/thirteenth century. They must have had the features of Jayavarman VII in a meditating attitude, and this example from the Guimet Museum may be one of them.*

*134 bottom Groups of dancing asparas (celestial nymphs), as in this relief at the Bayon temple (twelfth/thirteenth century), were one of the favorite ornamental themes of the period. The movements of the dancers converge symmetrically on the central figure, highlighted by a taller crown and the garland hanging from her shoulders.*

*135 Most of the buildings erected by Jayavarman VII have superstructures consisting of huge faces of Lokeshvara, the* bodhisattva *of compassion, who looks out towards the four cardinal points. The evident protective symbolism of this design alludes to the primary function of the king.*

The last great period of Khmer sculpture, the Bayong period, dates from the reign of King Jayavarman VII (1181-1218). The hieratic frontal views of the previous period were abandoned and an attempt was made to portray greater movement and spatial plasticity. The fact that Buddhism had become the state religion led sculptors to express a more human, intimate ideal of beauty in their statues. The faces have enigmatic smiles and mystical expressions, and the tendency to deify ancestors and relatives and the identification of King Jayavarman VII with the bodhisattva *Lokeshvara* led to the production of more realistic and psychologically studied images.

The short, almost engraved sampot suggests that the statues were dressed in fabric clothes that were changed for each ceremony, and the holes in the ears and other parts of the body indicate that removable jewelry and attributes were used. The female statues wore unpleated sarongs with flower patterns, embroidered edges, and a central drape in the shape of shark's fin, and their topknots were concealed under exquisite chignon caps.

Jayavarman VII's megalomania was also manifested in statuary, and some huge statues were included among the monumental symbolism of the city of Angkor Thom. The row of giants that protect the entrances and the huge faces of the sovereign-bodhisattva who guards the Bayon towers are the most impressive examples.

After the end of the great period of the Khmer Empire, sculptors returned to the use of wood, and the increasing power of the neighboring Thai kingdoms influenced the sculptures of later centuries.

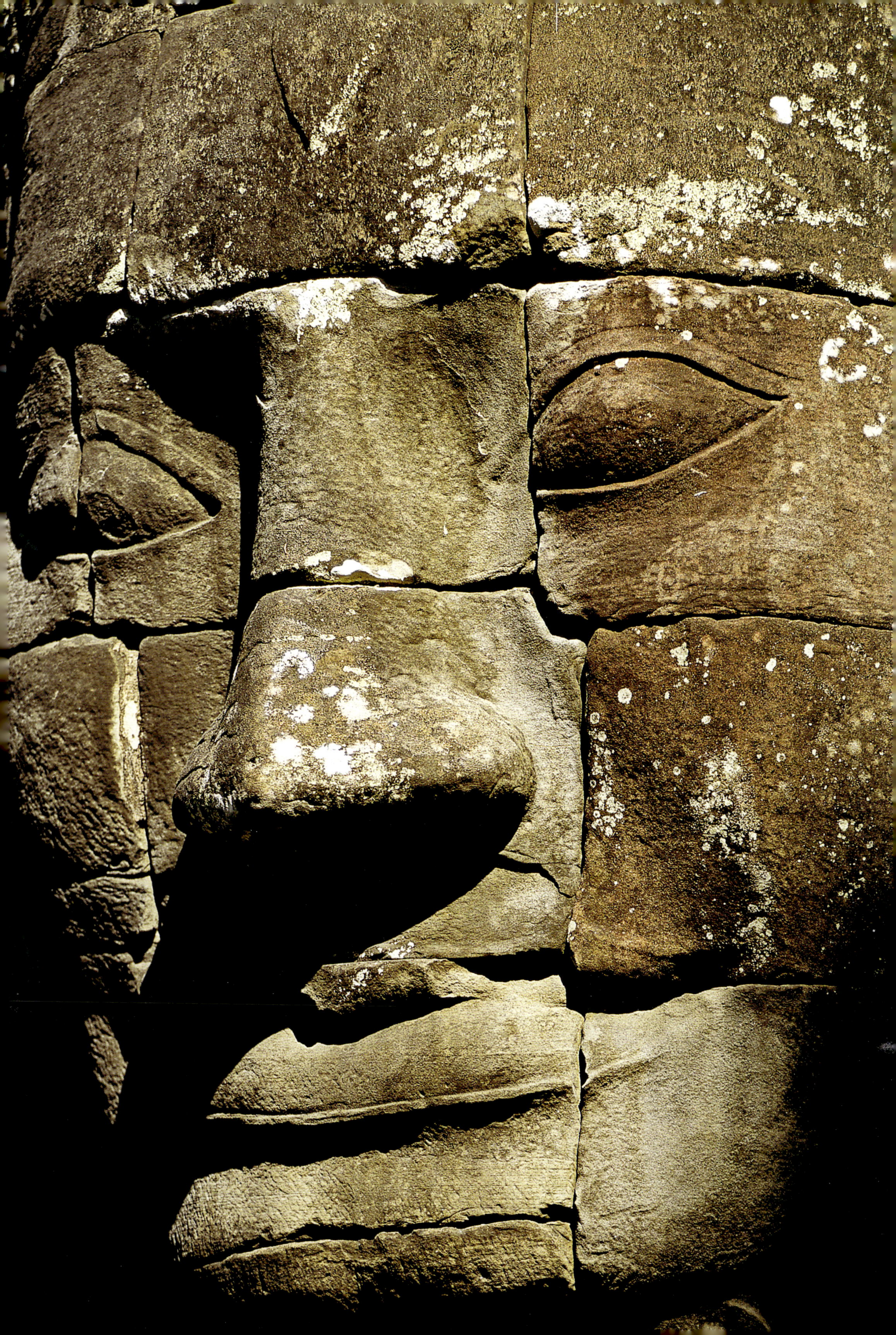

# CELESTIAL DWELLINGS

*136 The Khmer used precious metals in their buildings; the inner walls of the cells were covered with bronze plates, and the cusps of some temples may also have been plated. Everything has since been stolen, but this gold panel gives some idea of what the inserts must have been like.*

*137 left Two sheets of gold leaf were probably included among the symbolic objects placed in the foundation stones of the temples and the bases of the statues.*

*137 right At the corners of the temple roofs there were antefixes like this one, originally from Banteay Srei and now in Phnom Penh National Museum. They reproduce the structure of the shrine in miniature, as in the architecture of southern India, by which Khmer architecture was inspired.*

*Although Khmer architecture was considerably influenced by its Hindu counterpart, the Khmer architects elaborated upon Hindu structures and designs in a wholly original way. Although the temple complied with the symbolic criteria dictated by the Brahmans, the centralizing presence of the sovereign and his claim to deification more or less consciously required architectural procedures and ritual uses of the shrine which differed from their Indian counterparts.*

*The fundamental duties of each Khmer monarch included the task of building certain constructions, namely the temple of the ancestors, the temple of the* linga, *which symbolized the divine essence of the ruling monarch, and the temple dedicated to the cult of the* devaraja. *However, although the inscriptions refer to three temples, many kings only built two: the shrine dedicated to the ancestors, and the mountain temple which was the tabernacle of the* linga. *According to Philippe Stern, the reason for this discrepancy may be that the mountain temple fulfilled the dual function of housing the royal* linga *and being the place where the cult of the* devaraja *was performed.*

*In any event, the* prasat *(the Khmer temple) was inspired by Hindu cosmology, and its tower-shaped structure alludes to Mount Meru, legendary home of the gods and cosmic axis around which the manifest world that emerged from the primordial chaos was structured. Mount Meru, the hub of Indian mystical geography, rose in the middle of seven island-continents arranged concentrically, each surrounded by seven seas: one of salt water, one of sugar cane juice, one of alcohol, one of clarified butter, one of curds, one of milk, and one of fresh water. On the slopes and peaks of Mount Meru stood the paradises of the gods: the eight cities of the Lokapala (Protectors of the Universe), the Vaikuntha of Vishnu, sparkling with gems, and the golden citadel of Brahma on the main summit.*

*The concentric circles of the seven underworlds plunge beneath the mountain in a funnel-shape, an upside-down projection of the mountain itself, into the bowels of the earth, at the bottom of which lives the serpent Vasuki, who supports the universe on his seven-fold hood.*

*Mont Meru, due to its shape, is also a phallic symbol and therefore alludes to the* linga, *the aniconic representation of the god Shiva, who is the personification of the Absolute as First Principle from whom all beings emanate and to whom they return. The* linga *and Mount Meru are both images of the* axis mundi, *the imaginary focal point around which the universe unfolds in space and rotates in time, and the link between heaven, earth, and underworld.*

*The* prasat *was therefore a reproduction of Mont Meru and, being a mountain, was an almost solid building into which the tiny recess of the grotto cell, called the* garbhagriha *(embryo chamber), opened. This dark place reproduces the shadowy "womb" of primordial nature in which the potential world is enclosed, ready to evolve into manifest forms. In the* garbhagriha, *which is also a tabernacle, the sacred image constitutes the first formal manifestation of the Brahman (the Absolute), which becomes Presence. This process was supported by a fundamental architectural ritual which imitated the insemination or implant of the embryo: the laying of the foundation stone. It usually consisted of a rectangular block of laterite, a kind of ferruginous clay, with a varying number of holes containing symbolic objects including gold and silver leaf, quartz, metals, and precious stones associated with the* navagrah, *the nine planets of Hindu tradition, namely the Sun, Moon, Mars, Mercury, Jupiter, Venus, Saturn, Rahu, the demon of the eclipse, and Ketu, the personification of the node of the moon or the comets. These objects represented a kind of divine essence, a sacred bud from which the stony body of the temple sprouted, and were also included in the foundation stones of the pedestals of the statues and the* linga.

*The foundation stones of the temple were situated in a deep well that alluded to the subterranean world, the invisible, "upside-down" part of the upper world, or Meru, represented by the roof of the* prasat. *The various levels of the universe, namely the chthonian and celestial levels, were thus represented in the sacred building. The* prasat *also symbolized the synchronous rhythm of expansion and concentration of the cosmos, the former being represented by the centrifugal prolongation of the accesses to the temple (foreparts, avenues, and staircases), and the latter by the encircling galleries and the progressive upward taper of the pyramidal terraces.*

*Because the temple symbolized the tangible irradiation of the Divine towards the four corners of the universe, it was not supposed to have a façade. However, the building was oriented in accordance with a precise axial* layout, and in most cases faced east, the place where the sun began to shine anew every morning.

The huge pyramidal roof if the prasat has a strong upward sweep, and the hierarchical superimposition of the various architectural parts, which depart from the base and are united in the ideal place above the finial, alludes to the recomposition of the multiple into divine unity. The macrocosm and microcosm merge; the prasat represents the cosmic mountain and the infinitely large, while its reproductions in miniature on the superstructure tend towards the infinitely small.

The design of the temple can be symbolically interpreted in two different ways: as the emanation of the manifest world from the Divine (in which case the temple should be viewed from the summit to the base, from the smaller to the larger forms), or as the absorption of the universe into the First Principle (in which case it should be viewed in the reverse order, from the base to the summit).

The design of the temple was codified by a huge number of rules that regulated the choice of the site, the time when work began, its orientation, calculation of its dimensions, and the stages of building. The complex calculations performed prior to each architectural operation were designed to reproduce in the temple the harmony that governs the universe. The collection and installation of the architectural material was viewed as a ritual act because wood, brick, and stone were considered to be the body of the Essence that becomes visible through matter.

# Structure and composition of the Prasat

The position of the prasat in the sacred area differed, depending on whether it was a shrine to the ancestors or the temple of the linga and the devaraja. In the first case it stood on a base or a flat area, while in the second it was constructed on a pyramid, either by exploiting an existing hill or building an artificial one.

As the temple was a sacred area, it was separated from the rest of the town by one or more enclosures, and its axial entrances were often surmounted by a gopura. The gopuras were originally rectangular access areas with a superstructure taller than the enclosure wall but later transformed into cross-shaped monumental pavilions with side entrances and rooms that ran along the walls. They were first roofed with beams and tiles and later completed with false vaulted ceilings made of brick and sandstone. The gopuras projected outwards from the building towards the four cardinal points to celebrate the extension of royal power throughout the universe.

After the outer enclosure, the temple was approached by way of long, paved avenues lined with balustrades in the shape of nagas, mythical beings inherited from the Indian world that were originally part snake, part human, but transformed by the Khmer into many-headed serpents with some features, such as the crest, which made them more closely resemble the dragon of Chinese inspiration. The balustrade acted as a symbolic link between the city and the temple, between the world of men and the world of the gods, and recalls the rainbow that connects heaven and earth, and rain, which was believed to be brought by the naga. The naga-rainbow motif often recurs on the temple pediments too. The oldest naga balustrade is the one at the Bakong temple, built in 881. Here, the serpent is supported along its entire length by a base, whereas in later periods it only partly rested on supports. The access avenues, which were sometimes raised on a series of columns acting as stilts, were often lined with monolithic stelae five to six feet tall, at intervals of six to

138 In the Bayon style (twelfth/thirteenth century), the ends of the naga balustrades lining the avenues leading to the temple have the characteristic motif of a garuda riding a three-headed cobra and holding another serpent with six or eight heads in its arms.

thirteen feet. They resembled pillars with a base and capital, and were crowned with large cusps.

A platform made of laterite or sandstone with one or four access staircases led from the unconsecrated area to the sacred area of the temple. The oldest prasats resemble squat towers, having a single entrance without a portico that led into a square cell, the shape of which represented perfection in Hindu geometrical symbolism, and consequently in its Khmer counterpart, too. The outer walls were originally only ornamented by unparticular pilasters but gradually became increasingly diversified: corner pillars were emphasized, doors were inserted into projecting sections, and niches containing statues sculpted almost in the round were placed in the walls. Armed, hieratic young men acted as dvarapalas (gatekeepers), whose task was to protect the temple against evil intrusions. They stood on either side of the entrance; the figure on the right was usually portrayed in a benevolent attitude, while the figure on the left was menacing. Female figures known as devata (goddesses), with serene, enigmatic smiles, looked out from the stone. The upper corners of the walls bore nagas with three, five, or seven heads, which seemed to vibrate in the air.

*139 left The holy place was always protected by gatekeepers. At Banteay Srei (tenth century), the stairs leading to the platform of the central shrine were guarded by partly theriomorphic creatures like this one with a lion's features, the original of which is in the Phnom Penh National Museum.*

*139 right Sculptures of animals in the round placed in various parts of the temple are one of the typical features of Khmer art. One the most commonly portrayed animals was the lion, which did not exist in Cambodia. Its attitude was always aggressive, as in this specimen in the Phnom Penh National Museum, whose missing tail was made of metal.*

*140 top In this pediment from one of the temples of Preah Pithu (thirteenth century), now in the Guimet Museum, the figures are repeated to tell the story. Parvati, in the middle, covers her ears so as not to hear the tirade launched against Shiva by the ascetic shown on the left. Immediately to the right, Parvati is portrayed again, kneeling in front of the same ascetic; he was Shiva himself, who had decided to test her devotion.*

*140 bottom The figures on the bas-reliefs are often sculpted almost in the round, as can be seen in this antefix.*

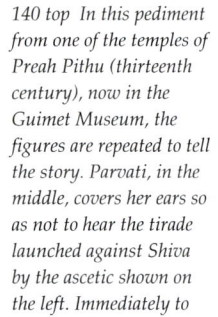

In addition to the actual entrance, false doors which reproduced wooden ones in stone were added on the other three sides of the prasat. The piers of the access chamber were originally merely slotted together, using pivots that fitted into holes in the threshold and architrave; later, all four parts of the door frame were cut and assembled to form a 45° angle. The architraves were particularly elaborate and their iconography allows the various architectural styles to be classified and dated. The oldest prototype consists of two makaras (mythical sea monsters) that spew out arches of leaves, garlands of flowers, and festoons of jewels interpolated between three medallions bearing figures: the one in the middle usually portrays Indra, king of the gods, riding the elephant Airavata, while the ones on either side depict two horsemen. Later, many-headed naga, masks of Kala (devouring Time), images of Vishnu riding Garuda (the mythical being that was part human and part vulture), and other celestial characters appeared among the volutes on the architraves.

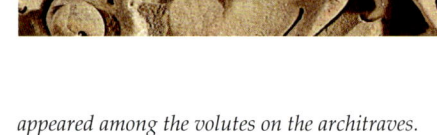

Each element was intended to emphasize the fact that the prasat was the dwelling-place of the gods. The hamsas (swans or geese) and the garudas at the base of the construction metaphorically carry it through the skies as if it were a vimana, the flying palace or chariot of the gods.

The linga, consecrated by the cult of the devaraja, and the statues, brought to life in the "eye-opening" ceremony, which involved making an incision in their eyes, acted as a tabernacle for the divine Presence in the cell, which was a secluded cavity, grotto, womb, and heart in a symbolism that identifies man with nature. On the king's death, his ashes were probably placed in the statue of the god whose incarnation the king believed himself to be. This theory may explain the persistence of raiders, who have broken nearly all the statues, in opening the T-shaped iron keys in their bases in search of treasure concealed in the foundation stones, which may never have been there at all, or merely amounted to a few symbolic objects.

The statues of the gods and deified kings were the object of complex rituals that included offerings of food, flowers, lights, incense, and draperies. They also involved ablutions, for which a drainage channel was installed; it led from the north wall of the cell into an elaborate, somasutra *(evacuation channel)*, which ended in a makara *head.*

The roof of the cell consisted of a series of diminishing tiers, usually four, each of which reproduced the façade of the temple and the architrave motif. This motif was repeated at each level, harmoniously marking the passage from one to the next, and at the same time emphasizing the vertical progression of the building. Later, miniature sculptures of the entire prasat, *including the pyramidal roof, were placed in the corners of the tiers as foreparts. The summit of the temple concluded with a circular motif in the shape of a vase called the* kalasha, *which was flattened to some extent, or a lotus blossom, on which three-pronged metal tridents* (trishula) *or five-pronged ones* (pancashula) *were probably placed.*

The interior of the cell had a false vaulted ceiling made with the corbelling technique, which prescribed laying the rows of bricks or blocks of stone so that they projected progressively, and rounding off the corners of each block to suggest the continuity of the vault, until reaching a tiny opening, where a chimney communicated with the cavity that housed the upper foundation stone at the base of the crown. The summit of the temple, like the foundations, had its own foundation stone, although it would perhaps be more accurate to call it a conclusion stone. The bare jutting corners of the intrados of the prasat *were concealed by a canopy, which was made of fabric until the tenth century and subsequently replaced by a painted coffered ceiling. The ceilings and roofs were supported by corbels, trusses, and entablatures. The true arch and vault were never used, because they were not part of the Indian tradition on which Khmer architecture was based.*

The false doors led to the development of foreparts which acted as porticoes. One of the first and most important examples of this kind is to be found in the Tak Keo, a mountain temple probably begun in 975. The ground-level temples gave particular emphasis to the main portico (usually the one facing east), which was turned into a mandapa *(pavilion). To the Indians, from whom it was borrowed, and the Khmer, this room was not a place of collective worship but a kind of waiting room in which worshippers enjoyed the* darshana *(vision of the god).*

140-141 *The portrayal of space on the architraves is highly dynamic, and rhythm is emphasized by the curvature of the iconographic elements such as the* nagas *spewed out of the mouth of the* makara, *a sea monster whose body is a garland. In this example from Prasat Pen Chang (eleventh century), now in the Phnom Penh National Museum, Krishna is portrayed in the center defeating Kaliya, the serpent that infested the Yamuna River.*

141

# The Ground-level Temple and the Mountain Temple

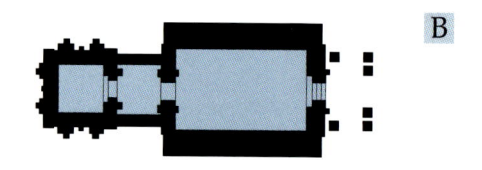

**A)** The simplest structure of the shrine on the mountain temple consists of a cell with a single entrance, as at Baksei Chamkrong (tenth century).

**B)** The ground-level temple had four parts: the cell, the vestibule, the rectangular pavilion, and the portico, as at Prasat Thom in Koh Ker (tenth century).

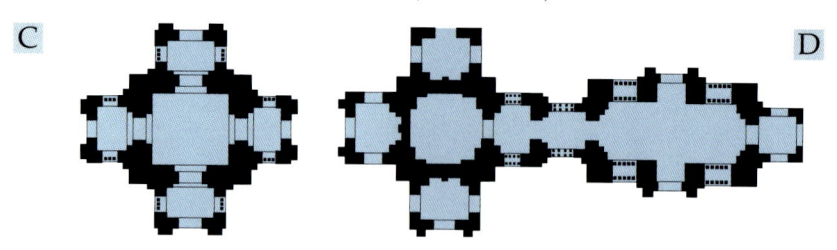

**C)** The shrine of the mountain temple acquired a cross shape with the addition of four vestibules to the cell, as at Ta Keo (tenth/eleventh century).

**D)** In the ground-level temple the cell also became cross-shaped with the addition of three more vestibules. Another room connected it to the pavilion, as at Banteay Samré (twelfth century).

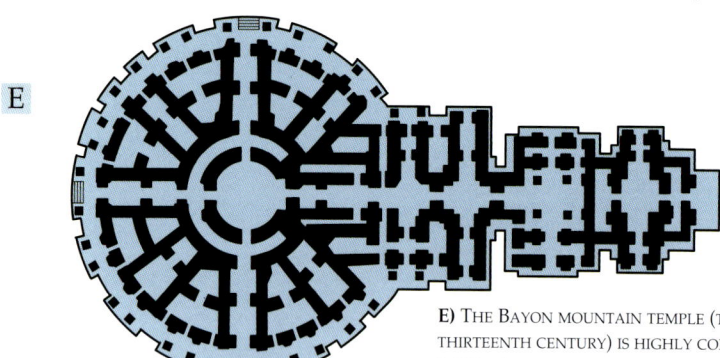

**E)** The Bayon mountain temple (twelfth/thirteenth century) is highly complex. Eight radial shrines with porticoes are built round the circular cell with its ambulatory; the eastern shrine is preceded by a forepart consisting of four rooms with double porticoes.

The parts which made up the ground-level temple, for which Sanskrit terminology was used, were the ardhamandapa (half pavilion), also known as the mukhashala (frontal hall), the mandapa (main pavilion), the antarala (vestibule), and the garbhagriha (cell). This design, which was used for the first time at Koh Ker in 921, reached perfection in the Banteay Srei temple, built in 967.

As the importance of the temple grew and the number of functions it performed increased—it was a place of education, culture and welfare, a store for valuables, a place of trade, etc.—its buildings also multiplied. Officials, dancers, officials, artists, and servants lived there permanently, and thousands of students and pilgrims also needed accommodation. In the more elaborate ground-level temples the central shrine was preceded by a series of porticoed rooms, illuminated by windows in the upper part, and terminating in roofs, which were originally made of wood, and later of stone. The extradoses were not made of simple, smooth slabs, but imitated ribbing and tiles, while the edges of the roofs were shaped like lotus blossoms, and the finials were crested and pinnacled. These designs derived from wooden architecture, as did the triangular pediments with volute-patterned uprights and statuary groups in the tympana, the most attractive examples of which are to be found in the Banteay Srei temple.

The buildings annexed to the temple stood in courtyards and cloisters. They included what are known as "libraries," which were originally built according to a square plan with thick brick walls and a single entrance, illuminated by slits, and later made of laterite or sandstone according to a rectangular plan simulating a nave and two aisles, with foreparts on pillars and false doors. Dancing was an essential part of the temple ceremonies, and special rooms (performance rooms and living space for the dancers) were set aside for this purpose, as at Preah Khan.

Although the mountain temple was inspired by Indian symbolism and architectural dictates, it was a type of architecture only found in the Khmer Empire. The first shrine to be built on a stepped pyramid seems to have been the Bakong temple, built in 881 by Jayavarman II in his capital Hariharalaya (now Roluos) to celebrate the cult of the devaraja which he promoted.

Unlike the ground-level temple, Mount Meru was no longer symbolized by the prasat in the mountain temple, but by a pyramidal structure obtained by exploiting a natural hill or creating an artificial one. The prasats, first one and then three or five grouped on a single base at the summit of the pyramid, became the mountain peaks where the gods dwelt. The scenic complex of the quincunx mountain temple (a temple with five towers, four in the corners of the square perimeter and one in the middle), which reached perfection at Angkor Wat, reproduced the five peaks of Mont Meru.

142-143 Architect Lucien Fournereau lived at Angkor from 1887 to 1888 and brought back plaster casts, relics, photos, and above all accurate drawings, some of which, like this one of the last level of Angkor Wat, were exhibited on large panels at the Paris Salon in 1889.

If there was no natural hill available for the mountain temple, it was necessary to build an artificial pyramid, made of filling material enclosed in laterite walls. Sandstone was used as cladding and for the terraces. The staircases that led to the summit had a gradient of between 45° and 70° and were often flanked by sculpted lions or elephants.

The enclosure walls of the ground-level temple were replaced in the mountain temple by galleries that ran along the edges of the terraces, and probably derived from the connection of a number of older rectangular perimeter buildings of unknown purpose, which were originally separate. The galleries of the mountain temple, seen from above, create concentric enclosures that surround areas of various levels of sacredness. From the eleventh century onwards they were also introduced into the ground-level temples. Being of various types, the galleries consisted of a solid outer wall, with or without blind windows, while the inner wall sometimes had open rooms or was turned into a colonnade with square pillars. In the most elaborate cases the main gallery replaced one or both walls of the colonnades and was flanked by one or two pillared half galleries; in this case, a kind of hypostyle room with multiple aisles was created. Towers that reproduced the prasat were built at the corners of the galleries. The galleries were originally roofed with tiles on a wooden framework, although later versions were closed with corbelled bricks and false vaulted roofs made of stone. The first temple to be built in this way was Phimeanakas, where the jutting slabs were arranged in three rows on each side, with closing blocks above.

The windows in the gallery walls were screened by colonettes with a cylindrical or octagonal shape depending on the period, which reproduced the wooden colonettes of the houses. A characteristic feature of the windows built during the reign of Jayavarman VII, who ruled from the twelfth to thirteenth centuries, was that half-lowered curtains and mats were reproduced in stone, leading to an evident reduction in labor. The last innovation in Khmer architecture, the four-faced prasat, was also introduced by the great Emperor. A dedicated Buddhist, Jayavarman VII modified the symbolism of the devaraja in light of Mahayana Buddhism, proclaiming himself the incarnation of the bodhisattva Lokeshvara. The obsessive multiplication of prasats with the faces of Jayavarman-Lokeshvara was the excessive conclusion of the cult of deified sovereigns, and marked the end of colossal stone architecture at Angkor.

From the fourteenth century onwards, temples were made of brick and above all wood, with structures and designs of the sober simplicity preferred by Theravada Buddhism, which had supplanted Hinduism and Mahayana Buddhism.

## CONSTRUCTION MATERIALS AND TECHNIQUES

*144 The windows are screened by elaborately shaped colonettes, like these at Angkor Wat (twelfth century). The limited natural lighting is not only due to climatic reasons but also has psychological and symbolic purposes; darkness is conducive to meditation, the sense of mystery, and the perception of the Divine.*

*145 The type of stone most often used by the Khmer for building was sandstone. The variety used at Banteay Srei, with its warm, pink shades, was particularly sensitive to changes of light.*

The first known Khmer religious buildings date back to the seventh century A.D., although there may have been earlier wooden buildings which have not survived. The oldest materials used were bricks, which usually measured up to 12 inches long, six inches wide and four inches high. They were laid by rubbing them against one another to smooth the edges, then assembled with great care and secured with a binder based on lime, palm sugar, and liana juice. After being laid they were sculpted and covered with a stucco made from lime and sand, which was made to adhere by scraping or making holes in the surface of the wall. Stucco was used from the ninth century onwards, and reached its peak in the tenth century, after which its use declined. Very thick walls were filled with broken bricks and soil.

Later, laterite and sandstone were used. Laterite, a kind of ferruginous clay that solidifies upon contact with air and is easy to cut, was used for bases, platforms, the terraces of the pyramids, and perimeter walls. It was cut into regular blocks around 16 inches thick, which were usually 12 to 20 inches wide and 23 to 32 inches long, and sometimes as much as seven feet long. Sandstone was detached by fire from rock and then cut into blocks weighing up to four tons. The blocks were laid without mortar by rubbing them together dry to smooth them.

The Khmer were not skilled engineers. Their buildings usually had shallow foundations resting on a layer of laterite rubble, and when the walls were built the stones were not always positioned in an ideal way. The building had a static cohesion based on inertia and was constructed with carpentry systems, using large blocks with iron anchorages, cramps, joints, and reinforcing pieces. Toothing was unknown. Reinforcing beams were inserted in hollowed-out stones, but when the wood decayed the stone could no longer support the weight resting on it and collapsed. More attention was paid to the horizontal laying of the stones than to vertical laying and staggering of the connections, causing discontinuity defects that led to breakage of the joints and consequent splitting of the wall mass.

In spite of their poor engineering skills, the Khmer used techniques that seem to be based on stereometric knowledge, in other words, the adaptation of architectural space to suit the visual perspective. One example is the gradual increase in height of the terraces of the mountain temples in which each one is twice as high as the preceding one while their surface area is reduced, thus preventing the gallery on the lower level from concealing the one on the upper level and at the same time giving the viewer the impression of a perfect pyramid.

The stones were transported by barges along the canals and overland on carts, and then laid with the aid of elephants. The visible holes in the stones served to attach ropes so that they could be pulled along.

The frames of the doors and windows, thresholds, and statue bases were made of schist and basalt. The sculptors' work started when the temple was finished; only the crowning stones, colonettes, and balustrades were roughly hewn out before work on the building began. When the wall surface had been leveled, they engraved it with the outline of the bas-reliefs and ornamentation, roughhewed the shapes, and then performed the actual carving and finishing work. The decorations show an evident desire for symmetry. For example, the moldings on the base were repeated upside-down on the cornice, and the colonettes of the door jambs and windows are decorated symmetrically relative to the central ring.

Tapestry-like decoration was widely used at Angkor Vat. It consisted of geometrical patterns as well as floral volutes with animals and people enclosed in them, which were flattened to the utmost and faintly engraved, as if they were patterns on fabric. According to Zhou Daguan, some temples also had walls covered with gilded bronze.

On the whole, despite its inconsistencies and construction defects, Khmer architecture with its axiality, symmetry, and repetitions is very evocative, and the jungle in which it is immersed merely increases its vaguely mysterious appeal.

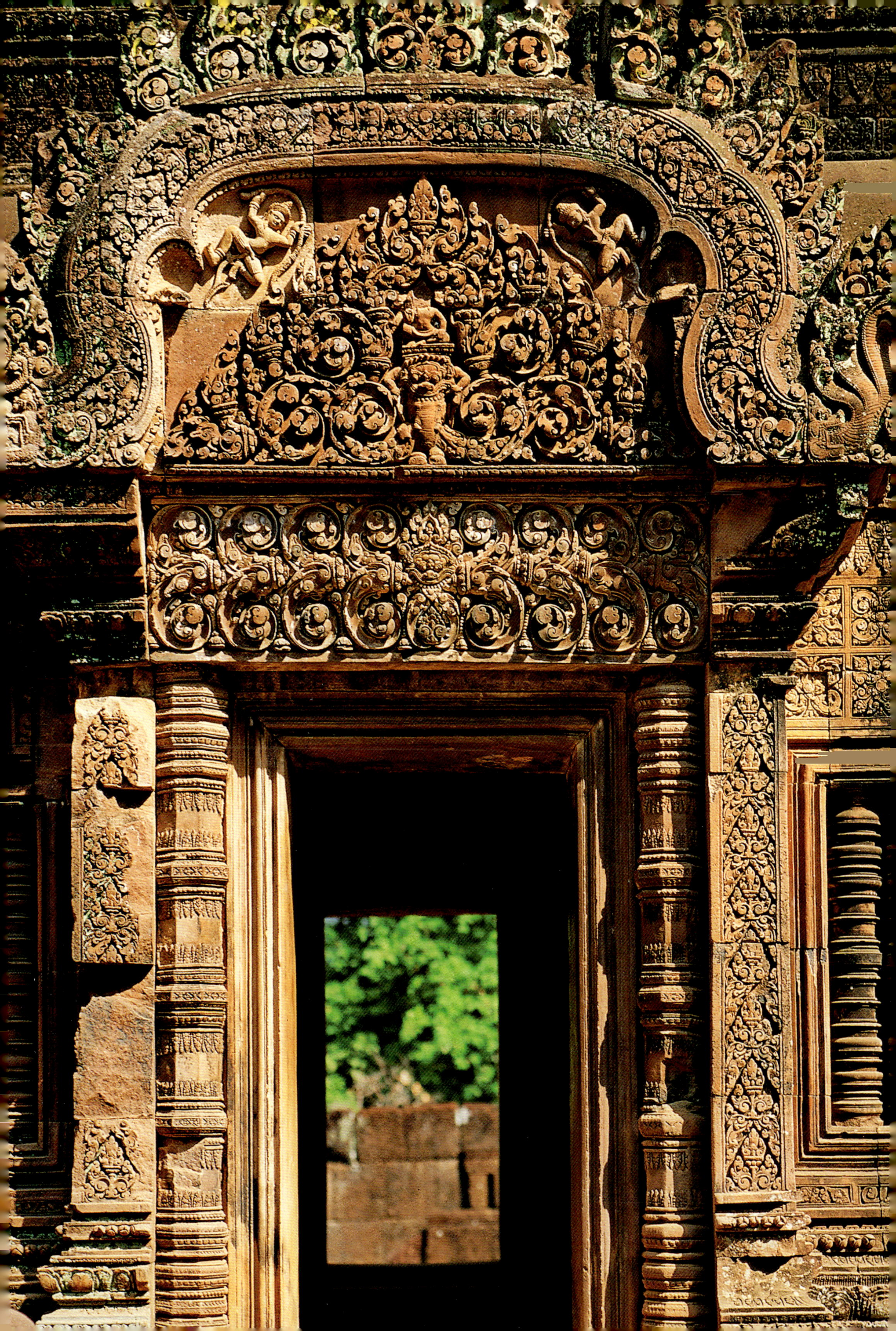

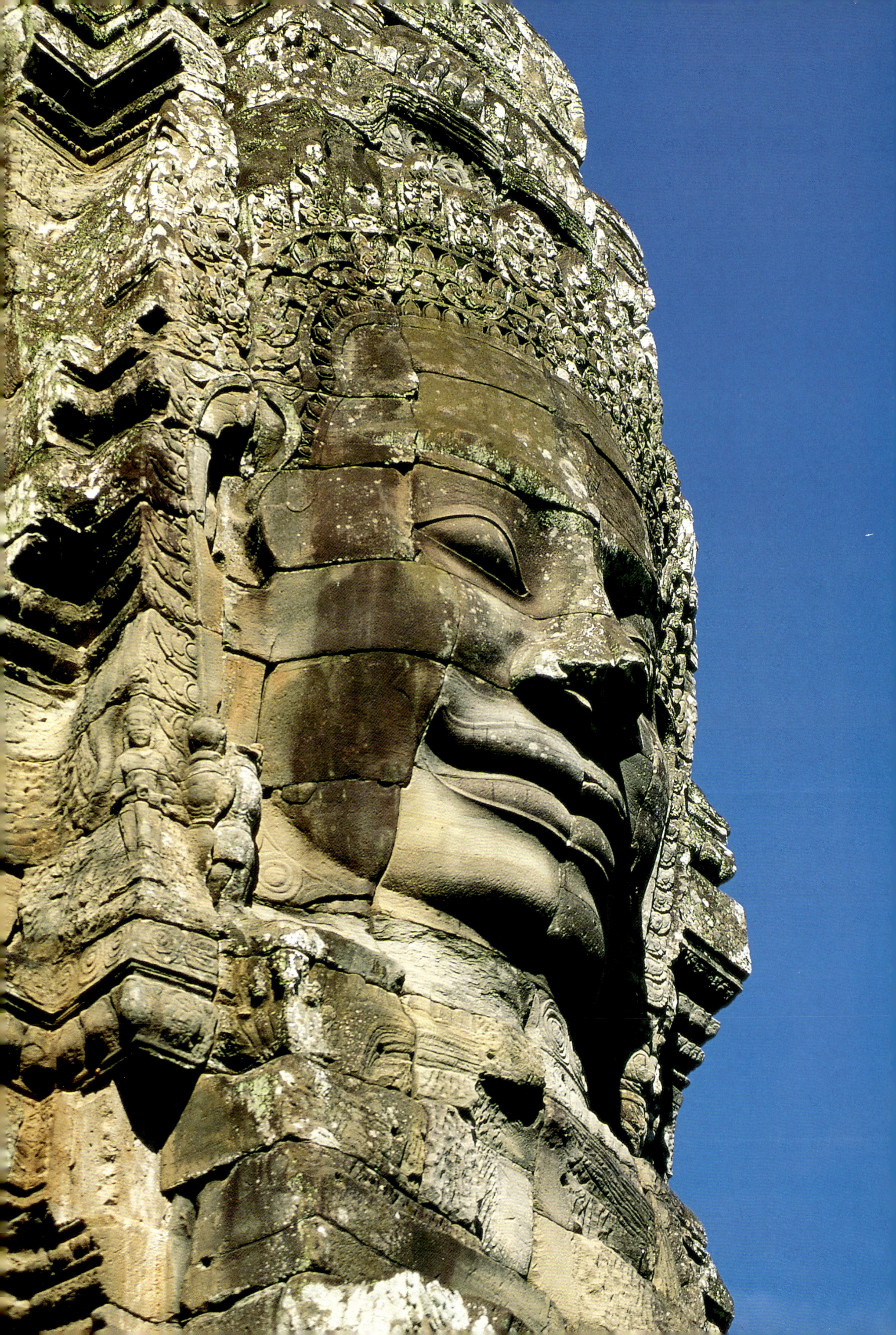

# REALMS OF IMMORTALITY
## ARCHAEOLOGICAL ITINERARIES

*146 Some artistic solutions are apotropaic (designed to ward off evil). For example, the faces of Lokeshvara on the Bayon towers and the temple of Jayavarman VII metaphorically place the building under the protection of the deities.*

*147 When the first French travelers saw Angkor they were astonished. Pierre Loti was overwhelmed by the enigmatic faces emerging from the jungle, and Delaporte expressed similar emotions in his "Album Pittoresque," shown here.*

## CONTENTS

| | | |
|---|---|---|
| INTRODUCTION | PAGE | 148 |
| SAMBOR PREI KUK: ISHANAPURA, CITY OF THE LORD | PAGE | 150 |
| ROLUOS: HARIHARALAYA, THE SEAT OF VISHNU-SHIVA | PAGE | 154 |
| ANGKOR: THE MOUNTAIN TEMPLES OF YASHODHARAPURA | PAGE | 162 |
| KOH KER: THE SHORT-LIVED CAPITAL | PAGE | 178 |
| BANTEAY SREI: THE GEM OF YAJNAVARAHA | PAGE | 182 |
| FROM ANGKOR TO BENG MEALEA: THE TRIUMPH OF THE GROUND-LEVEL TEMPLE | PAGE | 194 |
| ANGKOR WAT: THE STABLE OF THE CELESTIAL OXEN | PAGE | 200 |
| ANGKOR THOM: THE CITY PROTECTED BY THE GODS | PAGE | 226 |
| ANGKOR, BANTEAY CHMAR, KOMPONG SVAY: THE MONASTERY TEMPLES OF JAYAVARMAN VII | PAGE | 248 |
| FROM ANGKOR THOM TO PHIMAI: STAGES ON THE ROYAL ROUTE | PAGE | 272 |
| WAT PHU AND PREAH VIHEAR: THE DWELLINGS OF SHIVA | PAGE | 282 |

# INTRODUCTION

*148 A variety of tradesmen worked on the buildings. Chisellers were responsible for the smallest and most elegant decorations. This one adorns the walls of Angkor Wat (twelfth century).*

*149 As the eyes get used to the darkness, figures emerge from the walls as if appearing at that very moment. The temple then turns into a celestial palace, crowded with deities and animated by sounds and songs. This procession of* devatas *ornaments a corner pavilion at Angkor Wat.*

The Khmer civilization is often identified with the monuments that stand on the Angkor plain, where a series of urban settlements were built alongside, and sometimes on top of one another. Although most of the architectural masterpieces of Kambuja are located in this area, some very interesting constructions can be found at a number of other sites. In addition to the traditional destinations, the itineraries suggested here therefore include some sites located in little-known places, which are sometimes difficult to reach, but where the special characteristics and charm of the spot are worthy of the effort. The sites chosen encompass some of the most important of the numerous complexes built outside the borders of present-day Cambodia. In selecting these itineraries, a chronological order has been followed as far as possible in order to demonstrate architectural transformations and developments, with special emphasis on their symbolic interpretations.

Our first stop is at Sambor Prei Ku, to the north of present-day Kompong Thom, to see the ancient Ishanapura, one of the most important capitals of Chenla, with its numerous seventh-century brick temples decorated with sophisticated motifs.

Two centuries later, building commenced on the Angkor plain, which was chosen as the center of the Khmer Empire because of its geomorphological characteristics. The first great city, Hariharalaya, stands in the area of what is now Roluos, and its shrines are prototypes of the ground-level temples, devoted to ancestor worship, and the mountain temples, dedicated to the cult of the devaraja. The mountain temples, monumental structures with a wealth of symbolism, constituted the focal point of the various capitals built by the major kings. Yashodharapura, the "city that brings glory," is the most important example.

Some other important settlements were established outside the Angkor plain. In the tenth century, Chok Gargyal, situated in the Koh Ker area, was the short-lived capital of Jayavarman IV, whose architects built one of the largest pyramids in Kambuja. Just as other capitals were built outside Angkor, so were some temples built by non-royal personages, such as the two cultured Brahmans who commissioned Banteay Srei, one of the gems of Khmer art, built in 967.

Having now reached the classical age, the tour returns to Angkor to observe the development of the valley temples, exemplified by some magnificent specimens, and then travels some 25 miles to visit the majestic, intriguing Beng Mealea complex, lost in the jungle.

In the twelfth century the Khmer civilization, now mature, produced its masterpiece, Angkor Wat, a perfect work and the embodiment of paradise on earth, still watched over today by thousands of beautiful deities with ecstatic smiles.

The last great capital built at Angkor, Angkor Thom, reflects the genius and personality of an outstanding sovereign of contradictory appeal: Jayavarman VII. His complexity and mystery is represented by the Bayon Temple, an amazing symbol of a man and his spirit and the last great testimony to a declining royal cult. Jayavarman, a tireless builder, filled his capital and his huge kingdom with religious foundations. These gigantic monastery cities can be viewed in a long itinerary that leads from Angkor Thom and its monuments southward, to the Preah Khan at Kompong Svay, and northward, to the remote complex of Banteay Chmar at the foot of the Dangkrek mountains. On a spur of these mountains stands one of the loveliest Khmer temples, Preah Vihear, dwelling of the god Shiva and sentinel keeping watch over the empire of the devaraja.

One of the major royal routes that connected the capital with the outlying parts of the huge empire crossed the Dangkrek mountains. The penultimate itinerary follows part of its route, visiting shrines and rest areas as far as Phimai and its temple, the loveliest example of Khmer architecture in Thailand.

In conclusion, the journey must detour to Laos to visit the neglected but attractive Wat Phu complex, an ancient place of worship of the god Shiva and to some extent the cradle of the Khmer civilization. The Khmer seem to have begun their march to Angkor there, carrying in their hearts the image of the mountain, the dwelling place of the gods and symbol of royal grandeur. When they could not find any natural mountain on which to erect their celestial palaces, they built artificial ones in order to come closer to the heavens.

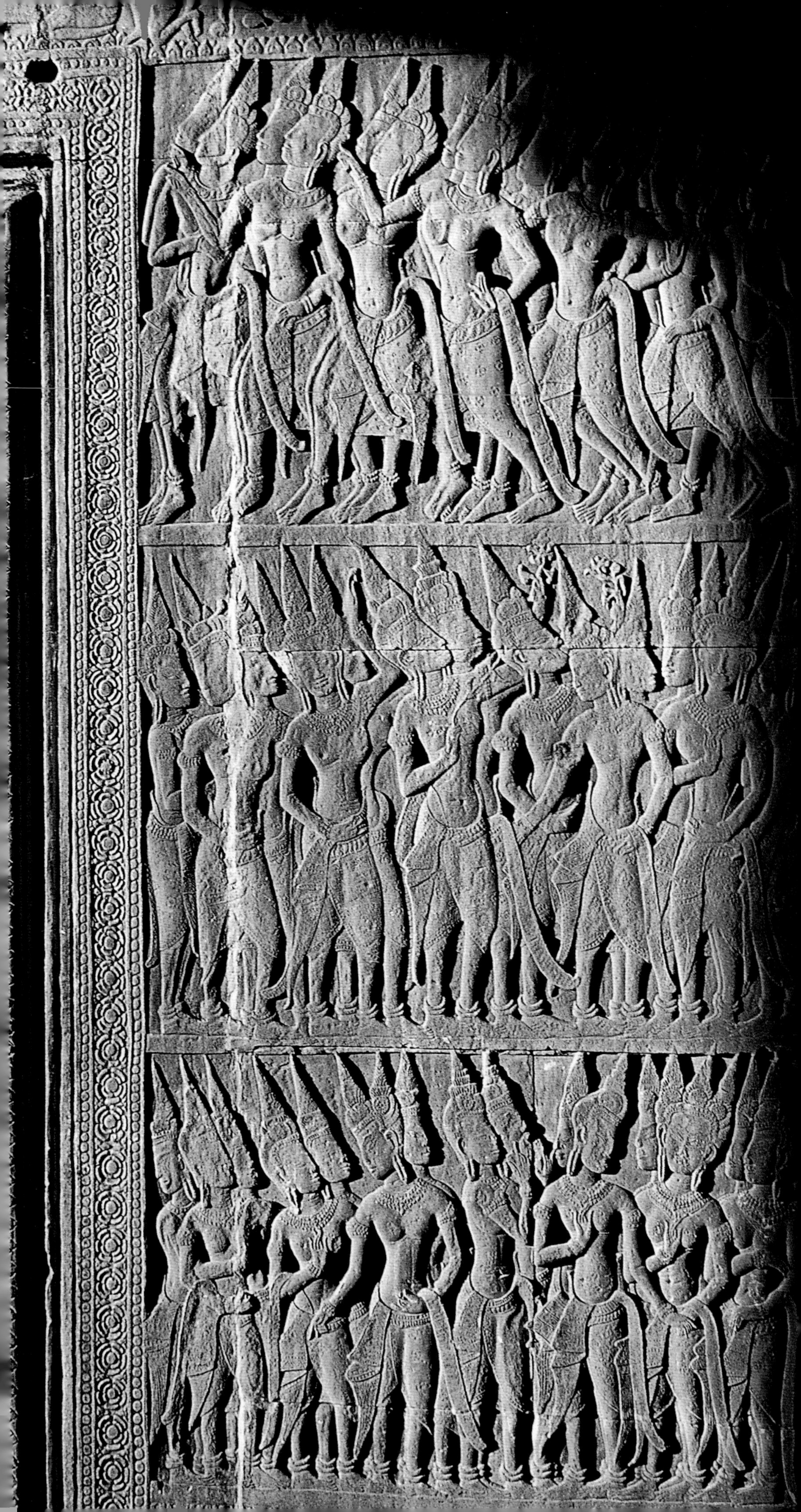

*150 top  Building N17 in the northern area of Ishanapura possesses a rare example of a flat roof. Under the plaster at the rear, the stone slabs of the walls fit into the grooves in the corner pillars.*

*150 bottom left  Octagonal sanctuaries were an isolated case in Khmer architecture and were not built for much time. This photo shows temple S8 in the southern zone.*

*150 bottom right  The typical pre-Angkor prasat was a square structure with thick, brick walls. One from the southern group is shown here. It has a single usable door, the other three being false doors carved in sandstone niches. The walls are ornamented by pilasters and miniature reproductions of buildings.*

*151  Lions ready to pounce keep watch from the staircase buttresses of temple C1 in the central area. The artist has depicted the mane and gaping jaws in a very realistic way.*

# SAMBOR PREI KUK

## Ishanapura, City of the Lord

Sambor Prei Kuk, situated 21 miles from present-day Kompong Thom, which is 86 miles southeast of Angkor, contains the ruins of a huge square settlement surrounded by an earth wall about a mile long per side, bordered by a moat supplied with water by the Stung Sen river which once ran near the city. The city's water supply was provided by a baray situated on the south side. The history of Sambor Prei Kuk is associated with that of ancient Chenla, which was not a united kingdom but divided into various principalities. Bhavavarman, who came from one of these principalities, settled at Bhavapura, which was probably situated in the area of Sambor Prei Kuk. When Bhavavarman died shortly after 598, his kingdom was inherited by his brother Citrasena, whose son Ishanavarman, crowned between 611 and 616, founded Ishanapura, meaning "city of Ishana," Ishana being a name of the god Shiva as well as the king. Chenla reached its maximum size during the reign of Ishanavarman, and the capital reflected its power and wealth.

However, Ishanapura was not built from scratch. There are settlements in the archaeological area of Sambor Prei Kuk which date from before the reign of Ishanavarman such as those in the northern area, although they were partly rebuilt during the Angkor period.

| ISHANAPURA | |
|---|---|
| A | NORTHERN GROUP |
| 1 | CELL N17 |
| B | MUSEUM |
| C | CENTRAL GROUP |
| 2 | C 1, MAIN TEMPLE |
| D | SOUTHERN GROUP |
| 3 | S 2, MAIN ENTRANCE |
| 4 | S 1, TEMPLE OF SHIVA |
| E | MODERN ROADS |

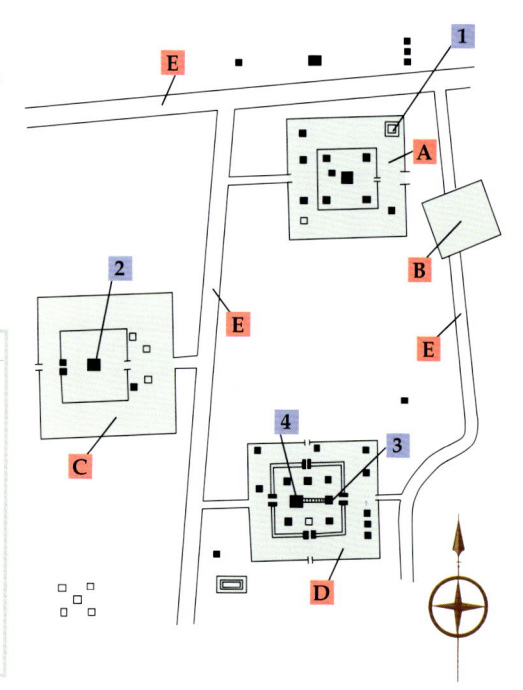

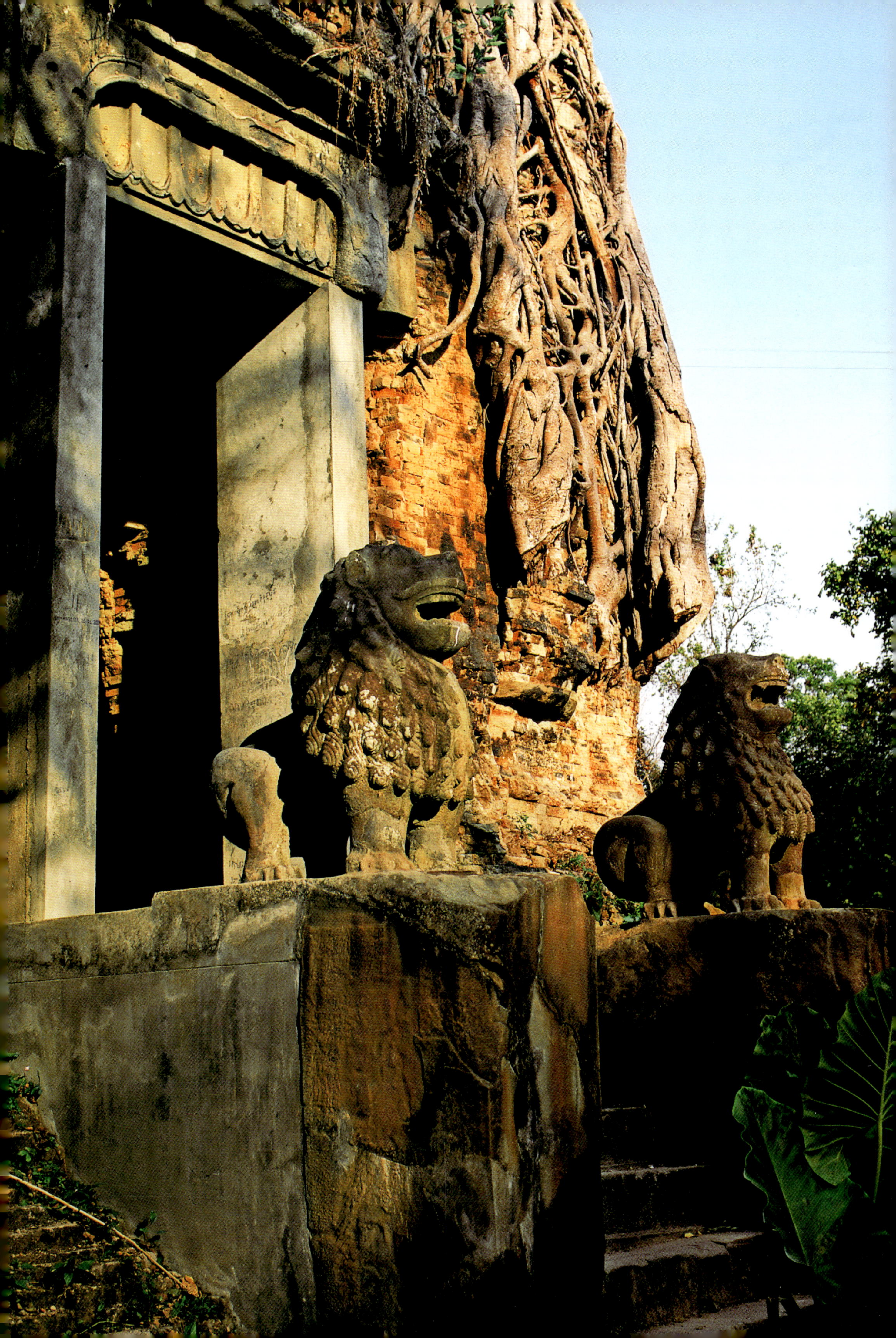

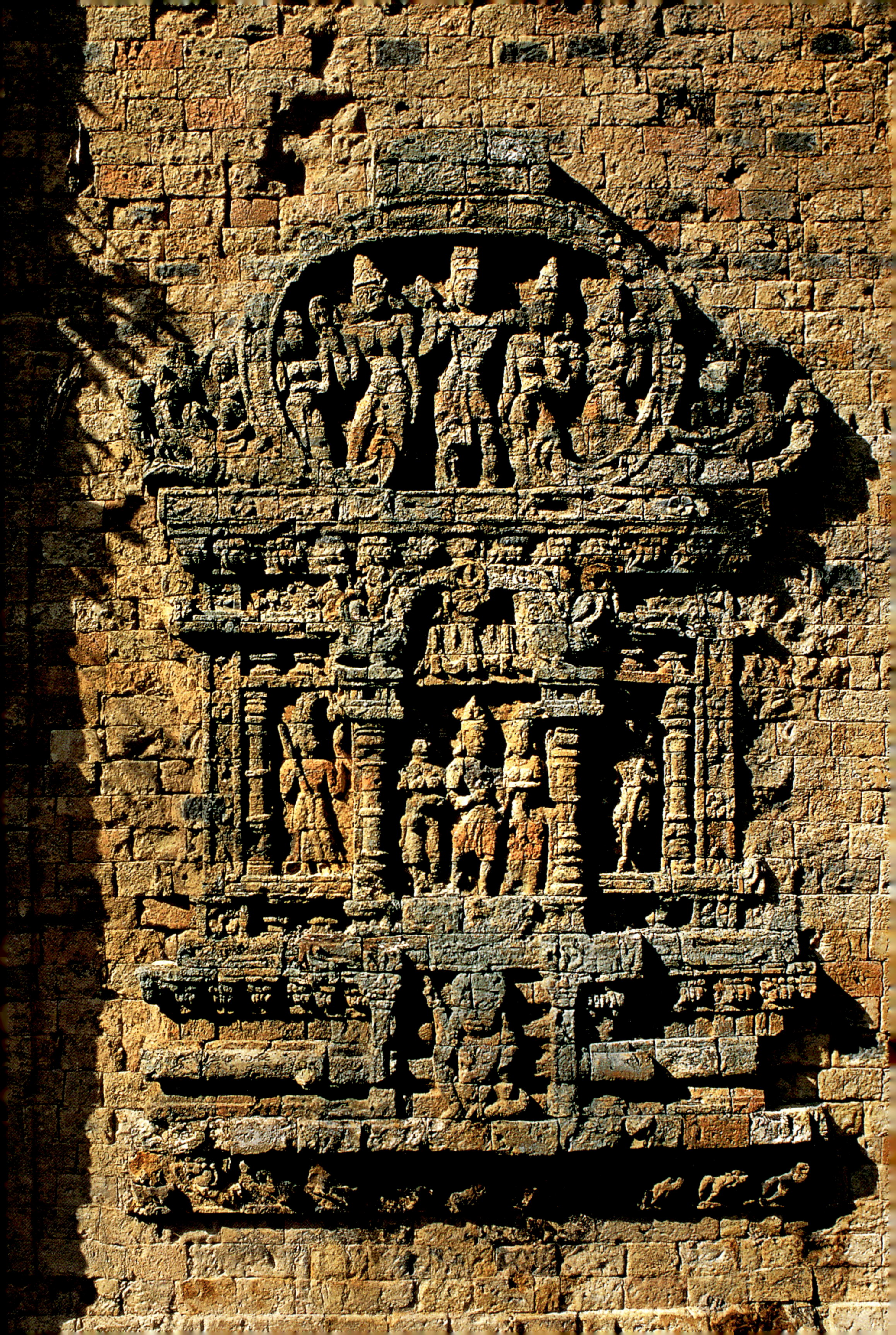

*152 The portrayals of buildings that decorate temple walls, as in temple N7, shown here, include some large* kudus, *skylight arches that constituted the pediments of oblong buildings.*

*153 left The festoons of garlands that run along the sandstone architraves probably reproduce the garlands of fresh flowers that were hung in wooden temples and household shrines.*

*153 right The bas-reliefs of Ishanapura, among the oldest in Kambuja, seem to demonstrate a Javanese influence, which is plausible in view of the historical events of the seventh century.*

The buildings in the southern quadrant can be definitely attributed to Ishanavarman in view of the inscriptions found on the site.

The buildings to the north are marked with the letter N followed by the number of the temple; N17 is unusual and seems to date back to the time of Bhavavarman. It is a square cell made of slabs of sandstone, built on a base and covered with a flat roof. The cornice is ornamented with kudus, the classic horseshoe-shaped Indian arches that enclose faces, a motif that simulates the dormer windows of the wooden buildings. The most important shrine in the northern group, which is surrounded by a double enclosure wall and made of brick like nearly all the buildings at Sambor Prei Kuk, has a quincunx arrangement, or in other words, a central temple-tower (prasat) surrounded by four corner towers. The most intriguing aspect of the complex is the magnificently decorated sandstone bases surrounding the main temple on which statues were probably placed.

The southern group of temples, marked with the letter S followed by a number, is also surrounded by a double enclosure, the outer one of which measures 853 by 779 feet. The walls of the inner enclosure are ornamented with medallions containing the earliest examples of bas-reliefs, although they are seriously damaged. The main entrance (S2) consists of a tower inspired by the monumental doors (gopura) of southern Indian temples and features a sandstone canopy that is a masterpiece of decoration. A statue of Nandin, the bull ridden by the god Shiva to whom the central temple (S1) is dedicated, was probably placed under the canopy. The remains of stilts suggest that a raised avenue connected the pavilion of Nandin to the shrine of his lord, anticipating a feature that was to be extensively developed and very popular at Angkor. In addition to the main rectangular temple, which has an east-facing entrance and three other bricked-up doors, there are also some minor prasat including five octagonal ones inside the first enclosure (their numbering starts from the center) and eight in the second. The octagonal structure is a feature particular to Sambor Prei Kuk.

The central complex, in which the monuments are marked C, is more recent. The most interesting building (C1), which like all the other shrines is surrounded by a double wall, is a rectangular temple approximately 26 by 20 feet (and therefore one of the largest), built on a raised base, with two entrance staircases flanked by pairs of lions.

The buildings of Sambor Prei Kuk provided the basic patterns for future Khmer architecture. The simplest, oldest prasat consists of a squat square or oblong cell with a single entrance and slightly projecting pillars on the outer walls, surmounted by a regularly stepped pyramidal roof. In the more complex later versions, the use of projections and recesses was accentuated and the number of outer pillars was consequently increased. In addition to the main door, which nearly always faces east, there is a false door on each of the other three sides of the prasat. The cell is roofed with a tiered structure of decreasing size in which each tier reproduces the temple façade.

With regards to ornamentation, the doors and architraves are made of sandstone. The openings are framed by round columns in which the upper bulb, in the shape of a turban fringed with garlands, is an Indian legacy. Traces of paint survive on the false doors, which are faithful reproductions of wooden doors. The architraves, which provide a vital clue to the development of Khmer architecture, consist of an arch disgorged from the mouths of two makaras (sea monsters with trunks and horns) from which rampant winged lions also emerge. Three medallions inserted in the arch depict animals or deities in relief, while garlands of flowers, festoons of stylized leaves, necklaces, and pendants hang in the lower register, recalling the offerings hung from the torana (the wooden arches that marked the entrances to Indian temples). In some cases, the arched motif of the architrave was constituted by a naga (many-headed serpent) and the makaras are replaced by men riding fantastic creatures, while the lower register is crowded with characters. One of the typical ornamental features of the walls of the Ishanapura prasat is the bas-relief depicting the miniature temple called the vimana, the flying chariot of the gods. One of the most attractive examples appears on octagonal tower N7. Traces of stucco consisting of a mortar made of lime and sand can be seen in a number of places and may have been colored.

# ROLUOS
## Hariharalaya, the Seat of Vishnu-Shiva

*154 left  The temple of Lolei, built in 893 by Yashovarman in honor of his father Indravarman I, stood in the middle of the Indratataka baray, on an artificial island measuring 344 by 262 feet. The barays (water reservoirs) symbolized the primordial sea that contained the seeds of the manifest world.*

*154 right  In addition to their east-facing entrance, the prasats (tower-temples) of Preah Ko, built by Indravarman I in 879, had three false doors that reproduced wooden doors.*

*155 The exquisite architraves of Preah Ko, like this one focusing on Garuda, are surmounted by a band of praying figures, often carved in a separate block of sandstone.*

Jayavarman II built four capitals for his kingdom: Indrapura, Hariharalaya, Amarendrapura, and Mahendrapura. Mahendrapura stood at the foot of Mount Mahendraparvata (now Phnom Kulen), about 20 miles northeast of Angkor. Mountains constitute a religious archetype in nearly all ancient civilizations as the meeting place between heaven and earth and site of the theophany. The Khmer world was no exception; in fact, the mountain was considered even more sacred than in the Indian culture in which Mount Meru or Sumeru is the fulcrum of mystical geography.

A king who declared himself chakravartin (universal monarch) could not choose a more suitable location for his capital than a mountain, which is why Jayavarman II chose Mount Mahendraparvata. This mountain was named after Indra, the ancient Vedic deity (a deity included in the Vedas, the earliest sacred Hindu texts) who constituted the prototype of the warrior and was thus particularly worshipped by the second Indian caste, the kshatriya (warriors). Indra was the king of the gods and the archetypal monarch, but over the centuries his power was overshadowed by that of Vishnu and Shiva, and the Khmer, inspired by the religious concepts of southern India, attributed supreme sovereignty in the divine world to Shiva. Tradition has it that Shiva appeared in 802 on Mount Mahendraparvata where Jayavarman II was about to be consecrated absolute monarch of Kambuja, and gave him the linga, a phallic symbol, the tabernacle of the essence of the god and at the same time the emblem of heavenly and earthly sovereignty.

Although Phnom Kulen was called Mahendraparvata it actually represents Kailasa, the legendary dwelling of Shiva, and Krus Preah Aram Rong Chen, which is unfortunately in very poor condition, may have been the building that contained the linga. It is divided into three overlapping terraces made of earth and bricks retained by laterite walls and surmounted by a pedestal on which the symbol of Shiva stood.

Jayavarman's most important capital was Hariharalaya (the seat of Harihara), named after the syncretic deity in which Vishnu and Shiva merged. It was located in the area of present-day Roluos, about seven miles southeast of Angkor, and the died there in 850. His son Jayavarman III is not associated with any monument, and the amazing expansion of the site is attributable to his successor Indravarman I, who succeeded to the throne in 877.

The construction of the Indratataka (pool of Indra) at Lolei, which exploited the water of the river Roluos, ensured a regular water supply for the paddy fields and the various temple complexes with annexed urban settlements in which, according to Stierlin, at least 15,000 people lived. The waters of Lolei supplied the canals of Preah Ko, Bakong, and Prei Monti, and around the latter temple Indravarman's palace was probably built.

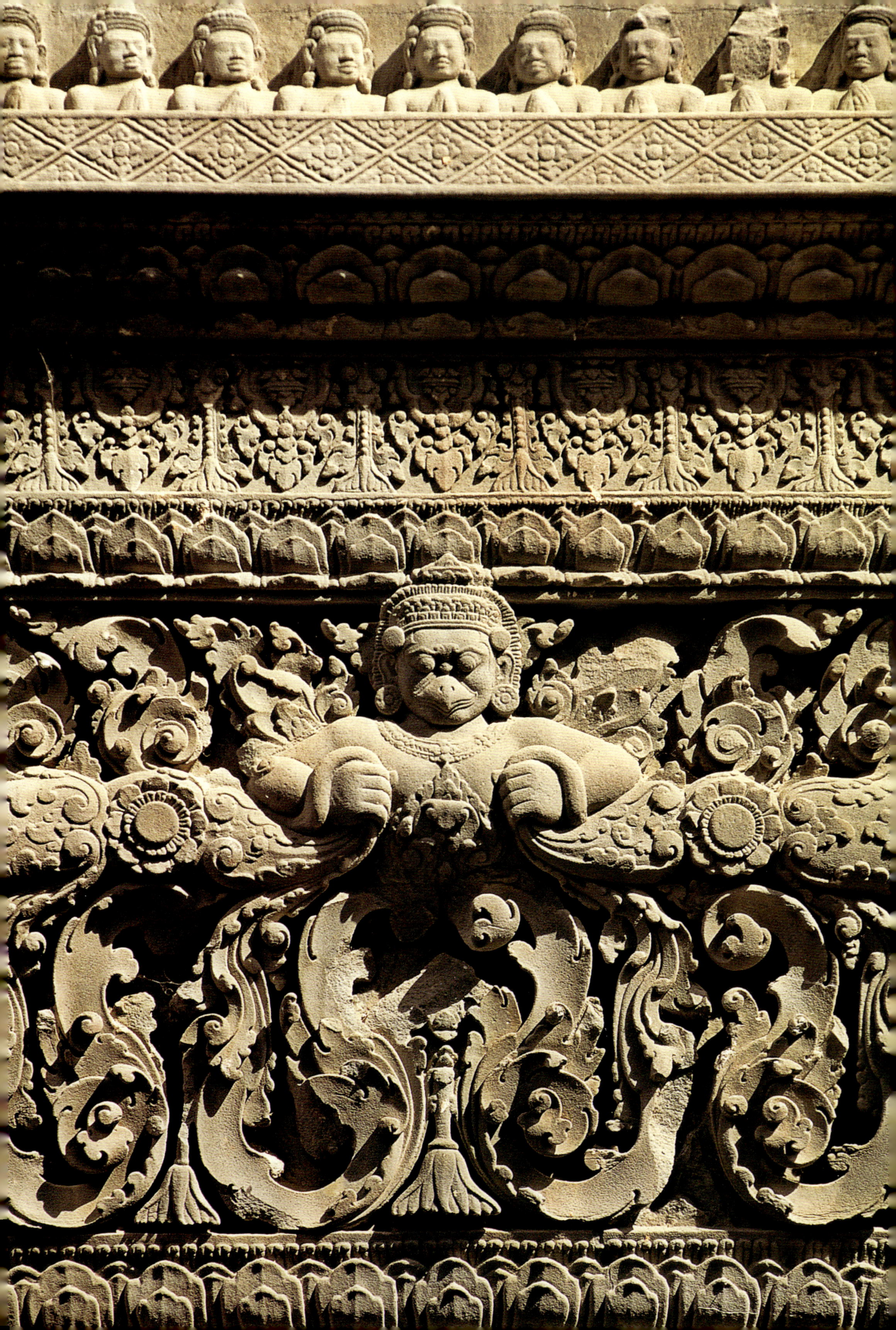

*156 top The only light to enter the* prasat, *like this one at Preah Ko, comes from the main door, since it has no windows and the other three doors are walled up. The dark cell is the* garbhagriha *(womb) which houses the germ of light, the image of divinity.*

*156 bottom left Lions, symbolizing warlike virtue, flank the stairways leading to the platform of Preah Ko.*

*156 bottom right The Divine radiates from the cell and is manifested for worshippers on the temple walls in a wide variety of forms. A* devata *(female deity) appears in this niche at Preah Ko.*

*156-157 This temple is named Preah Ko (sacred bull) after the statues of Nandin (Shiva's mount) that face it.*

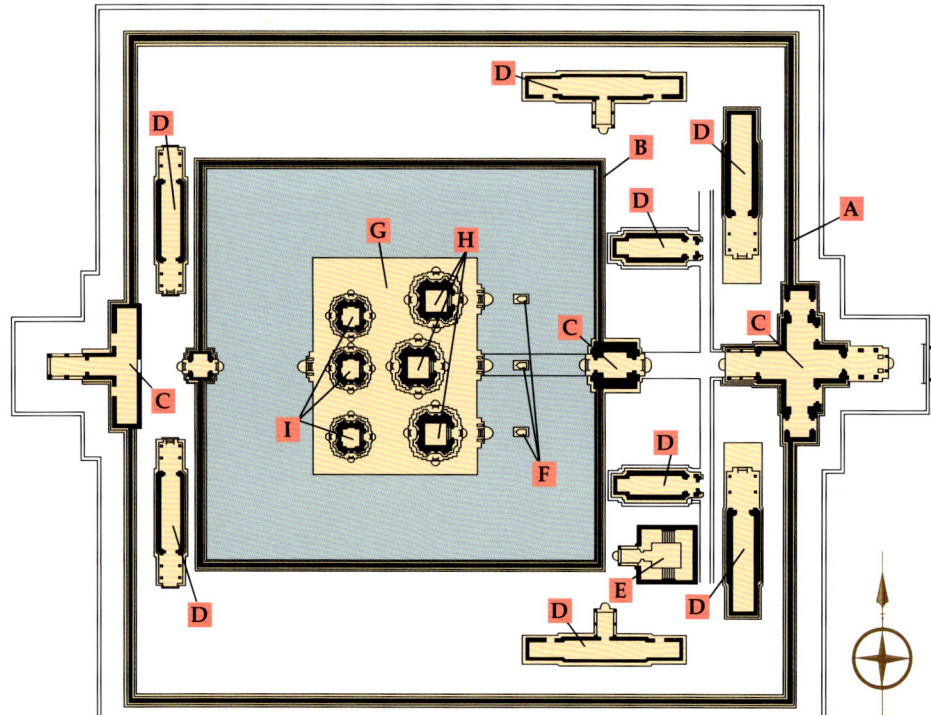

| | PREAH KO |
|---|---|
| **A** | OUTER WALL OR SECOND ENCLOSURE |
| **B** | INNER WALL OR FIRST ENCLOSURE |
| **C** | GOPURAS (ENTRANCE PAVILIONS) |
| **D** | RECTANGULAR BUILDINGS |
| **E** | SQUARE BUILDING OR "LIBRARY" |
| **F** | STATUES OF NANDIN |
| **G** | PLATFORM OF THE PRASATS |
| **H** | PRASAT OF THE KINGS |
| **I** | PRASAT OF THE QUEENS |

After inaugurating the great Khmer hydraulic architecture, in 879 the king built the temple **Preah Ko**, or "Sacred Bull," in honor of his ancestors. The temple was so called because of the three statues of Nandin it contained, which demonstrate that it was dedicated to Shiva. The outer perimeter of the temple area is delimited by a moat, which formed the borders of a residential area measuring roughly 1300 by 1600 feet and included two reservoirs within its margins. This is followed by two enclosure walls with gopura entrances in them. There are six rectangular buildings preceded by porticoes along the inner walls of the second enclosure (the enclosures are numbered in increasing order from the center of the monument to the perimeter) and two similar buildings perpendicular to the access avenue. A square brick building known as the "library," whose purpose is actually unknown, is situated in the southeast corner. The first enclosure contains the platform on which the temple stands. The temple consists of six prasat with the classic east-facing brick towers arranged in two rows. The three towers at the front, dedicated to the male ancestors, are larger than the three at the back, dedicated to their wives. The central prasat in the first row, the largest of all, housed the image of Jayavarman II in his posthumous form of Parameshvara. The northern prasat contained the linga Rudreshvara, emblem of Rudravarman, Indravarman I's material grandfather, while the southern one housed the linga Prithivindreshvara, the emblem of Indravarman's father Prithivindravarman. Their wives Narendradevi, Dharanindradevi, and Prithvindradevi were worshipped in their deified form; in fact, the suffix devi means "goddess."

The outer walls were covered with a lime and sand mortar which acted as stucco and is still visible in many places. Sandstone niches inserted in recesses in the walls contain armed figures of young dvarapalas (gatekeepers) on the prasat of the male ancestors and images of the devatas (female deities) on those of the female ancestors.

The doors, flanked by elaborate columns, were also made of sandstone, and the false doors featured exquisite floral decorations. The architraves are among the loveliest in Khmer art; the arch is replaced with a festoon ending in naga heads or diverging makaras. Figures of horsemen can be glimpsed among the foliage, and at the center of the festoon is the mask of Kala, or the god Vishnu riding his mount Garuda, which was part human, part bird of prey. A frieze, mostly depicting worshippers, runs above the architrave, connecting it to the pediment above.

In 881 Indravarman I had another shrine consecrated, the mountain temple of **Bakong**, center of the city of Hariharalaya and tabernacle of the royal **linga**, the symbol of the **devaraja** and of Indravarman himself. Although Ak Yum on the south bank of the West **Baray** and Krus Preah Aram Rong Chen on Phnom Kulen were built earlier, the Bakong is considered the first true mountain temple, partly because it was the first one to be made of sandstone, and partly because it is much larger and more structured than the other two.

In the middle of the complex stands a pyramid made of blocks of sandstone with an almost square plan, measuring 220 by 213 feet at the base and 66 by 59 feet at the summit, divided into five terraces, with a total height of 46 feet. This artificial mountain represented Mount Meru, and each of its five levels was connected with a category of mythical beings: the **naga**, **garuda**, **rakshasa** (demons), **yasha** (tree deities), and **deva** (gods). Four **gopuras** give access to the axial staircases, and on each floor the flight of stairs is preceded by an elegant semicircular threshold and flanked by lions. To provide the correct optical perception, the height and width of the stairs become imperceptibly smaller towards the top as the architects applied the law of proportional reduction, which until then had only been used for **prasat** roofs. Each terrace of the pyramid is slightly recessed to the west, again to correct the perspective.

There are statues of elephants at the corners of the first three steps of the pyramid that recall the legendary animals that support the earth; their presence is designed to transfer their force and stability magically to the building. The elephant was also the mount of Indra, king of the gods, and of the earthly king. There are 12 sandstone towers on the fourth terrace, each of which probably contained a **linga**, while traces of bas-reliefs can still be seen on the wall of the fifth and last terrace. The central **prasat**, reconstructed with the anastylosis technique by Maurice Glaize in 1940, proved to be a twelfth-century building with a denticulated plan on a tall base, three false doors and one real one, and a four-story superstructure with a lotus-shaped finial.

The pyramid is surrounded by a first enclosure wall made of laterite that forms a rectangle measuring 394 by 525 feet, is accessible from four gopuras with a cross-shaped plan, and includes numerous buildings.

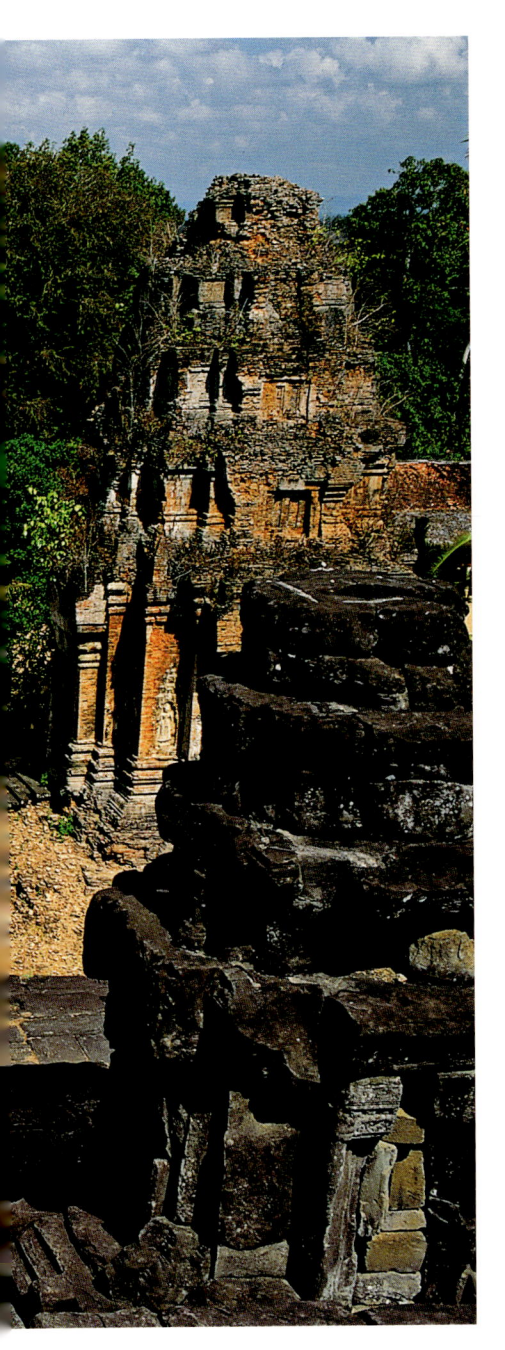

158-159 *The purpose of many buildings is still unknown, as in the case of the six* prasats *situated in the corners of the Bakong temple. This photo shows two of them, which are made of brick and have ventilation slits.*

159 top *Elephants, seen here at the Bakong temple, were believed to carry the world on their backs and favor its fertility because their shape and color were associated with the rain-bearing monsoon clouds.*

159 center *Laterite was used for bases and enclosure walls. It was laid in blocks, as shown here at Bakong, without considering the need to stagger them to prevent the joints from opening up.*

| BAKONG | |
|---|---|
| A | ENCLOSURE WALL |
| B | GOPURA |
| C | ACCESS AVENUE |
| D | PRASAT WITH VENTILATION HOLES |
| E | AEDICULES |
| F | RECTANGULAR BUILDINGS |
| G | "LIBRARIES" |
| H | PRASAT |
| I | STEPPED PYRAMID |
| J | SMALL PRASATS |
| K | CENTRAL PRASAT |

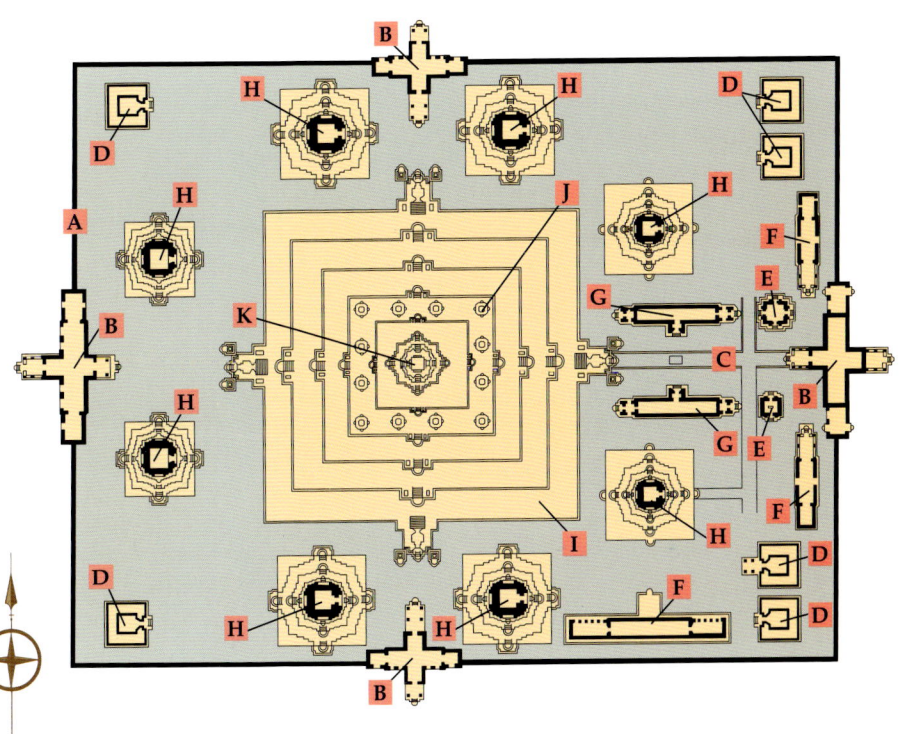

159

*160 top* As in most temples, the entrances on the north-south axis of the Bakong, shown in this photo, are smaller than those on the east-west axis.

*160 bottom* The Bakong, built by Indravarman I in 881, contained the linga Indreshvara, which symbolized the devaraja and the king. The foundation stele states that the building "amazed Tvashtar (architect of the gods) himself."

*161* The prasat that crowns the Bakong is a twelfth-century reconstruction. Its pyramidal structure symbolizes the emanation of the manifest world from the bindu, the point at which everything originated.

## ROLUOS: Hariharalaya, the Seat of Vishnu-Shiva

Six prasat of modest size with a square plan and thick brick walls stand in the corners of the enclosure wall; the ventilation holes at the top have led some researchers to suggest that they may have been cremation chambers. However it may be, their corner position anticipates the later towers situated in the corners of the enclosures. The two tripartite rectangular structures built perpendicular to the avenue of the east gopura formed the base on which perimeter galleries were to be developed, while the other three buildings, which were also rectangular but had porticoes at the end and were built horizontally to the avenue, are the prototypes of the rooms known as "libraries," whose actual purpose was unknown.

At the sides of the same avenue there are two aedicules. The foundation stela, found in the northern one, states that the other eight brick shrines built around the base of the Bakong pyramid were dedicated to the eight murti (aspects) of Shiva, namely the Sun, Moon, wind, earth, water, fire, ether, and atman (soul). It might also have a cosmic symbolism, in which the number eight alludes to the eight regions of space and their tutelary deities. The structure of the prasat is the usual one: a platform with four access staircases, a square structure on a base, a roof with diminishing tiers that reproduce the façade, and a succession of tall pediments one above the another, crowned with a finial in the shape of a lotus blossom. Inside, the walls were covered with red plaster and wooden ceilings concealed the intrados of the vault. The sandstone door frames and architraves with floral decorations, which also adorn the octagonal and round columns, are particularly interesting. The niches contain the remains of dvarapalas and devatas sculpted in stucco.

The second enclosure, of which some remains of the laterite wall still survive, formed the boundary of a strip of land some 82 feet wide where the personnel lived. A modern Buddhist monastery now stands in the northeastern corner. All around runs a moat 197 feet wide, which forms a rectangle measuring 1,050 by 1,150 feet. It is crossed by two dykes in an east-west direction, which are the continuation of two of the four axial avenues of the city of Hariharalaya. The road winds between rows of gigantic stone naga, which anticipate the magnificent serpent-shaped balustrades of the classical era.

Beyond the moat stood the city of Hariharalaya, which contained numerous buildings made of perishable materials that have now disappeared. It covered an area of over three million square feet and was situated on a strip of land 427 by 492 feet wide within a perimeter measuring roughly 2,300 by between 2,600 and 3,000 feet (the measurements supplied by the various surveys of numerous Khmer sites and monuments sometimes disagree). The outer enclosure wall of the city was bordered by a moat just over 65 feet wide.

Some features of the Bakong temple and the maturity of its construction have suggested to some experts, such as B. P. Groslier, that it may have been significantly influenced by Javanese art, especially Borobodur. Whatever the real genesis of Bakong, the Hariharalaya site as a whole is amazing for its adherence to Hindu cosmological symbolism: the Bakong temple represents Mount Meru, the first moat symbolises the cosmic sea from which it emerges, and the subsequent dry area is the land inhabited by men, which in turn is surrounded by mountain chains (the city walls) and another sea (the second moat).

Yashovarman, who succeeded to Indravarman I in 889, built the **Lolei** temple in the middle of the Indratataka reservoir as the first act of his reign, in memory of his father Indravarman and his royal ancestors. All that remains of the monument, which follows the pattern of Preah Ko, are four towers, and it is not certain whether the other two were ever built. Here again, the architraves are of excellent workmanship.

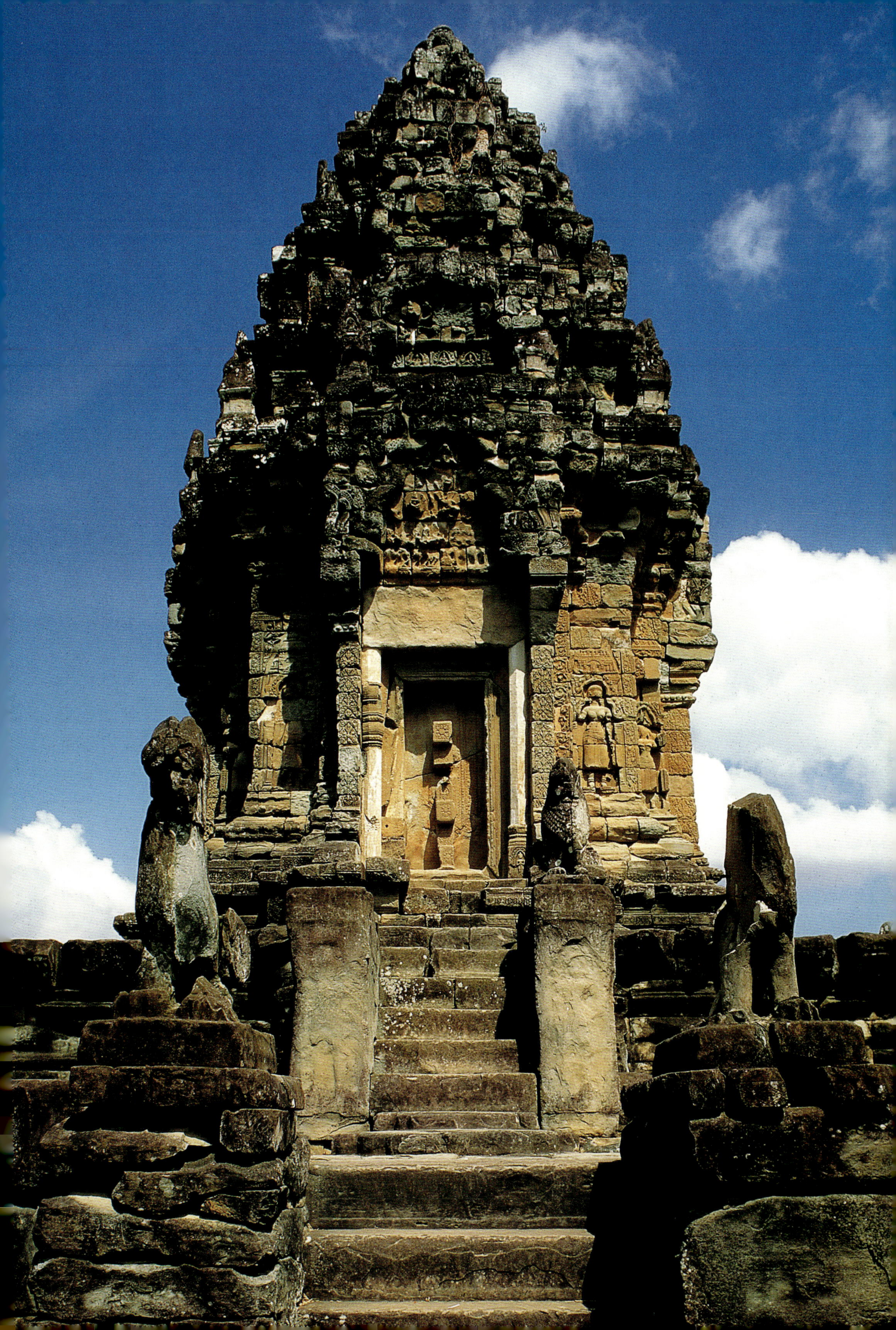

*162 top A pleated sarong, with a yoke folded over at the waist and the free edge trailing in a fishtail shape, characterizes this devata gatekeeper, wearing a conical crown, in a niche of the Bakheng.*

# ANGKOR
## The Mountain Temples of Yashodharapura

*162 bottom left This aerial photo shows the orderly arrangement of the 108 prasats of the Bakheng temple on the five terraces of the pyramid. The number and layout of the towers complied with astrological requirements.*

*162 bottom right This temple, built by Yashovarman on the natural hill called Phnom Bakheng between the late ninth and early tenth century, was the center of Yashodharapura. The photo shows one of its sandstone prasats.*

*162-163 The 44 brick towers that surround the Bakheng temple are built in groups of two, three, or four on the same base, and stand in pairs on either side of the four entrances. Very few of them are still intact.*

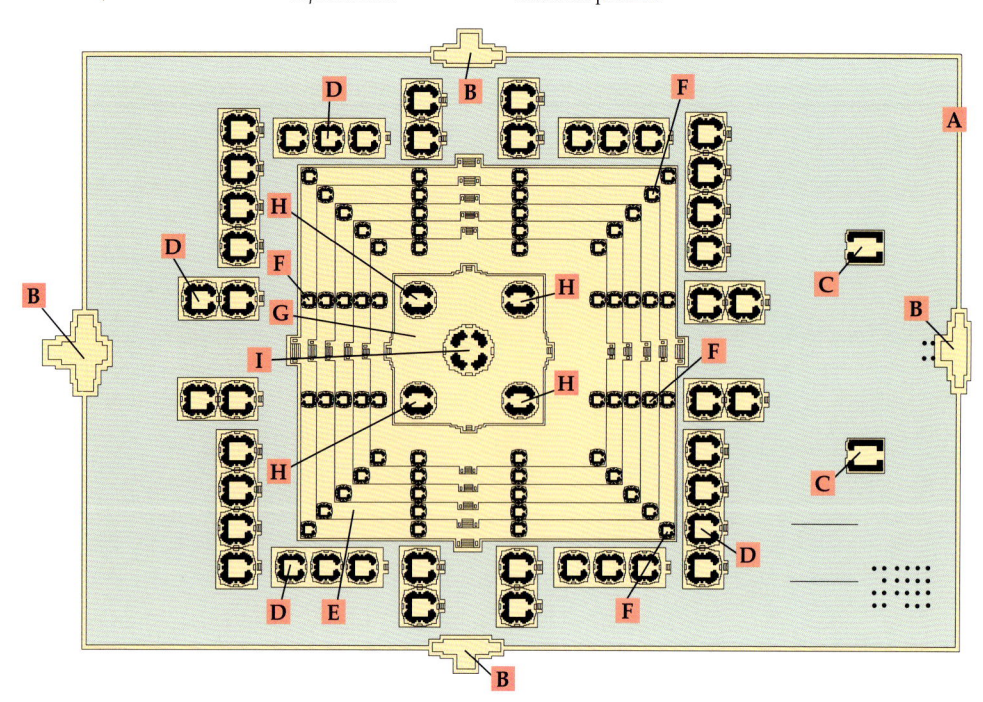

| BAKHENG | |
|---|---|
| A | ENCLOSURE WALL |
| B | GOPURAS (ENTRANCE PAVILIONS) |
| C | "LIBRARIES" |
| D | BRICK PRASATS, 44 AROUND BASE |
| E | PYRAMID TERRACES |
| F | SANDSTONE PRASATS, 12 PER TERRACE |
| G | BASE OF THE QUINCUNX |
| H | PRASAT OF THE QUINCUNX |
| I | CENTRAL PRASAT |

Before founding his new capital, Yashovarman had to ensure a sufficient supply of water to enable the cultivated areas to be extended. Emulating his father, the new king therefore built another reservoir called Yashodharatataka, known as the East Baray. It was 23,000 feet long and 5900 feet wide, and was supplied by the Siem Reap river. The river was partly turned into a canal, which formed the eastern moat of Yashovarman's new capital, Yashodharapura (the city that brings glory). This was the first of a series of urban settlements built in the area generically known as Angkor, a corruption of the Sanskrit term nagara (city), so called because it was an emblematic city, the capital of the kingdom.

Yashodharapura, which measured two and a half miles long per side, was one of the largest cities in the world at the time (the ninth century). Enclosed by walls and moats, it definitely included paddy fields and cultivated fields. It was accessed from four axial entrances, crossed by four avenues over 30 feet wide, and lined with canals and water reserves, of which there were apparently hundreds. The city was built around a natural hill about 200 feet high, destined to be the site of the temple of the devaraja to which axial avenues led. Although there is no trace left of it, the Royal Palace probably stood to the north of the temple and must have had a triumphal avenue parallel to the axial one.

The **Phnom Bakheng** hill was therefore exploited between 889 and 907 to build the mountain temple of the same name, which was situated in the middle of a rectangular reservoir measuring 2,133 by 1,430 feet, and surrounded by three enclosure walls with axial entrances surmounted by gopuras.

The access avenue ran through the gopura of the innermost enclosure wall, which measures approximately 625 by 400 feet, and then between two libraries to the temple pyramid. The pyramid consisted of five terraces of decreasing height excavated in the rock of the hill and covered with sandstone, with four axial staircases flanked by tall buttresses with lions on top. The impressive square structure measures 249 feet square at the base and 154 at the summit and is 43 feet high. There are 12 sandstone shrines on each terrace, four at the corners, and one on either side of each staircase, all facing east.

Five prasat, or sanctuary towers, also made entirely of sandstone, and all with four real doors, stand on the fifth terrace, a platform 102 feet square which is just over five feet tall, and are arranged in a quincunx pattern (four at the corners and one in the middle). The central prasat, which is the largest one, housed the linga Yashodhareshvara (the lord who brings glory) and, like the other four, now lacks a superstructure. The decoration of the octagonal pillars is simple and stylized; even the architraves are more modest than the earlier ones at Hariharalaya. The tangled plant decoration on the pillars and the niches containing the devatas at the sides of the doors is particularly attractive. The artists obtained a clearer, more elegant relief effect by carving and engraving the sandstone directly rather than the stucco.

The structure of the Bakheng, like the other mountain temples, represents Mount Meru rising from the cosmic sea, but also includes far subtler and more complex magical/esoteric symbolism, which has been studied by J. Filliozat and B.P. Groslier in particular. At Bakheng, a total of 108 prasat symbolically rotate around the central one (44 at the base, 60 on the terraces, and four on the summit). This number symbolises the totality of the universe and is also the result of multiplying 27, the days of the sidereal month, by four, the phases of the moon (new moon, crescent moon, full moon, and waning moon). Shiva has 108 principal names and the mala, the Indian crown-rosary, has 108 beads.

The central prasat constitutes the sum of all the others and, as its cell houses the linga, it symbolises the bindu, the instant when space and time, and therefore the universe, originated. The bindu is the first manifestation of the Absolute as Prince and the linga is its icon. However, both allude equally to the absorption of the manifest world which returns to its source and dissolves in it. The central prasat, the supreme peak of Mount Meru, is the beginning and end of the construction and the symbol of the ordering power that descends to earth, radiating from the cell, and of its guarantor (the king) who, on his death, ascends to heaven in deified form.

If the distribution of the other prasat is analyzed, it can be seen that there are 12 small towers on each of the five terraces of the pyramid for a total of 60. There are 12 signs of the zodiac in Indian tradition and 12 animals in the Chinese astrological cycle, by which the Khmer were also inspired. Moreover, the planet Jupiter takes roughly 12 years (precisely 11 years, 314 days, 20 hours, and 25 minutes) to orbit the Sun and cross the entire zodiac, which the sun does in one year. The cycle of Jupiter (Brihaspati in Indian astronomy), which lasted 60 solar years and was divided into five 12-year cycles, was also used in the Khmer region. Bakheng, with its five terraces and their 60 prasat, therefore appears to reproduce a complete year of Jupiter using the duodenary (12) and sexagesimal (60) counting systems.

In addition to these calculations, there was a mythical/religious symbolism: the seven levels of the Bakheng—namely the base, the five terraces, and the platform of the quincunx—symbolize the levels of Mount Meru and the saptaloka (the seven heavens of the Hindu gods). Moreover, there are 33 main deities, and the particular position of the towers and their different sizes is such that an observer standing in the middle of any side, therefore in correspondence with the cardinal points, could always see exactly 33 prasat. Mount Meru houses the court of the gods, and its

*164-165 The prasats on the terraces of the Bakheng temple, which are mostly intact, provide some complete examples of temple structure. The roof consists of diminishing tiers ending in a finial in the shape of a vase on an upside-down lotus blossom, as seen in the two buildings on the left.*

*165 top The mountain temple of Baksei Chamkrong was built in the tenth century by Harshavarman I to honor his parents and contained the statues of Shiva and the Devi (the Goddess).*

*165 center During the reign of Yashovarman inscriptions were often digraphic, i.e. written in two alphabets of Indian origin, Pallava (southern) and Nagari (northern), as demonstrated by the entrance piers of Baksei Chamkrong temple.*

*165 bottom The main prasat of the Bakheng temple frames the niches of the devatas in an elegant floral decoration.*

## ANGKOR: The Mountain Temples of Yashodharapura

reproduction in the middle of the city of men confirms the king's desire to build his capital in the divine image. This is emphasized by the inscriptions, which compare Yashovarman with Mount Meru, with Indra, king of the gods, and with Brahma, Vishnu, and Shiva, the deities of the Trimurti.

Yashovarman is also believed to have founded around 100 ashrama (hermitages), whose location gives some idea of the size of the kingdom. The most northerly one was situated near Wat Phu in present-day Laos, the most southerly one at the southernmost tip of Cambodia, the most easterly one in the Cambodian region of Phnom Rung, and the most westerly one in the Thai region of Chantaburi. The foundation of the ashrams was not only an act of religious piety, but a way of controlling the country and strengthening the king's authority, as they constituted communities of priests and hermits dependent on and therefore loyal to the crown. Foundation stelae indicate the existence of the ashrams but no other trace of them has been found, as the buildings were made of perishable materials. **Baksei Chamkrong**, the small mountain temple to the north-east of Phnom Bakheng, was commenced by Yashovarman's son, Harshavarman I and is believed to have been completed by his successor, Rajendravarman.

However, not all experts agree with these attributions. The name given to the temple by the local people, which means "bird that shelters under its wings," is associated with a mythical event said to have occurred in the area: a Khmer king who was about to be captured by his enemies was saved by a great bird that spread its wings to shield him.

Baksei Chamkrong consists of a small building on a square pyramid that has four laterite terraces measuring 89 feet square at the base and 49 at the summit and is 43 feet tall. The single prasat, on a molded sandstone base, which adds another 36 feet to its height, is made of brick and stucco, with the door frames and false openings made of sandstone as usual. The roof consists of three tiers which are decreasing reproductions of the façade. Four axial staircases with stout buttresses lead to the summit of the temple, which was once surrounded by the usual enclosure wall and whose entrance was surmounted by a gopura.

*166 top According to an inscription, Prasat Kravan, a ground-level temple probably built by a courtier, was consecrated in 921 to the god Vishnu, portrayed here on the north wall of the central prasat between two worshippers, riding his mount Garuda, which was part human, part bird of prey.*

*166 bottom left and right The north prasat is dedicated to Shiva's wife Lakshmi, portrayed on the wall facing the entrance, surrounded by worshippers kneeling in prayer, as shown by the detail in the left-hand picture.*

*166-167 Prasat Kravan has been rebuilt with the anastylosis technique; it was dismantled and reassembled in accordance with a meticulous reconstruction and consolidation plan. Those parts which had to be replaced blend in harmoniously with the others, but are recognizable by their special markings.*

# ANGKOR: *The Mountain Temples of Yashodharapura*

At Yashodharapura ground-level temples were built as well as mountain temples. One example is **Prasat Kravan** (the cardamom temple), also attributed to the period of Harshavarman I but perhaps built by a courtier. The five brick prasat aligned on a platform overlook a small reservoir and face east, like nearly all the Angkor temples. The roof of the central tower has been reconstructed with the anastylosis technique and is divided into four diminishing tiers, separated by pediments which emphasize their vertical height. Inside, the temple hosts some magnificent bas-reliefs, once covered with multicolored paint, portraying various aspects of Vishnu. The Lord of Providence, second member of the Trimurti, is portrayed on the left-hand wall while performing the three paces in the form of Vamana (the dwarf), an appearance taken on by Vishnu to humiliate the arrogant King Bali, who believed himself to be the master of the universe. Vishnu appeared to the king in the guise of a dwarf and asked for a plot of land that measured three paces as a gift. King Bali haughtily granted his request. Vishnu then returned to his own shape; with his first pace he crossed the earth, with the second, the atmosphere, and with the third, the sky, acquiring the Triple World and relegating the evil man to the underworld. On the right-hand wall of the cell, Vishnu is portrayed on his mount Garuda, and on the central wall he is shown with eight arms, in all his majesty. Lakshmi, his wife, appears in the northern prasat holding the discus, an attribute of her husband, together with the trident, symbol of Shiva, confirming the religious syncretism of the Khmer.

After the Koh Ker interval, the Khmer kings returned to the Angkor area. Rajendravarman, the cousin of Harshavarman II, restored and completed the Baksei Chamkrong.

He consecrated it in 948 and installed in it a golden statue of Parameshvara, the posthumous name of Jayavarman II, whom Rajendravarman wished to emulate. The new king chose the south side of the East Baray for his capital and had a canal dug to convey some of the water from the Siem Reap river.

Many of Rajendravarman's buildings were the work of Kavindrarimathana, a highly versatile person who was commander-in-chief of the army, a poet, and an architect, as indicated by his name, which means "king of poets and destroyer of enemies."

*167 bottom  The bas-reliefs of Prasat Kravan are among the rare examples found inside a cell. On the south wall of the cell of the central* prasat, *Vishnu, framed by a* torana *(triumphal arch), is shown performing the three steps which made the gods the rulers of the earth, atmosphere, and heavens. The temple is dedicated to Vishnu in his manifestation as Trialokyanatha (lord of the three worlds).*

Kavindrarimathana's first great creation was the **East Mebon** temple, built on an artificial island in the middle of the East Baray which measured 394 feet long per side. It was consecrated in 953 to Rajendreshvara, the "Lord of Rajendra," and is not exactly a mountain temple because although its pyramid has three terraces it is not very tall. The temple, for which all the currently available materials were used (stone, brick, laterite, and stucco), could only be reached by boat, and four jetties flanked by lions project from the outer enclosure wall. The presence of the jetties prevented the cross-shaped *gopuras* from projecting away from the building, so they were placed inside the walls of the second enclosure and slightly recessed.

A continuous row of rectangular buildings, which once had double-pitched wooden roofs, runs along the walls beyond the entrances. The pyramid, which was wholly artificial, stands in the innermost enclosure. On the second terrace there are eight square brick prasat, dedicated to the eight aspects of Shiva, and five rectangular buildings, four of which are in the corners. Magnificent monolithic elephants stand on the edges of the first and second terraces. Five **prasat** arranged in a quincunx shape, the central one of which was on a higher base, stand on the upper platform, which measures 100 feet square. The holes in the walls demonstrate generous use of stucco, and the gods Indra Skanda, son of Shiva and leader of his armies, and Shiva himself appear on the sandstone architraves.

In the same year (953) Kavindrarimathana, who was a Buddhist, built **Bat Chum**, consisting of three brick towers on a reservoir, each of which bears an inscription lauding the great architect composed by different authors. To the north of the temple Kavindrarimathana excavated Srah Srang, a small reservoir measuring roughly 2,300 by 1,150 feet, which was later modified.

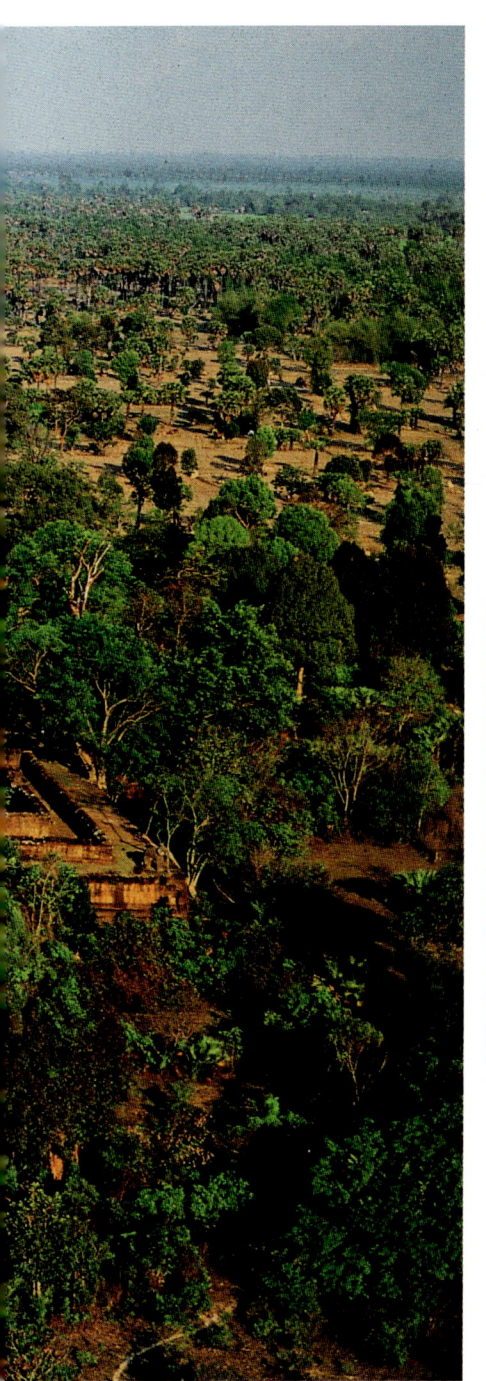

*168-169 The East Mebon temple stood in the middle of the Yashodharatataka baray, which supplied the city of Yashodharapura with water. It was bordered to the east by the canalized Siem Reap River and on the other sides by moats 650 feet wide, enclosed between parallel dykes on which raised roads were built.*

*169 top and bottom The Mebon temple was commissioned in 953 by Rajendravarman and built by Kavindrarimathana, the only Khmer architect whose name is known today. The building combines the architectural characteristics of the mountain temple with the dedicatory function of shrines to the ancestors, as shown in these photos. The foundation stela records that two statues of Shiva and Parvati in the likeness of Rajendravarman's parents were erected there.*

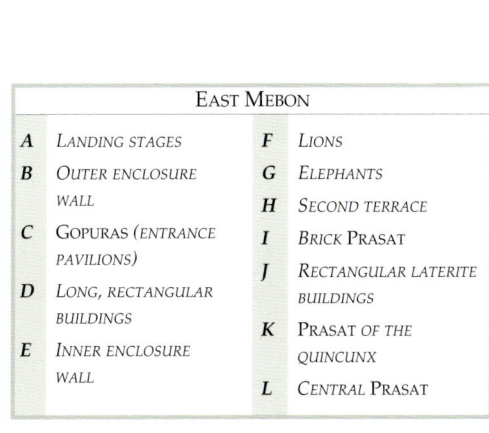

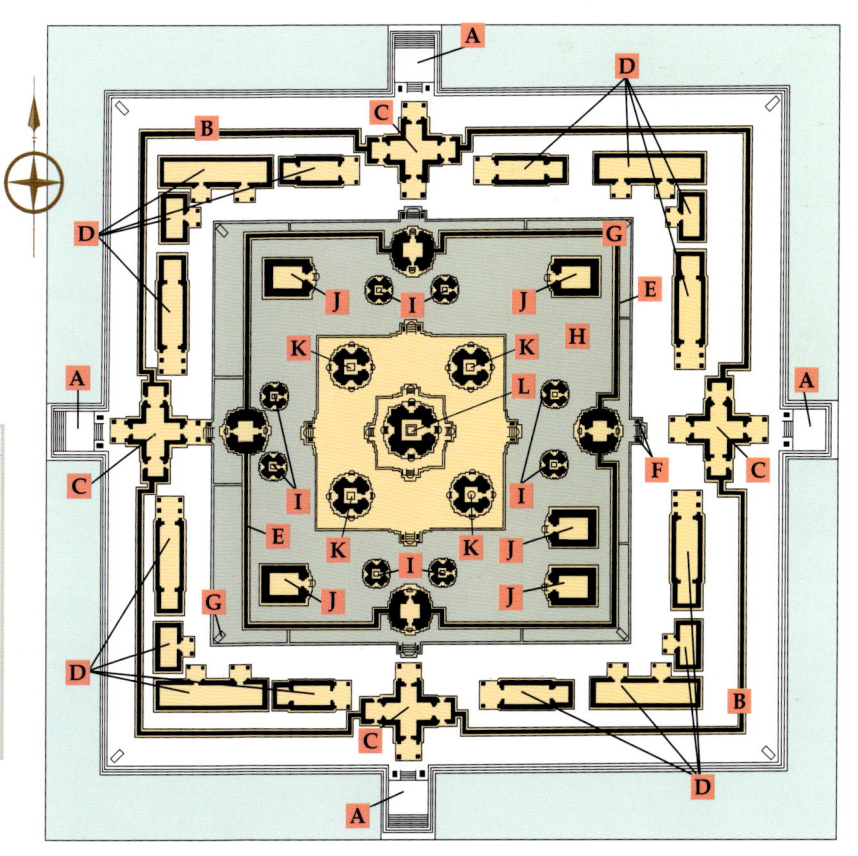

| East Mebon | | | |
|---|---|---|---|
| A | Landing stages | F | Lions |
| B | Outer enclosure wall | G | Elephants |
| C | Gopuras (entrance pavilions) | H | Second terrace |
| | | I | Brick Prasat |
| D | Long, rectangular buildings | J | Rectangular laterite buildings |
| E | Inner enclosure wall | K | Prasat of the quincunx |
| | | L | Central Prasat |

However, the masterpiece of Rajendravarman's architect was the **Pre Rup**, one of the most important mountain temples, which marked the changeover from the pre-classical to the classical period. Pre Rup, which perhaps formed the center of a new capital, was built on an artificial laterite hill and was consecrated in 961 or early 962. Its name, which means "body-turning," refers to a funerary practice in which the shape of a body was recreated several times with the ashes of the deceased and was turned to face in different directions. The name derives from what was thought to be a sarcophagus at the temple entrance but must actually have been the pedestal of Shiva's mount, the bull Nandin; like the vast majority of the other temples, Pre Rup was dedicated to Shiva.

The temple, which was surrounded by two rectangular enclosure walls of different levels, was built on an embankment and consisted of a pyramid with three laterite terraces of different heights, crowned by the brick quincunx, with the central prasat standing on two more terraces. As always, a moat which symbolizes the cosmic sea runs alongside the outer laterite enclosure wall, which measures 394 by 367 feet. The four axial access pavilions, surmounted by gopuras, consist of a central chamber surrounded by four rooms, each preceded by a portico, a structure which was to be very popular during the classical period. There were five brick towers on the eastern façade of the temple between the first and second enclosures, and rectangular buildings running parallel to the wall on the other three sides.

The inner, or first, enclosure was entered through four small gopuras. Here again, nine long, rectangular brick buildings, once roofed with a tiled wooden framework, run along the wall. Continuous perimeter galleries were soon to develop from these elongated structures of unknown function. Beyond the east gopura stands the famous Nandin base, with two libraries parallel to it. In the northeastern corner of the enclosure there is a small laterite kiosk with a false corbelled ceiling, which once housed a stela. The Pre Rup foundation stela contains one of the longest Sanskrit compositions, containing 298 verses.

The three-terraced laterite pyramid, whose sides are each 164 feet long and which is 39 feet high, has 12 small prasat containing lingas on the first level. The quincunx towers on the summit

# ANGKOR: The Mountain Temples of Yashodharapura

*170-171 With the building of Pre Rup, commissioned by Rajendravarman perhaps as the center of a new city or as his mausoleum, the mountain temple came to perform a dual function: it was the seat of the* devaraja *with whom the living king identified, and his funeral dwelling after his death.*

*171 top The central* prasat *of the quincunx that crowns Pre Rup stands on another double base. The stuccoed brick towers have sandstone doors framed by exquisite octagonal colonettes.*

*171 bottom The kiosk built with large blocks of laterite in the northeast corner of the first enclosure probably contained the foundation stela, which was found not far away.*

### PRE RUP

- **A** OUTER ENCLOSURE WALL
- **B** GOPURAS (ENTRANCE PAVILIONS)
- **C** PRASATS
- **D** LONG, RECTANGULAR BUILDINGS
- **E** INNER ENCLOSURE WALL
- **F** BASE OF NANDIN
- **G** KIOSK OF THE STELA
- **H** "LIBRARIES"
- **I** PRASATS OF THE LINGAS ON THE FIRST TERRACE
- **J** PRASATS OF THE QUINCUNX
- **K** CENTRAL PRASAT

are made of brick, and the deities in the niches were once covered with a stucco made of sand and lime. The decoration on the sandstone architraves and doors is of excellent workmanship, and the octagonal colonettes that frame the entrances feature some sophisticated ornamentation. The central *prasat* housed the linga Rajendrabhadreshvara in which the sovereign was associated with Shiva Bhadreshvara, the ancient tutelary deity of Chenla. The linga Rajendravarmeshvara was honored in the southeast tower, and Vishvarupa, a legendary ancestor of the king, Jayadevi or Jayendradevi, Rajendravarman's aunt and Jayavarman IV's wife, and Harshavarman II, Jayadevi's son and Rajendravarman's predecessor, in the others.

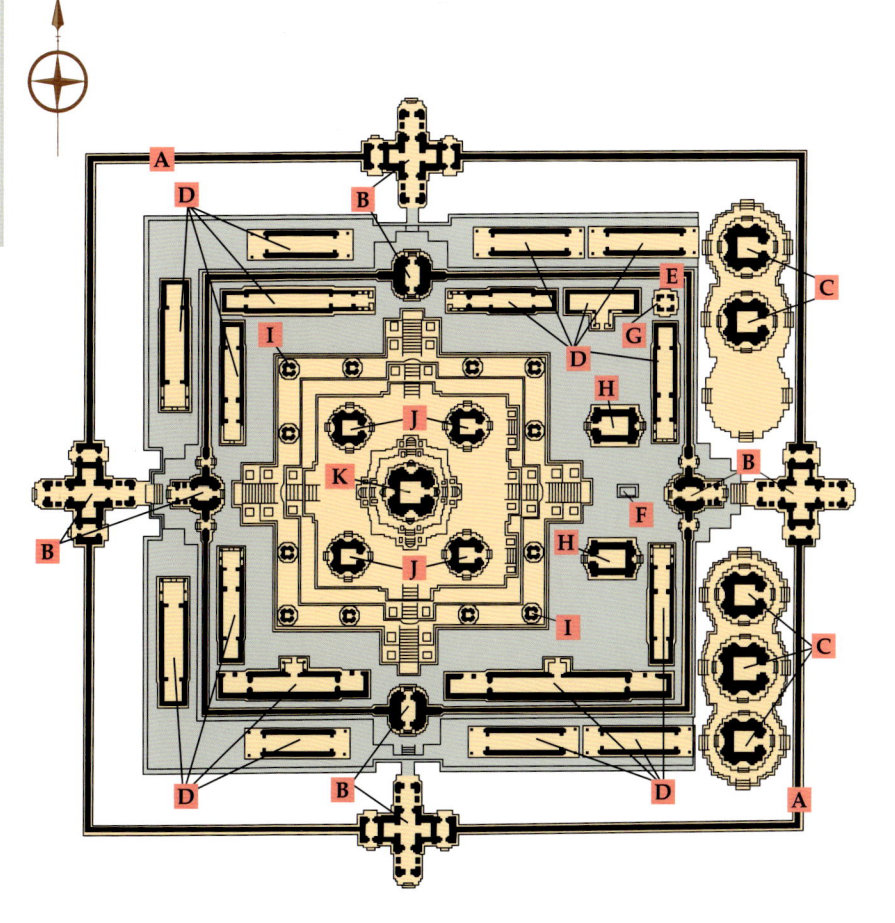

*172 top Despite the inscriptions on the walls of Ta Keo, which include the genealogies of Brahmans who performed important functions at court, its attribution is still doubtful.*

*172 bottom left The first perimeter gallery was built at Ta Keo to connect the earlier long, rectangular buildings.*

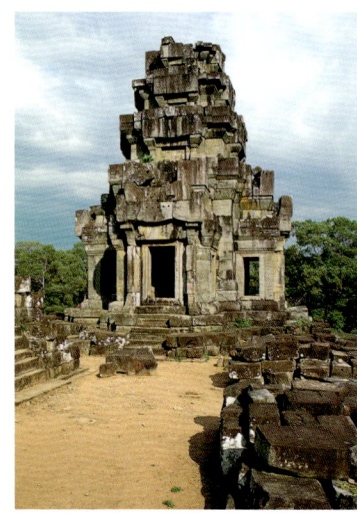

*172 bottom right The* prasats *of Ta Keo face towards the four cardinal points, with foreparts illuminated by real windows, thus inaugurating the Greek cross plan, which was to become common later.*

*172-173 The impressive, severe Ta Keo was the first mountain temple to be built entirely of sandstone. It was started in 975 but never finished. According to local tradition it was struck by lightning, a sign of the gods' disfavor. Suryavarman I apparently gave it to his guru Yogishvarapandita, who was of royal descent.*

Rajendravarman's son, Jayavarman V, built a new capital on the west side of the East Baray, which he called Jayendranagari (city of Indra the conqueror). Its mountain temple, the **Ta Keo**, was begun in 975 but never finished. Preceded to the east by a processional avenue lined with two rows of pillars, it consists of a huge rectangular laterite pyramid entirely covered with sandstone and is one of the most attractive examples of its kind. The first level, built on a plinth five feet eight inches tall, consists of an enclosure wall measuring 400 by 348 feet and a blind wall with axial gopuras, the main one of which faces east. Two rectangular buildings preceded by porticoes run parallel to the east wall.

The second level rises to a height of 18 feet 9 inches and has an innovative feature, namely a continuous gallery measuring 263 by 246 feet with a false vaulted ceiling of corbelled bricks, blind colonetted windows on the outer side, and open colonetted windows on the inner side. The gopuras are incorporated in the walls, at the corners of which angular towers begin to emerge. The gallery, which was formed by combining the previous rectangular buildings, is inaccessible, which suggests that it had a purely symbolic function. Inside the enclosure two rectangular buildings run along the east wall, and two libraries flank the access avenue. To make room for these buildings, the east side of the terrace is wider than the others. The libraries have an interesting structure: they have a single room inside, but from the outside, because of the two lowered half-barrel vaults resting on the perimeter walls, they appear to have a nave and two aisles.

The pyramid, which is recessed to the west, has three molded terraces, measures 200 feet long per side at the base and 154 at the summit, and is 46 feet tall. The prasat, arranged in a quincunx, are made entirely of greywacke, a kind of very hard feldspathic sandstone. They had a cross-shaped plan, and the cell was preceded by four porticoes. In the central tower, which stood on a double cross-shaped base, there are four vestibules between the cell and the porticoes. The roof, which consists of four gradually diminishing tiers, culminates 148 feet above ground level, and is impressive and almost cyclopic in its bare, unfinished state.

Work on the Ta Keo probably continued during the reign of Jayavarman V's successor,

## ANGKOR: The Mountain Temples of Yashodharapura

Jayaviravarman or, as some experts believe, may actually have been started by him. The building of the north **Kheang** is attributed to Jayaviravarman; it contains inscriptions by him, but they cast no light on the use of the building. It is a rectangular structure measuring 131 feet long and 15 feet wide, with sandstone walls five feet thick which were open on both sides, and probably had a tiled roof. Some small rooms give onto the annexed courtyard, which is surrounded by a laterite wall; however, they were not storerooms as the recent name Kheang suggests.

| TA KEO |
|---|
| A  OUTER ENCLOSURE WALL |
| B  GOPURA |
| C  LONG, RECTANGULAR BUILDINGS |
| D  PERIMETER GALLERY |
| E  "LIBRARIES" |
| F  HALLS |
| G  PYRAMID |
| H  PRASATS OF THE QUINCUNX |
| I  CENTRAL PRASAT |

173

Suryavarman I, who was probably a usurper, settled in Yashodharapura in 1010 and was consecrated king two years later. The building of the gigantic West Baray, which was over 7,000 feet wide, began immediately, and the king located his court in the area still called the Royal Palace. **Phimeanakas**, about which experts disagree, stands within this enclosure, which measures approximately 820 by 2,000 feet and has a gopura entrance. No trace of dwellings survives there because the king's palace was made of perishable materials. This small rectangular temple, measuring 115 by 92 feet at the base, 100 by 75 at the summit, and 39 feet high, is built on a three-story laterite pyramid crowned with a single prasat, made partly from blocks of sandstone. The gallery that surrounds the last terrace, which is interrupted by real and false windows, was the first to be wholly built in sandstone, including the roof, which consists of three rows of projecting stones with a closing row above. The bell-shaped extrados is patterned to imitate tiles. The name Phimeanakas is a corruption of the Sanskrit terms vimana (palace of the gods) and akasha (heaven). According to Zhou Daguan, it was made of gold. This presumably means that the dome of the temple was gilded, a feature perhaps borrowed from the architecture of the Mon kingdoms where buildings were often covered with gold. Zhou Daguan also recounts that the king coupled every night in the Phimeanakas with the nagini, the incarnation of the genius loci, who was half woman, half snake.

Suryavarman also built the oldest nucleus of the temple of Suryagiri or Suryaparvata (Mountain of the Sun God), now called **Phnom Chisor**, 37 miles south of Phnom Penh, where the king had erected a linga which probably marked the southernmost border of the kingdom. A spectacular stairway with 400 steps leads to the summit, and buildings of different periods stand on the platform, which measures 330 by 260 feet. The

*174-175 The Royal Palace, which was commenced by Rajendravarman, completed by Suryavarman I, and renovated by later kings, was surrounded by a laterite wall 16 feet tall that enclosed a 42-acre area, divided into quarters, separated by walls, and interspersed with reservoirs. The houses, which stood on stone bases, consisted of wooden pavilions. The famous oath in which officials swore in the presence of the sacred flame to obey no king other than Suryavarman I is carved on the wall of the eastern gopura, the largest of five which led into the palace enclosure.*

*175 top The lingayoni, the symbol of Shiva and his wife Parvati, symbolizes the mystery of the One that becomes two and the duality that merges into unity. The base with the yoni and the drain for ablutions, together with the hole into which the linga was inserted by means of a pivot, can be seen at Phimeanakas.*

*175 center Phimeanakas, the palatine temple, was built in the eleventh century on the site of an earlier shrine, as demonstrated by the reuse of older material, and later renovated. The single-flight scenic staircase runs between buttresses wulched over by lions.*

*175 bottom Two "spirit houses," models of homes dedicated to the neak-ta (tutelary deities), can be seen at the base of one of the gopuras of the Royal Palace. Animism is the oldest form of popular worship in Cambodia and is still the most common today.*

main temple, made of laterite and brick with the doors and niches framed with sandstone, is surrounded by the ruins of a wide gallery.

Udayadityavarman II, the son or close relative of Suryavarman I, built yet another Yashodharapura and completed the huge reservoir called the West Baray begun by Suryavarman. The **West Mebon** temple, which stood in the middle of the reservoir, has almost entirely disappeared. The temple was dedicated to Vishnu Anantashayin (which means "reclining on the serpent Ananta") as demonstrated by the discovery of part of a huge bronze statue of the god, now in Phnom Penh Museum.

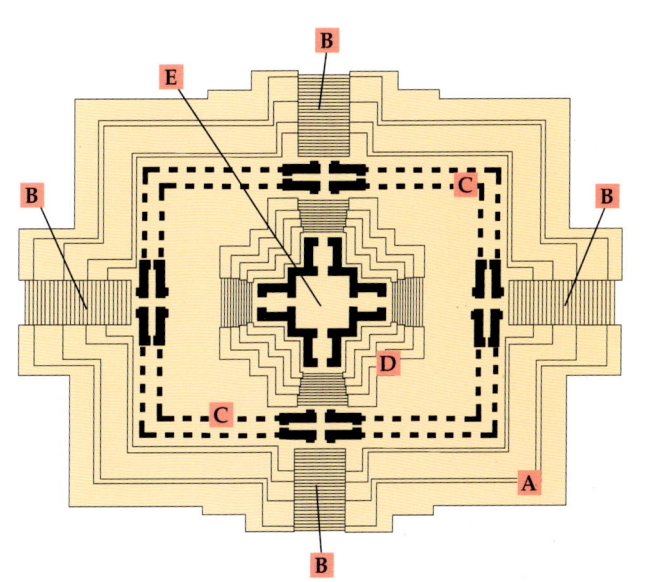

| PHIMEANAKAS |
|---|
| **A** PYRAMID |
| **B** AXIAL STAIRCASES |
| **C** PERIMETER GALLERY |
| **D** BASE |
| **E** CENTRAL PRASAT |

*176 top  One of the most interesting features of the Baphuon temple is the avenue on stilts, interrupted three-quarters of the way along by a pavilion that originally constituted the access gopura.*

*176 bottom  There is a reservoir on the south side of the same pavilion, and there was probably another to the north. Water was a fundamental element in Khmer architecture.*

*177  The Baphuon collapsed as result of a series of construction defects and is currently being rebuilt. The gopura of the outer enclosure, roofed with an unusual dome structure, has already been completed using the anastylosis technique.*

### BAPHUON

- **A**  RECONSTRUCTED GOPURA
- **B**  AVENUE ON STILTS
- **C**  PAVILION
- **D**  RESERVOIR
- **E**  INNER ENCLOSURE WALL
- **F**  GOPURA
- **G**  "LIBRARIES"
- **H**  PYRAMID

The center of Udayadityavarman II's capital was constituted by the exceptionally large **Baphuon** mountain temple. Sadly, the architectural aspirations of the Khmer were not matched by their engineering skills, and the huge weight of the galleries, gopuras, and corner towers on the terraces of the Baphuon caused its collapse. The builders had tried to prevent this from happening by fitting staples between the blocks and wooden reinforcing beams inserted into hollowed-out blocks of stone. It was this latter expedient that doomed the temple: when the wood rotted, the stone in which it was housed could not support the weight above. Extensive anastylosis work is now under way and will continue for several years.

The Baphuon temple is surrounded by a rectangular enclosure measuring 1,400 by 410 feet, unusually made of sandstone. It consists of a pyramid that measures 427 by 341 feet at the base, 138 by 118 feet at the summit, and is 79 feet tall. If the crowning prasat is included, the total height of the temple probably reached 164 feet.

An avenue 564 feet long, raised more than three feet above ground on a walkway consisting of a triple row of colonettes, which evidently acted as stilts, led to the temple. Halfway along the route stood a cross-shaped pavilion to the south of which there is a reservoir with sandstone steps, and there was probably another one to the north.

The gopura which gives access to the first level, bounded by a perimeter gallery with corner pavilions, has been entirely reconstructed with the anastylosis technique, and has a very interesting tripartite structure. A square central chamber flanked by wings divided into two rooms, one inside the other, giving a telescopic effect, is preceded by a twin vestibule towards the outside and a single one towards the inside. The side chambers have a false vault, while the central one is surmounted by another smaller storey crowned with an unusual dome with a square base, known as the "domical vault" or "cloister vault," which ends with a lotus blossom-shaped finial. The gallery into which this magnificent gopura led had blind windows in the outer wall and real windows in the inner wall, all screened by colonettes; the roof must have been a tiled wooden structure.

The ruins of four libraries stand on this first level of the Baphuon, two on the east side and two on the west, and the pairs of buildings were probably connected by a raised walkway. The second level formed a double platform and was crowned by a narrow sandstone gallery with a pseudo-vault consisting of four rows of stone blocks closed by two adjacent blocks, with real windows on both sides. There are some magnificent bas-relief panels here, which cannot be seen at present due to the reconstruction work.

The third level was also divided into a double platform ending in a gallery. Between the second and third levels there are signs of stairways in the corners that lead to the corner towers but they are in any event unusable. A single cross-shaped prasat, the structure of which has yet to be discovered, stood on the summit.

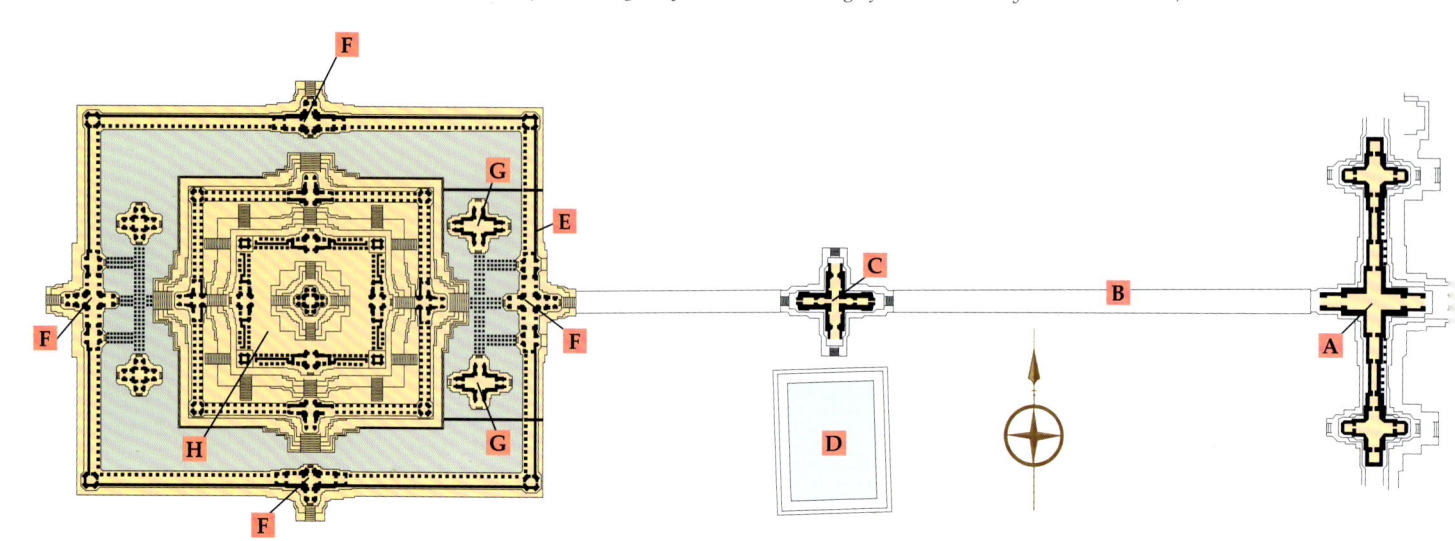

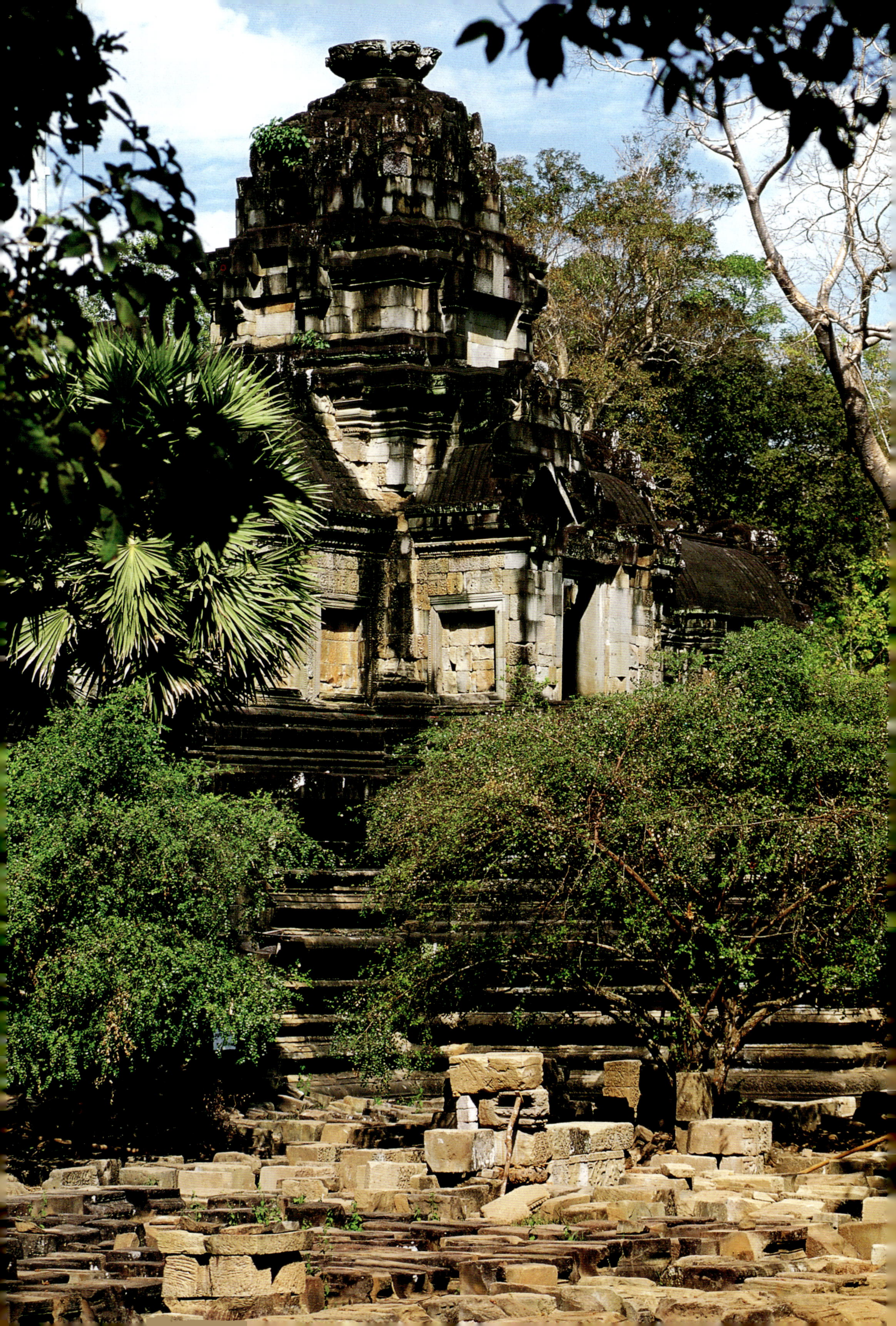

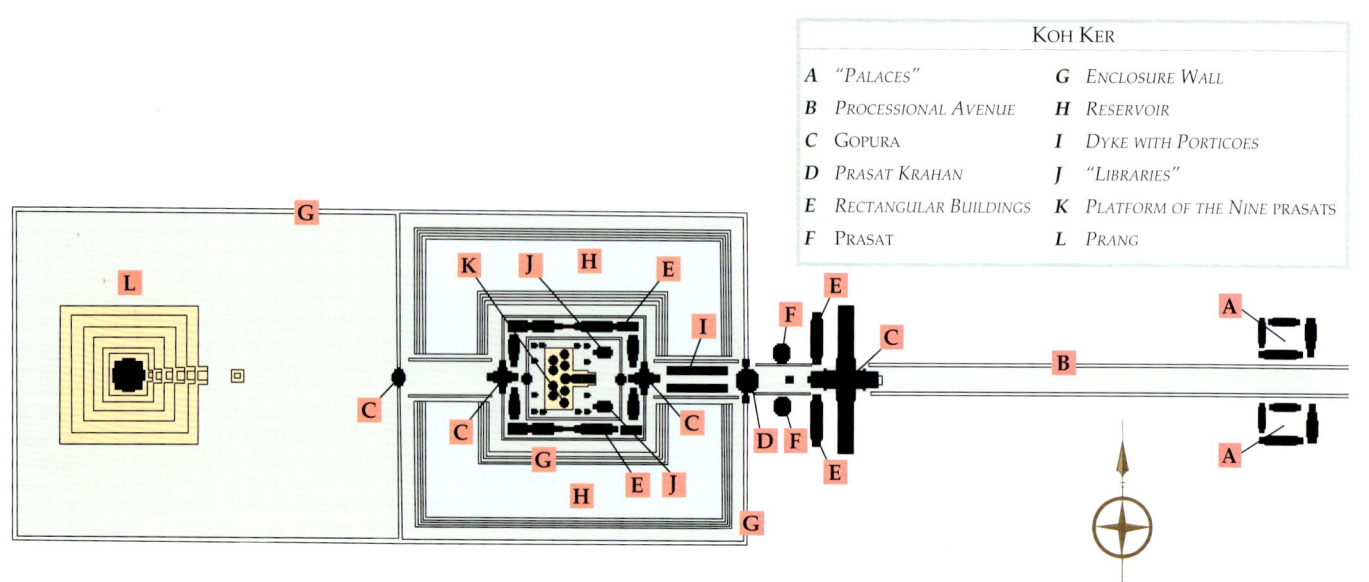

| | KOH KER | | |
|---|---|---|---|
| A | "Palaces" | G | Enclosure Wall |
| B | Processional Avenue | H | Reservoir |
| C | Gopura | I | Dyke with Porticoes |
| D | Prasat Krahan | J | "Libraries" |
| E | Rectangular Buildings | K | Platform of the Nine prasats |
| F | Prasat | L | Prang |

# KOH KER
## The Short-lived Capital

In 921, during the reign of Harshavarman I, a maternal uncle of his rebelled against the legitimate king and had himself crowned with the name of Jayavarman IV in his fief, situated 53 miles north-east of Angkor. As he would not or could not move to Yashodharapura, he chose his birthplace, Chok Gargyar, now Koh Ker, to be the capital of his kingdom and built a baray measuring 3,900 by 1,800 feet, called the Rahal, by exploiting a depression in the terrain and a nearby river. The Rahal was partly excavated in rock, and the laterite lock which controlled the outflow of water to irrigate the paddy fields still survives. The capital had an area of 14 square miles, and part of its enclosure wall can still be seen to the north and west of the Rahal.

There are numerous buildings at Koh Ker but they are sadly in a very poor state of repair. However, a visit to the **Prasat Thom** complex, dedicated to Tribhuvaneshvara (lord of the triple world) is worth a visit because of its innovative characteristics. The desire for a temple which reproduced the sacred mountain had required up to this point a construction that was tightly amassed around a center and built upwards. Probably as a result of the increasing complexity of ceremonial procedures and the inclusion of parades, a series of axially rising structures was placed in front of the palace of the gods. Prasat Thom is situated on an east-west axis 2,000 feet long and is divided into three architectural blocks: the processional avenue with its innovative approach buildings, the triple enclosure with the shrine to the ancestors, and the mountain temple at the end of the route.

The long processional avenue is flanked at the start by two quadrangles, improperly called "palaces." They consisted of long buildings, each divided into three rooms, with pillared porticoes and windows screened by colonettes, which surrounded a kind of patio. After about 590 feet a huge cross-shaped sandstone gopura extends to the north and south with two galleries around 70 feet long, which have a solid wall on the east side and a series of porticoes on the west and must have had a tiled roof laid on a wooden framework. Immediately after this there are two elongated buildings positioned perpendicular to the access avenue, followed by two prasat. Not far away is the third enclosure wall, made of laterite,

*178-179 At Koh Ker, which was the capital of the Khmer kingdom between 921 and 944, architects experimented with new construction solutions, including the use of centering to facilitate the installation of false ceilings. The quoins were hollowed out and specially shaped to receive the supporting beams. This expedient proved disastrous because the hollow stones were unable to support the weight resting on them when the wood rotted.*

*179 top Many of the buildings at Koh Ker had pitched roofs consisting of tiles laid on a wooden framework. The gable was made of stone which also demonstrates the appearance of the first buildings with foreparts.*

*179 bottom The Prang, a seven-terraced pyramid, emerges from the jungle that concealed the ruins of Koh Ker. The largest linga temple in Kambuja was to have stood on the pyramid, but it was never completed.*

*180 top To suit the landscape, the enclosure wall of Koh Ker consisted of earth ramparts bordered by moats at some points. The temples were surrounded by walls, and some* gopuras *(entrance portals) were transformed for the first time into shrines called* prasats.

*180 center The central figure in the sandstone architraves is particularly important, emphasizing the symmetrical arrangement of the ornamental features.*

# KOH KER: *The Short-lived Capital*

the entrance to which is a full-scale temple in its own right. This building, known as Prasat Kraham, was probably a later addition. It had four floors and was the tallest building at Prasat Thom after the mountain temple. A few fragments of the huge statue of a dancing Shiva it contained have survived.

After Prasat Kraham, there is a reservoir measuring 427 feet square, lined with two interesting balustrades. The balustrades consist of two seven-headed nagas alongside Garuda, the mythical creature, part man and part vulture, who was Vishnu's mount and the sworn enemy of serpents. The combination of naga and garuda became one of the typical ornamental motifs of Khmer architecture. The avenue that runs along the dyke is lined with two rows of porticoes, a design not found in any other temple complex in Kambuja. A second laterite wall measuring 213 by 184 feet surrounds the embankment on which the prasat stand. A cross-shaped gopura leads immediately to another smaller one in the first sandstone enclosure wall. A continuous row of elongated laterite buildings with porticoes and colonetted windows, once roofed with a tiled wooden framework, stands in the narrow space between the two walls, which is around 70 feet wide. Although they are not properly joined together, these buildings constitute the prototype for the continuous perimeter galleries that were to develop later, reaching their peak at Angkor Wat.

Inside the first enclosure, there are two libraries in the right- and left-hand corners, while the other half of the

*180 bottom In Khmer art, the ornamentation of the colonettes of the door jambs is hierarchical; in other words, it varies according to the building, reaching the height of complexity at the main entrance of the temple. This photo shows the octagonal colonettes of Prasat Krahan.*

*180-181 The use of brick, which was predominant in the pre-Angkor period, gradually declined in favor of sandstone. Laterite continued to be used for bases. Bricks were held together by a plant-based mortar, while stones were laid dry.*

*courtyard is occupied by a terrace with nine* prasat. *There are five in the first row and four in the second, which are larger and staggered. The central* prasat *is preceded by a* mandapa, *the traditional pavilion of Indian temples in which the worshippers gathered while waiting to see the god in the cell; in a way it was the counterpart of the audience chamber in the royal palace. The* mandapa, *preceded by a portico, communicates through the* antarala *(vestibule) with the* garbhagriha, *the cell of the* prasat. *Twelve smaller towers stand around the nine towers.*

*The axial route continues, passes through the two western* gopuras *in the first and second enclosures, and then crosses the reservoir on the dyke, finally reaching another enclosure wall measuring 560 by 490 feet on which the* **Prang** *mountain temple stands.*

*The architects of Jayavarman IV, probably inspired by Baksei Chamkrong, built a huge seven-story sandstone pyramid. The first story measures 203 by 210 feet and the last 56 by 56 feet, and its total height is roughly 118 feet. The base of the pyramid measuring 39 feet per side may have supported a huge* linga *shrine, according to Stierlin. The emblem of Shiva at Koh Ker must have been one of the largest in Kambuja; Parmentier believes that it was 15 feet high and weighed 24 tons. The Prang* prasat, *which was probably never finished, had a roof formed by diminishing tiers that would have brought the height of the mountain temple to 200 feet. This architectural colossus, accessible on the east side by a single-flight staircase, contains 150,000 tons of material and is one of the boldest Khmer buildings.*

*One of the typical features of the Koh Ker style is enormous size; huge blocks of stone were used for buildings and sculptures alike and their dimensions were pushed to the limit. Wooden reinforcing beams inserted in hollowed-out blocks of stone may have been first used at Koh Ker, but they proved to be a disastrous expedient because when the wood rotted, the stone that housed it could not support the pressure from above.*

*182 top  The Khmer temples were crowned with two types of finial, either an upside-down lotus blossom or a kalasha (vase), like the one shown here at Banteay Srei, which symbolized the cosmic waters from which life was born.*

*183  In the east tympanum of the south library, Ravana, the demon with a thousand heads and a thousand arms, attempts to uproot Mount Kailasa, the dwelling-place of Shiva. The god sits impassively on the summit while the terrified Parvati clings to him.*

# Banteay Srei

## The Gem of Yajnavaraha

By the tenth century, Khmer architects had made so much progress that they were ready to review their past and indulge in deliberate, sophisticated archaisms. This was the context in which the magnificent temple of Banteay Srei, rightly considered to be the gem of Angkor, was built about 12 miles northeast of the East Baray. It was planned and commissioned not by a king but by two Brahmans, Yajnavaraha and his younger brother Vishnukumara, who owned land and possessions in the area then called Ishanapura. The modern name Banteay Srei (citadel of women) seems to have been attributed to the temple by the local people, fascinated by the sensual devatas carved in the temple niches.

The complex was completed in 967 and the foundation stela, dated the following year, describes the men responsible for its construction who had royal blood, and in particular Yajnavaraha. He was a grandson of Harshavarman I and had been a purohita (chaplain) of Rajendravarman and tutor to his son, Jayavarman V, from whom he received the prestigious title vrah guru (holy spiritual master). Yajnavaraha, a cultured aesthete, wanted to build a ground-level temple that followed the purest Hindu architectural tradition and was therefore inspired by Indian models but at the same time reflected the indigenous structure of the shrines to the ancestors designed a century earlier at Hariharalaya. In the meantime, however, there had been the interlude of Koh Ker and its Prasat Thom, where the layout of the ground-level temple on the longitudinal axis had been "elongated" into a series of approach buildings and features.

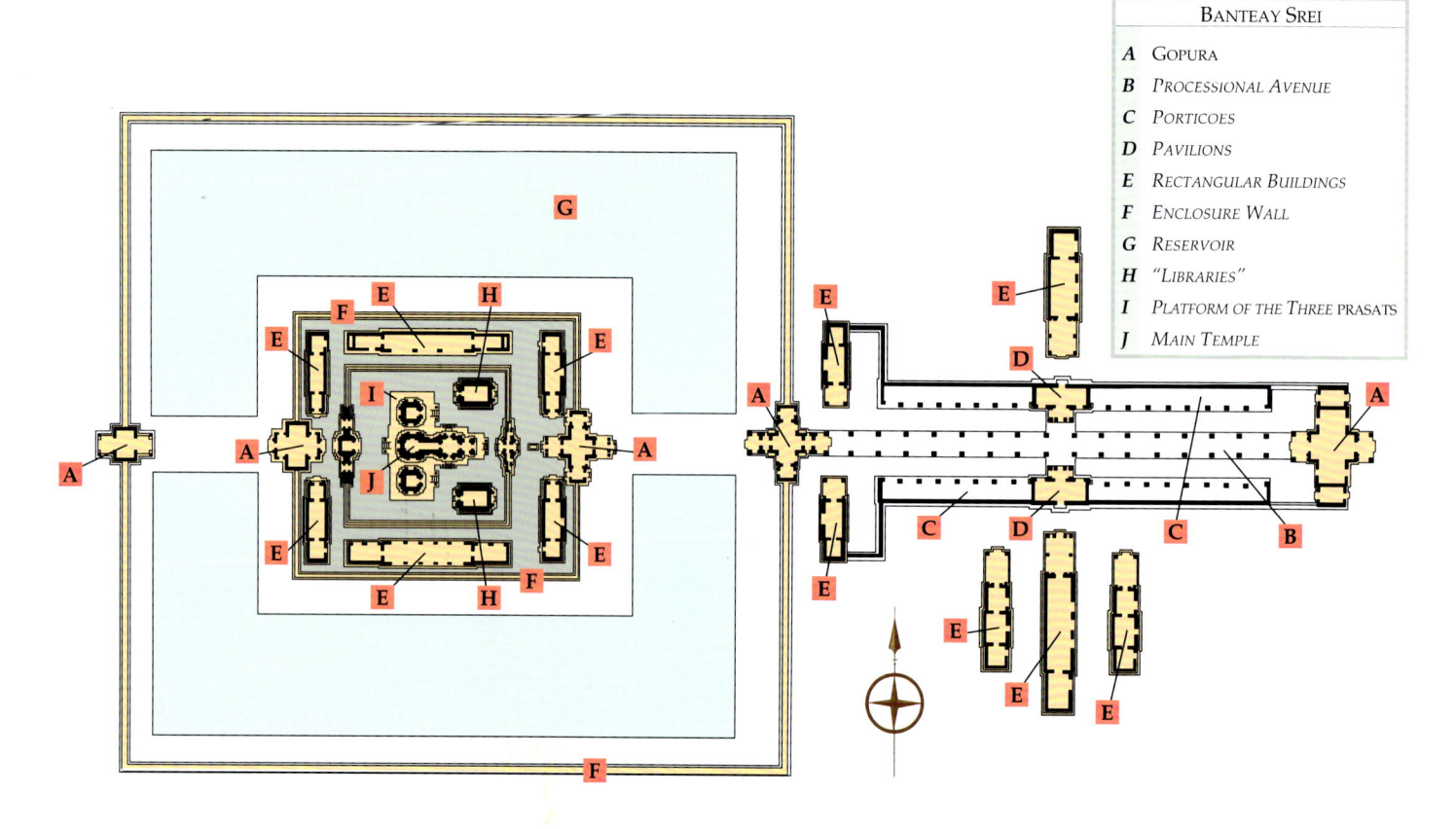

| | Banteay Srei |
|---|---|
| A | Gopura |
| B | Processional Avenue |
| C | Porticoes |
| D | Pavilions |
| E | Rectangular Buildings |
| F | Enclosure Wall |
| G | Reservoir |
| H | "Libraries" |
| I | Platform of the Three prasats |
| J | Main Temple |

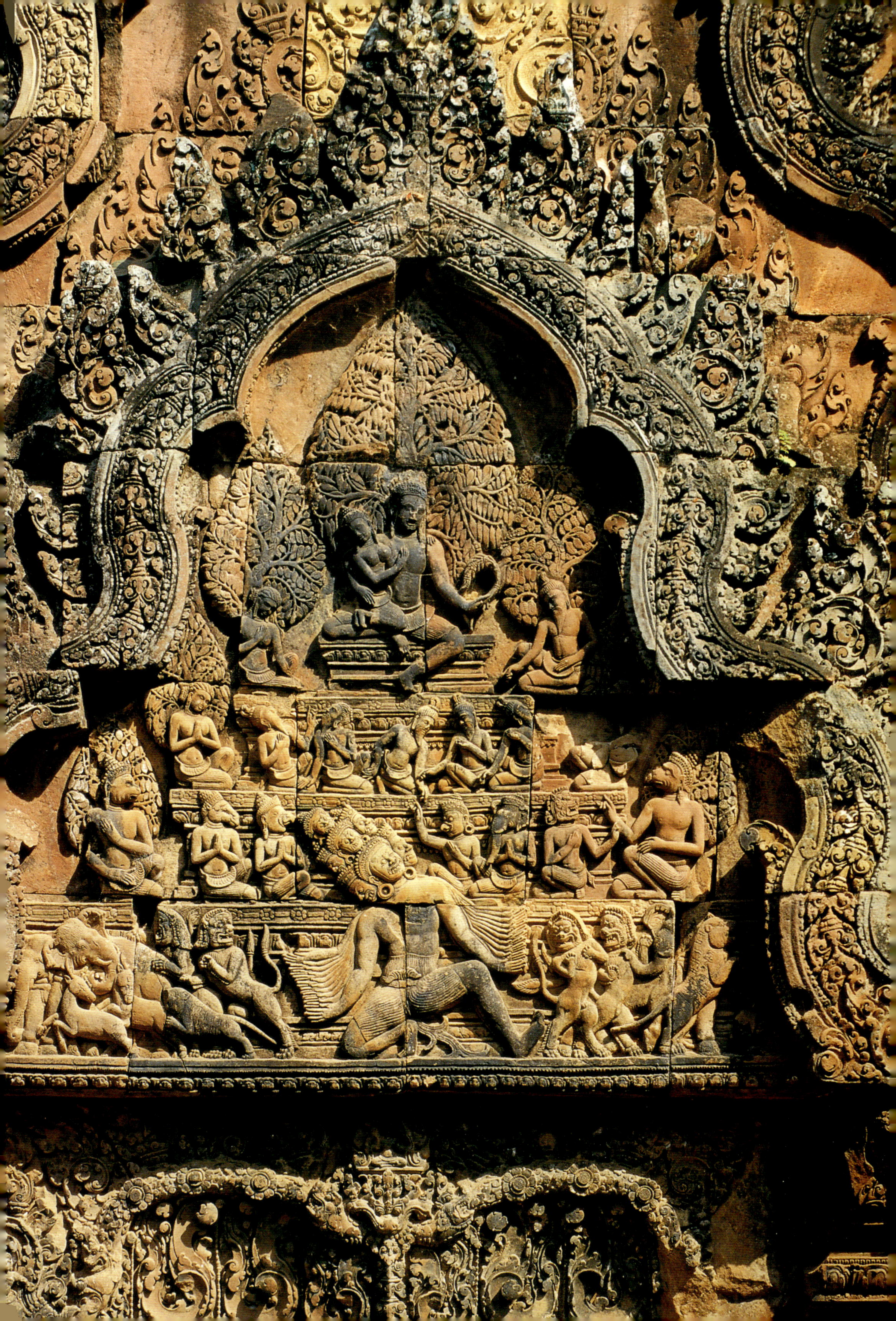

*184 top  The access avenue approaches the temple gradually. The purpose of the buildings lining the route is unknown.*

*184 bottom left  In the east tympanum of the north library, Indra unleashes a terrible downpour on the Vrindavan forest, the place where Krishna spent his childhood and youth. Krishna is pictured in the center, with his brother Balarama.*

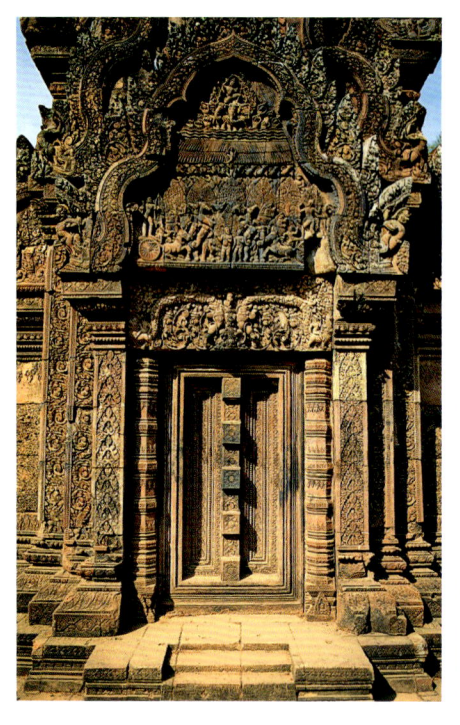

*184 bottom right  The dikpalas, protectors of the spatial directions, watch over the quarters of the world entrusted to them. The eastern quarter is under the protection of Indra, so the god, riding his three-headed elephant Airavata, is portrayed on the tympanum of the eastern entrance to the mandapa.*

## Banteay srei: *The Gem of Yajnavaraha*

Banteay Srei was inspired by these principles and the main temple imitated the system of prasat aligned on a single platform that was inaugurated at the Preah Ko in Roluos, but in this case, the central shrine was divided into cell, vestibule, pavilion, and portico in accordance with the Indian practice, and an innovative approach route to the temple was added outside the outermost enclosure. The complex therefore has a triple enclosure, preceded on the east side by a processional avenue some 230 feet long, accessed through a roughly cross-shaped pavilion with two porticoes and two wings with small passages on very high thresholds. This is not a true gopura, as there is no trace of a fourth enclosure, but a kind of propylaeum.

The access route runs between two rows of pillars, lined by porticoes along its whole length. These buildings, which consist of a blind laterite wall towards the outside and square sandstone pillars towards the inside, once had a roof made of tiles laid on a wooden framework. They are interrupted roughly halfway along by two pavilions, each of which has two windows and a portico overlooking the avenue and a door leading to the exterior on the opposite side. At right angles to these pavilions there is a building with a portico

*184-185 Banteay Srei was discovered by the French in 1914 and became famous some ten years later when author and adventurer André Malraux removed four statues of apsaras and was sentenced for theft. The temple was rebuilt by Henri Marchal using the anastylosis technique between 1931 and 1936. This photo shows the east gopura of the second enclosure wall.*

*185 bottom left  The pediments of the libraries consisted of a triple series of arches formed by the bodies of the nagas in the corners. The south library is shown here.*

*185 bottom right  The perfect joins of the cornices, at 45° angles, indicates the use of templates. The colonettes were inserted on the spot with a system of slots and pivots.*

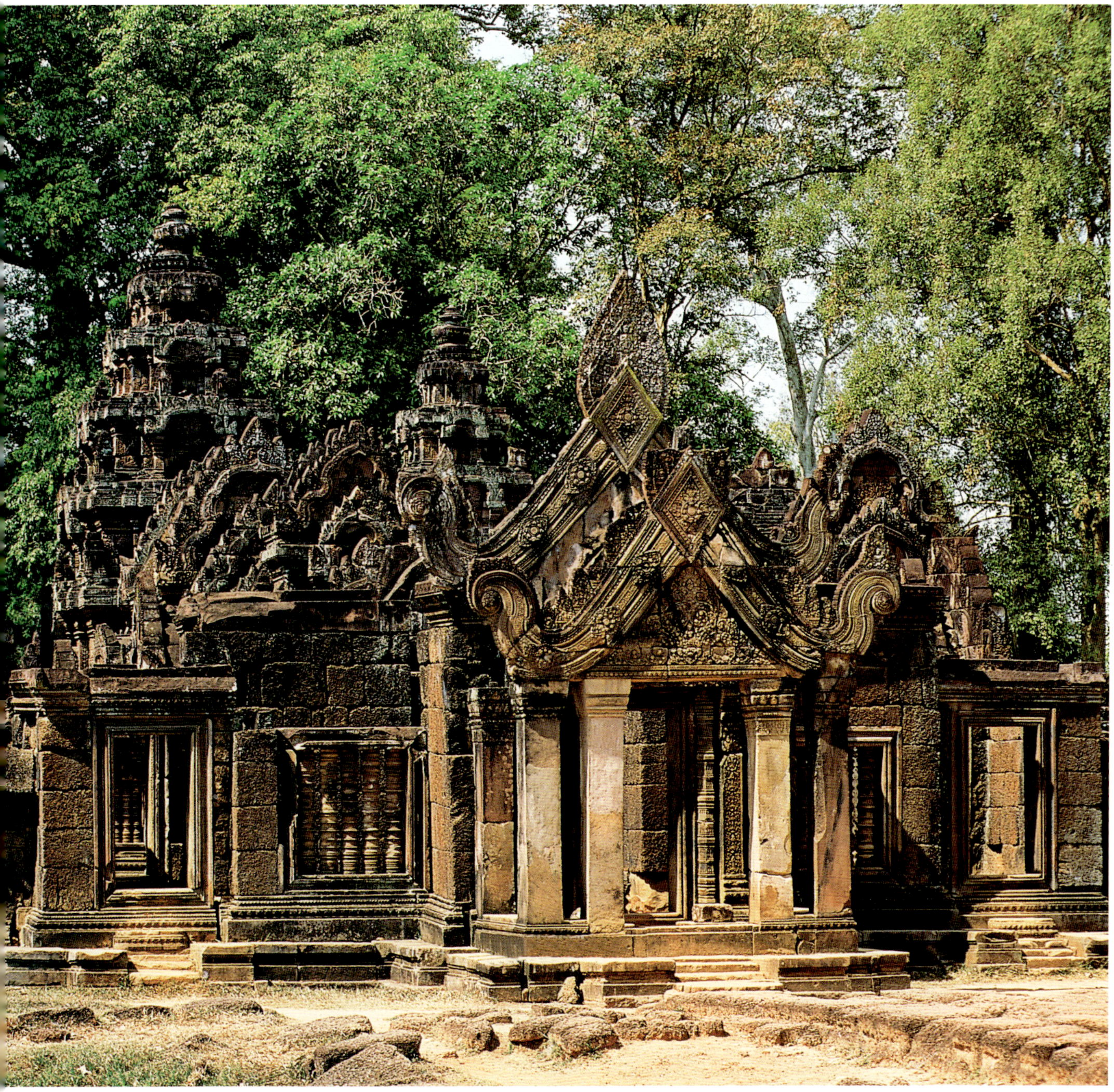

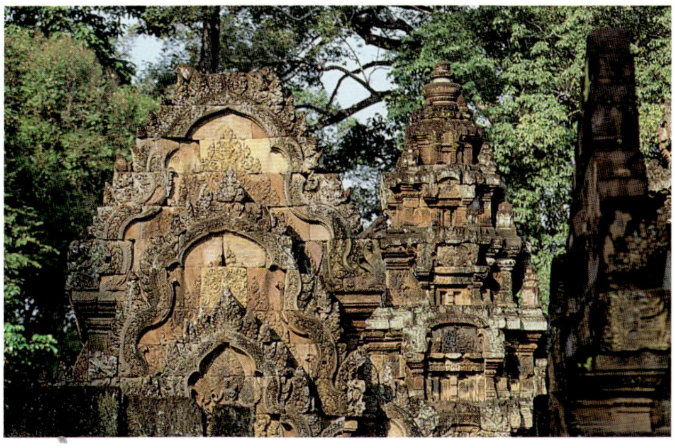

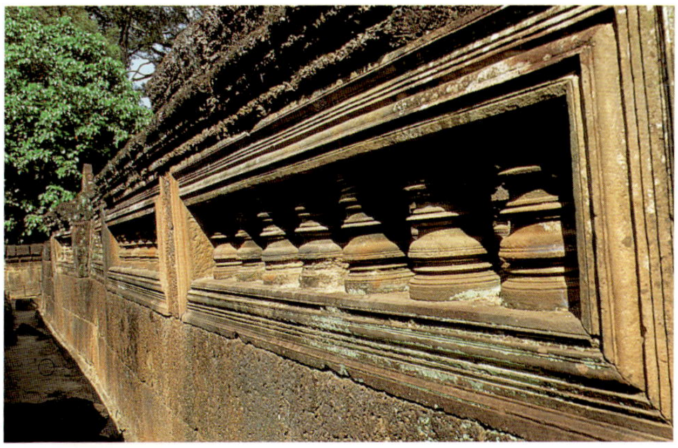

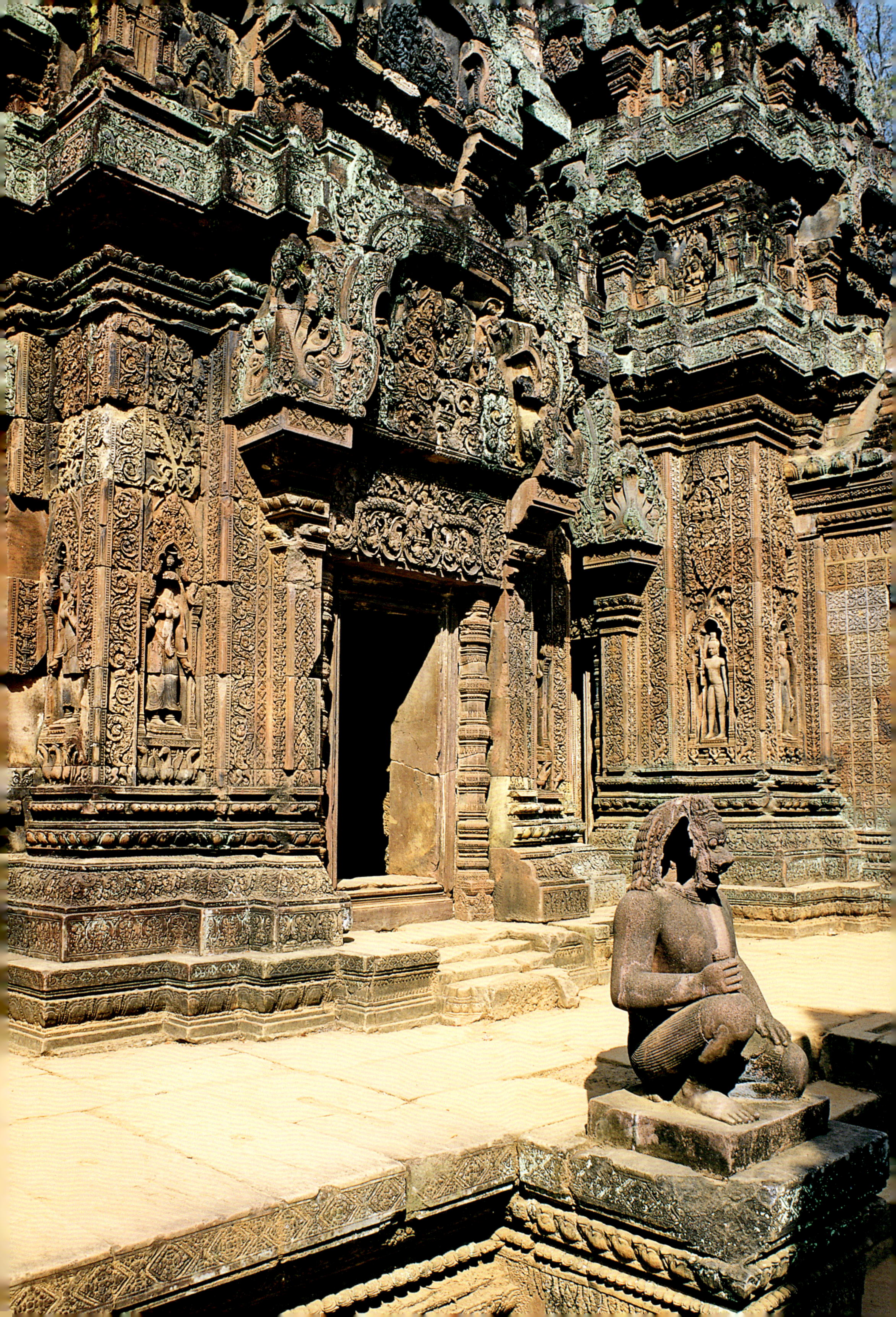

*186 The base of the temple consists of a series of moldings which follow a precise arrangement: band, ogee, cavetto, and ovolo moldings, with leaf, petal, and diamond patterns. The same motifs are repeated on the cornices.*

*187 top Little remains of the innermost enclosure wall of the temple, which was made of brick. Some of its ruins can be seen here, in front of the south library. A residential complex was built around the temple, and the area was known as Ishvarapura (city of the Lord), a name also used for other towns.*

## BANTEAY SREI: The Gem of Yajnavaraha

and two windowed rooms to the north and three similar buildings to the south; the central one is larger and the side ones smaller, and they have an extra room. The avenue continues and widens into a courtyard with two small tripartite structures perpendicular to it.

The third enclosure, made of laterite, which measures 213 by 361 feet and contains the reservoir surrounding the temple, has a cross-shaped gopura with two porticoes, which once had a wooden roof. During the rainy season, the temple is reflected in the reservoir as if it were Mount Meru emerging from the cosmic sea. The second enclosure wall, also made of laterite, surrounds a courtyard measuring 138 by 125 feet, accessible through another cross-shaped gopura, which is preceded and followed by porticoes and flanked by two side rooms, each with one entrances. The triangular pediment with flamboyant finials and spiral tips is very elegant. Hardly anything remains of the west gopura, made of brick. Six laterite buildings, each of which has three rooms, run along the walls of the second enclosure. They were originally roofed with tiles laid on a wooden framework.

The first enclosure, which was 79 feet long per side, is made of brick, while its eastern entrance pavilion is made of sandstone and has a "telescopic" structure. The axial passage with false vaulted ceiling is flanked by two rooms on each side of decreasing height that are so small that it is almost impossible to enter them. The entire temple has small proportions, which was appropriate for a building erected by someone other than the king.

The west gopura of the first enclosure is rather unusual, because it has a single entrance. It was therefore probably another shrine rather than an access pavilion.

In the northern and southern corners of the entrance wall of the first enclosure there are two sandstone libraries with some laterite inserts, covered with corbelled bricks and a false nave with two aisles, made from a false attic with real windows, which is flanked by half-roofs with lowered barrel vaults. Three polylobate pediments, one inside another, streamline the two buildings and surround the loveliest tympana in Khmer architecture. The ones on the north library portray Vishnuite themes, as this building is opposite the prasat dedicated to Vishnu, while the two on the south library portray Shivaite themes, because that library overlooks the prasat that houses the linga. Their great narrative sweep, the dynamism of their sculptural composition, and their psychological expressiveness suggest wooden and pictorial precedents.

*187 bottom left The three shrines stand on a platform with attractive moldings, accessed by six staircases flanked by tall buttresses on which the gatekeepers keep watch. The staircase leading to the south side of the mandapa is shown here.*

*187 bottom right The base of the libraries consists of a double plinth which imitates the denticulated plan of the buildings. The front entrance door and the false rear door, like this one belonging to the south library, are inserted in foreparts which were later transformed into porticoes.*

# BANTEAY SREI: *The Gem of Yajnavaraha*

*188 top Floral decorations cover the walls of the Banteay Srei temples like tapestries. The faces glimpsed through the foliage represent* yakshas *and* yakshis, *the male and female spirits which, according to Hindu tradition, live among the plants.*

*188 bottom left and right The corners of the ends of the volutes on the pediments are brilliantly resolved; a* simha *(a kind of rampant lion with four arms) or a four-headed* naga *emerge from the jaws of two* makaras *(sea monsters), whose bodies have turned into garlands. The edge is marked by the head of the lion and the main head of the cobra.*

*189 The* devakoshthas *(niches of the deities) are framed by floral responds, the base of which forms the body of an animal, probably a lion, while the upper part turns into sprigs of greenery. The* hamsas *(sacred geese) that support them suggest that the temple was a* vimana, *a flying palace or chariot that sped through the sky.*

The tympana and pediments are the most significant elements of Banteay Srei. The temple has three types of pediments: triangular, with flamboyant finials and wide lateral volutes, mostly having a tympanum with floral decoration; polylobate, the undulated contour being particularly developed, with a triple superimposition enclosing mythical scenes; and arched, deriving from the kudu (the horseshoe-shaped motif of Indian architecture). The triangular pediments derive from wooden architecture and were still used for buildings roofed with wood and tiles. The polylobate pediments were used with brick and sandstone roofs, especially on the temple annexes, while the kudu type were mainly used on the shrine. All three forms are particularly elaborate at Banteay Srei. A good example of this is constituted by the corners, most of which have three-headed nagas issuing from the jaws of a lion or a makara with a highly elongated trunk. Garudas with their wings spread were also used to turn the corner into a decorative element.

The temple consists of three prasat aligned on a molded, T-shaped platform, accessed by staircases with tall buttresses on which the sculpted gatekeepers of the sacred place kneel. They are magnificent in-the-round figures, some of which had the faces of lions and monkeys. The central prasat consists of a portico that gives access to a mandapa, the pavilion from which worshippers could contemplate the image of the god in the cell. It was roofed with bricks and communicated via the antarala (vestibule) with the garbhagriha, the denticulated square cell, which had three false doors and one real one. Alongside the main prasat, dedicated to Tribhuvanamaheshvara, namely Shiva in his form as "great lord of the triple world," stand two secondary prasat, simple towers with an entrance and three false doors; the northern one was consecrated to Vishnu, and the southern one to Shiva. The roofs of the three shrines consist of four tiers, which imitate the façade on a decreasing scale with antefixes at the corners

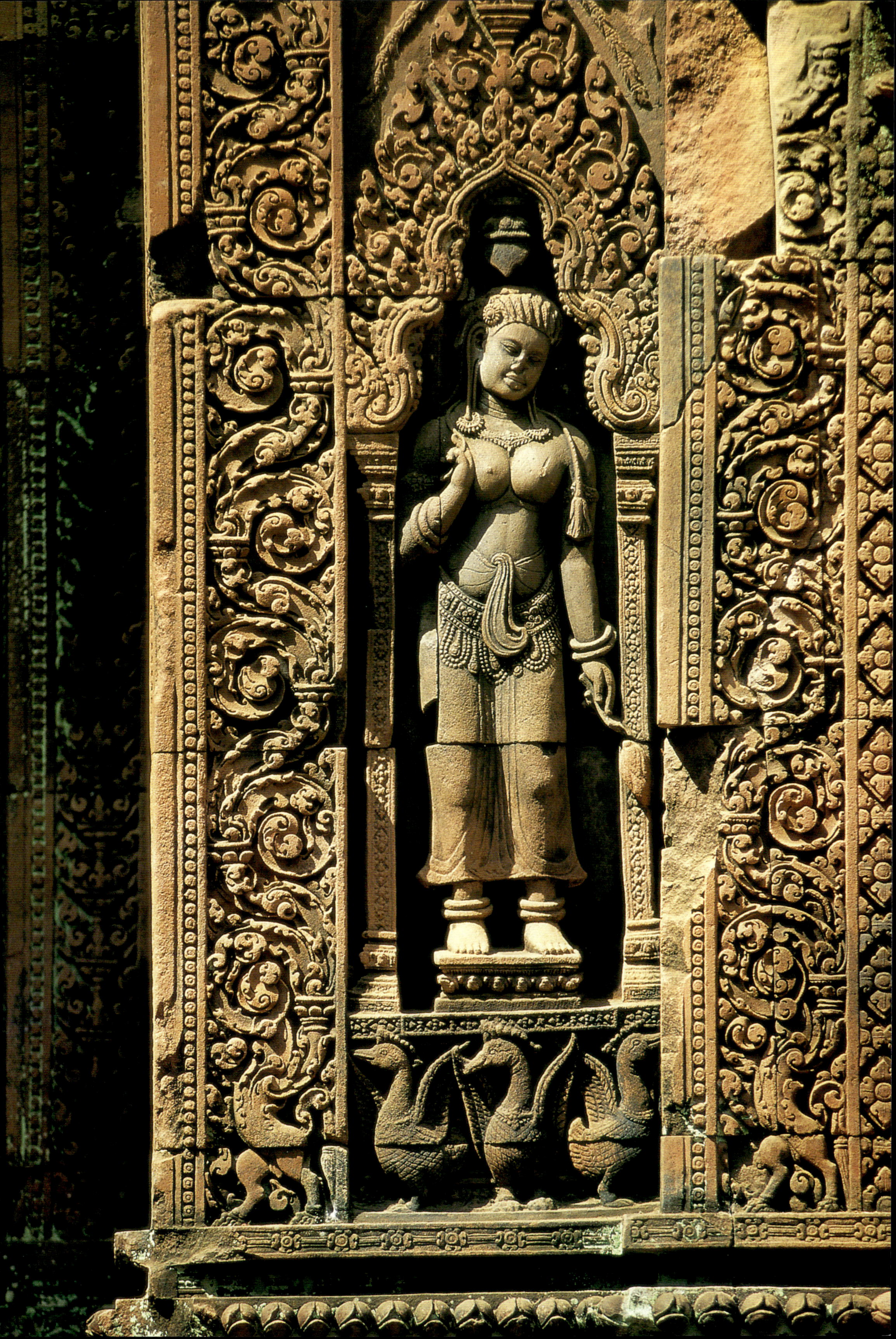

*190-191 Indra, though unimportant in India, was frequently portrayed by the Khmer, especially in the center of architraves where his three-headed elephant cleverly connects the two parts of the decoration.*

*191 top Narasimha, the incarnation of Vishnu in human and animal form, can be seen among the tangled greenery with praying figures in the act of disemboweling the demon Hiranyakashipu, who persecuted his own son Prahlada because he worshipped Vishnu.*

*191 bottom The portrayal of the details on the tympanums is very realistic. The east tympanum of the south library, shown here, depicts the different expressions of the* rishi *(ascetics and fortune tellers) and the agitation of Parvati, who clings to her husband.*

## BANTEAY SREI: *The Gem of Yajnavaraha*

*that reproduce the entire* prasat *in miniature. The bow-shaped pediments, deriving from the* kudu, *are repeated on all four tiers and connect them with a series of arches.*

As already mentioned, the temple is small. The central prasat is under 33 feet high and the cell is no more than six feet wide. Visitors have to bend down to enter it because the door is only just about three feet high. However, the total length of Banteay Srei, measured from the outermost east access pavilion to the west pavilion in the third enclosure, is over 650 feet.

The entire surface of the three prasat is covered with exquisite floral decoration, which produces a tapestry-like effect on the walls and surrounds elaborate niches consisting of two columns surmounted by flamboyant arches, with two flying spirits on the cusp. The young gatekeepers and the devatas with their deliberately archaic clothes and hairstyles smile enigmatically, as if lost in inner contemplation. The architraves consist mainly of two arched festoons connected by a figure in the center.

The play of volumes, the stereometric effects, the superior-quality sandstone with warm pink shades which is particularly sensitive to changes of light, and above all the decoration make Banteay Srei one of the masterpieces of Khmer art. The first of the Angkor monuments to be reconstructed with the anastylosis technique in 1931, it is now one of the best preserved.

192

*192-193 Carved on the stones of the Kbal Spean river bed, the deities emerge from the water, symbolizing the liquid primordial chaos that incorporated all forms of life, which were brought into existence by divine intervention.*

*192 bottom left and right The* linga *is one of the most frequent motifs, as its connection with water was very important. The photo on the left shows six* lingayonis *and the one on the right, nine: one in the middle and eight forming a* mandala *shape.*

*193 top and center A* makara *(top) has turned into a crocodile. At the bottom, three deities are bathing in a stream.*

As if such beauty were not enough, visitors who continue along the road for a few miles will reach the clearing from which the trail to Kbal Spean begins. There, hermits once carved religious symbols and images in the river bed and on the surrounding rocks. It is an enchanting spot, and a walk in the jungle reveals little by little, once the eyes have grown accustomed to the surroundings, the vestiges of a faith so deep that it has left traces even in such unusual places.

*193 bottom In a scene well suited to its setting, Vishnu, watched over by Lakshmi, reclines on the serpent Ananta, floating on the cosmic waters in the pause between the end of one universe and the appearance of another. When life recommences, a lotus sprouts from the god's navel and Brahma, Lord of the origins, appears.*

*194 top* The devatas of Thommanon are highly detailed and their feet are portrayed in a more natural way.

*194-195* Thommanon, attributed to the reign of Suryavarman II, is a prasat of great uniformity and harmony, which was reconstructed by Bernard-Philippe Groslier in the sixties. The concrete reconstruction of a coffered ceiling demonstrates what the inner space in the temple was actually like.

*194 bottom* The five temples of Preah Pithu, which are now considered to be a set but were probably designed and built independently between the thirteenth and fourteenth centuries, are identified by the letters of the alphabet for lack of other information. They are all Hindu apart from Temple X, which is Buddhist.

*195* Temple V, which is preceded to the west by a 230-foot avenue that leads to a terrace with a naga balustrade, consists of a forepart and a cell 13 feet square that contains a large linga.

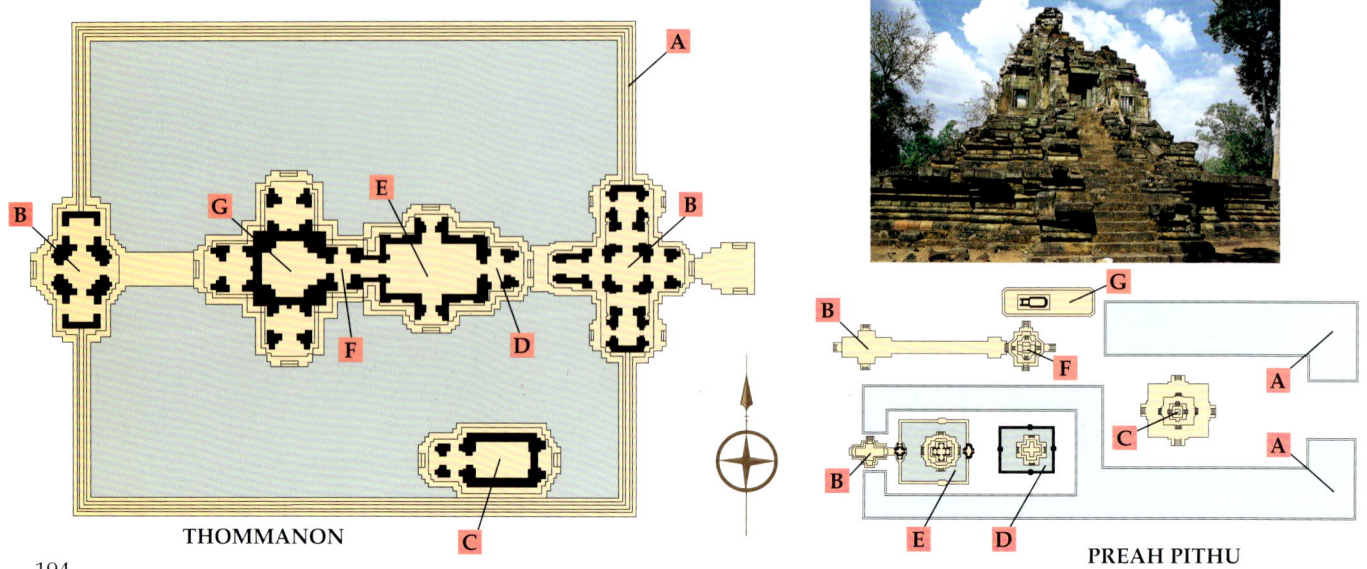

**THOMMANON**

**PREAH PITHU**

# From Angkor to Beng Mealea

## The Triumph of the Ground-level Temple

Khmer architecture reached the height of its glory in the twelfth century with the building of Angkor Wat, one of the most spectacular religious complexes in the world. However, the magnificent temple was not created out of the blue but was based on a long process of development which included other monuments worthy of attention. Chau Say Tevoda, Thommanon, Beng Mealea, Banteay Samré, and other buildings in the huge Preah Khan complex at Kompong Thom, also known as the Preah Khan of Kompong Svay, are attributed to the same king who built Angkor Wat, Suryavarman II. Although it is unlikely that these temples were all built by him, and some were probably built, or at any rate completed, by his successors, in view of their characteristics they are classified within the Angkor Wat style, the golden age of Khmer architecture.

Apart from Angkor Wat, the buildings erected by Suryavarman II were all ground-level temples with the same layout: a raised processional approach avenue to the temple interrupted by cross-shaped terraces; one or more concentric enclosure walls consisting of continuous galleries with **gopura** entrances on the axes and turreted structures at the corners; and two or more libraries. The central temple, consisting of a **prasat** with four porticoes (the eastern one being smaller, so as to connect it to the **antarala**, or vestibule), is preceded by the **mandapa** (pavilion), which also has one or three porticoes. The buildings stand on tall bases and are connected to one another by corridors raised on stilts. The highly denticulated, multi-tiered roofs of the **prasat** have an ogival pattern and end in a lotus-shaped finial.

At Angkor, the development of the ground-level temple can be seen by visiting Chau Say Tevoda, the Thommanon, Preah Pithu, Beng Melea, and Banteay Samré.

The **Chau Say Tevoda** and **Thommanon** temples stand opposite one another and their small size makes it possible to see their structure clearly and admire it in detail. Both temples stand inside an enclosure wall; Chau Say Tevoda has four gopuras, while Thommanon has two. They were once reflected in their reservoirs. The first temple has two rectangular libraries in the northeast and southeast corners while the second only has one. The shrine has the same structure in both temples: a prasat with three porticoes, a fourth portico transformed into a vestibule, a pavilion, and a porticoed entrance to the east.

Chau Say Tevoda is currently being restored, while Thommanon has already been restored to its original form thanks to reconstruction work performed in the sixties with the anastylosis technique. The eastern entrance pavilion is a magnificent cross-shaped building with two annexed wings and a portico facing the temple. The structure is "telescopic," in other words, it has rooms of decreasing size that give onto one another, connected by a dome with a false vaulted ceiling that covers the central room. In the southeast corner of the enclosure there is a library that is preceded by a small portico on the western side and has a false door on the eastern side. Like the gopura, it stands on a tall molded base, as does the temple. The wall decoration is a delicate veil of floral motifs, and the stylized devatas in the niches are particularly graceful.

| THOMMANON | |
|---|---|
| A | ENCLOSURE WALL |
| B | GOPURA |
| C | "LIBRARY" |
| D | ENTRANCE PORTICO |
| E | MANDAPA |
| F | VESTIBULE |
| G | CELL WITH PORTICOES |

| PREAH PITHU | |
|---|---|
| A | RESERVOIRS |
| B | CROSS-SHAPED TERRACES |
| C | TEMPLE X, BUDDHIST |
| D | TEMPLE U |
| E | TEMPLE T |
| F | TEMPLE V |
| G | TEMPLE Y |

### Banteay Samré

- **A** Outer Enclosure Wall
- **B** Angular Shots of Inner Enclosure Wall
- **C** Gopura
- **D** Quay
- **E** "Libraries"
- **F** Entrance Portico
- **G** Mandapa
- **H** Vestibule
- **I** Cell with Porticoes

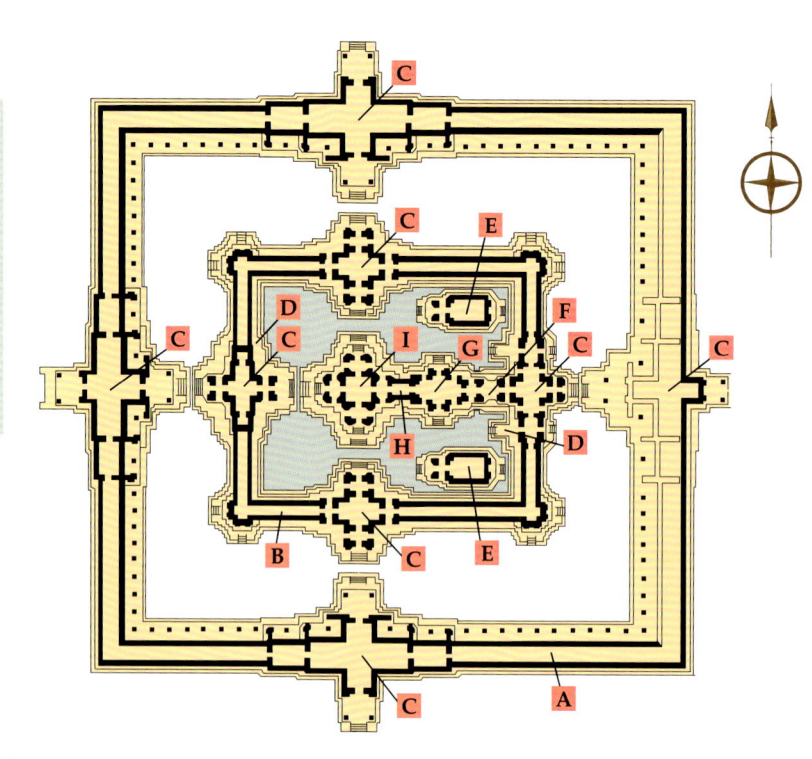

## FROM ANGKOR TO BENG MEALEA: *The Triumph of the Ground-level Temple*

The **Preah Pithu** complex, situated in a secluded spot, comprises five shrines, once surrounded by walls, with reservoirs between them. It is now mostly in ruins. The cross-shaped terraces with the naga motif, the bases intersected by axial staircases guarded by lions, the false doors, the deities in the niches, and the details of the decoration demonstrate great sophistication and surprise visitors who are willing to depart from the usual Angkor itineraries.

After Angkor Wat, the most important temple dating from the period of Suryavarman II is **Banteay Samré** (attributed wholly or partly to his successor Yashovarman II by some experts), which stands in an isolated spot at the end of the East Baray. Here, the structure of the ground-level temple reaches perfection. Its name, which means "Citadel of the Samrés," associates it with the Samré people who once lived in the area around Phnom Kulen. A processional avenue 656 feet long, which may originally have been roofed with a wooden structure, leads to the temple. The avenue is divided into two levels, is lined with serpentine balustrades, and culminates in a staircase flanked by crouching lions. A laterite terrace forms the base of the east gopura in the outer laterite enclosure, a rectangle measuring 272 by 253 feet, with axial entrances marked by cross-shaped gopuras with elongated wings and two more lateral rooms. The wall consists of four galleries, originally covered with tiled wooden roofs, that have a solid wall on the outside and a window screened by colonettes on the inside. The galleries stand on a tall base and are flanked on the temple side by a colonnade designed to support a portico made of perishable materials. The innermost enclosure wall, which measures 144 by 125 feet, is made of laterite and has telescopic axial sandstone gopuras with false vaulted ceilings. It consists of four galleries, the corners of which are emphasized on the outside by projecting sections with staircases, and false doors with pediments above them. The galleries, all of which have intact roofs, consist of one blind wall and one with colonnaded windows facing inwards. Standing on tall bases like all the other buildings in the enclosure, they are bordered by a continuous platform that allowed worshippers to perambulate the temple. The temple rose from the water stored in the reservoir, which was floored with laterite and bounded by the enclosure walls. In the northeast and southeast corners, connected to the temple by walkways on stilts, there are two libraries preceded by porticoes with corbelled vaults and false naves with two aisles. Their most noteworthy features include the decorations on the walled-up doors and the staircases bordered by many-headed serpents of exquisite workmanship. The sandstone temple, dedicated to Vishnu, is divided into the usual rooms (cell, vestibule, pavilion, and porticoes) but is elongated because of the new importance acquired by the vestibule.

The stages in its development can be seen at Chau Say Tevoda and Thommanon: in the first case the vestibule is merely the eastern arm of the cross-shaped prasat, while in the second it begins to emerge as a separate room, vying for space with the arm of the prasat, which is consequently shortened. At Banteay Samré, the vestibule is located before the arm of the prasat, considerably elongating the connection between the prasat and the mandapa. The pavilion, a rectangular structure with a false vaulted ceiling, was lightened by inserting colonetted windows into the curtain wall alongside the side doors. The portico of the mandapa almost merges with that of the gopura, accentuating the impression of longitudinal expansion of the temple. The prasat, which has three false doors and double pediments, has a very tall first tier, which is higher than the pediments of the porticoes, and four more highly denticulated tiers which culminate in a lotus-shaped circular finial 39 feet above ground level.

196 left The gallery of the first enclosure consists of a blind wall towards the outside and balustraded windows towards the inside. There are no other openings, which is as odd as the fact that there was no way of getting through from one side to the other.

196 right The cross-shaped terrace opposite the eastern entrance of Banteay Samré is guarded by two lions ready to pounce. In front of it runs a raised avenue, dating from a later period, which was lined with naga balustrades and possibly roofed with a wooden structure.

196-197 The gopuras have a cross-shaped plan and "telescopic" wings, and their tympanums portray scenes from Hindu mythology. The roof ridge is crowned by pinnacled finials.

197 bottom The corners of the laterite enclosure wall are emphasized by projections with staircases and false sandstone doors surmounted by pediments. The fortified temple structure is called the banteay (citadel).

Among the lesser-known but more interesting complexes of the Angkor period is the majestic temple of **Beng Mealea** (the lotus reservoir), situated 25 miles east of Angkor, on the southeastern slopes of Phnom Kulen. Now in a deserted jungle area which is difficult to visit, Beng Mealea once lay on the road that led southeast from Angkor to the Preah Khan of Kompong Thom, and north to Chok Gargyar. The date of the monument and its chronological relationship with Angkor Wat is still controversial, although most experts attribute it to Suryavarman II and believe that it was begun after Angkor Wat but finished earlier.

Beng Mealea combined the structure of the ground-level temple with that of the mountain temple to form a complex that develops outwards but is still centered thanks to the concentric galleries. In the near future, these galleries were to indicate the changes of level and sacredness that in mountain temples were expressed by the terraces of the pyramid. The gradual approach along routes that converged on the main cell symbolized the process of internalization and replaced the climb. Though the spatial approach is different, the meaning is not; man can encounter the Divine either by climbing the cosmic mountain or by descending into the depths of the heart.

The huge Beng Mealea complex includes three galleried enclosure walls, the outermost of which measures 594 by 499 feet, connected to one another by cross-shaped roofed passages that form cloisters, numerous prasat (apparently 11), and annexed buildings. It is in a sad state of disrepair but should soon undergo more detailed study and restoration work, which is certainly desirable in view of the importance of the site. Delaporte, years ago, planned a somewhat fanciful reconstruction. An avenue leading from a large dried-up baray leads to the east façade of the temple, and opens out into a scenic cross-shaped terrace in front of it. Each of the other three entrances also apparently had a similar avenue and terrace.

## FROM ANGKOR TO BENG MEALEA: *The Triumph of the Ground-level Temple*

A triple series of concentric galleries encloses the central shrine, which is the usual **prasat** preceded by a forepart. The north and south galleries of the first enclosure are prolonged to intersect with the east galleries of the second and third enclosures. As a result of the presence of another corridor perpendicular to the second and third enclosures, a series of cloisters are thus created which lead to three entrance **gopuras** on the east façade. These entrance pavilions have a cross-shaped plan, and similar structures also appear in the corners of the galleries, marked by towers. On the south side of the third enclosure stand two huge buildings in courtyards, called "palaces," and were possibly used for ceremonies and dancing.

The most interesting feature of Beng Mealea is the wide, vaulted galleries made entirely of sandstone without the expedient of wooden beams inserted into hollowed-out stones. In addition to the usual design feature of the solid wall and the windowed wall, an innovation was introduced, namely a continuous wall on one side and a row of pillars on the other. In some cases the architects daringly rested the false vaulted ceiling on two rows of pillars, but the gallery collapsed. The intrados is no longer leveled because the corbelled stones were concealed by a wooden ceiling. As the half-vaults were visible, they were smoothed and sometimes decorated in relief. Although the temple was probably dedicated to Vishnu, Buddhist iconographic motifs are also present.

The beauty and intriguing charm with which Beng Mealea is imbued make up for the difficulties of access and offer the excitement of discovery.

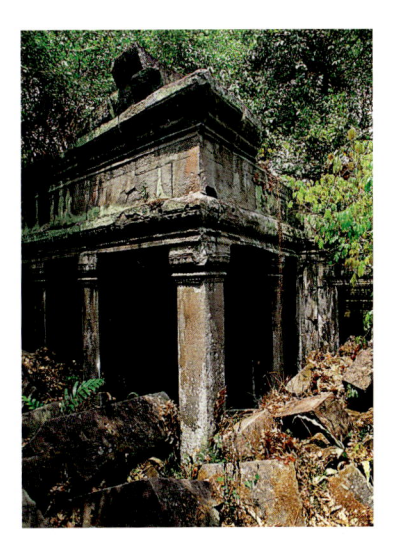

*198-199 The interiors of Beng Mealea are full of shadow, which is barely dispelled by the balustraded windows, screened by monolithic colonettes.*

*199 top Raised walkways were used extensively. They had both practical and symbolic functions, as they enabled the temple to be circumambulated under shelter during the monsoon season and processions to be held above ground level.*

*199 center The blocks of sandstone were so accurately rubbed together when they were laid that their horizontal joints are often indistinguishable.*

*199 bottom Larger sandstone galleries with the vaults resting on pillars, without the expedient of centering (wooden beams inserted into hollowed-out stones), appeared at Beng Mealea.*

# ANGKOR WAT
## The Stable of the Celestial Oxen

Was it a palace, a temple, or a mausoleum? Angkor Wat, the most famous monument in Angkor, built by Suryavarman II between 1113 and 1150, was all this and more; it was also the dwelling-place of the gods. Once called Brah Bishnulok or Vrah Vishnuloka (the sacred dwelling of Vishnu), it was dedicated by Suryavarman to the second deity of the Trimurti with whom he identified. On his death the great king took the posthumous name Paramavishnuloka (he who has gone to the paradise of the supreme Vishnu), and the temple became his mausoleum. The name by which it is now known means "royal monastery city" because after the religious revolution introduced by Jayavarman VII in the thirteenth century, the Khmer empire embraced Buddhism and Angkor Wat was transformed from a Vishnuite shrine to a Buddhist wat, a term of Thai origin which means "monastery." Local legend has it that Angkor Wat was turned into a monastery by Buddhaghosha, a famous Indian monk who received the magnificent complex as a gift when he returned from Sri Lanka with the texts of the Buddhist law. Be that as it may, its conversion to a Buddhist temple meant that Angkor Wat was never totally abandoned.

It was a temple, mausoleum, and monastery, but was it also a palace? There is no doubt that a city, Suryavarman's capital, lay

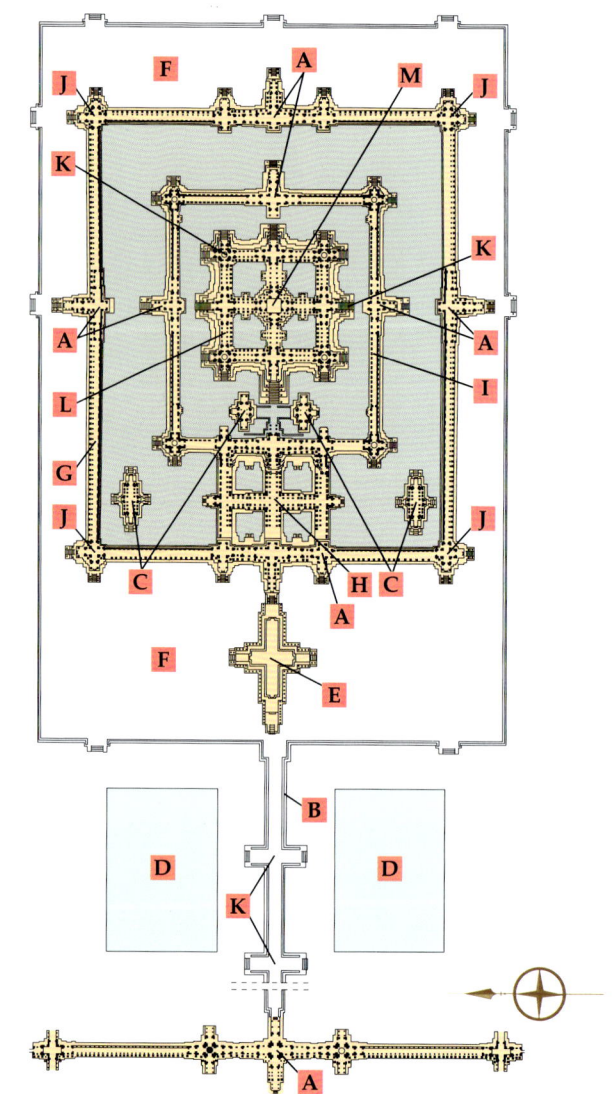

*200 left* The female figures that decorate the walls of Angkor Wat are estimated to number between 1500 and 2000, and no two are alike.

*200 right* Unlike other temples, where they are pictured alone, the devatas of Angkor Wat are also portrayed in groups.

*200-201* A city once stood inside the perimeter of Angkor Wat, built by Suryavarman II between 1113 and 1115, but no trace of it has survived. The Royal Palace was probably situated to the north of the temple as usual.

200

| ANGKOR WAT | |
|---|---|
| A  Gopura | H  Cross-shaped |
| B  Raised Avenue |    Cloister |
| C  "Libraries" | I  Second Gallery |
| D  Ponds | J  Corner Prasats |
| E  Cross-shaped | K  Staircases |
|    Terrace | L  First Gallery with |
| F  Platform |    Quincunx |
| G  Third Gallery | M  Central Prasat |

inside the outermost enclosure of the shrine, and that Suryavarman's court was situated there, probably to the north of the temple. In addition to the historical evidence that parts of the now empty spaces in the complex were used for residential purposes, there is a delightful Cambodian legend involving Ket Mealea, in Sanskrit Ketumala (prince of flowery light), son of a Khmer princess and the god Indra. The young man was taken to heaven by his father on reaching adolescence but rejected by the other gods because of his unpleasant "human odor." His grief-stricken father sent him back to earth to rule over Kok Thlok (Kambujadesha) and gave him Angkor Wat to compensate in some way for the divine legacy of which he had been deprived. There are various versions of the legend: one of the two main ones recounts that Indra ordered Vishvakarman, architect of the gods, to build a palace similar to the celestial dwellings for his son, while the other says that when he was asked to choose which of the heavenly buildings he would like to take back to earth with him, Ket Mealea, not daring to ask for too much, chose the stables of the oxen.

Zhou Daguan adds his version to the legends of Angkor Wat. He says that the place was the tomb of Lou Pan, the Chinese god of architects, translating into his culture the information that connected the architectural colossus to Brah Bishnukar (Vishvakarman in Khmer).

The Angkor Wat complex is situated in the southeast quadrant of Yashodharapura and forms a rectangle measuring 4,900 feet from east to west and 4,250 feet from north to south, covering an area of roughly one square mile. The huge, attractive moat that forms the perimeter, which is filled by a canal leading from the Siem Reap river, is about 650 feet wide and edged with steps leading down to the water.

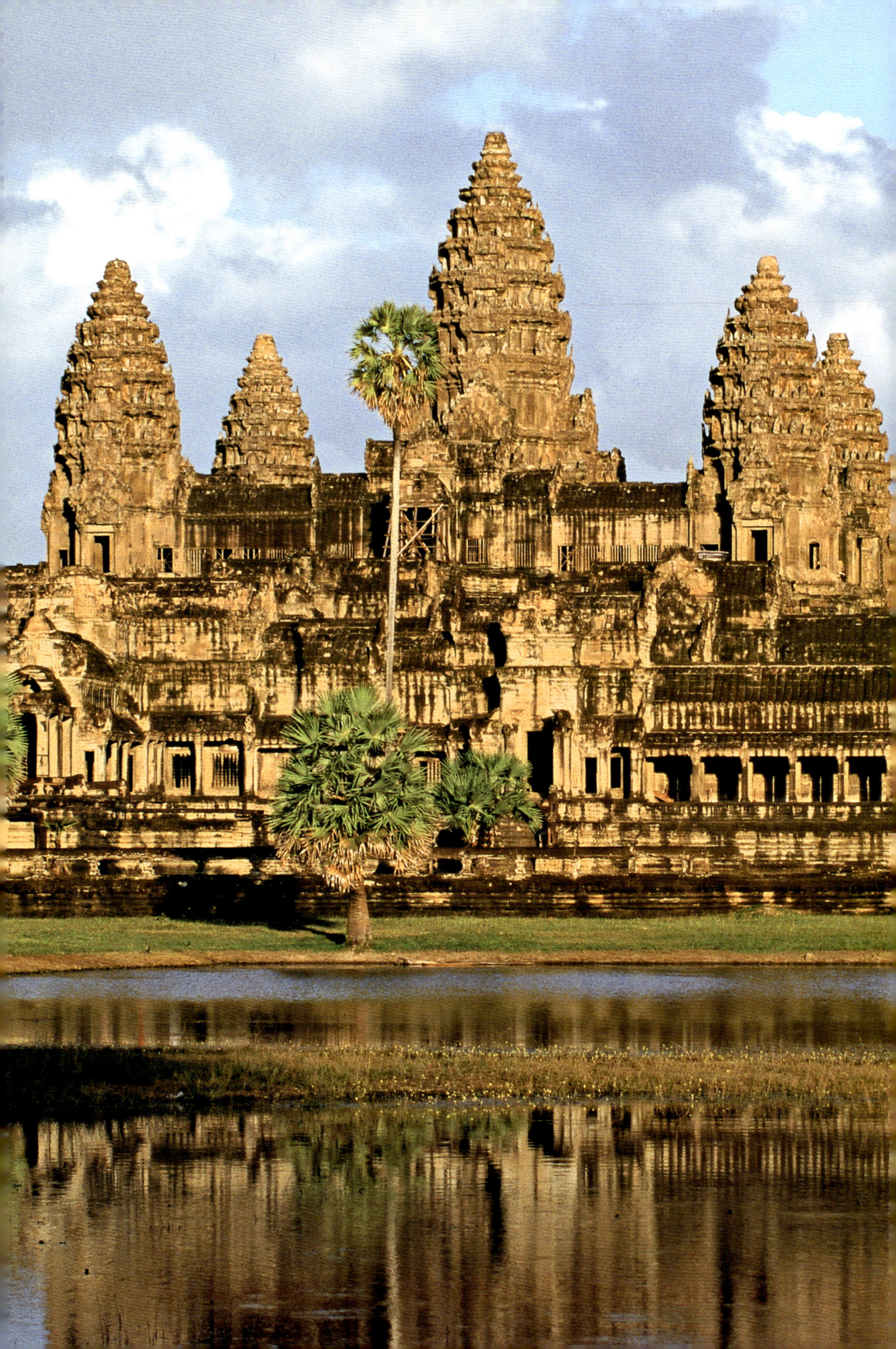

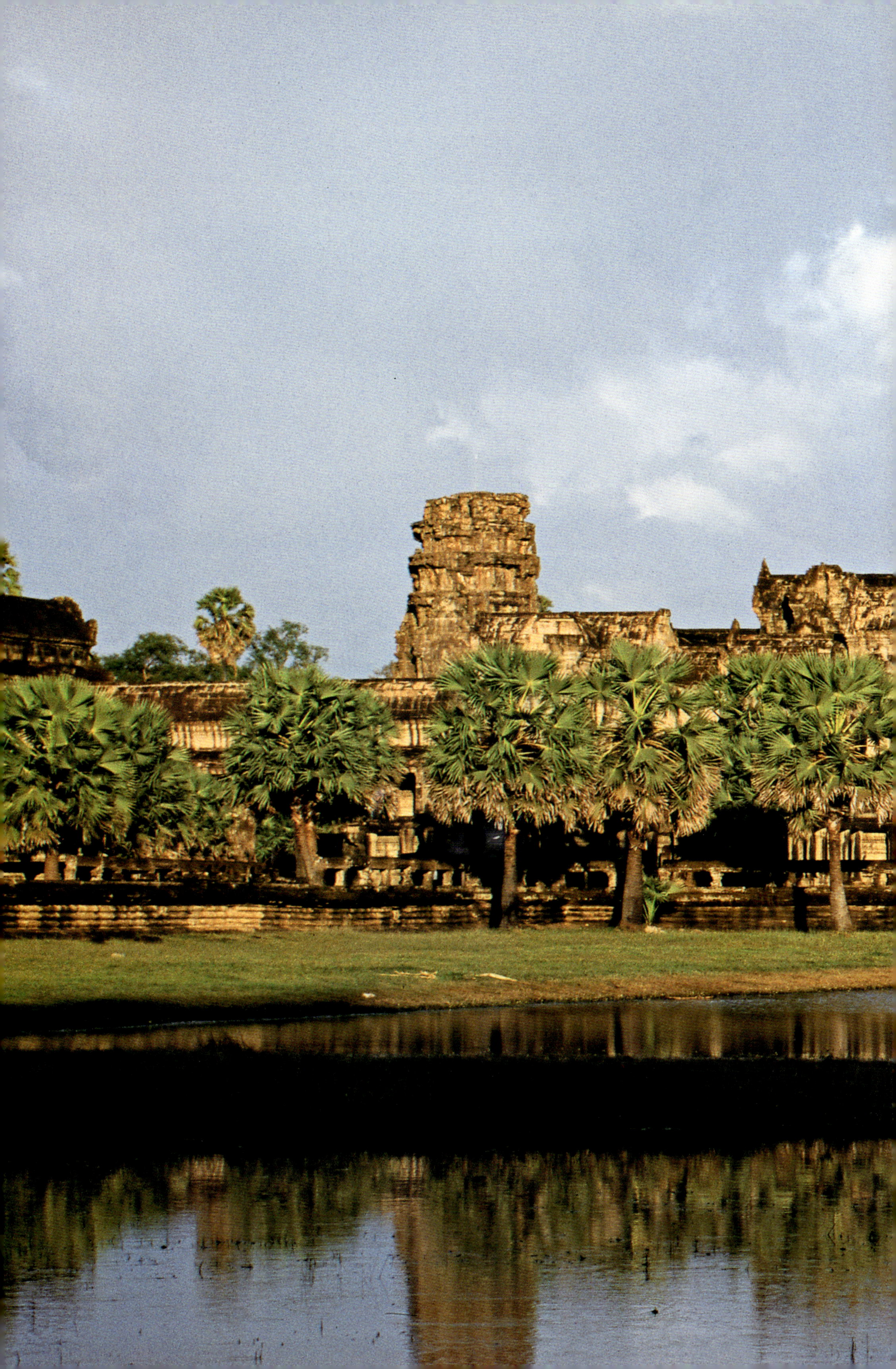

# ANGKOR WAT, The Stable of the Celestial Oxen

*202 Angkor Wat combines the concentric structure of the ground-level temple with galleries with the vertical structure of the mountain temple. Both the progression towards the center and the ascent to the summit have the same purpose: to come closer to the Divine.*

*203-206 The architectural symbolism of Angkor Wat is cosmographic: the moat symbolizes the primordial sea, the galleries are the mountain chains that surround the earth, and the five prasats of the quincunx are the peaks of Mount Meru.*

*207 The reservoirs surrounding the temples supplied drinking water to the population and water for agricultural use, thus strengthening the charisma of the King, who managed the water system and thus became the dispenser of life. Work on such constructions required thousands of laborers and a strong central power able to maintain the structure when it was built. This photo shows the moat of Angkor Wat with steps leading down to the water.*

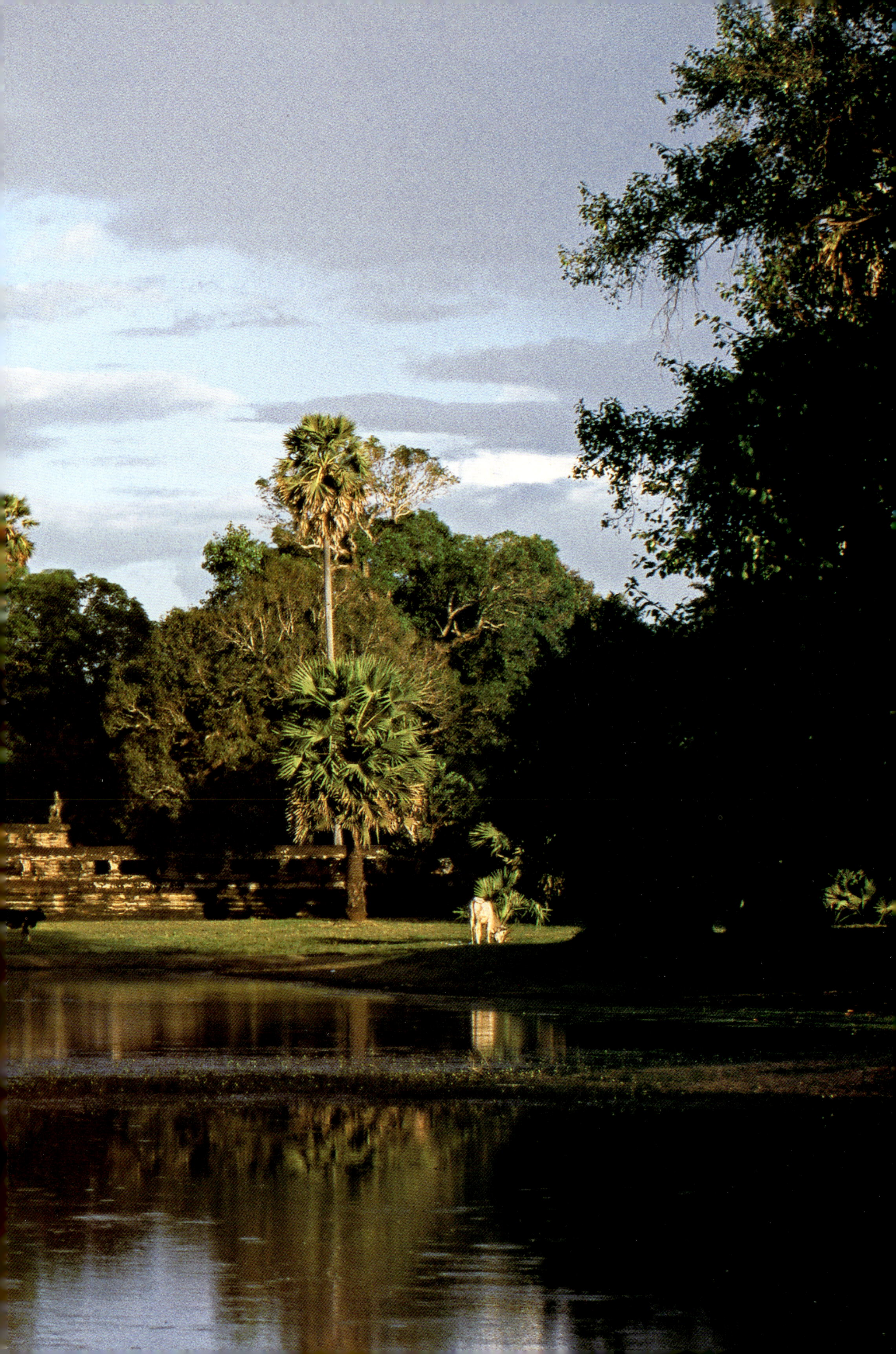

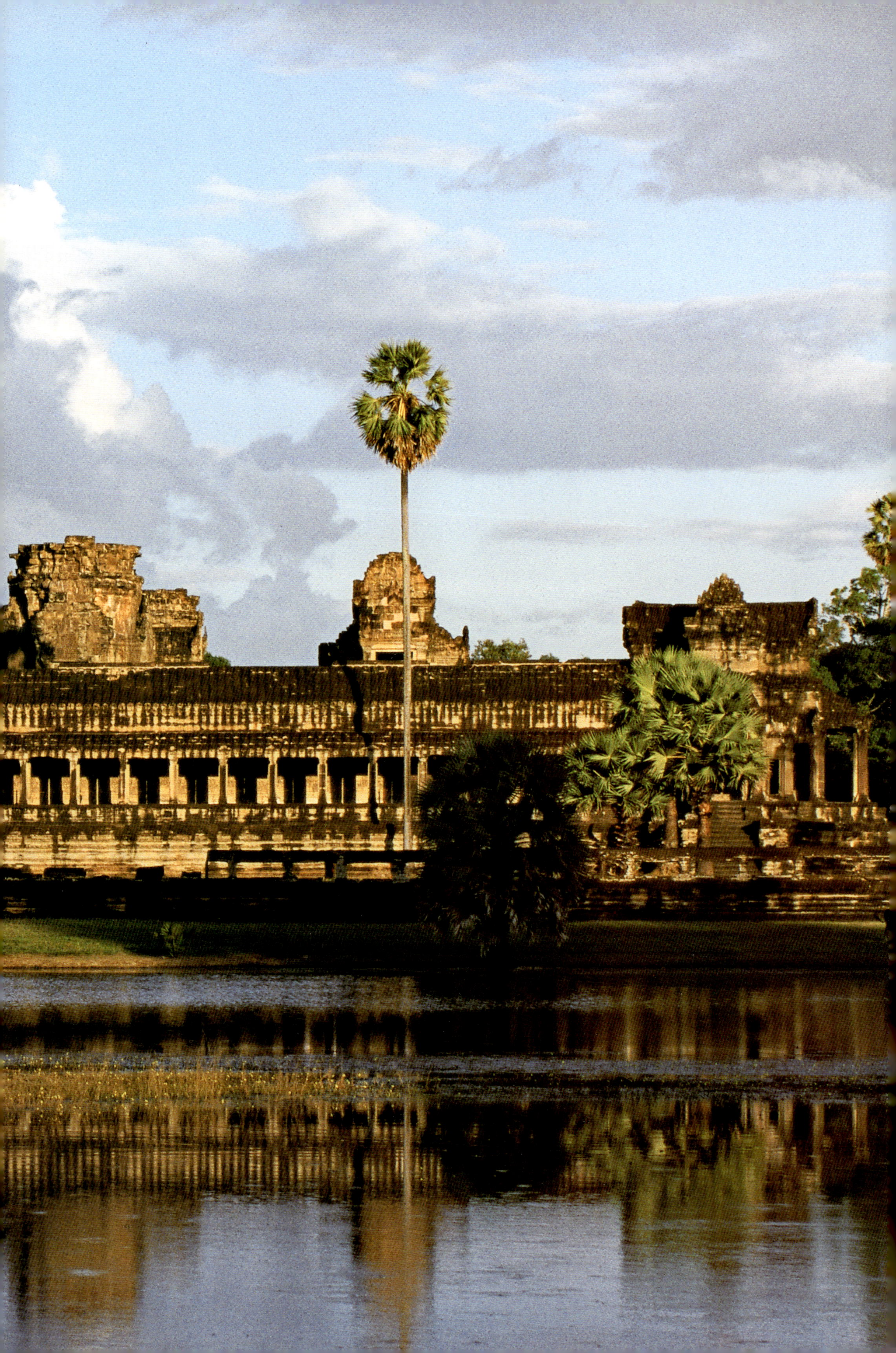

*208 top Halfway along the west dyke there is a terrace with two landing stages, guarded by lions.*

*208 center The telescopic gopuras of the outer enclosure wall, seen here from the inside, join to create a series of staggered tiers that break up the horizontal appearance of the building as a whole.*

*208 bottom This weather-beaten naga, with the façade of the outer enclosure wall in the background, demonstrates the need for restoration work.*

*208-209 At the ends of the front of the outer (fourth) enclosure wall there are entrances for carts and elephants, which were once connected by wooden bridges that spanned the moat.*

On the huge Angkor Wat site, stone buildings and the annexed structures (over 12 million cubic feet of material) only occupy one million square feet because nothing remains of the buildings made of wood and other perishable materials. As mentioned, the king and his court and the population that revolved around it lived inside the outer enclosure of Angkor Wat in addition to the temple personnel. According to Stierlin, it may have had as many as 20,000 residents.

Unusually, the complex is west-facing, thus conflicting with the ritual criteria of Hindu and Khmer architecture, according to which temples should face east. Experts have given various explanations for this fact: its dedication to Vishnu, who was associated with the western quadrant of the universe; its use for funerals, as the west was considered to be the quarter of the dead; or the fact that the new complex was inserted into the existing Yashodharapura and if it faced east, it would have looked away from the previous residential area, which would have been highly inauspicious. Although this last reason seems the most likely, the other two cannot be wholly ruled out.

Angkor Wat is divided into four enclosures and stands on a three-stepped pyramid. Its central tower soars over 200 feet above the Angkor plain (the survey measurements range between 207 and 213 feet). The outermost (fourth) enclosure is made of laterite and

## ANGKOR WAT, *The Stable of the Celestial Oxen*

measures 3,380 feet from east to west and 2,750 feet from north to south (3,363 by 2,631 feet according to Jacques). The moat that surrounds it is crossed by two axial dykes. The east dyke is made of earth, and must have been a service passage. A paved sandstone avenue 820 feet long and 39 feet wide, flanked by a naga-shaped balustrade, is built on the main west dyke. Although the naga, a serpent with five or seven heads, was an Indian motif, it incorporated the local ancestral figure of the water dragon, bringer of rain and symbol of the rainbow that connects heaven and earth, and was consequently used to decorate the avenue that connects the unconsecrated area of old Yashodharapura to the sacred area of Suryavarman's new temple-capital.

Halfway along the avenue there is a cross-shaped platform with stairways leading down to the water to form landing stages. At the end of the avenue visitors see the front of the outer enclosure, consisting of a sandstone gallery with a false vaulted ceiling that rests on a blind wall and a row of square pillars. The portico is 756 feet long and is preceded by a lower half-nave which has almost disappeared, apart from a few pillars. In the middle stands the raised scenic main entrance (which anticipates the one in the third enclosure), consisting of three cross-shaped gopuras surmounted by tall turret-shaped structures, connected by a series of rooms. The central room is larger than the side rooms and is preceded by a double hypostyle portico. At the ends of the gallery front there are two more ground-level passages for animals and carts, while on each of the other three sides of the enclosure there is an axial opening, again in gopura form, but with a simpler structure.

Once inside the enclosure of the sacred city, another paved avenue almost 33 feet wide, raised five feet above ground, stretches for 1,150 feet, flanked by nagas. At regular intervals six stairways on either side descend to ground level where the houses of Suryavarman's city once stood.

*210 top The evidence of Angkor Wat's conversion to a Buddhist temple includes this brick stupa. Originally a reliquary, the stupa became a cosmic symbol. Its five parts symbolize the elements that make up the universe: earth, water, fire, air, and ethereal space.*

*210 center The raised avenue is interrupted by a cross-shaped platform guarded by lions, which was used for ceremonial purposes. The third gallery, which contains the bas-reliefs, can be seen in the background.*

*210 bottom The* nagas *always had an odd number of heads; those portrayed at Angkor Wat had seven.*

*210-211 The tall molded base of the outer enclosure wall is guarded by lions seven feet tall. A second base resting on this first one makes the building appear slenderer, while the balustraded windows with elaborate colonettes lighten the masonry.*

About halfway along the avenue there are two libraries over 130 feet long with a cross-shaped plan, a nave and two aisles 20 feet wide, and a vaulted ceiling, with hypostyle porticoes accessed by staircases on all four sides. A little further on there are two rectangular reservoirs measuring 213 by 164 feet beyond which can be seen the perimeter of a platform around three feet high, measuring 886 by 1,115 feet (846 by 1,089 feet according to Jacques), and accessed from three staircases on each side. The actual temple, divided into three stories, each surrounded by a gallery, stands on this platform. The avenue ends at a cross-shaped platform with two levels, the lowest of which stands on short, squat stilts that herald the main entrance of the third gallery, which surrounds the first of the three levels on which Angkor Wat stands.

The third gallery, which measures 614 by 705 feet, is built on a tall plinth with exquisite moldings, roofed with a false vault, and has a blind inner wall with false colonetted windows and a pillared outer portico on which a hypostyle semi-nave rests. There are four axial entrances in the gallery; the western one is divided into three cross-shaped pavilions connected by rectangular rooms accessed via staircases. The same structure is repeated symmetrically on the east side, while on the other two sides the entrances consist of a single cross-shaped pavilion preceded by porticoes and staircases. The expedient of the cross-shaped pavilion with staircases was used ingeniously at the corners of the perimeter gallery too, where the horizontal design was interrupted by the verticality of the superimposed roofs.

## Angkor Wat, *The Stable of the Celestial Oxen*

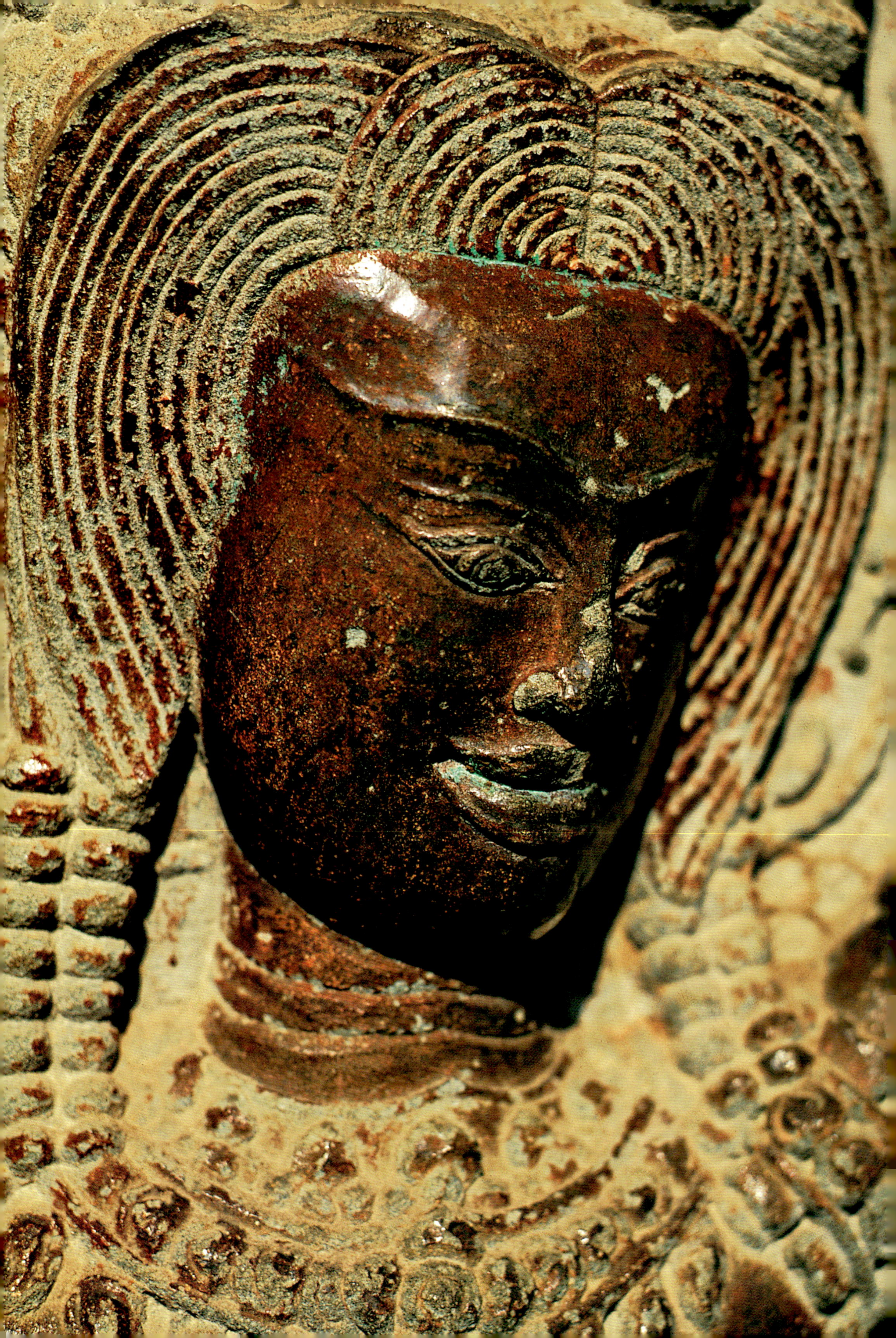

# ANGKOR WAT, The Stable of the Celestial Oxen

*212 One of the favorite hairstyles of the Khmer princesses, whose features inspired those of the* devatas, *was hair plaited from the roots. Their eyes were lined on top and bottom, and perhaps lengthened with soot. This figure, which shows traces of painted stucco, has open eyes, but many other deities are portrayed with their eyes closed.*

*213 top The arched fingers shown in the detail of this* devata *are still a characteristic feature of classical dancers in present-day Cambodia, who practice these finger positions from childhood.*

*213 bottom The sandstone extradoses of the galleries, with their horizontally cut stones and undulations, simulate tiled roofs. The last tiles on the pitched roof are shaped like petals or animals' heads. Antefixes in the shape of* nagas *mark the joints between the staggered tiers of the roofs.*

The blind wall in the third gallery supports an amazing row of bas-reliefs, which unwind for over 1,970 feet (not counting those in the corner pavilions) in a band about six feet high, like illuminated stone manuscripts. Some particularly shiny sections suggest that they were originally covered with a coat of protective paint or lacquer, although the shine may have been caused by the rubbing action of visitors' hands. The first theory is borne out by the presence of traces of red, black, and gold paint in some places. All the subjects relate to the mythology of Vishnu, with whom Suryavarman II, the builder of Angkor Wat, identified, and their overall dynamics have been given different interpretations.

If the temple is viewed in accordance with the pradakshina, the traditional practice of keeping it to one's right, upon entering one should turn left from the entrance pavilion of the west gallery into the north wing. The Battle of Lanka, the crux of the epic poem "Ramayana" whose protagonist is Rama, incarnation of Vishnu and prototype of the perfect king, is portrayed here. Scenes from the same poem also appear in the pavilion in the northwest corner.

Taking the west wing of the north gallery the great Hindu theme of the battle between the deva (gods) and asura (demons) is depicted, presenting a Khmer version of Varuna, god of the waters, portrayed sitting on a many-headed naga instead of the makara (legendary sea monster) which is Vishnu's vahana (vehicle) in Hindu tradition. The theme portrayed in the east wing is once again the battle against evil forces. It celebrates the victory of Krishna over the asura Bana, who was eventually saved by the intercession of Shiva. This panel was sculpted between 1546 and 1564 during the reign of Ang Chan I, who transferred the capital of the Khmer kingdom to Lovek but continued to sponsor the main religious foundations at Angkor.

Passing through the east gallery, the bas-relief of the victory of Vishnu over the demons also dates from the reign of Ang Chan, while the "churning of the sea of milk" depicted in the south wing is inspired by the "Bhagavata Purana" and is contemporary with the foundation of Angkor.

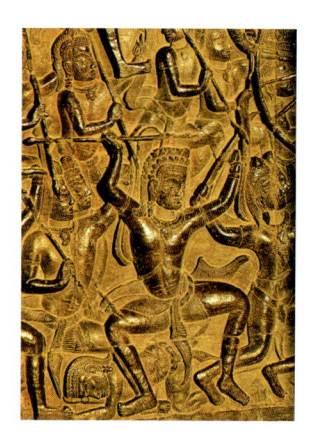

*Continuing a clockwise tour of the south gallery, Suryavarman II dominates the scene. In the east wing, Yama, god of the dead, has the King's features, and presides over the distribution of rewards and punishments, the latter being described in bloodthirsty detail. In the west wing Suryavarman stands out majestically amid the courtiers and soldiers, among whom the mercenary troops and those recruited in provinces inhabited by non-Khmer ethnic groups are recognizable by their clothing, as in the case of the Siamese and the contingents from Lobpuri.*

*Back in the west gallery, the* pradakshina *concludes with the portrayal of the Battle of Kurukshetra, the field to the north of Delhi where*

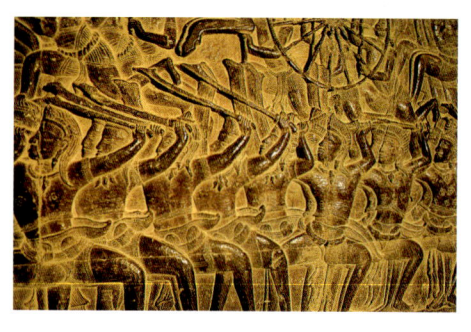

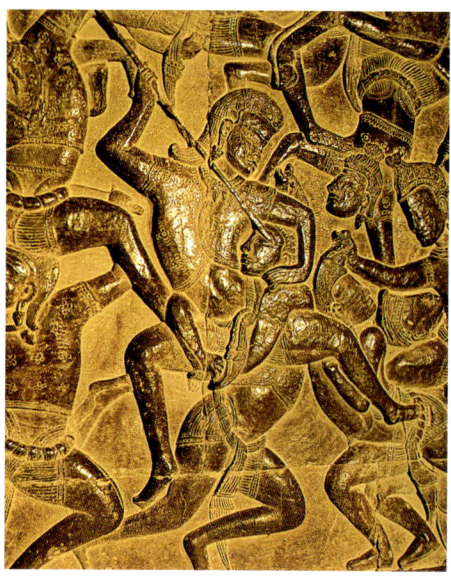

214

# ANGKOR WAT, The Stable of the Celestial Oxen

*214 top  Hundreds of feet of bas-reliefs cover the blind wall of the third gallery of Angkor Wat. These pages show details of the Battle of Kurukshetra, which are portrayed in the west wing.*

*214 center  After tracing the outline, the engravers modeled the figures with a technique borrowed from painting. As a result, the bas-reliefs resemble illuminated manuscripts in stone and form a continuous composition.*

*214 bottom  Heroic figures stand out from the frenzied throng of bodies, catalyzing the dynamic lines of the narration and attracting the viewer's attention.*

*214-215  The postures of the combatants, especially when they are deities as in the case of the protagonists of the Battle of Kurukshetra, often resemble dance steps, and the artists may actually have been inspired by theatrical performances. Khmer culture, which was influenced by Indian culture, must also have cultivated the dramatic arts and represented mythological events.*

216-217 *Violent displays of emotion were considered a sign of instability and lack of self-control and detachment. As a result, they were only portrayed in villainous characters or those of lower rank, as in this detail of the Battle of Lanka, in the north wing of the west gallery, which shows a horde of monkeys and demons.*

the armies of the Pandavas and the Kauravas, the heroes of the great epic poem "Mahabharata," clashed.

The themes of the bas-reliefs symbolize the king's career. In the churning of the sea, the regulatory and saving intervention of Vishnu alludes to the king's social and religious function, the legendary battles against the demons herald wars with the Khmer Empire's neighboring kingdoms, which were considered evil, Suryavarman's triumphal procession celebrates his earthly glory, and his identification with Yama confirms his divine apotheosis.

However, in view of the funerary purpose of Angkor Wat, J. Przyluski and F.D.K. Bosch maintain that the bas-reliefs were meant to be viewed in the reverse order, keeping them on one's left and not on the right. In fact, in funeral rites, the Hindus replace the **pradakshina** with the **prasavya**, an anticlockwise perambulation

*217 top The floral jerkins worn by the warriors may have been made of leather, or even been breastplates. On the powerful chest of the monkey there is a typical banded jewel fastened at the breastbone.*

*217 bottom In the confusion of this scene, the shield that acts as the background to the encounter between the warriors' arms and the monkey's constitutes the center of balance of the action.*

*218-219 Khmer artists were mainly inspired by the Indian epics "Mahabharata" and "Ramayana." The battle of Lanka, a crucial moment in the "Ramayana," whose protagonist is Rama, the incarnation of Vishnu and prototype of the perfect king, is depicted in the north wing of the west gallery of Angkor Wat.*

## ANGKOR WAT, *The Stable of the Celestial Oxen*

around the monument.

Whatever their exact interpretation may be, the bas-reliefs are highly evocative, although their perspective is rather poor. The narration proceeds in two ways, which seems to indicate that they were sculpted at different times, both contemporary with the building of Angkor Wat and after the death of Suryavarman. In the first case the bas-reliefs portray large-scale scenes in which the one or more characters stands out from the throng and the movement converges on a crucial point, while the eye is attracted by psychological features. In the second case, the action is divided into parallel, separate planes and registers, as in the portrayal of the churning, Suryavarman's procession, and the last judgment. The spectator's eye defines the field of vision, which in any event is calibrated to the viewer, and clever details attract the eye to the main elements of the scene.

Between the first and second levels of Angkor Wat stands one of the most brilliant features of the entire building: the cross-shaped cloister. Three parallel corridors lead from the three entrances of the third gallery to staircases with successive landings. These stepped passages, roofed by intradoses with false vaults and extradoses with pediments that fit inside one another, constitute the foreparts of the three cross-shaped entrance pavilions of the upper floor.

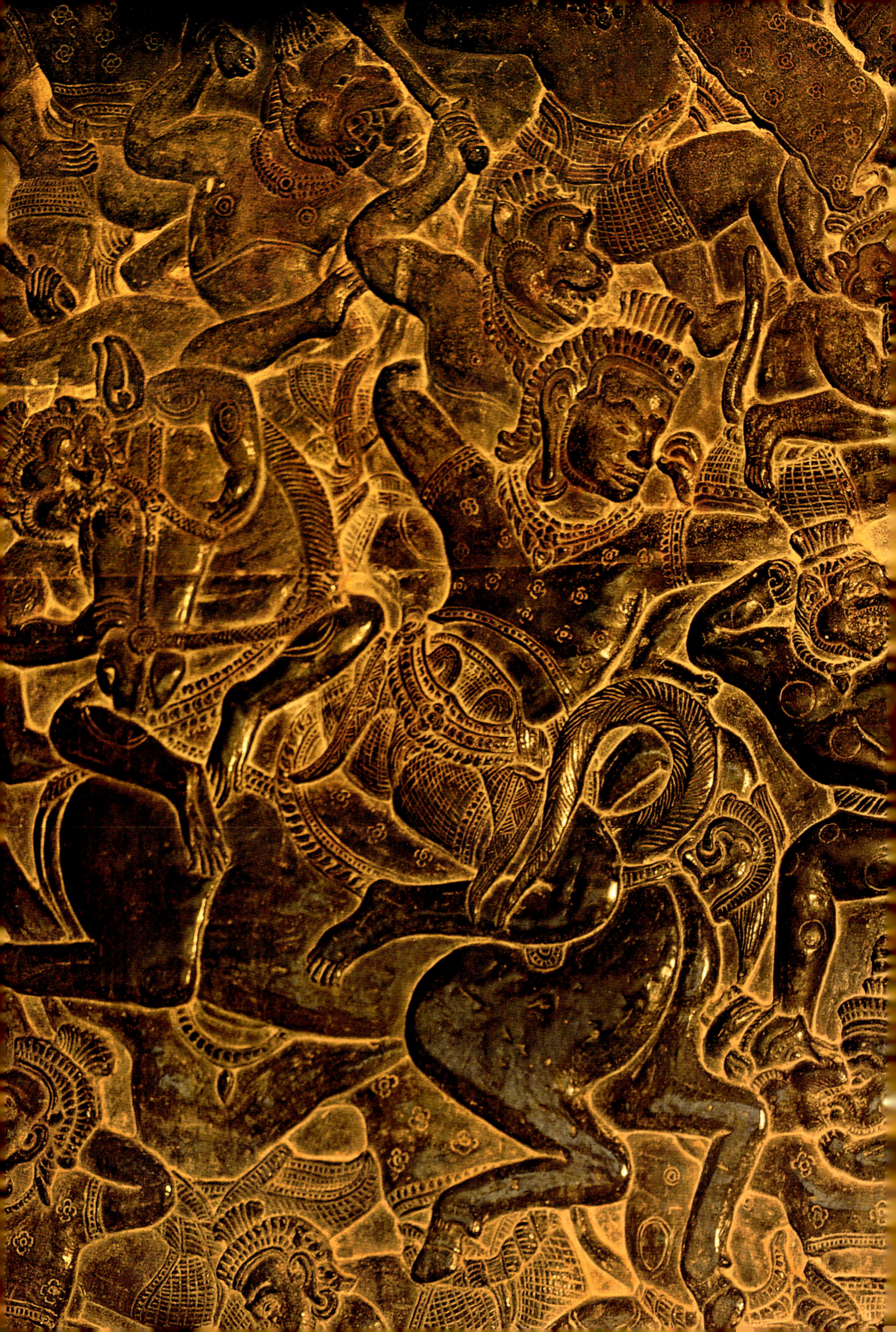

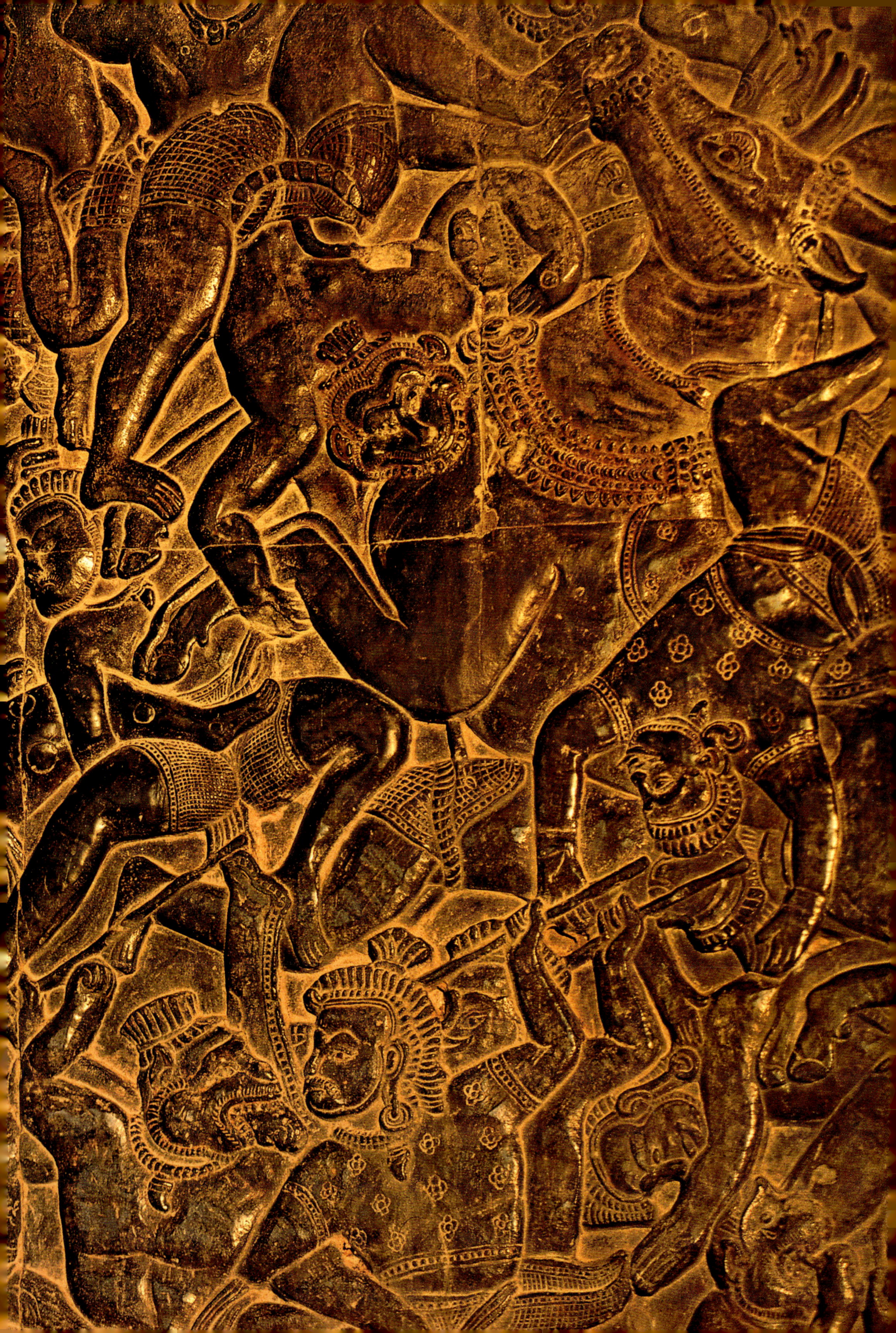

A fourth corridor lies at right angles to the other three, forming four small inner courtyards. This corridor has a nave and two aisles with four rows of pillars; the nave has a false sandstone roof and the aisles have half-vaults. The high plinth on which the courtyards stand, and the steps leading to ground level, identify them as basins for lustral water, which was essential for temple ceremonies. In the corners of the western façade of the first level there are two libraries, one on either side of the cross-shaped cloister, which has two side porticoes facing the courtyard.

The second level is accessed not only from the cloister but also from the courtyard via the terraced entrance pavilions on the other three axes of the second gallery, and from its corner towers, which are full-scale prasat. At the end of the central staircase of the cross-shaped portico there are two more small libraries connected to one another and to the entrance by a raised platform on short stilts. This second level of Angkor Wat was prohibited to the general population; the dark aisleless gallery which borders it, measuring 328 by 377 feet, consequently has no openings in the outer walls, although it is lightened by false colonetted windows.

In the courtyard of the second level stands the base of the third level, a quadrilateral measuring 246 feet per side and 43 feet high (36 feet according to Jacques), which is divided into two highly molded terraces. Twelve steep single-flight staircases with a gradient of up to 70°, each enclosed between four pairs of stout buttresses, lead to the third gallery, which measures 200 feet square. In the outer wall there is a row of colonetted windows, while towards the inside, the gallery, which has the usual false vaulted ceiling, rests on pillars and is bordered by a colonnade that supports a lowered half-vault. The third level reproduces the cross-shaped cloister of the first and connects the central prasat to the axial entrance pavilions by corridors with a nave and two aisles on pillars, thus forming four small courtyards which probably acted as lustral basins. Unlike the cloister on the first level, which had no superstructure at the point where the four corridors met, the stout central prasat, 138 feet tall, dominates the area and subordinates all the other structures to itself, as if sucking them into the spiral of its tiers in a strong vertical sweep.

The prasat, which has a denticulated plan and four vestibules, each preceded by a portico, originally had four real doors and contained a statue of Vishnu. Some experts suggest that it was the one currently housed in the west gopura of the outer enclosure. When the temple was converted to a Buddhist wat, the doors were walled up and images of Buddha carved on them. When the south door was reopened in 1908, the foundation deposit, consisting of two rectangular superimposed blocks of laterite, was found in the cell in a 82-foot well under the torn-out pedestal of the missing statue. In a circular cavity in the lower block there were two sheets of gold leaf and four smaller ones covered with fine sand that contained two white sapphires. Nothing else was found of the treasure that probably once lay there.

Above the buttresses constituted by the pediments of the vestibules and porticoes, the prasat *rises for four more floors until it is crowned by a triple ring of lotus petals and concludes with a lotus bud. The four corner* prasat *imitate the structure of the central one, but on a smaller scale. This third level, which symbolized the palace of the gods on Mount Meru, was only accessible to the high priest and the king, who identified with the god portrayed in the statue in the central shrine.*

*The five* prasat *of the quincunx were not the only tower shrines at Angkor Wat: the corner towers in the second gallery were also temples, as were the three above the entrances of the outermost enclosure. There were consequently a total of 12* prasat. *C. Jacques points out that this number recurs: there are 12 staircases in the second access avenue, 12 on the platform on which the main temple stands, 12 leading to the third level, and the third enclosure has 12 entrances. This number obviously had a particular significance in addition to the number of signs of the zodiac and animals in the Chinese calendar.*

220 top *The planning of the complex is attributed by some experts to Divakarapandita, a famous Brahman who was minister and spiritual adviser to Suryavarman II and his two predecessors.*

220 bottom *The central prasat of Angkor Wat, with its projections and recesses, symbolizes the center of the universe, the cosmic mountain which is the dwelling-place of the gods.*

220-221 *As there were no natural hills available, the hill on which the pyramid stands was built artificially using earth and rubble.*

*222 The devata with the improbable hairstyle wears garlands of flowers visible at the sides of her face which, according to the canons of beauty of the period, was supposed to resemble a full moon. Other signs of beauty were fleshy lips and cheeks as fresh as fruit, firm breasts resembling flowers about to blossom, and a deep navel.*

The decoration admirably completes the monument. The multifaceted colonettes are divided into ten or twelve rings which make them light and vibrant and the flat interweave of plants carved on the walls produces a tapestry effect that recalls the silk brocades with large floral patterns imported from China, which were used, among other things, to conceal the intradoses. The extradoses imitate tiles, reproducing them down to the smallest detail. More than 1500 **devatas** (goddesses with complex hairstyles) and **apsaras** (dancing nymphs) decorate Angkor Wat, materializing on the bare walls, peeping out from niches, and smiling enigmatically against a background of trees in blossom. Sinuous many-headed **nagas** surround the pediments, softening their contours, while on the tympana, crowded mythological scenes stand out dynamically against the uniform background of the roofs.

Although the construction had some technical defects, such as the unsolved problem of the vault, made by corbelling, and the little attention paid to vertical staggering of the stones, which could have prevented the spaces between them from widening, Angkor Wat is undoubtedly a masterpiece from an architectural standpoint. Its perfection is due to the observance of a few stereometric principles. For example, the avenue between the entrance pavilion and the temple is almost twice as long as the west façade, permitting the entire monument to be seen because it is at a perspective distance twice as long as its largest dimension. Each of the three terraces is twice as high as the previous one, and its area is no more than half that of the previous one, thus preventing the gallery on the lower terrace from concealing the one on the terrace above and at the same time giving the viewer the impression of a perfect pyramid. Moreover, each terrace is recessed east from the previous one, or in other words, in the opposite direction from the entrance, so that the monument does not appear to lean forwards.

At the height of its power the Khmer Empire produced the perfect building, making manifest the dream of paradise on earth and giving mankind a masterpiece of supreme beauty.

*222-223 The face of this devata, with her eyes closed as if intent on inner contemplation, is not at all stylized, and the earlobes deformed by heavy earrings are taken from real life.*

## ANGKOR WAT, *The Stable of the Celestial Oxen*

# ANGKOR WAT, The Stable of the Celestial Oxen

*224 top* This **devata** under a canopy of flowers, portrayed against the background of an attractive balustraded window, is inspired by the Indian motif of the Yakshi, the dryad associated with trees in blossom.

*224 bottom* The **devatas** were a fertility symbol and evoke pleasure, although their sensuality was always restrained. In esoteric terms they were aspects of Shakti, the divine female energy that underlies the cosmos.

*225 top and bottom left* These two **devatas** wear the same amulet round their necks. The one on the right is weaving flowering tendrils in her hair, emphasizing her connection with the world of plants, against the background of which the figure on the pilaster is portrayed.

*225 right* The floral context and its symbols emphasize that the **devatas** embodied the vital forces of nature. This one, like many of her companions, is holding a root of **utpala** (blue lotus).

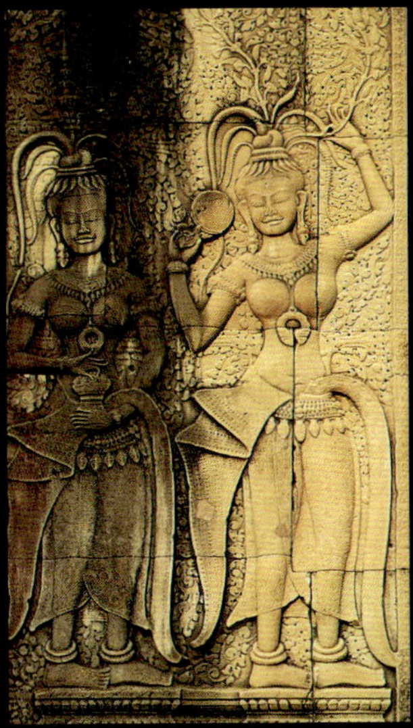
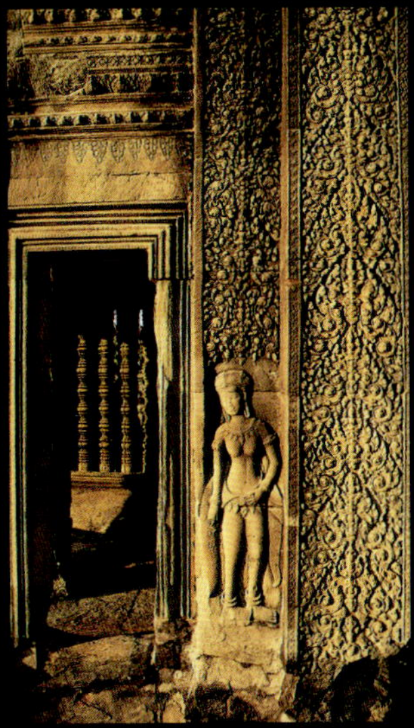
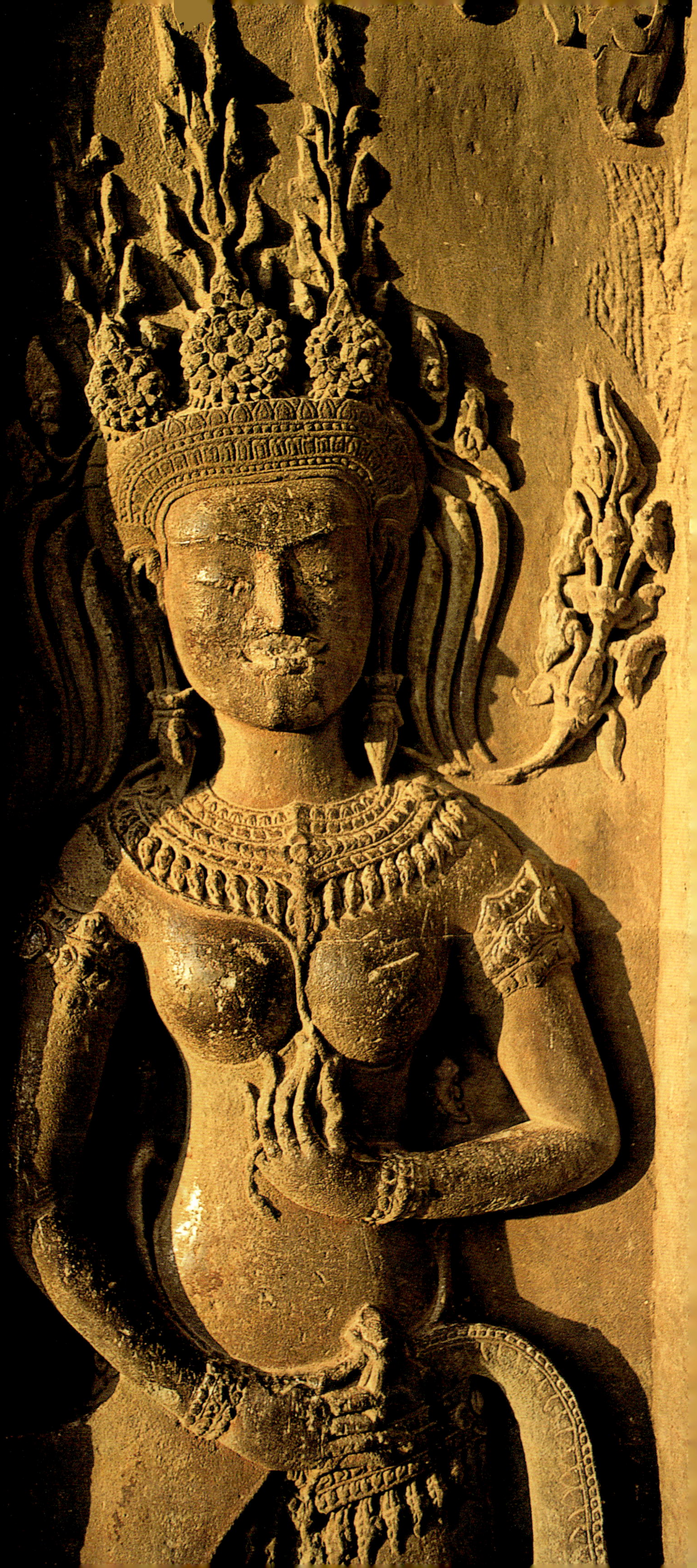

*226-227 Angkor Thom, the capital built by Jayavarman VII after the sack perpetrated by the Cham in 1177, was surrounded by walls. It had five gates, four of which were axial (this photo shows the west gate), and a fifth on the east side, aligned with the Royal Palace and known as the "Victory Gate." In accordance with Indian customs the city was laid out as a vastupurushamandala, a grid divided into* padas *(squares), each of which was protected by a particular deity, while each building, caste, and guild had its own specific location.*

*227 top The east gate, on the left, and the Victory Gate, on the right, like the others, are surmounted by faces of Lokeshvara-Jayavarman.*

# ANGKOR THOM
## The City Protected by the Gods

After the terrible sack of Yashodharapura in 1177 by the Cham, led by Jaya Indravarman IV, an energetic commander who had not forgotten the Khmer incursions into his land and who reached the capital by sailing up the Mekong, the Tonlé Sap, and perhaps the Siem Reap Rivers, Jayavarman VII drove out his enemies and decided to build an invincible city, once firmly ensconced on the throne.

Now known as **Angkor Thom** (great capital), it is believed to have hosted a million inhabitants, including the court, priests, high officials, and civil servants, while some of the common people lived outside the fortifications. Constructed on the site of the previous settlement built by Udayadityavarman around Baphuon, Angkor Thom is surrounded by a stout laterite wall measuring two miles square, edged by a moat 328 feet wide and up to 20 feet deep. On the inner side of the walls, which are up to 26 feet tall, is a rampart 82 feet wide along which the parapet walk runs. At the corners stand four small temples, all called Prasat Chrung, which contain stelae bearing details of the construction of the city. Around 300 feet away from the walls, a canal up to 130 feet wide formed an additional inner perimeter at that time. Along it ran a road that served for troop movements and ritual processions involving the perambulation of the town.

Angkor Thom was accessed by way of five laterite dykes that crossed the outer moat and led to five monumental gates; four stood on the axes and a fifth, known as the "Victory Gate," was added on the east side to access the Royal Square and the Palace. Five avenues 100 to 130 feet wide, flanked by moats 26 feet wide that flowed into the inner perimeter canal, led from the gates. The city was divided into padas (residential squares) according to the traditional Hindu urban grid, which featured right-angled roads and precise positioning of buildings in accordance with their function. According to H. Stierlin, Angkor Thom had 144 padas which measured 820 feet square, and therefore covered an area of 672,700 square feet each.

The city's water requirements were supplied by the Jayatataka, the new "victory baray" measuring 11,480 by 2,950 feet built by Jayavarman, and a complex system of canals. Waste water flowed into a lake in the southwest corner, Beng Thom, whose contents were discharged into the southern outer moat through five vaulted canals 200 feet long, which ran beneath the walls. The moats, canals, and water intakes and outlets were lined with laterite and constituted one of the most perfect hydraulic networks in Indochina.

Each of the five entrance gates, which are up to 75 feet tall, is surmounted by a turret-shaped structure consisting of four faces reproducing the bodhisattva *Lokeshvara*, with whom Jayavarman VII identified. The faces of the lord of compassion with the king's features, which probably appeared for the first time at the Preah Khan of Kompong Svay, turn their solicitous gaze towards the four corners of the kingdom, guaranteeing their protection.

The defense of Angkor Thom did not rely only on buildings but also on the complex apotropaic symbolism on which their construction was based.

227

| ANGKOR THOM | | | |
|---|---|---|---|
| **A** | Moat | **L** | Royal Palace |
| **B** | Dykes | **M** | Phimeanakas |
| **C** | Gates | **N** | Elephant Terrace |
| **D** | Walls | **O** | Terrace of the Leper King |
| **E** | Axial Roads | **P** | Prasat Suor Prat |
| **F** | Victory Road | **Q** | Khleang |
| **G** | Royal Square | **R** | Preah Pithu Complex |
| **H** | Bayon | **S** | Beng Thom, Drainage Reservoir |
| **I** | Baphuon | | |
| **J** | Gopura | | |
| **K** | Reservoirs | | |

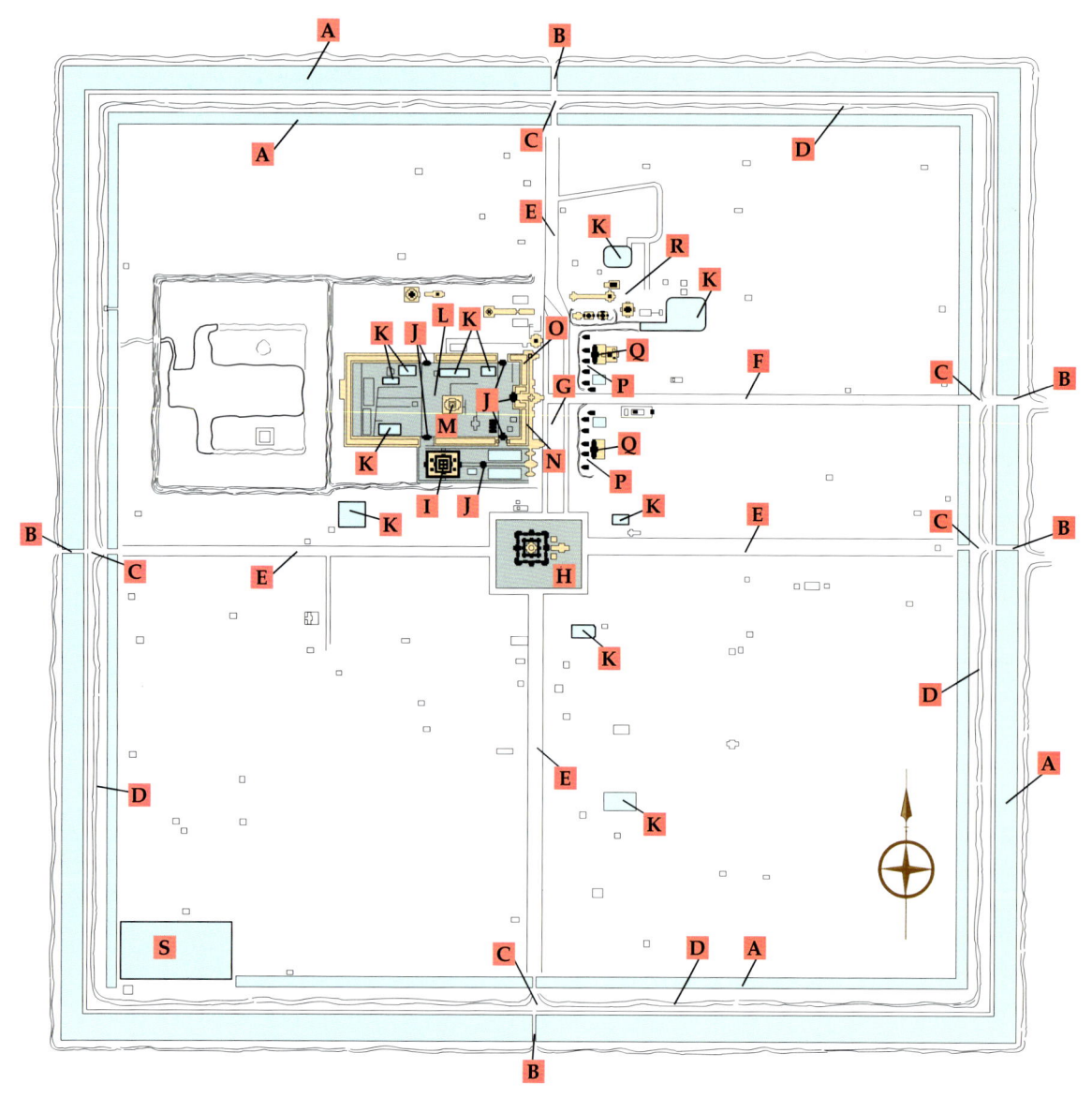

*228 top and bottom To increase the magical/religious power of the city, Jayavarman had 54 figures of gods and 54 of demons installed at the sides of the avenues built on the dykes that crossed the perimeter moat of Angkor Thom at the gates. They alluded to the legend of the "churning of the sea" and reproduced the Tavatimsha (paradise of Indra). This photo shows the south gate with the gods (top) and demons (bottom).*

*228-229 Gopuras with four faces became a particularly impressive sculptural element. The one on the south gate is shown here.*

The architects continued to reproduce Hindu cosmography. The city rotates around the Bayon, the mountain temple that symbolises Mont Meru, just as Jambudvipa, the "rose-apple continent" which incorporates India, lies at the foot of the cosmic mountain, surrounded by another six rings of earths alternating with seas. When Angkor Thom was built, Buddhist cosmography was also taken into account, which encloses the world in a wall of rock beyond which lies the great cosmic sea, symbolized by the enclosure wall and moat .

However, the city of Jayavarman VII was also associated with the myth of the "churning of the sea of milk," and after the first experiment at the Preah Khan of Angkor, the builders aligned two rows of "giants" in front of each gate at Angkor Thom. There were 54 devas (gods) on the left and 54 asuras (demons) on the right, totaling the sacred number of 108 protectors of the city. The asuras, which were subjugated to the royal power, kept away evil influences and enemies. The devas and asuras support a many-headed naga, which is both the primordial serpent Vasuki of Hindu myth and the Khmer symbol of the rainbow, a bridge between heaven and earth, which is the emblem of the pact of benevolence of the celestial powers that send fertilizing rain. The nagas, with their seven heads ready to spit poison, open the rows of giants and close them with their erect tails.

The gods at the south gate are matched by the demons at the north gate and vice versa, and the same applies to the east and west gates. The movement of gods and demons which alternatively pull the serpent ensures the life of the city, protected by the powers of light and darkness, which are both essential as they are polar forces, whose opposition generates the dynamism of life. As a result, the rotation of the cosmic mountain, Meru-Bayon, achieves the extraction of amrita, the ambrosia of immortality that makes Angkor Thom impregnable. Jayavarman therefore built a city protected by divine forces and at the same time used them to ensure his own immortality.

The gopuras, which were transformed from an architectural element to a gigantic statuary group, also performed a protective function. In the corners of the doors Indra, the warlike sovereign of the celestial ranks riding a three-headed elephant, stands guard armed with the vajra, the divine thunderbolt that destroys enemies. Boisselier considers the giants of Angkor Thom to actually be yaksha, in this case attendants of Indra, who celebrate the victory of the god over the demons, and that Jayavarman VII's capital was consequently identified with Tavatimsha, the paradise of Indra.

From the top of the doors Lokeshvara also stands guard, his attentive, compassionate faces looking in all directions, and the Hindu myth is redefined in the Buddhist context. Everything combines to reinforce the protective symbolism of the city, which was finally made comprehensible to the populace, who until then had had no access to the innermost or highest parts of the temples and who understood little or nothing of the esoteric meaning of the Indian myths.

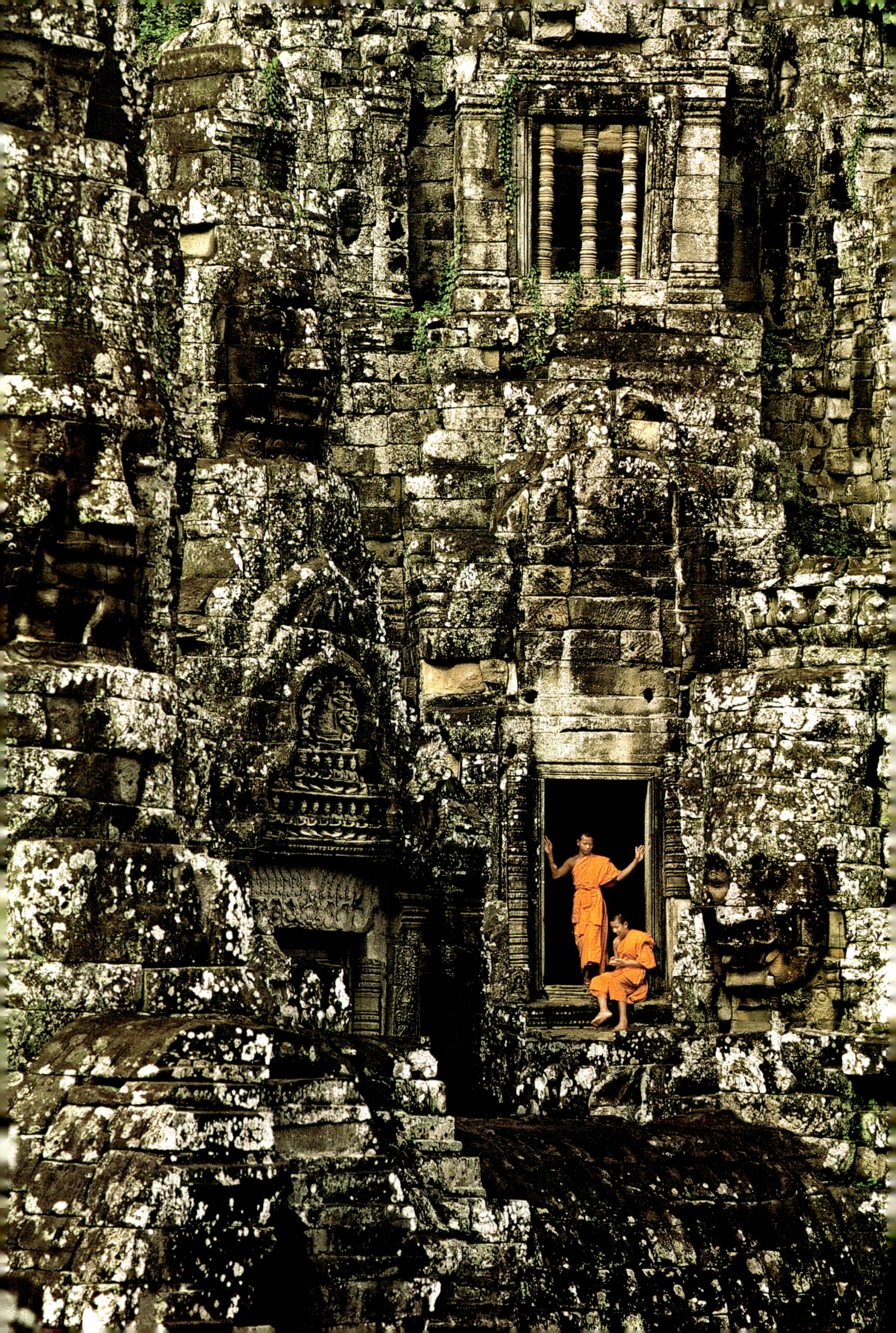

*230 The mountain temple of Angkor Thom, the Bayon, symbolically represents the center of the universe. It therefore stands in the middle of the city, where the two main roads crossed. Complex and enigmatic, it is one of the most evocative religious buildings in the world.*

*231 top The Bayon complex consisted of an unknown number of prasats, perhaps 54 to equal the number of gods and demons in the city's access avenues. The temple contained not only Buddhist deities but also Hindu and local gods, thus symbolizing the unity of the Empire.*

*231 bottom Whether it represented Lokeshvara, the bodhisattva of compassion, or the Enlightened One himself as the Buddharaja, the face on the Bayon bears the features of Jayavarman VII. Some experts believe that above the prasats with four faces there was a fifth made of gold.*

## THE BAYON, Faces in the Jungle

At the center of Angkor Thom, Jayavarman built the **Bayon**, his mountain temple, an awesome symbol of the megalomania of the king, who was obsessed by the desire for immortality and at the same time hungry for power and mysticism. The temple, which is difficult to interpret because it was renovated on numerous occasions, stands on the site of an earlier building that probably had a Greek cross plan. The Bayon was initially believed to be a Hindu shrine; it was not until 1925 that it was recognised as Buddhist. It was correctly dated by Coedès in 1928 as a result of Stern's studies.

The first structure encountered when approaching from the east is a platform on two levels that measures 236 feet, flanked by two reservoirs which are 82 feet square. The temple is surrounded by three enclosure walls and stands on three levels.

The outermost enclosure, a rectangle measuring 512 by 463 feet, consists of a gallery with a blind wall towards the inside and a double row of pillars towards the outside, which suggests the addition of a half-nave. On the blind wall, which is 15 feet tall, there is a magnificent set of bas-reliefs that celebrate Jayavarman VII's victory over the Cham in the great naval battle of Tonlé Sap. At the edge of the battle scenes, everyday life continues on the banks of the lake in the houses on stilts. At the market, the men drink brandy and watch cock and mastiff fights. In the palaces, princesses dress and noblemen play chess. The common people walk, carrying their goods on the heads, while the rich are carried in litters. The natural backgrounds are portrayed in great detail, and the lake fauna is depicted with fresh precision. The scene is no longer dominated only by gods and kings, but by the ordinary people, who in the twilight of the Empire's history finally gained the right to appear alongside their dominators.

The corner towers and access pavilions of the gallery are cross-shaped with wide projecting porticoes, and the four central pillars of the main hall are larger than the eight surrounding ones. These hypostyle buildings, measuring 66 feet square, had a false vaulted ceiling which did not hold up because of the size of its span and its design faults. The techniques used were borrowed from carpentry and involved the use of cross-gables, a system that proved inadequate to support the roofing stones.

Two libraries stand in the eastern corners of the courtyard bounded by an outer gallery. The bases of 16 rectangular buildings, possibly demolished upon the death of Jayavarman, are also partly visible. They are arranged in a perpendicular pattern, four on each side, between the third and second galleries, creating 16 small courtyards. They are entered through simple doors in the wall featuring bas-reliefs. The 16 buildings seem to have been shrines which contained images of the main Khmer deities and those of the various subjugated provinces.

The second gallery, measuring 230 by 260 feet, is accessed by climbing four feet four inches. It has a nave and two aisles, a blind wall towards the outside, which is also decorated with bas-reliefs, and a series of pillars, and inside it has a windowed nave and a pillared portico. There are a total of 16 towers, surmounted by the four faces of Lokeshvara, on the triple gopuras of the four axial entrances and on the four corner towers. The second gallery was probably added to the primitive cross-shaped structure to transform it into a rectangle with four perpendicular wings. In any case, the open spaces are very small, reduced to small courtyard-wells at the corners, because the cross-shaped platform on the third level occupies nearly the whole area of the second.

| | BAYON | | |
|---|---|---|---|
| A | RESERVOIRS | F | GOPURA |
| B | TWO-TIERED PLATFORM | G | CORNER TOWERS |
| | | H | "LIBRARIES" |
| C | FIRST LEVEL AND BAS-RELIEF GALLERY | I | PRASAT |
| | | J | CENTRAL PRASAT |
| D | SECOND LEVEL | K | RADIAL SHRINES |
| E | THIRD LEVEL | L | FOREPART OF CENTRAL PRASAT |

*232-233 Initially planned as a ground-level temple with 16 shrines, the Bayon was rebuilt on numerous occasions, and its height was increased. The central prasat, situated on the third level shown here, probably had a cross-shaped plan originally. Its present shape is the result of the addition of the radial chapels.*

*233 top This aerial view shows the Bayon and the annexes of the Royal Palace behind it. The jungle has encroached on what was once the urban area. The boundary of the city was marked by a wide moat with roads built on the embankments, while a network of right-angled canals separated the various districts, providing them both with clean water and drainage for their dirty water. The streets intersected at right angles, and the main road that ran from east to west was known as the "royal road."*

*233 center Part of the false ceiling of the south wing of the inner (second) gallery still survives. The base of one of the 16 shrines which were apparently demolished by Jayavarman VII's successor can be seen in the bottom right-hand corner of the photo.*

*233 bottom left The hasty builders failed to decorate the cornice of this door, which offers one of many views of the faces on the Bayon.*

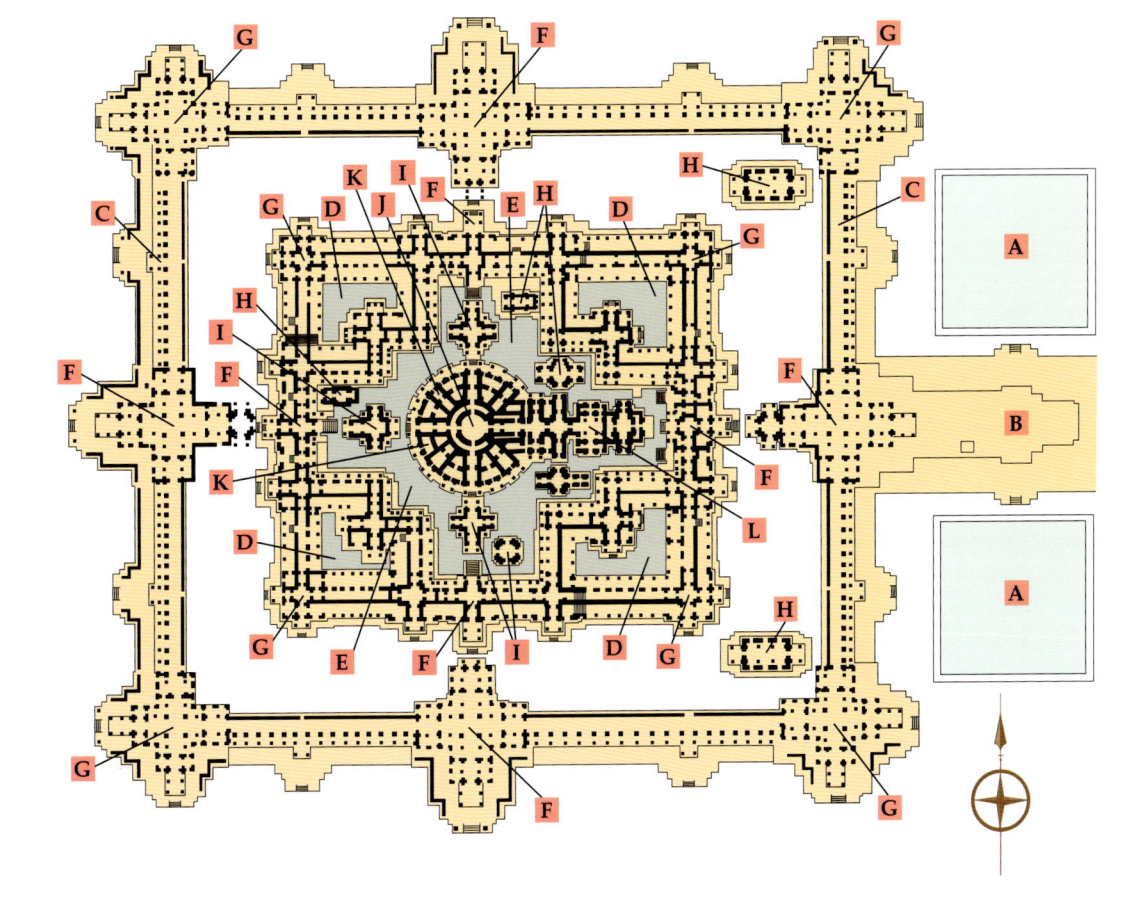

233

The feeling of claustrophobia disappears when, ten feet higher up, we come out onto the third floor and find ourselves in a forest of petrified faces dominated by the formidable central prasat, which has a diameter of 82 feet and stands 141 feet above ground level. Inside the dark grotto-cell which has a diameter of 16 feet, stood a 12-foot tall statue of Buddha sitting on the coils of the serpent Mucilinda, whose seven heads acted as his canopy. Its features were those of the king. The statue, which was hacked to pieces and thrown into the foundation well during the Brahmanic restoration after Jayavarman's death, was found in 1933, restored, and replaced on a terrace to the east of southern Khleang.

The central prasat and its cell have a circular plan as they are inspired by the stupa, the first Buddhist monument to be built in India as a funerary mound for the ashes of the historical Buddha. Around the cell runs the pradakshinapatha, the corridor used to perform the pradakshina ritual, during which worshippers had to walk around the stupa, keeping it on their right in sign of veneration. The stupa thus came to replace the shrine of the devaraja.

The circular shape alludes to the mandala, the sacred pattern of Buddhist initiation and meditation, and to the Wheel of the Doctrine, consisting of eight spokes, representing the eight-fold path of rectitude, which is the symbol of Buddhism. Around the cell there are eight radial shrines with porticoes. The eastern shrine is preceded by a large forepart divided into four rooms, each with a double portico. The shrines

*235 center The Khmer army is shown on the march on a number of registers in the south wing of the east gallery of the first enclosure. The character in the left-hand corner is striking a gong.*

*235 bottom There are intriguing details, like this scene in which a soldier appears to be urinating, looking towards the spectator, almost as if the artist were making fun of his client.*

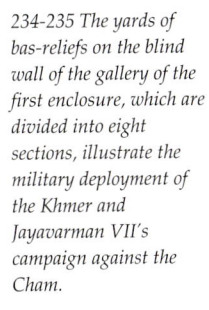

*234-235 The yards of bas-reliefs on the blind wall of the gallery of the first enclosure, which are divided into eight sections, illustrate the military deployment of the Khmer and Jayavarman VII's campaign against the Cham.*

*235 top A dvarapala and a devata, inserted into floral niches, guard the south entrance to the second gallery. The front edge of the woman's sarong is folded over into a shark-tail shape.*

## THE BAYON, Faces in the Jungle

*236 top and center Ritual dances accompanied the army to the sound of tambourines, a double-headed drum, and a horn.*

*236 bottom left  The naval battle between the Khmer and the Cham on the Tonlé Sap is portrayed in the east wing of the south gallery.*

*236 bottom right  This devata holding a dove shows the hasty assembly of the sandstone blocks, which are no longer smooth.*

*236-237  A lush forest, with coconut-laden palms and trees in blossom, full of birds, can be glimpsed behind the infantry, with their protective breastplates and shields. The portrayal of nature is highly accurate.*

probably housed members of the deified royal family, and eventually the spaces between them were transformed into additional porticoed areas, bringing the total number of radial shrines to 16. The central prasat is also connected to the first gallery on the other three sides via three porticoed cross-shaped prasats.

According to Paul Mus, there must originally have been 54 prasats, which means over 200 faces of Lokeshvara with the features of Jayavarman smiled down at visitors. The faces of the compassionate lord, looking towards the cardinal points, watched over the Khmer people. However, although Lokeshvara is a bodhisattva, it is the symbolism of the Buddharaja (Buddha-king) that is evoked. The Bayon complex celebrates not only the functional role of the king, who was identified as Lokeshvara and therefore the solicitous guardian of his subjects' welfare, but also his innermost essence, his Buddhahood, from which the bodhisattvas emanate. The faces, gradually illuminated by the sun, reflect the alternation of light and shade, the passing of time, and the incessant rhythm of the universe. Not only space is celebrated and crystallized in the sacred architecture, but also time, as the building represents and transcends the two ways of measuring human beings and their lives.

The Bayon, a gigantic three-dimensional spiral, appears to coil upwards towards the sky, rising from the levels of everyday life to the heights of the spiritual dimension. But nirvana, the extinction of life and ultimate goal in the Buddhist path to liberation, must have unconsciously attracted Jayavarman. The proliferation of the king's faces, which was intended to symbolize the ubiquity of his protection and benevolence, betrays his thirst for power and fear of death.

*239 and 240-241 Lokeshvara-Jayavarman always wears a diadem, crown, and heavy earrings, and sometimes a bejeweled collar. The particular shape of the eyes makes them appear to be open or closed, depending on the light and the perspective. The fleshy lips, whose raised corners suggest a serene, detached smile, are often disquieting.*

## THE BAYON, Faces in the Jungle

*238 top  As a result of the enormous amount of building work carried out, high-quality sandstone had become very scarce by the reign of Jayavarman VII, as the quarries to the north of Beng Mealea had nearly been depleted.*

*238 center  Here, the faces rest on a more or less elaborate cornice. However, the buildings were erected in such haste that the cornice is often missing. At the time of Jayavarman VII, a tower 40 feet high and 16 feet square could apparently be built in a month.*

*238 bottom  This photo shows the structure of the Bayon towers. The four faces wholly or partly replace the tiers of the roof, and the finial always consists of a double lotus blossom. Despite its apparent uniformity, the roof structure varied considerably, depending on the monument it covered.*

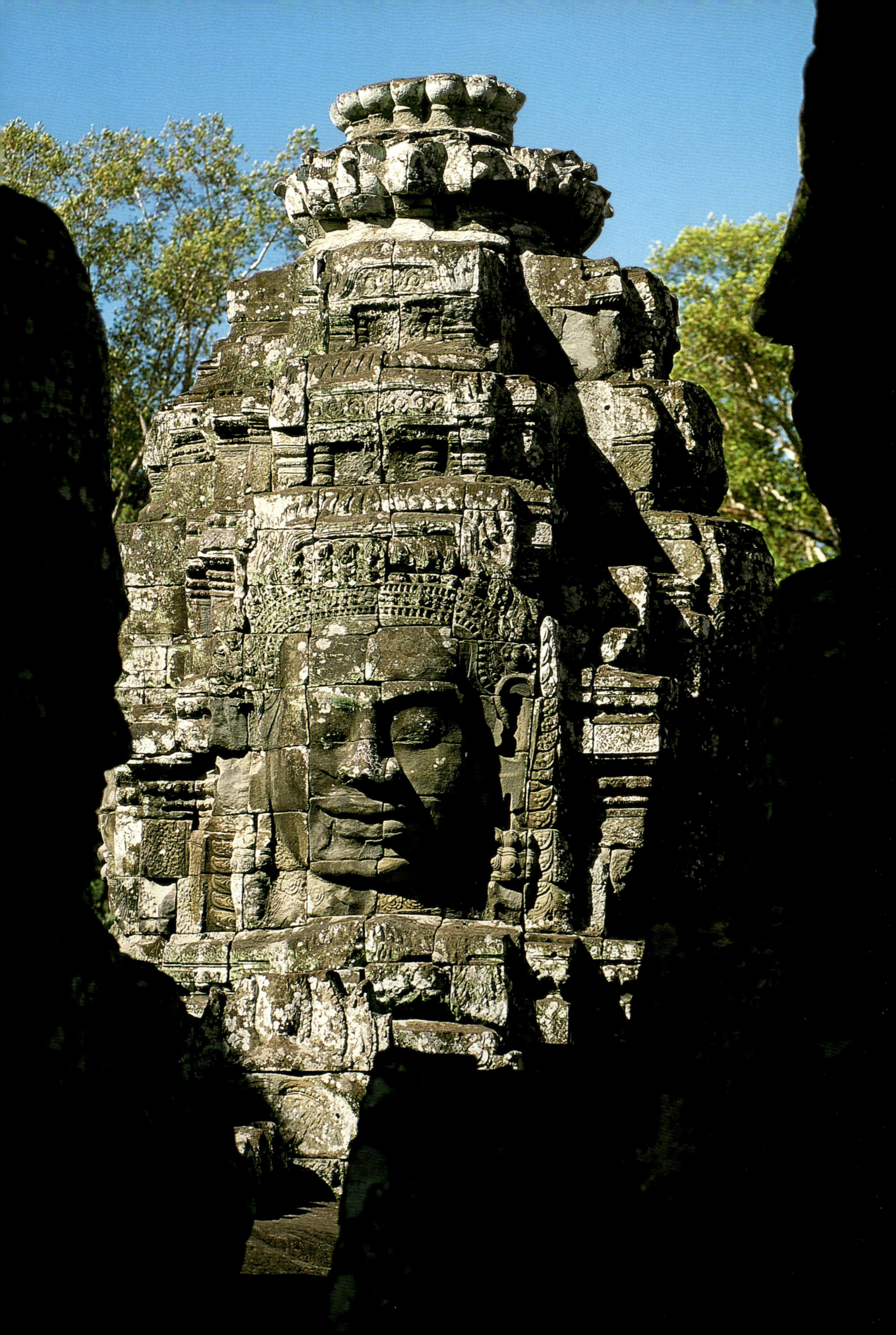

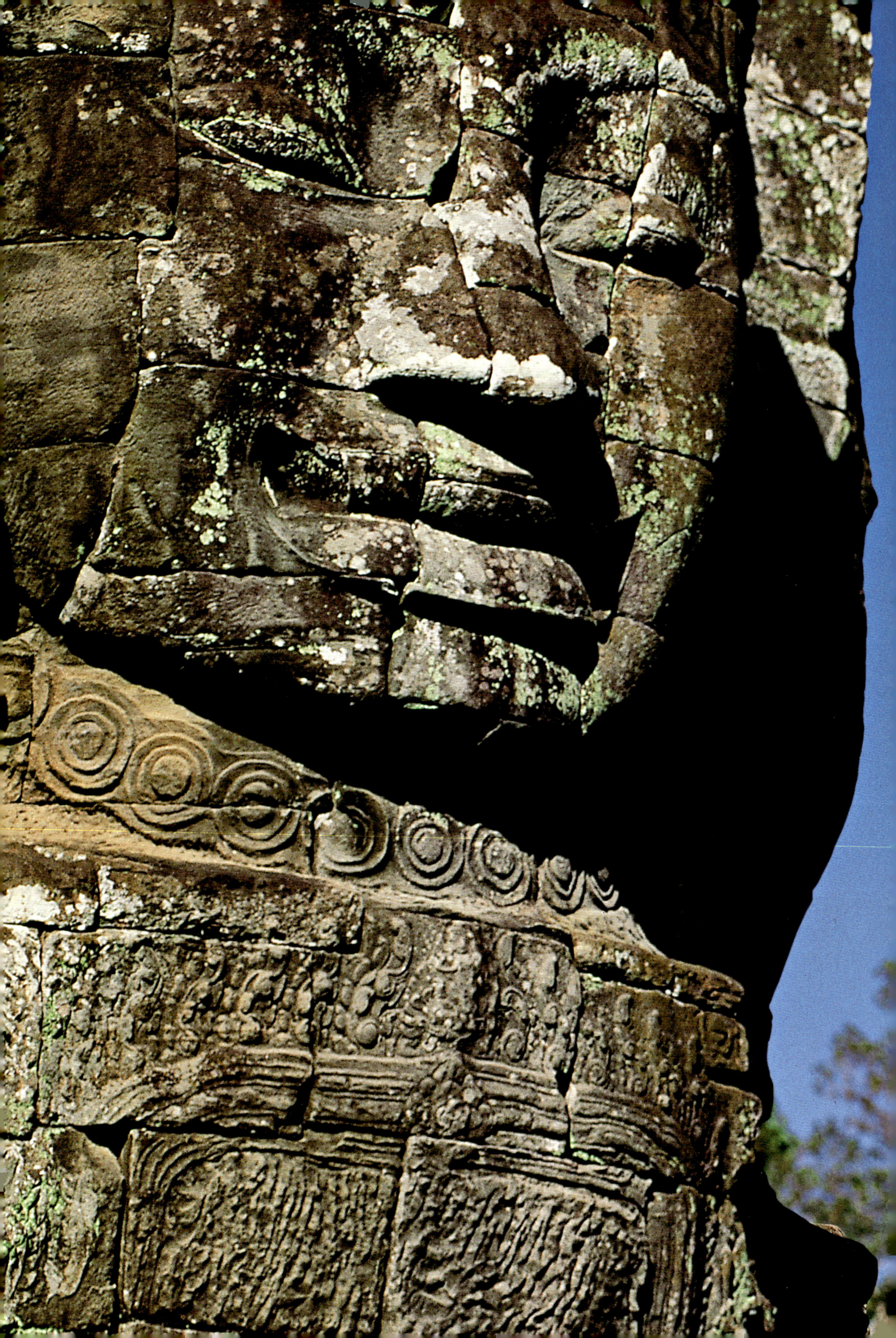

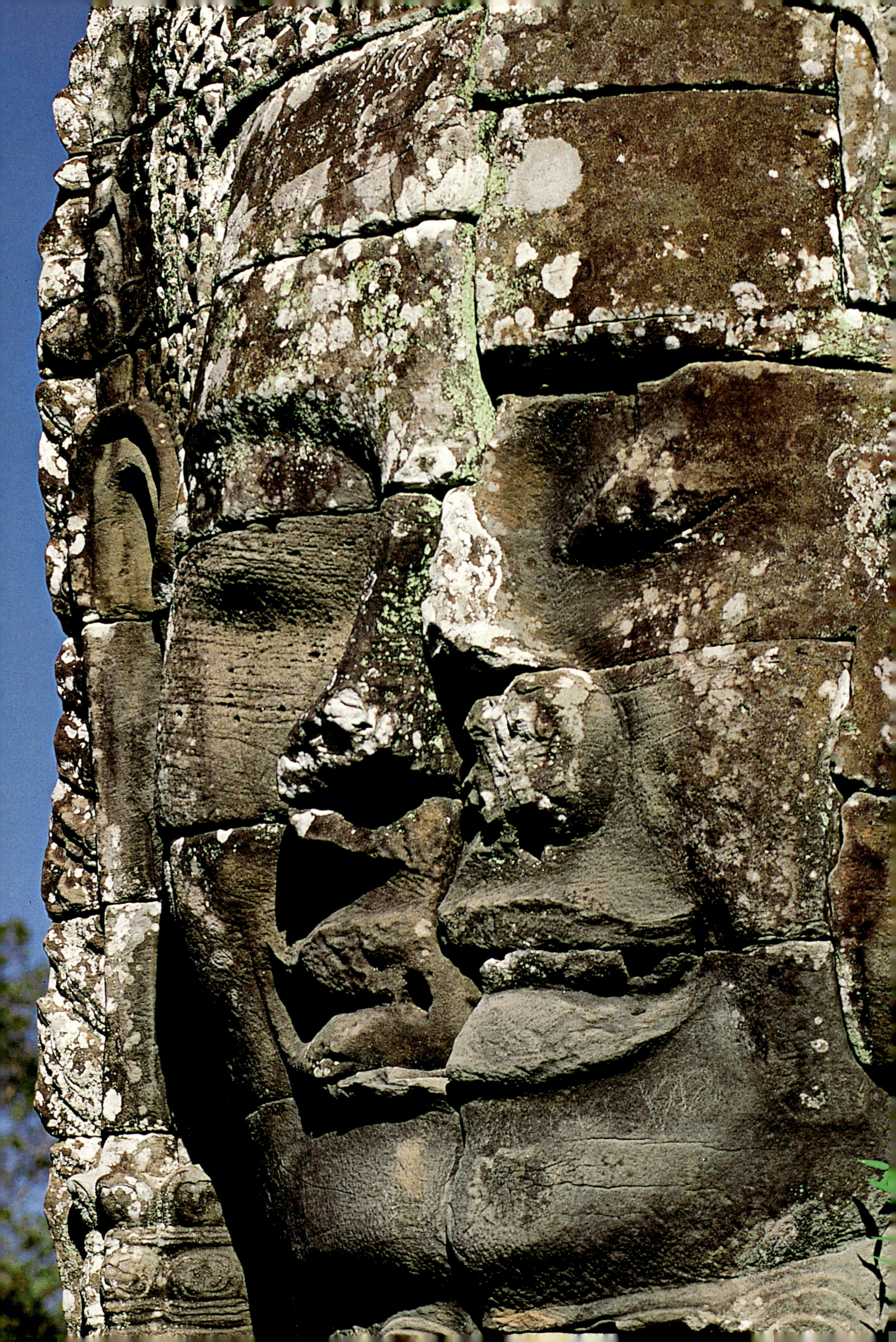

242 top  The purpose of the twelve towers known as Prasat Suor Prat, on the east side of the Royal Square, is still unknown. They may date from after the reign of Jayavarman VII.

242 bottom left  When the Elephant Terrace was successively extended, some parts were covered, like this five-headed horse on the wall at the northern end, in front of which another wall was built.

# ANGKOR THOM, the Royal Palace and the Elephant Terrace

Although he was the greatest builder of all the Khmer kings, Jayavarman VII lived in wooden structures, choosing as his residence the ancient **Royal Palace** built around Phimeanakas, situated in the northwest quadrant of Angkor Thom. All that remains of the great complex is the laterite walls with the access gopuras, built earlier than Jayavarman's reign, and two reservoirs, the largest of which appears to have been renovated by the king. This pool, known as the "queen's bath," measures 410 by 150 feet, and is bordered with steps decorated with reliefs of garudas, nagas, fish, and other aquatic creatures.

The scenic layout of the **Royal Square**, which overlooks the eastern façade of the palace and was used for parades, triumphal performances, and ceremonies, is also attributed to Jayavarman. The avenue that runs from the Victory Gate leads into the east side of the square between two rows of six towers. These 12 laterite buildings, surmounted by two floors, are known as **Prasat Suor Prat** (rope dancers' towers) because popular tradition has it that ropes were slung between two buildings and used for tightrope walking shows. However, Zhou Daguan says that parties to a dispute were shut up in it, and the one who was in the wrong would fall ill after a few days. As Prasat Suor Prat gives onto the Royal Square, the most likely theory is that they were places from which dignitaries and ambassadors could watch parades. The towers, which were perhaps built after than the reign of Jayavarman VII, were accessed through a porticoed entrance and illuminated by windows on three sides, and the door frames and pediments were made of sandstone.

The same comments apply to the use of the **Khleangs**, the twin buildings behind Prasat Suor Prat, which were perhaps annexes for distinguished visitors. One was built in the tenth century, and the southernmost one in the eleventh century.

The most spectacular side of the square is the west side, where a series of magnificent terraces supported wooden pavilions. The base of the **Elephant Terrace** stretches nearly 1000 feet, partly concealing the walls and the entrance to the Royal Palace. The terrace is the result of successive renovations, and the remains of older parts can still be seen such as a majestic five-headed horse at the northern end. Sequences of pachyderms, depicted with surprising realism and naturalness, are sculpted on the ten-foot high walls, alternating with garudas and rampant lions acting as Atlases. Two lateral and three central staircases, all on foreparts and watched over by three-headed elephants and lions, give access to the terrace, edged with nagas, on which stands a second base decorated with hamsas, the swans or geese that were Brahma's mount. Wooden pavilions roofed with lead tiles, recently discovered behind the terrace, once stood here.

*242 bottom right
The buttresses of the foreparts of the five staircases of the Elephant Terrace consist of* garudas *and lions acting as telamones.*

*242-243 The trunks of the three-headed elephants gathering lotus sprigs on the wall above the south platform of the terrace turn into columns.*

*243 bottom The Elephant Terrace in front of the ancient Royal Palace constituted the base for the court pavilions. It was built in the Bayon style and renovated on several occasions up to the sixteenth century.*

# ANGKOR THOM, the Terrace of the Leper King

To the north of the Elephant Terrace is the **Terrace of the Leper King**, whose present layout seems to be attributable not to the builder of Angkor Thom but to one of his successors: Jayavarman VIII. The front of the terrace overlooking the Royal Square is 82 feet long, and the 20- to 26-foot-high wall is decorated with up to seven registers of divine characters, nagas, and sea creatures. Behind this first wall there is a second one, discovered by chance during the EFEO excavations, which is decorated with the same bas-reliefs as the first. The existence of this wall is interpreted differently by the experts. Some, including Stern, consider that it is an extension of the structure, while others, especially Coedès, believe that the wall was deliberately concealed by another one because it alludes to the chthonic world and the deities of the underworld beneath Mount Meru.

This interpretation, certainly more fascinating, is based on the fact that the terrace probably had a funerary function; it may have been used for royal cremations. The statue of the Leper King after which the terrace is named has been identified with Yama, lord of the dead. What was thought to be a portrayal of leprosy on the body of the mysterious, naked, sexless figure was probably actually caused by lichen. However, Khmer folk tradition has it that Jayavarman himself was a leper, which is why he built so many hospitals. According to popular accounts, other kings apart from Jayavarman also suffered from the terrible disease.

244-245 The Terrace of the Leper King is one of the most controversial monuments of Angkor Thom. It consists of a series of sculpted walls, some of which are hidden, and this fact has been interpreted in various ways. In this detail from the north wing, the character standing on the right in the first register appears to be a sword-swallower entertaining a king and his wives.

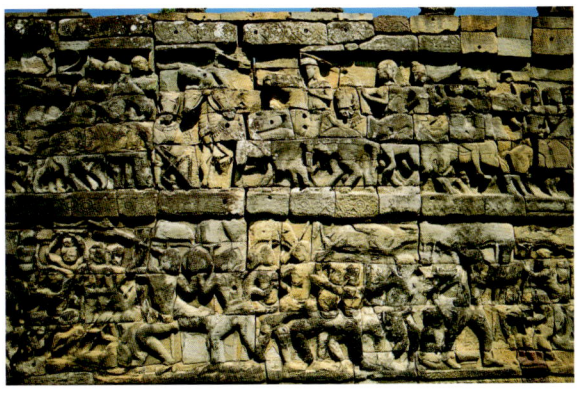

245 top Some experts believe that sculpture was considered a magic rite and sometimes performed even in places where it would not be seen. They consequently interpret the hidden bas-reliefs as representations of the underworld, which were deliberately concealed when they were finished.

245 center and bottom This photo shows the south side of the Terrace of the Leper King, seen from the end of the Elephant Terrace, with a naga balustrade in the foreground. This detail shows two of the seven registers of the bas-reliefs depicting animated scenes of combat.

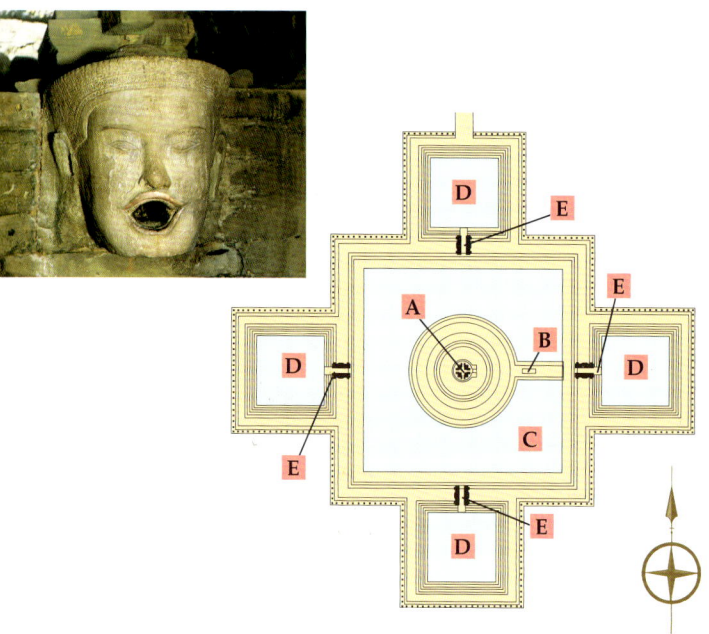

### Neak Pean

- **A** CENTRAL PRASAT
- **B** BALAHA, THE HORSE
- **C** CENTRAL RESERVOIR
- **D** LATERAL RESERVOIRS
- **E** BUILDING WITH FOUNTAINS

Jayavarman VII built one of the most important monuments at Angkor for curative purposes: the complex of reservoirs at **Neak Pean**. This site, which was called Rajyashri (fortune of the kingdom) at the time, covers an area of 3,800 square feet in the middle of the Jayatataka, the baray excavated by Jayavarman for the Preah Khan. Neak Pean, a popular place of pilgrimage, is described in great detail on the stela of Preah Khan, which says that the images of 14 deities and no less than "a thousand lingas" were situated there.

The site once included 13 reservoirs, five of which have now been restored. In the middle of the main reservoir, which measures 230 feet square, stands a circular island with a diameter of roughly 46 feet, whose laterite base is formed by two "coiled nagas," the literal meaning of the name

246

*246-247 The horse Balaha in the Neak Pean reservoir is the manifestation of Lokeshvara, and the underlying symbolism alludes to the crossing of the sea of rebirths.*

*246 bottom In the eastern building of Neak Pean, water gushed from a spout with human features.*

*247 top and bottom right Ta Prohm Kel is one of the 102 hospital "chapels" built or restored by Jayavarman VII. The stelas begin with a homage to Buddha and the two bodhisattvas Candravairocana and Suryavairocana, who protected against disease, and continue with a eulogy of the King. They indicate that up to 100 people worked in the major foundations, including an astronomer and two priests.*

*247 bottom left The platform on which the central prasat stands is formed by two nagas immersed in the reservoir, alluding to the connection between cobras and water.*

## ANGKOR THOM, Neak Pean

Neak Pean, with their tails curled up. A small prasat, which rests on a base in the shape of a lotus blossom, stands on the island. Its three walled-up doors contain statues of Lokeshvara, while the pediments portray episodes from the life of Buddha.

Four smaller reservoirs are arranged in a cross shape around the central one, and four vaulted buildings stand at the arms of the cross. Here, conveyed by taps with differently shaped spouts, the waters of the large reservoir bathed the pilgrims, dispensing their curative powers. The spout in the eastern building had human features and was connected to the element earth. In the northern building, the elephant was the emblem of water. In the southern building the lion sprinkled water on the sick, evoking the element fire, while in the western building the horse symbolized the air. The fifth cosmic element, ethereal space, was probably represented in the central prasat.

Traditional Hindu medicine, Ayurveda, obviously had great influence in this context. According to Ayurveda, the composition of the elements in the human structure is crucial and a surplus or deficiency can cause disease. This is why people took the waters in the one of the four reservoirs associated with the particular element out of proportion. According to some researchers, the Neak Pean reproduced the Anavatapta, the mythical warm water lake in the Himalayas in which divine beings bathed and from which the four great rivers of India gushed forth.

Between 1181 and 1220, Jayavarman VII built an astonishing number of buildings and also restored and modified numerous existing ones. In addition to the buildings described above, he built the great royal foundations of Ta Prohm, Preah Khan, and Banteay Kdei, the temple of Ta Som, hospital chapels, and "fire houses." This mass of buildings featured quantity rather than quality, and numerous expedients were used to deceive the eye and finish the buildings in the shortest possible time. For example, the colonetted windows were sculpted directly in the wall rather than being inserted into specially constructed rooms, and the upper part of the wall was often left smooth, to simulate a partly lowered blind.

However, despite their engineering faults, the sculptural solutions are interesting and innovative. Material was amassed and given shape in an operation that was no longer architectural, but sculptural. The Bayon complex is the most outstanding example. By means of this gigantic "spatial sculpture," the great religious themes were represented in a theatrical, esoteric way, no longer reserved for a small elite but offered to the populace in simpler and more touching terms. It is as if the rulers realized that the end was nigh and attempted to reach the hearts of their subjects to regain their credibility. But the Empire of the **devaraja** was drawing to an end, and not even the **Buddharaja** would be enough to save it.

*248 top This devata at Ta Prohm watches visitors with open eyes. Statues were consecrated with rituals which included the blowing on and opening of the eyes, intended to "animate" the stone so that it became a receptacle for the divine.*

*248-249 Ta Prohm has been invaded by the jungle, and huge trees like this Ficus religiosa entwine their tentacular roots around it.*

*249 The positions of the hands of these two devatas are borrowed from dancing. In accordance with Indian tradition, dancers used the mudras (codified gestures that formed a kind of language), most of which are included in the repertoire of the dancers belonging to the modern Phnom Penh Royal Ballet Company.*

# Angkor, Banteay Chmar, Kompong Svay

## The Monastery Temples of Jayavarman VII

The frenzied building with which Jayavarman VII endeavored to achieve immortality, the growing number of deified persons who required specific temples, and the king's belief in Mahayana Buddhism, composed of large monastic communities, led to a proliferation of royal foundations at Angkor and in the provinces.

The operation of these huge complexes is evidenced by a great deal of epigraphic material, which enables the process that led to the institution of these places and their upkeep mechanisms to be reconstructed. In this context the foundation stone, which contains invaluable information, inherited the tasks of boundary stones and testified to the rights of the monastery temple, dictating the duties of those who supported it. If the temple was not supported by the king, the person who intended to institute a religious foundation (usually a dignitary or a relative of the king) asked the king for permission to give the temple part of the revenues he received from land given in usufruct, actually purchased land specifically for use as a prebend, or applied for a vacant site on which to build the foundation. In each case it was essential to obtain a royal mandate so that the applicant and his family could receive the agricultural product exclusively and forever, and administer it to support the foundation. The temple was not only exempted from paying taxes but also received subsidies of various kinds from the royal warehouses, although these emoluments sometimes appear to have been more symbolic than real. Nevertheless, the institution of a religious center always brought the promoter prestige and power and contributed to the centralization and redistribution of food surpluses.

The architectural layout of the great royal institutions derives from Beng Mealea. They usually had three concentric enclosures, the first of which enclosed the central prasat, preceded by a mandapa. The first and second enclosures were connected by a series of corridors and roofed hypostyle galleries that created a labyrinth, which was increased by continual extensions. Between the second and third enclosures stood the cross-shaped cloister deriving from the Angkor Wat prototype, but in using a modified version it became more of a corridor than an independent structure. The gradual reduction of the four courtyards transformed them into impluvia, cisterns for the monsoon rains and wells to capture the light, which tended to make the building as a whole darker.

The emphasis given to the enclosures and concentric galleries is based on a reinterpretation of Hindu cosmology which focuses not so much on Mount Meru, the hub of the universe, as on

*250 top  A tall tree that features prominently at Ta Prohm is Ceiba pentandar, which can grow up to 160 feet tall. It has shiny silver bark, and kapok is obtained from its fruit.*

*250 bottom  A tree grows from the seed dropped by a bird, and its roots are insinuated between the joints until they reach the ground, dislodging the stones but at the same time holding them together.*

*250-251 The east gopura of the fourth enclosure wall of Ta Prohm, preceded by a cross-shaped terrace, marks the entrance to the main temple area. The huge city that lay around this area was surrounded by another enclosure wall, which formed the outermost perimeter of the site.*

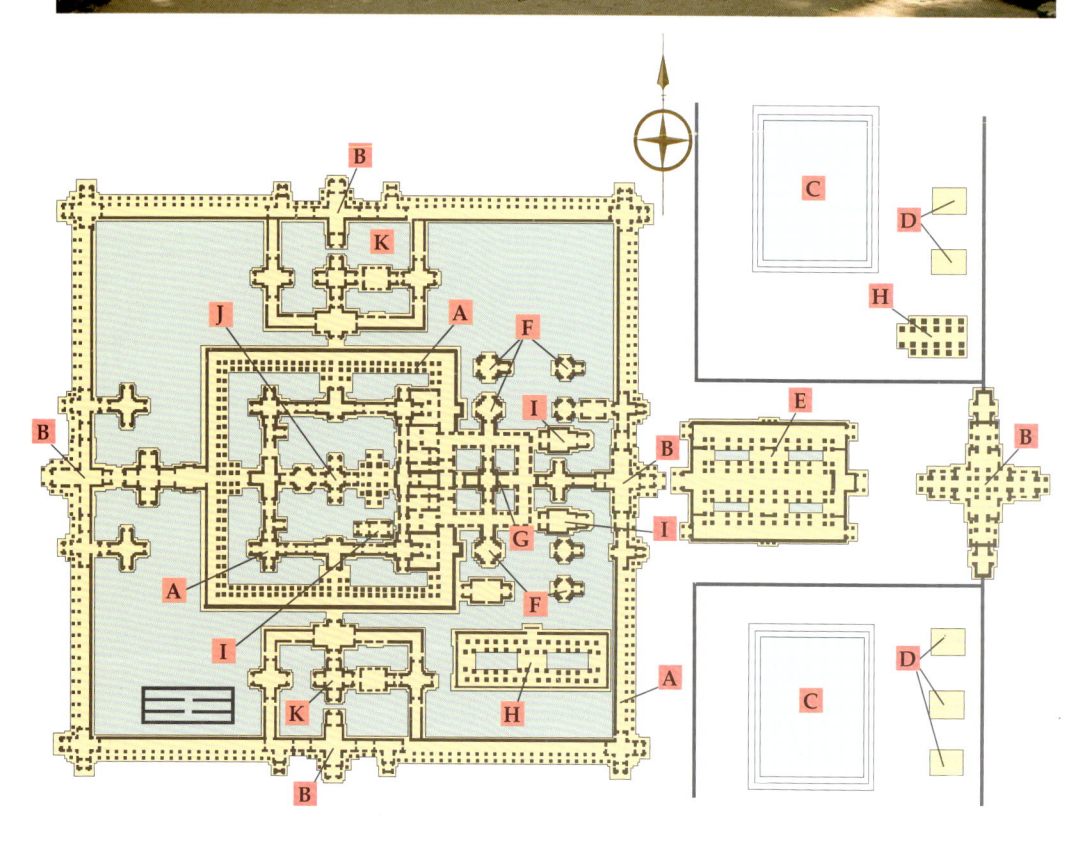

### TA PROHM

A  ENCLOSURE WALL
B  GOPURA
C  RESERVOIRS
D  CELLS
E  PROBABLE DANCERS' PAVILIONS
F  PRASAT
G  CROSS-SHAPED CLOISTER
H  HYPOSTYLE ROOM
I  "LIBRARY"
J  CENTRAL PRASAT
K  TEMPLE COMPLEXES

the surrounding mountain chains. At the same time the symbolism of ascent, which is so evident in the mountain temples, is replaced in these labyrinthine constructions by complex routes leading to the center. The layout reflects that of the mandala, the esoteric motif which the performer/meditator makes by proceeding from outside to inside, to search in the depths of his consciousness for Truth, represented in the central prasat by the image of Buddha. The importance of the outer enclosure gradually increased because it bounded and protected the sacred area while also defining the area over which the protective power of the king and the deities was exercised. The French term enceinte du domaine (royal enclosure), attributed to the outer enclosure, effectively expresses this concept.

Unlike the earlier Hindu temples, which were only partially accessible by the populace, the sacred foundations of Mahayana Buddhism were open to the faithful, and more room for worship was therefore needed.

Jayavarman VII built three great foundations at Angkor: the Ta Prohm, Preah Khan, and Banteay Kdei. In the provinces, two more monumental complexes are associated with his name: Banteay Chmar and the Preah Khan of Kompong Thom, also known as the Preah Khan of Kompong Svay. In some cases the king may have merely modified or extended existing shrines.

251 bottom Thanks to a play of light that gives them dimension, the devatas of Ta Prohm seem ready to emerge from their niches, with their polylobate arches.

251

*252 top left One of the prasats situated between the third and second enclosure walls demonstrates the structure of the typical Khmer shrine, roofed by a number of diminishing tiers which conclude in a lotus blossom.*

*252 top right During the reign of Jayavarman VII, buildings were decorated with rows of praying figures that were inserted in the architraves and pediments, as in the photo, to fill the spaces quickly with stereotyped motifs.*

What is now known as the **Ta Prohm** (the ancestor Brahma) was consecrated in 1186 by Jayavarman VII in the name of his mother, deified as Prajnaparamita, divine mother of all Buddhas and lady of the "perfection of knowledge." The temple was deliberately left to the ravages of the jungle and today evokes in visitors the excitement experienced by the first explorers of Angkor.

An inscription now housed at the Angkor Conservation Bureau gives some idea of the gigantic size of the complex, known in Jayavarman's time as rajavihara (the royal monastery). 12,640 people lived inside the Ta Prohm enclosure and its personnel comprised 18 high priests, 2,740 officiants, and 2,232 assistants, as well as 615 dancers. 3,140 villages were given as prebends, and if their inhabitants are included, a total of 79,365 people gravitated around Ta Prohm. The temple's property included over 1,100 pounds of gold plate, 35 diamonds, 40,620 pearls, 4,540 precious stones, 876 Chinese veils, 512 silk litters, and 523 parasols. Furthermore, the inscription of Ta Prohm states that the temple also controlled and managed the 102 hospitals built or restored by Jayavarman, and some 20 stelae found in various areas give more details about these institutions. After invoking the Bhaishajyaguru (the healing Buddha) and singing the praises of the merciful King Jayavarman, the Sanskrit texts set out the regulations of the hospital and a list of its personnel. In most cases there were 98 people, plus an astrologer and two

*252 bottom The number of buildings erected or started by Jayavarman VII is equal to those built by all his predecessors of the classical age put together. This huge amount of construction work left little time for decorative details, as shown by this false door at Ta Prohm, in which only the central strip is decorated, while the door leaves are smooth.*

## The Monastery Temples of Jayavarman VII

252-253 *After the death of Jayavarman VII, a Brahmanic reaction led to the elimination of Buddhist iconographic motifs from the temples or their transformation into Hindu motifs. The Buddhist figures on the tympanum of the east gopura of the third enclosure wall of Ta Prohm were chiseled away, leaving only the praying figures.*

253 bottom *Pillars are a vital part of architectural and iconographic development. In accordance with the symmetrical taste of the period, those of Ta Prohm, in the Bayon style, have the same frieze under the capital and at the base of the shaft, edged by a fillet that constitutes a characteristic feature of the period.*

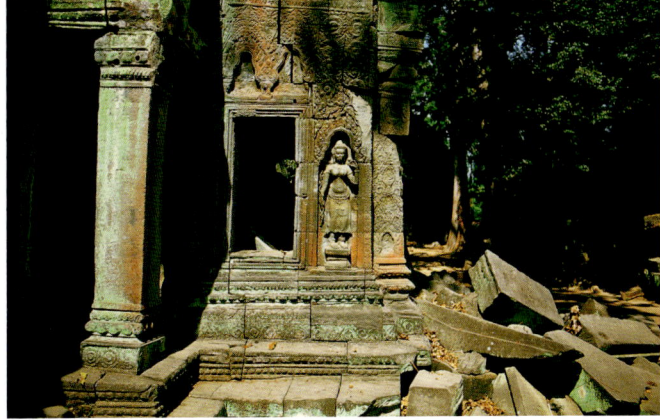

*254-255 Gentle faces characterize the Bayon period, which was divided into three stylistic stages by P. Stern. Ta Prohm belongs to the first stage (from the coronation of Jayavarman to the consecration of the Preah Khan in 1191), during which huge temples in honor of parents were built.*

officiants, but the hospitals of the capital had a workforce of up to 200.

The Ta Prohm temple, situated on a 180-acre site, covers three acres and is surrounded by a rectangular laterite enclosure measuring 3,280 by roughly 2,300 feet. Beyond the east **gopura** of this enclosure and a cross-shaped terrace follows another laterite enclosure wall (the fourth) measuring 820 by 720 feet with its own **gopura**, after which there are a number of rectangular cells parallel to the enclosure wall. In front of the temple there is a sandstone building with stout square pillars which was perhaps a pavilion for ritual dances considering the dancing **apsara** decoration with which it is ornamented.

Proceeding to the west there is the third enclosure measuring 367 by 354 feet, which has a blind wall with a double colonnade towards the outside, corner pavilions and triple axial **gopuras**, and contains numerous buildings.

*255 top  The expedient of portraying lowered blinds considerably reduced the amount of work needed on the windows. In this detail from Ta Prohm, the blind consists of a panel with floral patterns which demonstrates the wealth of the temple's furnishings.*

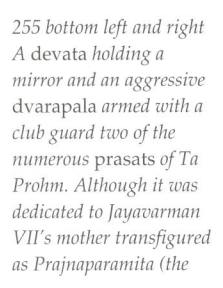

*255 bottom left and right A* devata *holding a mirror and an aggressive* dvarapala *armed with a club guard two of the numerous* prasats *of Ta Prohm. Although it was dedicated to Jayavarman VII's mother transfigured as Prajnaparamita (the perfection of awareness from which Buddhas emanate), the great monastery temple also contained shrines to other deified personalities, including the King's guru Jayamangalarthadeva and older brother Jayakirtideva.*

## The Monastery Temples of Jayavarman VII

A number of prasat flank the corridor leading to a cross-shaped cloister that probably derives from the one at Angkor Wat, resting on the second gallery. In the southeastern corner there is another pillared room with a small courtyard, while on the north and south sides there are more temple complexes surrounded by walls with access gopuras dedicated to the guru of Jayavarman VII and an older brother of the king.

After leaving the second gallery, lined with a double colonnade, a series of rooms on the east side connects it to the first gallery, consisting of a wall with corner towers and four entrance pavilions. The central temple, a cross-shaped prasat of modest size preceded by a hypostyle room and flanked by a library, is connected to the west wing of the gallery by another corridor. The cell looks bare, but it was probably stuccoed and gilded or covered with metal plates, as the holes in the walls suggest. Proceeding axially, we reach the triple west gopura of the third enclosure, and come out again into what was once the residential area.

The Ta Prohm is difficult to interpret. According to P. Stern there were 39 prasat, 566 stone houses, and 288 brick houses. In all, 260 divine images were housed in them, in addition to the statue of Jayavarman's mother.

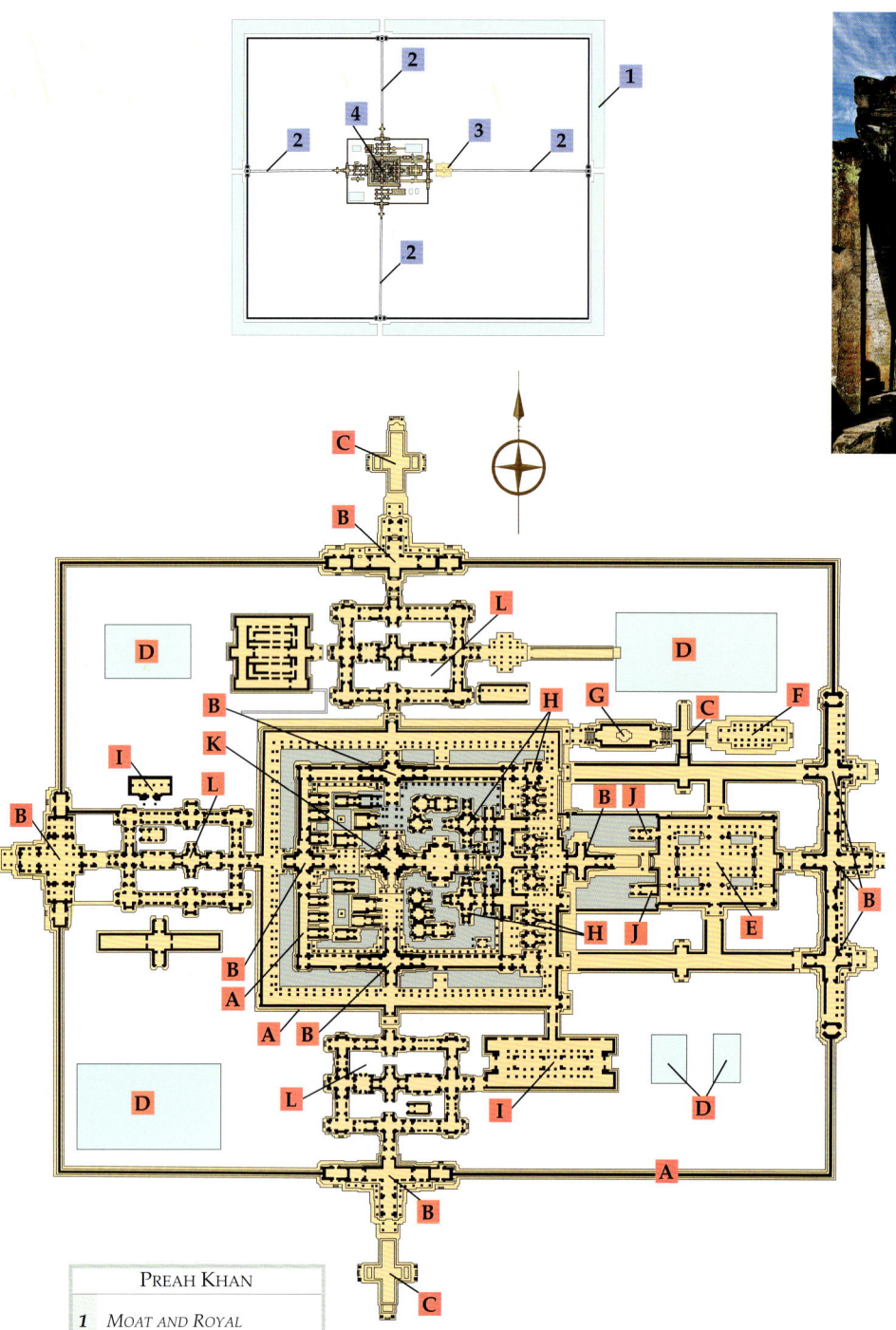

*256 top right* Preah Khan, which belongs to the first stage of the Bayon style, includes the dancers' pavilion, so called because it is decorated with friezes of dancing apsaras.

*256-257* This two-story building on stilts is the only example of its kind in Khmer architecture. Its purpose is unknown; some experts suggest that it may have contained the preah khan (the sacred palladian sword of the kingdom), whereas others believe that it was a granary.

*257 bottom left* The hordes of gods and demons supporting the nagas lining the access avenues, which appeared for the first time at the Preah Khan, inaugurated the second stage of the Bayon period.

*257 bottom right* The laterite base next to the building on stilts supported a wooden structure.

### PREAH KHAN

1. MOAT AND ROYAL ENCLOSURE SURROUNDING THE TOWN
2. AXIAL AVENUES
3. CROSS-SHAPED PLATFORM
4. TEMPLE OF PREAH KHAN

---

A. ENCLOSURE WALL
B. GOPURA
C. CROSS-SHAPED TERRACE
D. RESERVOIRS
E. "DANCERS' ROOM"
F. BUILDING WITH COLUMNS
G. PLATFORM
H. PRASAT
I. HYPOSTYLE ROOM
J. "LIBRARY"
K. CENTRAL PRASAT
L. TEMPLE COMPLEXES

Equally complex is the plan of Nagarajayashri (the fortunate city of victory), now known as **Preah Khan**, the dwelling place of the sacred palladian sword of the Khmer kingdom, a more recent copy of which is still kept in the Royal Palace in Phnom Penh. Built by Jayavarman VII between 1184 and 1191, the huge temple was dedicated to his father Dharanindravarman, also identified with the bodhisattva Lokeshvara. A full-scale city with 102 prasats and hundreds of stone buildings, it was supplied with water by the Jayataka reservoir, and included the Ta Som temple. The foundation stela celebrates the gift of 5,324 villages, responsible for supplying ten tons of white rice a day, and calculates that 97,840 people gravitated around the Preah Khan. As well as being a royal foundation, the Preah Khan was a famous school and followed the Indian model of the great Buddhist universities.

The temple stands on a 15-acre site and is surrounded by four enclosure walls, the outermost of which measures roughly 2,300 by 2,620 feet (as usual, the various surveys disagree) and is encircled by a moat 131 feet wide. The avenues leading to the east and west entrances are flanked by a row of pillars three feet high, on each of the sides of which four monstrous animals support a niche that once contained seated Buddhas, crowned with a finial in

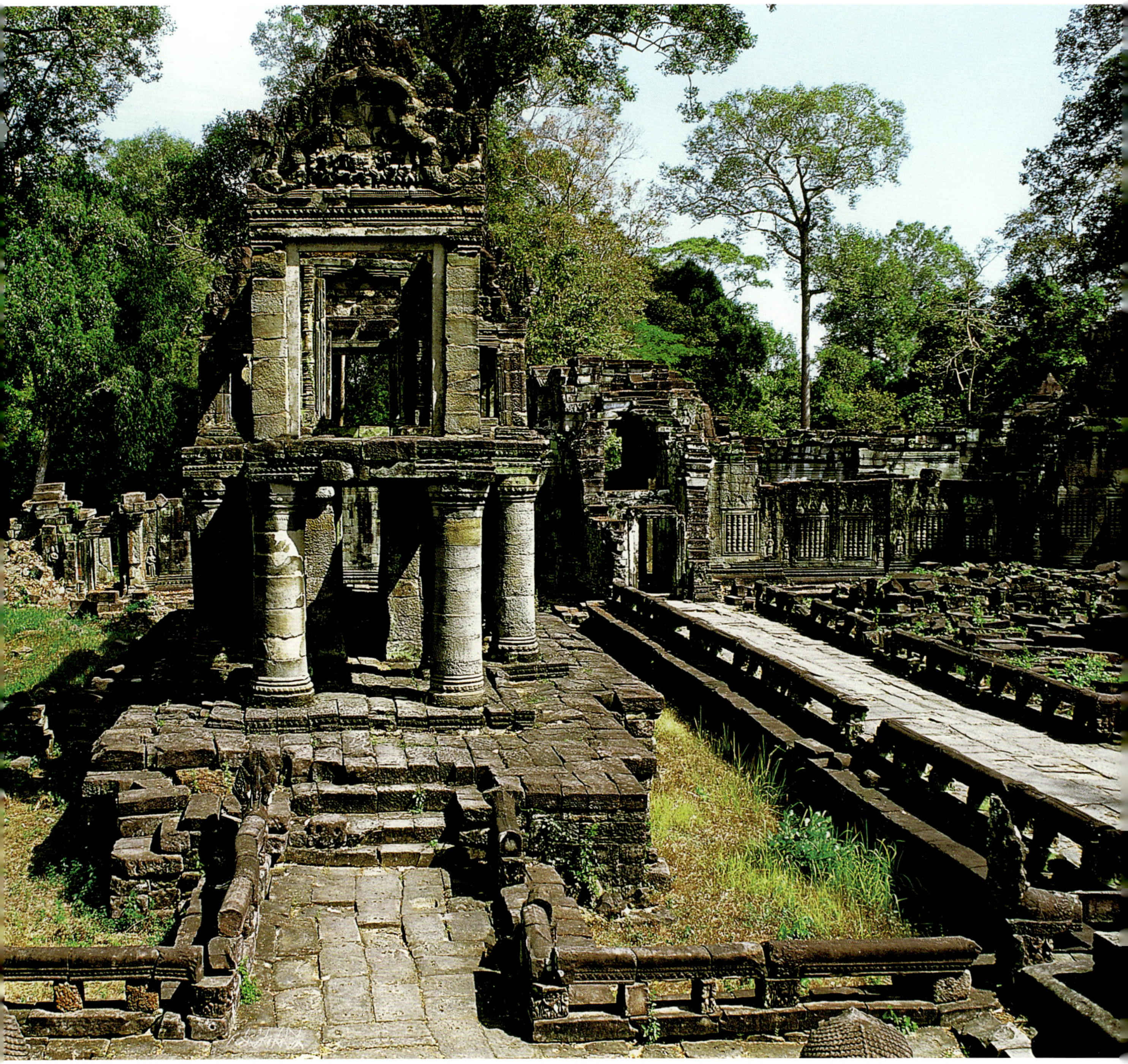

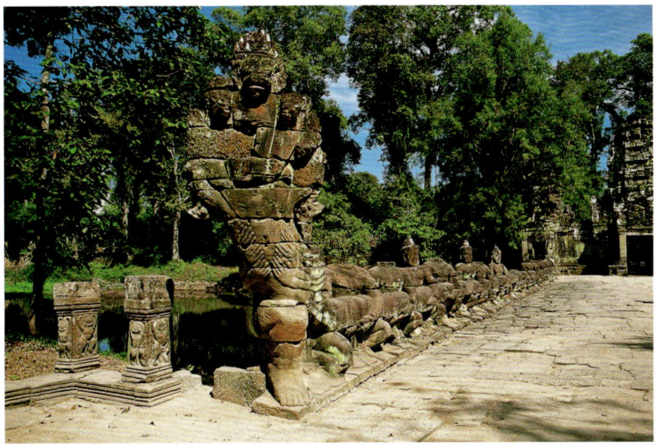

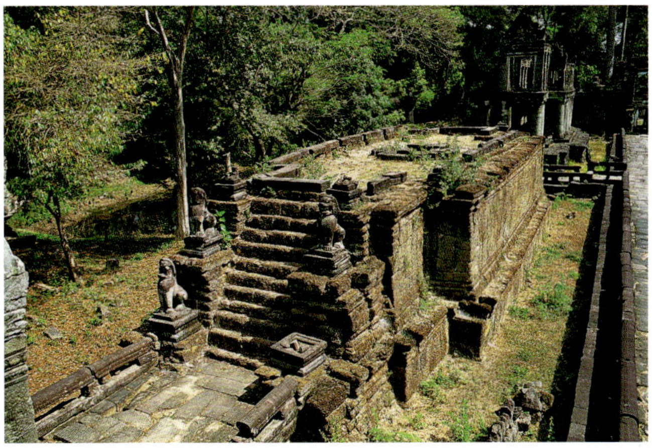

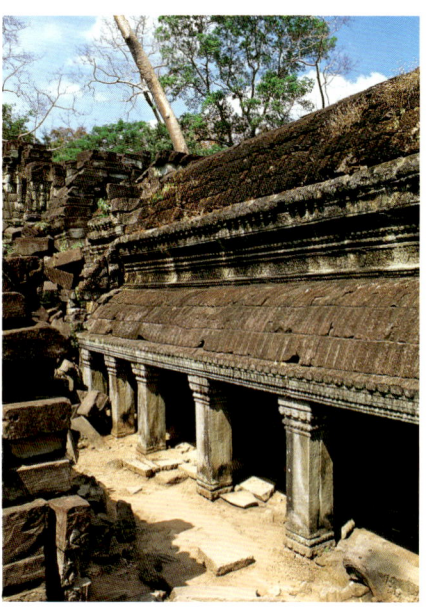

the shape of an upside-down lotus blossom. At the end of the pillars, the paved avenue is lined with rows of devas and asuras that support the many-headed naga. The laterite wall of the outermost enclosure is over ten feet tall and decorated with spectacular garudas on the walls situated in the corners 148 to 165 feet apart from each other. Four axial gopuras, each with three entrances, the central one being for elephants, lead into the area once occupied by houses and now reclaimed by the jungle. From the east entrance a track leads to the temple, in the area of which a "fire house" has been found. This structure was probably designed for religious use, and hostels for pilgrims made of perishable materials were built around it.

At the third enclosure, a rectangle measuring 656 by 574 feet, an impressive platform with a staircase flanked by lions, leads to the triple cross-shaped gopura, which opens to the outside with a double colonnaded gallery, while the wall with blind windows at the end prevents the inner courtyard from being seen. A number of interesting buildings await the visitor in this courtyard. In the northeastern corner stands a strange two-story pavilion resting on heavy cylindrical columns, which appear here for the first time in Khmer architecture. Because there are no stairs and no other apparent method of access to the first floor, it was perhaps reached by a wooden staircase. It has been suggested that this was the place where the sacred sword was kept, but there is no evidence to support this theory. The building extends into a cross-shaped terrace lined with nagas.

On the north, west, and south sides of the enclosure, in communication with the entrance pavilions, stand another three temple complexes surrounded by galleries and dedicated to Shiva

## The Monastery Temples of Jayavarman VII

*258-259 This photo of one of the gopuras of the third enclosure wall shows its uneven roof. Some of the sandstone used contains bentonite, a type of clay that swells after rainfall.*

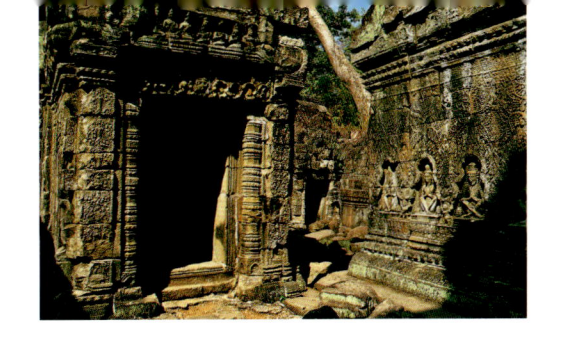

*258 bottom The false half-vault of the gallery of the cross-shaped cloister in the Preah Khan rests on an architrave consisting of a frieze, and its decorative motifs repeat those of the base and capital of the pillars.*

*259 top The ascetics portrayed in yoga postures in the niches of the wall covered with tapestry-like floral decoration were originally images of Buddha, converted during the Brahmanic reaction.*

*259 bottom left Colossal headless dvarapalas guard the entrance to the north gopura of the third enclosure wall. To prevent the theft of their heads, which is very common, many statues are now stored in the Angkor Conservation Bureau.*

*259 bottom right The stupa in the main prasat of Preah Khan dates from the sixteenth century; it originally contained the statue of Jayavarman VII's father. Note the holes in the walls, used to fix the bronze plates which covered it.*

(unusually represented by his footprints), Vishnu, and the dead Khmer kings. The Preah Khan was not only a Buddhist temple but also contained a shrine dedicated to other deities of the Hindu pantheon, local spirits, royal ancestors, and deified human personalities. The 430 sacred images included those of heroes Arjuna and Shridharadevapura, who died defending Yashovarman II when he was attacked by the usurper Tribhuvanaditya. The southern religious complex was dedicated to the deposed king and the royal ancestors. A building even seems to have been consecrated to Tribhuvanaditya in which Tribhuvanavameshvara was worshipped. Though a usurper, the dead king automatically became a protector of the country.

Opposite the east gopura of the third enclosure, on the entrance axis, stands a hypostyle structure deriving from the cross-shaped cloister. It is called the "dancers' room" because of the rows of dancing apsaras that decorate the walls. According to the foundation stela, the Preah Khan had over a thousand dancers. The west exit of what is believed to have been their pavilion is flanked by two libraries.

Yet another cross-shaped structure leads to the second enclosure wall, consisting of a double-portico gallery measuring 280 by 250 feet (272 by 322), with no gopura or corner towers. A series of buildings with false vaulted ceilings which resemble oratories are distributed along the eastern front of the first enclosure, which opens onto this side with three cross-shaped entrance pavilions. We finally reach the innermost temple courtyard, which is almost square, measuring 180 feet and lined with columns. A mandapa leads to the central prasat with four porticoes, which is connected to the other three entrance gopuras of the first enclosure by three axial pillared corridors. The stupa that now stands in the cell is a sixteenth-century addition. The numerous holes in the walls indicate that they were covered in bronze, as at Ta Prohm, and this was probably also the case with the exterior of the shrine. The Preah Khan stela states that no less than 1,500 tons of bronze were used in the construction of the temple. The courtyard is crowded with other buildings which resemble small cells, minor prasat, and unidentified constructions, making it difficult to interpret its layout. There are numerous traces of rebuilding, and above all the images of Buddha have often been eliminated, chipped away, or replaced with lingas, demonstrating the Brahman reaction on the death of Jayavarman and the attempt to convert the Preah Kham, like other Buddhist monasteries, to a Hindu temple.

The **Ta Som**, annexed to the Preah Khan, is a much smaller building and consequently easy to interpret. It is surrounded by a triple enclosure wall with the classic faces of Lokeshvara on the gopuras and has a simple central prasat flanked by two libraries.

**Banteay Kdei** (citadel of cells), of more modest proportions than Ta Prohm and Preah Khan, was built in 1181, probably on the ruins of a Buddhist temple erected by the famous architect Kavindrarimathana during the reign of Rajendravarman. The same architect excavated the **Srah Srang**, the adjacent reservoir renovated by Jayavarman VII, which now measures 1,150 by 2,300 feet. Its most interesting feature is the terrace/landing stage, lined with the usual naga balustrades and guarded by lions, which once supported a light pavilion.

Although its foundation stela has not been found, it is believed that Jayavarman dedicated Banteay Kdei to Buddha, thus completing his homage to the Buddhist triad constituted by Buddha, Prajnaparamita (after whom Ta Prohm was named), and Lokeshvara, who was worshipped at Preah Khan. Some experts suggest that the temple may have been built in honor of the king's tutor. The complex is surrounded by four enclosure walls. The outermost one measures 2,300 by 1,650 feet and included the town. This enceinte de domaine, a later addition made of laterite, is in the classic Bayon style with garudas at the corners and four axial gopuras surmounted by faces of Lokeshvara.

*260-261 The fourth enclosure wall of Banteay Kdei, which belongs to the first stage of the Bayon period, was a later addition, as demonstrated by the faces of Lokeshvara, which were characteristic of the buildings dating from the second Bayon period. The east gopura is shown here.*

*261 top The idyllic baray of Srah Srang (the "Royal Swimming Pool"), excavated in the tenth century opposite the temple of Banteay Kdei, was renovated towards the end of the twelfth century by Jayavarman VII, who added a scenic landing stage. The naga on the balustrade of the landing stage is here.*

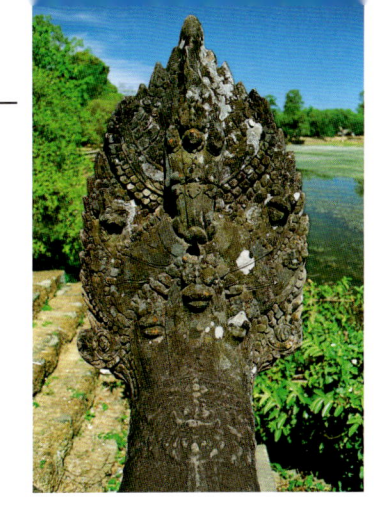

*261 center Ta Som is well worth a visit thanks to its atmosphere and some excellent sculptures. This photo shows a view of the inner enclosure wall seen from the north-west.*

*261 bottom The cross-shaped terrace with naga balustrades is a characteristic feature of the temples of this period. The one overlooking the east gopura of the third enclosure wall of Banteay Kdei is shown here.*

## The Monastery Temples of Jayavarman VII

**BANTEAY KDEI**

- **A** TERRACE
- **B** GOPURA
- **C** ENCLOSURE WALL
- **D** AVENUE WITH NAGAS
- **E** "DANCERS' ROOM"
- **F** HYPOSTYLE ROOM
- **G** PRASAT
- **H** "LIBRARIES"
- **I** CENTRAL PRASAT

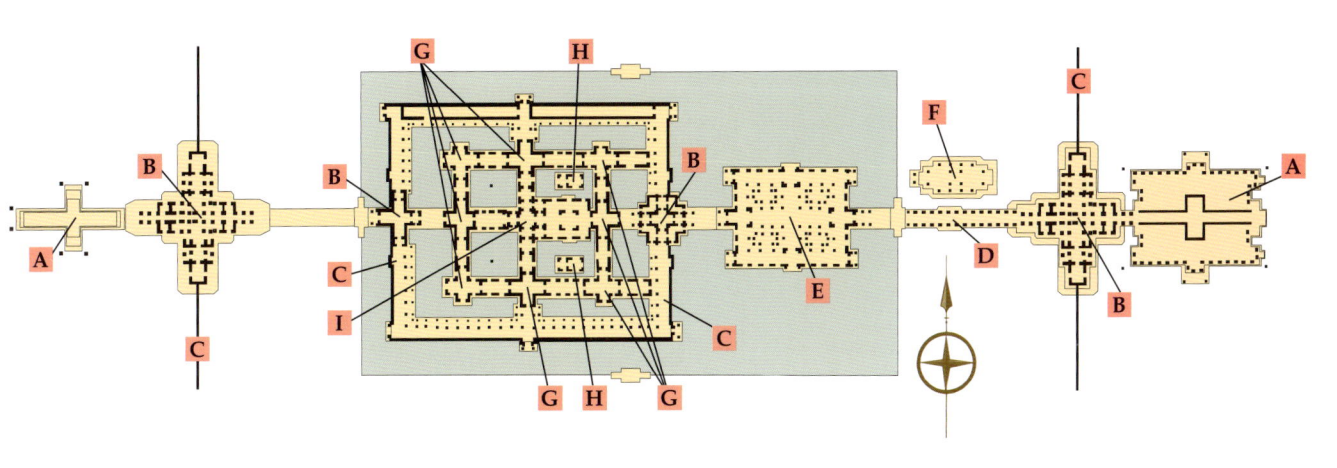

## The Monastery Temples of Jayavarman VII

*262 top and center  These* devatas *from Banteay Kdei were probably a later addition. They are attributable to the third stage of the Bayon style, which portrays them with a triangular hairstyle consisting of lanceolate elements and discs, pushing aside or picking a sprig of flowers with their raised hand and holding a garland-scarf in the other.*

*262 bottom  A conical chignon cap decorated with lotus petals and a low diadem that follows the contours of the temples constituted the classic male headgear of the Bayon period, as demonstrated by the* dvarapala *of Banteay Kdei.*

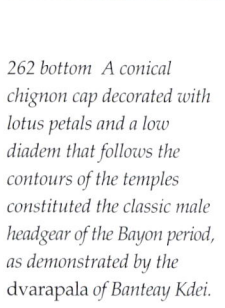

*262-263  The* devata *of Banteay Kdei, which split when the joints between the stones were dislodged, keeps smiling at her inner vision, reminding the viewer that the divine mystery housed in the cell of the temple is actually enclosed in the heart of every being.*

*263 bottom  At Banteay Kdei as elsewhere,* dvarapalas *with threatening expressions discouraged the unworthy from crossing the threshold of the temple.*

By following a 650-foot path we reach the usual cross-shaped terrace with **nagas** overlooking the third enclosure, a laterite wall measuring 1,050 by 980 feet, surrounded by a moat. Proceeding along the **naga**-lined avenue after passing through the attractive **gopura**, we come to the cross-shaped cloister, which was transformed into the "dancers' room," and as always was decorated with friezes depicting dancing **apsaras**. A gopura with three entrances leads to the second courtyard, whose enclosure wall opens into a double colonnade. It is connected to the first courtyard by three galleries on the eastern façade and by hypostyle passages on the other sides.

Eight minor prasat stand in the front part of the first enclosure, four in the corners, and four on the axes, where the extended arms of the central **prasat** are joined, preceded to the east by a **mandapa** flanked by two libraries. However, the plan is hard to interpret due to the numerous collapses caused by the fragility of the sandstone used.

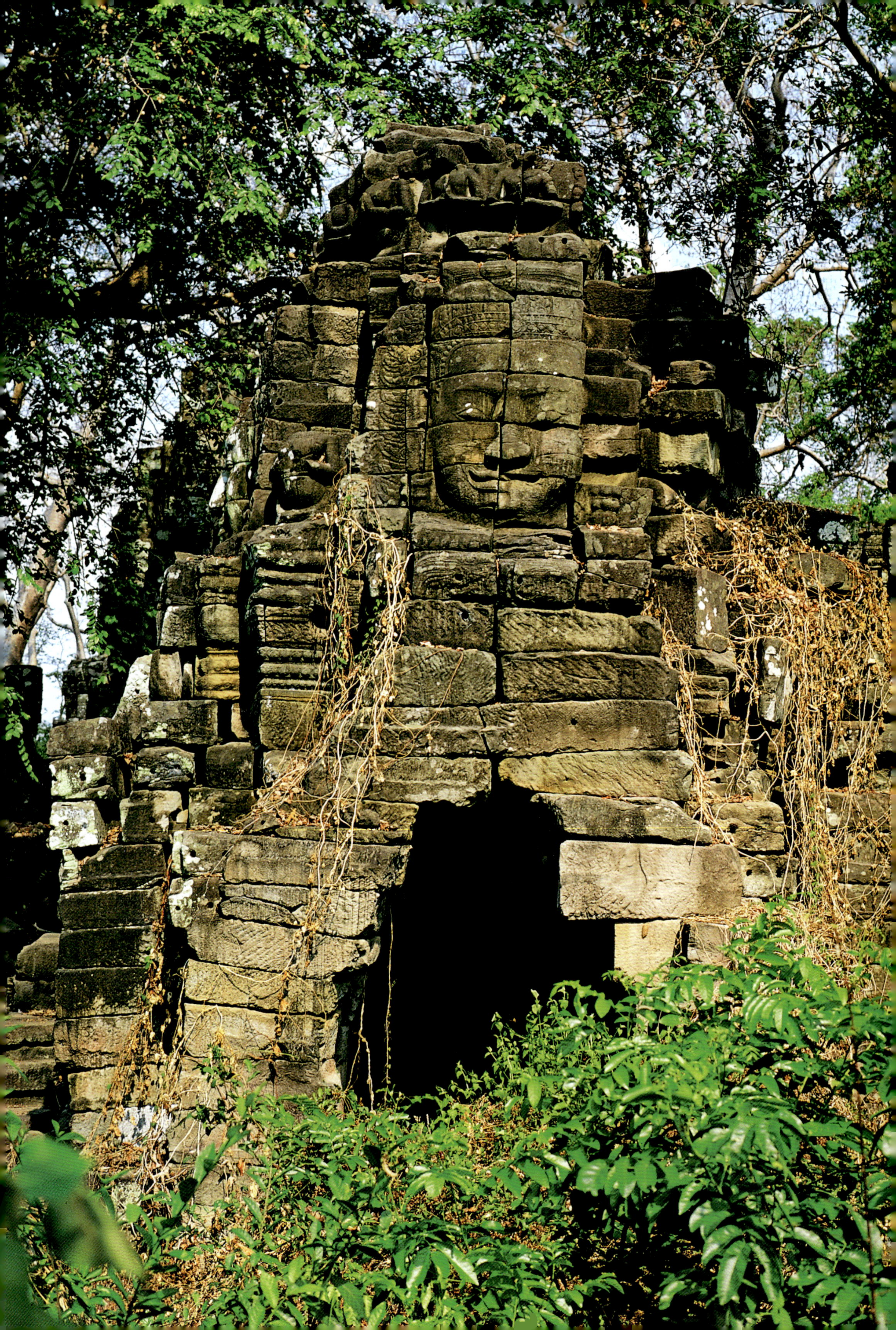

Outside the capital, Jayavarman VII converted and extended a number of existing buildings. **Banteay Chmar** (citadel of the cat), a huge complex whose oldest nucleus is believed to have been founded by Jayavarman II and renovated by Suryavarman II, lies 44 miles from Sisophon, which in turn is around 60 miles from Angkor. The settlement, situated at the foot of the Dangrek mountains, controlled the access route to the upper Mun valley, and was dedicated by Jayavarman VII to his son Indravarman, who was nominated rajakumara (Crown Prince) but was killed in a battle with the Cham. Two samjaks (a term which designated a military office), who had sacrificed their lives for the Prince and been deified, appear to have been worshipped too.

Banteay Chmar was a veritable city, surrounded by an earth embankment around ten feet high, which formed a rectangle measuring 6,500 by 8,200 feet. A large reservoir measuring 2,300 by 4,900 feet with a small prasat in the middle supplied the necessary water, and an avenue connected it to the temple. The temple is surrounded by another laterite wall measuring 2,000 by 2,600 feet, edged by a 160-foot moat, which is crossed by a dyke lined with devas and asuras supporting a naga. Triple towers with the faces of Lokeshvara crown the gopuras, as at Angkor Thom. Another laterite wall runs about 30 feet away from the outer enclosure wall, except on the eastern façade, and paved axial avenues lead to the two innermost enclosure walls (the second and the first).

264 Banteay Chmar belongs to the second stage of the Bayon period, which featured rows of gods and demons, garudas with raised arms acting as telamones, the addition of the "royal enclosure," and towers with four faces of Lokeshvara on the gopuras, as shown in this photo.

265 top left Banteay Chmar, which is situated in a remote border area, has been looted repeatedly. In 1999 the Cambodian police intercepted a truck bound for Thailand carrying 117 blocks of stone, comprising over 36 feet of bas-reliefs.

265 top right The remains of the frieze in the dancers' room shows apsaras with raised arms, in an attitude that is far more similar to those of the garudas and lions acting as telamones than those of the other dancers at the Bayon and Preah Khan temples.

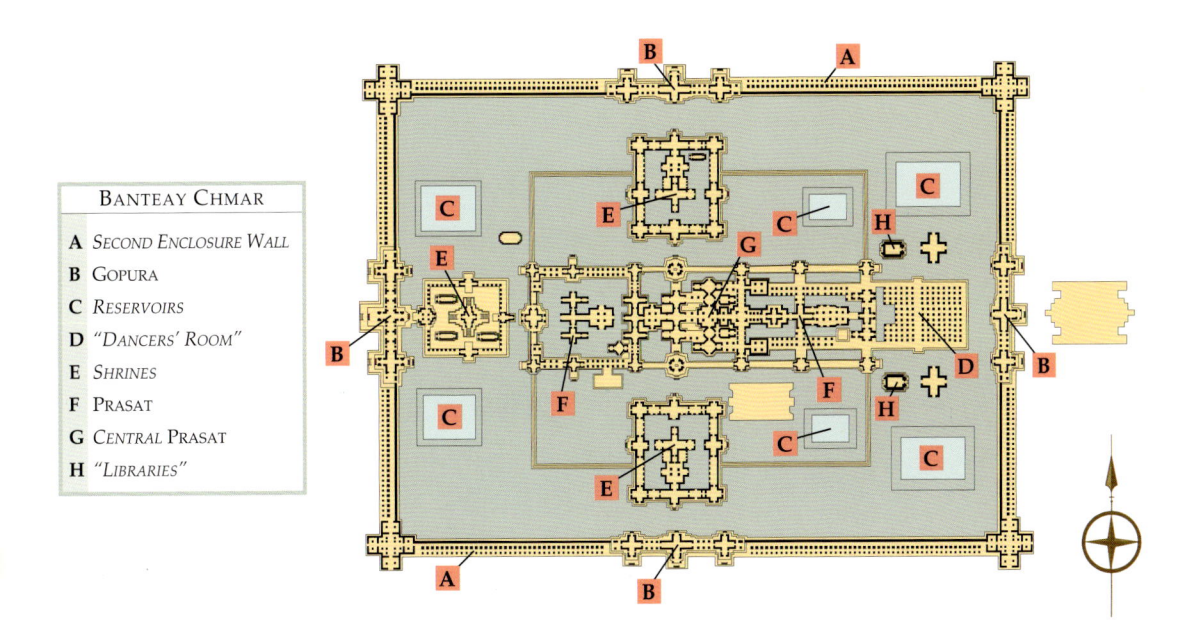

| BANTEAY CHMAR | |
|---|---|
| A | SECOND ENCLOSURE WALL |
| B | GOPURA |
| C | RESERVOIRS |
| D | "DANCERS' ROOM" |
| E | SHRINES |
| F | PRASAT |
| G | CENTRAL PRASAT |
| H | "LIBRARIES" |

The second enclosure wall forms a gallery of 650 by 820 feet, consisting of a portico resting on a blind wall which is decorated with a row of magnificent bas-reliefs. Despite damage during Thai raids and the serious state of neglect of the temple, its remains still demonstrate a high degree of artistic skill. There is a reservoir in each of the four corners of this second enclosure, which is entered through four gopuras, each with three entrances. On the north-south axis, two buildings with a similar structure penetrate into the first enclosure, while two more buildings are situated along the east-west axis. The eastern building, which rests directly on the gopura of the first enclosure, is larger and was probably dedicated to the female dancers, while the western one is a minor shrine with a cloistered gallery. There is a library on either side of the dancers' rooms. The first enclosure is occupied by a rectangular complex measuring 400 by 130 feet, consisting of three prasat connected to one another. According to P. Groslier, the central one is Vishnuite and is the oldest of the three, while the other two are Buddhist, as indicated by the towers with the faces of Lokeshvara, and were added during the reign of Jayavarman VII. The disastrous state of the temple prevents its component parts from being reconstructed but the atmosphere with which it is imbued is among the most evocative of all the Khmer sites, and those who are not afraid of a little discomfort will find the adventurous visit very exciting.

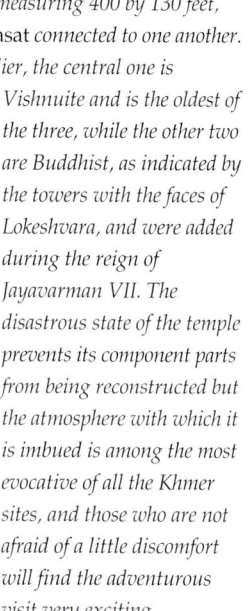

*266 top On the wall of the second enclosure of Banteay Chmar there are several registers of bas-reliefs which celebrate historical events transformed into myths. The most easily understandable are those in the west wing.*

*266 center To move the blocks of stone, which weighed one to ten tons, pairs of holes were made and bamboo wedges inserted into them. The bamboo swelled when it was wet and adhered to the stone, thus forming a suitable support for handles.*

*266 bottom This detail shows the* puja *(act of reverence to the gods), involving gifts and gestures symbolizing the five elements: food alluded to the earth, aspersions to water, lights to fire, flowers to the air, and draperies to space.*

*266-267 Buddhist motifs are portrayed in the south wing of the west side of the bas-relief gallery at Banteay Chmar, including these two images of the* bodhisattva *Lokeshvara with 32 arms.*

*267 bottom The temple-city of Banteay Chmar has never been excavated, and many of its treasures are still to be discovered. Its bas-reliefs are attributable to the third stage of the Bayon period, inspired by the temple of the same name.*

*269 Bows and arrows were used in battle and for hunting. The arrows were kept in decorated quivers. Blowpipes were also used for small game. When particular freedom of movement was needed, the* sampot *was rolled up to form a loincloth.*

## The Monastery Temples of Jayavarman VII

*268 top  The characterization of the faces in this detail from the Banteay Chmar bas-reliefs reveals that they were given the final touches by an artist. Bas-reliefs were made in several stages by different workers, who outlined, rough-hewed, and finished them.*

*268 center  The naturalness of the scenes sometimes verges on the comical, as in the case of this infantryman drinking from a flask that probably contains palm brandy while he is watched by an amazed, envious bystander.*

*268 bottom  Food and water are still carried on yokes in the Cambodian countryside today, just as in this scene, which depicts a market or a camp kitchen. Note the detail in the weave of the basket.*

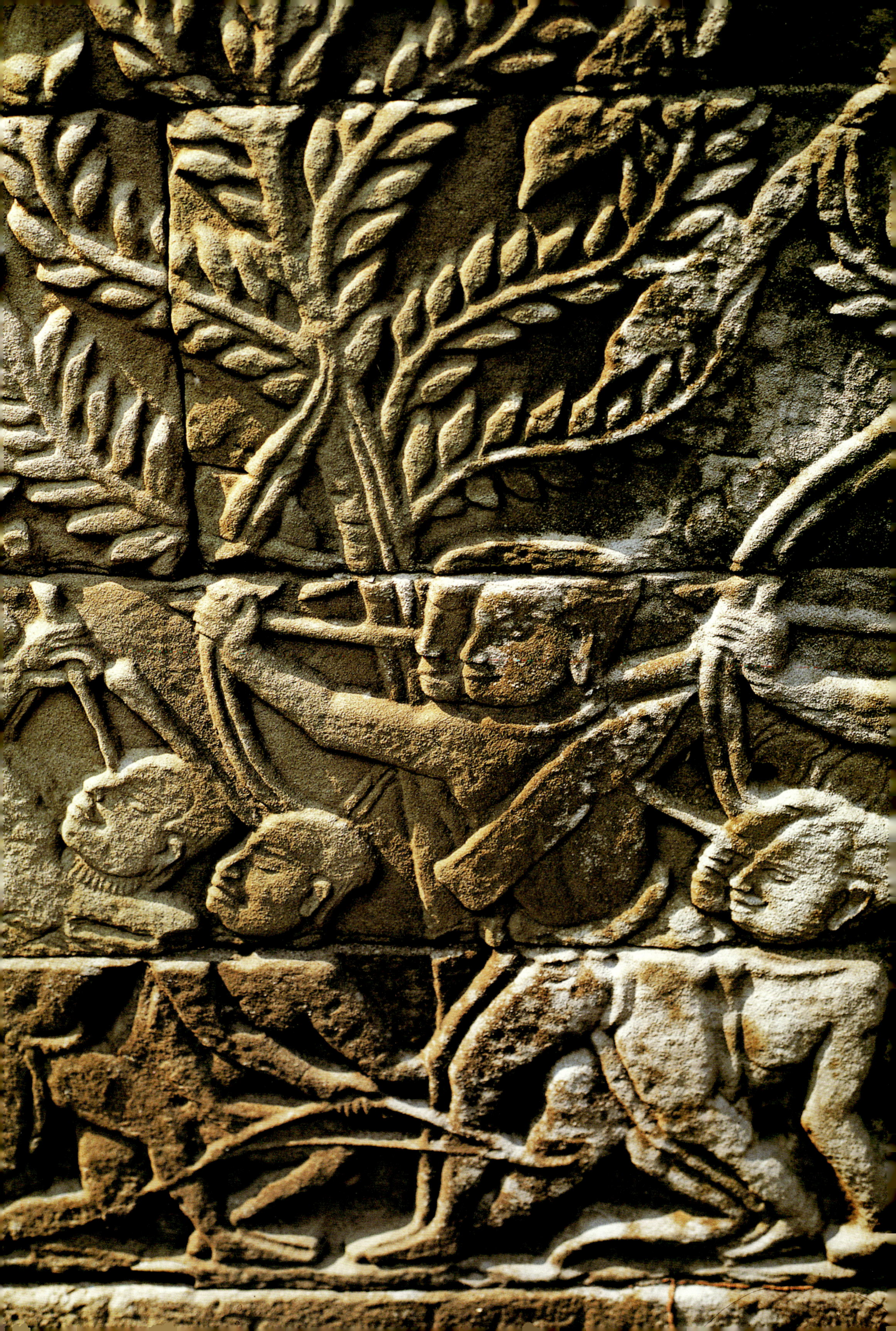

The other great provincial foundation of Jayavarman's reign was the **Preah Khan of Kompong Thom** or Kompong Svay. Kompong Thom is around 90 miles from Angkor, and the Preah Khan is situated 60 miles further north, at Kompong Svay. A wide road lined with "fire houses" once led there from the capital. It continued north-east for 25 miles to Beng Mealea and then descended to the south-east, reaching what is now Kompong Svay after another 37 miles.

A triple earth dyke between two moats, which is 820 feet wide in all, surrounded a residential area measuring three miles square, the largest in Cambodia. On the eastern axis, the baray can still be seen. It measures 9,800 by 1,700 feet and forms a right angle with the triple dyke. Four temples with annexed buildings of different periods demonstrate that this place had been very important since ancient times. The oldest buildings seem to have been erected by Suryavarman I, while some of those in the second enclosure were built by Suryavarman II. Jayavarman VII rebuilt some of the existing buildings, added more structures in the third and fourth enclosures, and excavated, or at any rate extended the baray.

On an island in the middle of the baray stands Preah Thkol, a **prasat** with two annexed libraries boasting particularly attractive decoratation. Another temple, Preah Damrei, a square pyramid about 50 feet high, stands on the east bank of the baray. Majestic elephants stood in the corners of the 12 low terraces, and lions and dvarapalas lined the staircases. On the west bank stands the Preah Stung, whose roof is a tower with the face of Lokeshvara repeated on all four sides, a motif that was to be perfected at the Bayon temple. Two cross-shaped terraces supported by hamsas (the geese or swans which were Brahma's mount) precede the prasat.

Proceeding east there is the third enclosure, a laterite wall measuring 2,300 by 3,600 feet, edged by a moat, and enclosing another reservoir, with four axial gopuras. Hardly any of the monuments have survived, apart from a small pavilion that houses a stela containing a great deal of information about the place.

After the second enclosure, preceded by a cross-shaped platform that leads to a gopura with five access pavilions, one reaches the first enclosure, another gallery with axial gopuras that measures 130 by 190 feet and contains the few remains of a cross-shaped sandstone prasat standing on a two-tiered platform.

The intricate architecture of these great royal foundations is very different from the linear constructions of the Classical age, and its sometimes mysterious complexity demonstrates that the decline of the Khmer civilization had by this point begun.

## The Monastery Temples of Jayavarman VII

270-271 The first roofs with the faces of Lokeshvara, which were to become common in the second stage of the Bayon period, appeared on the Preah Stung at the Preah Khan of Kompong Thom.

271 top The Preah Khan of Kompong Thom, a huge and very important site, was built in various stages. Jayavarman VII perhaps took refuge there between 1165 and 1177.

271 center The gopuras of the third enclosure wall are inspired by those of Angkor Wat. The central opening was for elephants, which were trained in special enclosures called kraals.

271 bottom The Preah Stung had one of the most innovative layouts of the period. It features a hypostyle mandapa with three porticoes and a triple vestibule, and four corner chambers were built onto the cross-shaped porticoed cell.

*272 top and 272-273 Ta Muen Thom, an importing staging post on the road to Phimai from as early as the eleventh century, includes two sandstone towers, one of which was blown up by the occupying Khmer Rouge in the 1980s. During the same period all the removable statues were smuggled to Thailand, still a transit center for the many works of art that are regularly stolen from Khmer archaeological sites.*

*272 bottom left The cell houses a* svayambhulinga, *a natural linga consisting of a stone jutting out of the ground, which was considered sacred.*

*272 bottom right The temple stands on a platform made of laterite, an easy-to-cut stone that, on exposure to the elements, oxidizes as a result of its iron content and hardens. Because of its limited capillarity and a honeycomb structure, it prevents any rising dampness and facilitates the evaporation of moisture from the temple, thus constituting a solid base.*

# From Angkor Thom to Phimai
## Stages on the Royal Route

At the time of Jayavarman VII there were seven major roads, which reached the furthermost corners of the Empire. They were very wide, paved with laterite, and built on embankments up to 20 feet tall. One of the main royal roads of Kambuja started at the north gate of Angkor Thom and led north across the Dangrek Mountains as far as Phimai. Along the arduous 140-mile route there were several important towns used as stopping points which are still partly identifiable from their ruins. The most interesting examples are the Ta Muen Thom and Phnom Rung complexes in what is now Thailand, the former in the Kab Choeng district of Surin province, and the latter in Buriram province.

The temple of **Ta Muen Thom** stands in a beautiful, secluded, wooded spot near one of the main passes over the Dangrek Mountains. Long occupied by the Khmer Rouge, it has sadly been damaged, and nearly all the removable statues have been stolen by smugglers. Facing south, perhaps so that it looked towards distant Angkor, the shrine contains a natural linga, a rock formation recognized as the symbol of Shiva, and it was probably this that influenced the orientation of the temple, which was apparently built during the reign of Udayadityavarman II, in the eleventh century.

A laterite stairway leads to the hill on which the sacred buildings stand, surrounded by a gallery measuring 151 by 125 feet with four entrances; three are simple pavilions with side chambers, while the southern one has a larger gopura. The temple is made of pink sandstone and consists of a porticoed **mandapa**, a vestibule, and a cell open on all sides. Two secondary towers stand in the northeast and northwest corners, and there are two other laterite buildings, one square and one rectangular, to the west and east of the main shrine. One of the most intriguing features of the complex is a long laterite channel that runs along the entire platform of the temple, originating from the cell. It has been identified as a **somasutra** (evacuation channel) for the lustral water poured onto the linga but has a very unusual size and layout.

The theory that Ta Muen Thom stood on the royal route is borne out by the ruins of Ta Muen Toch, just under a mile away, and Ta Muen, just over a mile away. Both are attributed to the reign of Jayavarman VII (twelfth-thirteenth century) and are in a good state of repair. Ta Muen Toch is the shrine of a hospital, consisting of a tower preceded by a portico with a small annexed "library" and a reservoir, inside an enclosure with a gopura. Ta Muen is a "firehouse," a rectangular laterite building with a tower, which was also a place of worship, around which wooden pavilions for travelers stood.

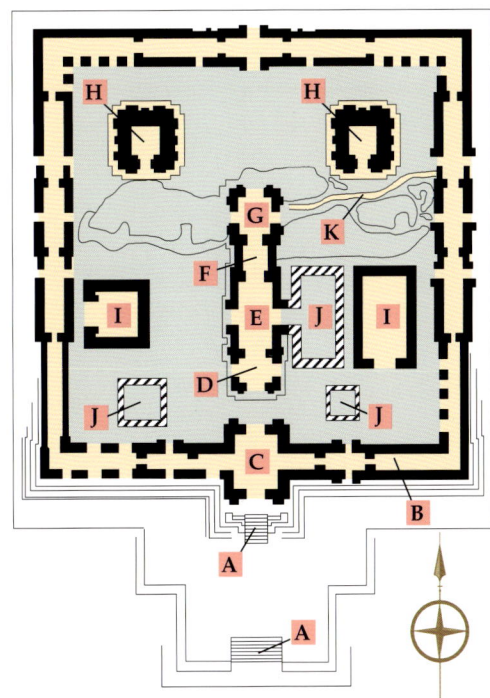

| TA MUEN THOM | |
|---|---|
| A | STAIRCASES |
| B | GALLERY |
| C | GOPURA |
| D | PORTICO |
| E | MANDAPA |
| F | VESTIBULE |
| G | CELL |
| H | TOWERS |
| I | BUILDINGS OF UNKNOWN FUNCTION |
| J | FOUNDATIONS OF OTHER BUILDINGS |
| K | SOMASUTRA |

273

*274 top The Phnom Rung* prasat *was dedicated to Shiva, who appears in the tympanums in various guises. Here, on the eastern entrance of the* mandapa, *the god is portrayed as Nataraja (Lord of the Dance), whose dance dissolves the universe and permit its reappearance.*

*274 bottom The east* gopura, *preceded by a platform guarded by* nagas, *leads into the temple enclosure.*

*274-275 This view from the south-western corner shows a* dvarapala *guarding the entrance of the double west portico of the* prasat. *In the foreground is Prang Noi, interrupted above the cornice, with some attractive finials in the corners.*

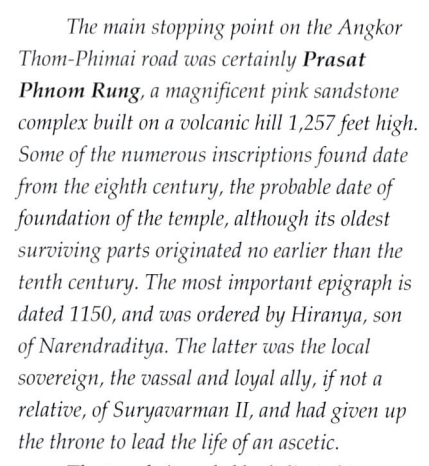

The main stopping point on the Angkor Thom-Phimai road was certainly **Prasat Phnom Rung**, a magnificent pink sandstone complex built on a volcanic hill 1,257 feet high. Some of the numerous inscriptions found date from the eighth century, the probable date of foundation of the temple, although its oldest surviving parts originated no earlier than the tenth century. The most important epigraph is dated 1150, and was ordered by Hiranya, son of Narendraditya. The latter was the local sovereign, the vassal and loyal ally, if not a relative, of Suryavarman II, and had given up the throne to lead the life of an ascetic.

The temple is probably dedicated to Shiva, although there are some Vishnuite images. It is built axially from east to west, preceded by a long series of cross-shaped terraces and staircases. Next to the first terrace is the "white elephant room," a porticoed rectangular building made of laterite and sandstone, surrounded by walls and galleries.

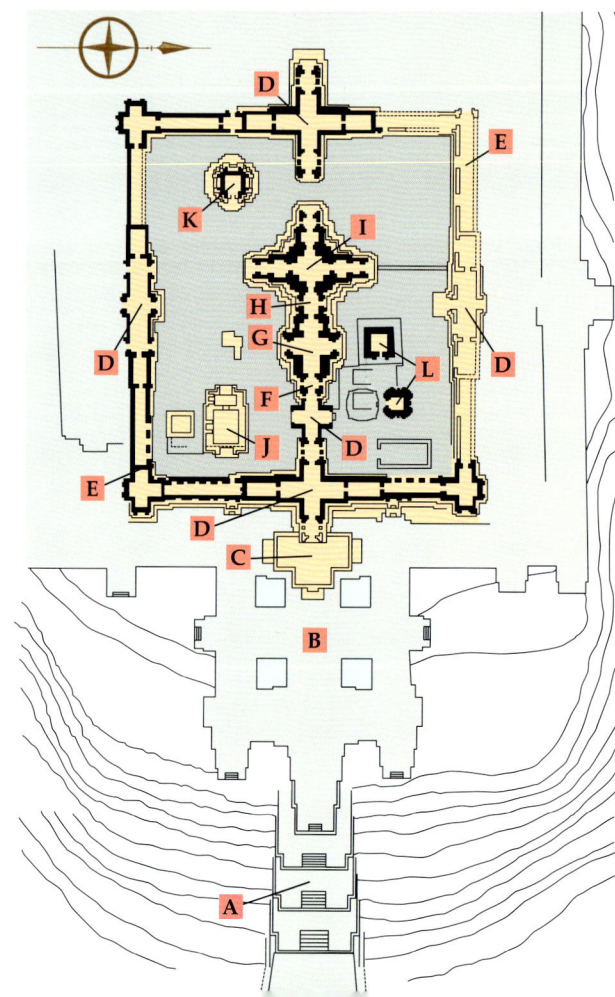

| Phnom Rung |   |
|---|---|
| A | Ramps |
| B | Third Terrace with Lustral Basins |
| C | Platform |
| D | Gopura |
| E | Gallery |
| F | Portico |
| G | Mandapa |
| H | Vestibule |
| I | Cell |
| J | "Library" |
| K | Prang Noi |
| L | Brik Prasat |

Its name derives from the recent popular belief that Phnom Rung was a palace, and the building in question housed stables for the elephants. A laterite avenue 525 feet long, lined with 67 pillars surmounted by stylized lotus blossoms, leads from the terrace to a second terrace surrounded by magnificent five-headed nagas. This is followed by five wide flights of steps leading to another terrace with four lustral basins. Another platform in the shape of nagas disgorged from the mouths of makaras (legendary sea monsters), once sheltered by a wooden pavilion, gives onto the east gopura. The entrance to the shrine is an interesting structure, with "telescopic" side chambers decorated with magnificent architraves and tympana.

On leaving the portico of the gopura one comes to the portico of the mandapa, an elongated cross-shaped structure that leads through the vestibule into the prasat. A magnificent dancing Shiva is portrayed on the tympanum of the mandapa, resting on an equally magnificent architrave in which Vishnu reclines on the serpent Ananta, which has turned into a dragon, probably as a result of Cham influence. The exquisite Hindu scenes depicted on the architraves of the vestibule and the porticoes of the prasat contribute to the well-deserved fame of Phnom Rung. The extrados of the prasat recalls the design of the one at Phimai. It has a highly denticulated pyramidal structure with five stories including the cornice, crowned by a kalasha, the water vessel that symbolized abundance and prosperity.

The enclosure wall, which has three more secondary gopuras, surrounds a number of other buildings: a library, a small temple known as Prang Noi, which means "small prang" (the Thai word for prasat), and two brick buildings dating from the start of the tenth century.

Michael Freeman, who has studied the Khmer temples in Thailand, says that on April 13th, as the plane of the ecliptic is aligned with the axis of the temple, the sun's rays shine through the doors and rooms of the temple one after another, from the east gopura to the west. The festival of Phnom Rung is consequently celebrated on that date, and the Khmer, who were very interested in astronomical events, probably consecrated the temple on that very day.

*Phimai: Stage on the Royal Route*

*277 top Two types of sandstone were used at Phimai: red sandstone, colored by its high iron content, which is easily oxidized and friable, and the white sandstone used in the* mandapa *shown here, which is more compact and durable.*

*277 bottom right The cross-shaped platform on stilts overlooking the main entrance to the temple almost seems to fly, borne by the arched nagas. The temple was neglected until 1950, when it was restored by the last curator of Angkor, B. P. Groslier.*

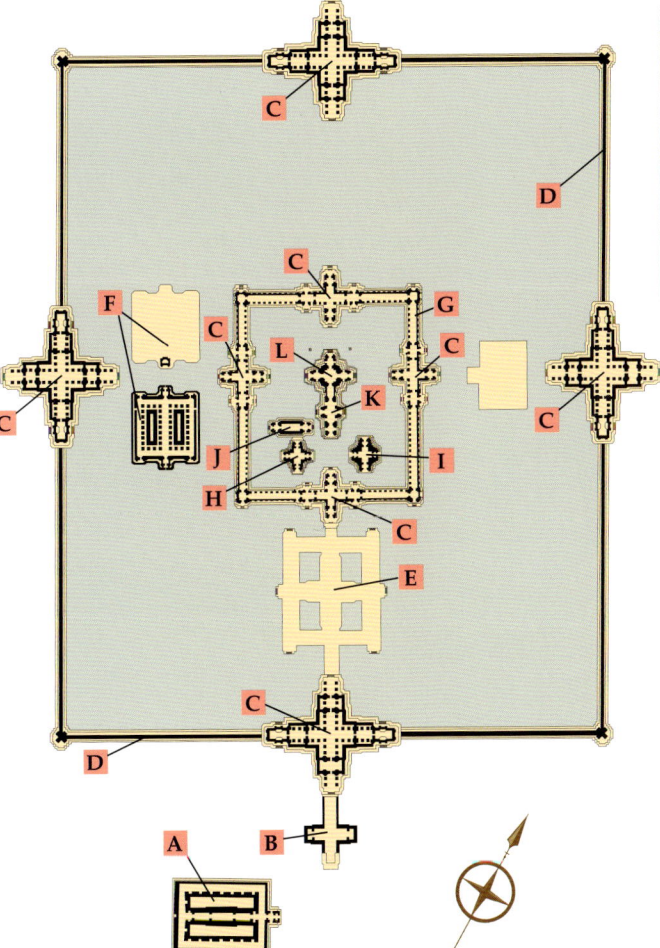

### PHIMAI

| | |
|---|---|
| **A** | TREASURY PAVILION |
| **B** | CROSS-SHAPED TERRACE |
| **C** | GOPURA |
| **D** | OUTER ENCLOSURE |
| **E** | TERRACE WITH LUSTRAL BASINS |
| **F** | TWIN PAVILIONS |
| **G** | INNER ENCLOSURE |
| **H** | PRANG HIN DAENG |
| **I** | PRANG BRAHMADAT |
| **J** | "LIBRARY" |
| **K** | MANDAPA WITH PORTICO |
| **L** | CELL WITH VESTIBULE |

*276-277 The last inscription on the temple of Phimai, one of the most important provinces in the Khmer Empire, dates from 1112, which means that the* prasat *tower may have influenced the later towers of Angkor Wat.*

*276 bottom left The slenderness of Phimai Temple is emphasized by its tall, slightly splayed base, and the pointed arch of the* prasat *is set by the antefixes on the offset corners, lightening its bulk.*

*276 bottom right The ruins of Prang Hin Daeng, a* prasat *added in the early thirteeth century, can be seen in the southwest corner, behind the south gopura of the innermost enclosure wall. A similar one stands in the southeast corner.*

The royal road finally reaches **Phimai**, which lies on the left bank of the Mun river. Already inhabited at the time of Chenla (seventh-eighth century), it is referred to as Vimayapura in an inscription dating from 1082, during the reign of Jayavarman VI, originally from the principality of Mahidharapura which was situated in the area. Suryavarman II and Jayavarman VII, who carried out renovation and construction work at Phimai, apparently bragged to be related to the Mahidharapura dynasty.

The temple faces south, and its unusual orientation may have been chosen so that it faced towards Angkor, or because it was dedicated to Jayavarman's ancestors (according to Hindu belief, the dead live in the southern quarter of the universe). However, the temple is not Hindu but Buddhist, and belongs to the Mahayana school, which was present in the Mun valley from the seventh century on. The place where the Mun joins its tributary, the Klong Chakrai, is a highly suitable site for a temple because it is protected on three sides and above all creates a sangama (confluence), which was considered sacred. A laterite wall measuring 3,350 by 1,900 feet surrounded the temple-city, edged by a moat

277

278

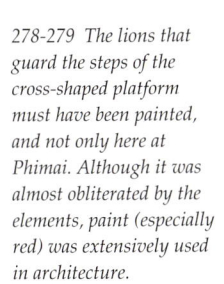

278-279 *The lions that guard the steps of the cross-shaped platform must have been painted, and not only here at Phimai. Although it was almost obliterated by the elements, paint (especially red) was extensively used in architecture.*

278 bottom left *The cell of Prang Brahmadat, one of the two* prasats *in the southern corners, contains a copy of an image of Buddha with the features of Jayavarman VII, the original of which is now in the Bangkok Museum.*

278 bottom right *Floral decoration was an essential element in temples, because it alluded to the sap or lifeblood that pervaded the building.*

279 *The cell of Phimai, a temple of the Mahayana school, contains an image of Buddha meditating on the coils of the* naga *Mucilinda.*

supplied with water by the rivers. The main entrance of the four was the south entrance, the "Victory Gate," to which the royal road from Angkor Thom led.

The temple stands between two enclosure walls, the outermost of which measures 900 by 720 feet, while the innermost measures 272 by 243 feet. In front of the south gopura there is a cross-shaped naga terrace, preceded to the left by a rectangular building inaccurately described as the "treasure pavilion." The gopura is a large red sandstone building, in which inserts of white sandstone are used for the door and window surrounds and for the pillars that divide the gopura and its porticoes into a nave and two aisles. In the outer courtyard, two reservoirs flank the approach avenue, which then crosses a wide terrace. Four depressions suggest that four lustral basins once stood there. Twin rectangular pavilions of unknown use stand on the west side of the courtyard.

On reaching the innermost enclosure, which is slightly asymmetrical, with colonetted windows and corner pavilions, one passes through a gopura similar to the previous one but smaller. The path leading to the central temple is flanked by two prasat added in the thirteenth century, the one on the left made of red sandstone and the one on the right of laterite.

The right-hand prasat contains a copy of a statue of Jayavarman VII with the features of Buddha (the original is in Bangkok Museum). This magnificent white sandstone building consists of a porticoed mandapa and a square cell with four porticoes, the one connected to the mandapa being elongated and transformed into a vestibule. The architraves and pediments, crowded with figures, are of excellent manufacture. A library stands on the left-hand side of the mandapa.

The 92-foot-tall tower, with a denticulated plan, stands on a highly molded base, taller than those of the porticoes and the mandapa, and has an ogival contour that heralds the structure of the Angkor Wat prasat. The five diminishing tiers of the roof rest on a projecting cornice supported by garudas. Its corners were rounded by inserting antefixes ornamented with nagas, male and female deities, and mythical creatures. The multiple pediments on the porticoes of the prasat, with their telescopic effect, emphasize its vertical sweep, concluded by a row of lotus blossoms that support the vessel of abundance.

The attractive design, the color effects of the sandstone, and the elegant sculptures, many of which are now in the Phimai National Museum, make this temple the most outstanding example of Khmer architecture in Thailand.

*280 top Various populations (Mon, Khmer and Thai) settled in Lobpuri, in present-day Thailand, situated in a fertile area which was second only to the Angkor plain for rice production at the time. The thirteeth-century Wat Mahatat complex can be seen in this aerial photo.*

*280 bottom and 280-281 Sam Yod has an unusual structure, with three cross-shaped shrines that communicate with anterooms. The temple constituted a highly influential example for later Thai architecture. In fact, the Thai* prang, *the equivalent of the* prasat, *retained many Khmer characteristics.*

*281 top right The cross-shaped structure of the* prasat *also symbolizes the expansion of the sacred in the Buddhist religion, in this case the expansion of Dharma, the doctrine of the Enlightened One.*

*281 bottom right The praying figures or* rishi *(the ascetics/fortune tellers who first transmitted the sacred science) standing at the base of the pillars began to appear during the Angkor Wat period, and became widespread in the Bayon period.*

A more extended tour of Thailand should also include Lavo, now called **Lobpuri**, which was an important outpost in the Chao Phraya valley, adjacent to the Mun valley. Lavo was founded by the Mon and conquered by Suryavarman I in the eleventh century, from which period the first Khmer inscriptions date. Although it was subjugated to Angkor, it enjoyed a great deal of independence, to that point of sending independent delegations to China. Its armies were so famous for their discipline and loyalty that a Lavo contingent with its commander Rajendravarman is immortalized in the Angkor Wat bas-reliefs.

The surviving temples, made of laterite with stucco decorations, date from the thirteenth century. The most important monument is Sam Yod with three prasats in the Bayon style. The middle one is dedicated to Buddha, seated on the serpent Mucilinda, and the ones on either side to Lokeshvara and Prajnaparamita. However, the presence of a linga suggests that the shrine was originally Hindu and only later converted to Buddhism. The three towers are connected by vaulted passageways and have attractive stucco decorations.

Other Khmer remains are to be found in the huge, often rebuilt Wat Mahathat, whose central sanctuary recalls that of Phimai, and at Prang Khaek, which has sadly been relegated to a traffic divider.

# Wat Phu and Preah Vihear
## The Dwellings of Shiva

| Wat Phu |
|---|
| **A** Portico |
| **B** *Traces of Earlier Prasats* |
| **C** Mandapa |
| **D** Vestibule |
| **E** Modified Cell |

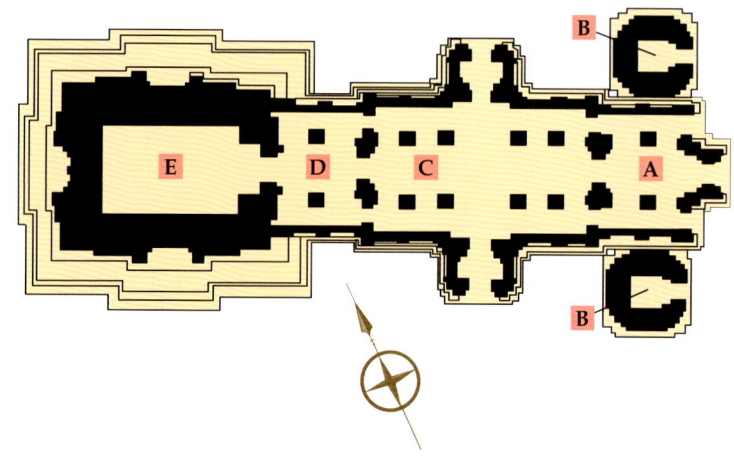

282-283 Wat Phu, originally devoted to the worship of Shiva, was a temple for bloodthirsty rites, traces of which survive in a ceremony still performed today by the local group of the Lao Theung, who sacrifice a buffalo to the spirit of the earth and sprinkle its blood on the ground to enhance its fertility.

283 top The "palaces", the southern one of which dates from the eleventh-twelfth century, consist of four rooms built round an inner courtyard. Their purpose is unknown, but they were not merely residential. An interesting theory maintains that they were seminaries for priests.

283 bottom This view of the shrine shows the portico with three entrances that leads into a mandapa with a nave and two aisles. The triangular pediments of Wat Phu are the last of their kind; the polylobate type had already begun to appear locally.

One of the most sacred places in Chenla was Lingaparvata (mountain of the linga), a mountain 4,619 feet high which had a natural monolith with a phallic shape on the summit. It is now called Phu Kao (mountain of the coiled hair), clearly referring to Shiva's chignon. According to Coedès, Shreshthapura, one of the first capitals of Chenla, lay at the foot of the mountain in the sixth century. The attractive complex of Wat Phu, five miles south of Champassak in what is now southern Laos, still stands on a 230-foot-high hill. The temple may have been built earlier and was probably founded by the Cham, who dedicated it to Shiva Bhadreshvara, their tutelary deity.

A sixth-century Chinese text, the "Chronicles of the Sui," states that human sacrifices were performed in honor of the god. Seven centuries later, Zhou Daguan reported that in bygone days the King of Champa offered to the gods thousands of gallbladders removed treacherously from the people. Although this seems very unlikely, it is probably an imaginative transposition of bloodthirsty rites actually performed in honour of Shiva. Shiva has a terrifying appearance, both because of his destructive function and because disquieting sacred ancestral figures converge on him. This was much more evident in Indian than Khmer architecture, where the positive functions of Shiva prevail. However, considering the age of Wat Phu, at which time the religion would have adhered more closely to the Indian sources, the god must have retained his terrifying, bloodthirsty aura.

When the Khmer arrived in the area and supplanted the Cham, they inherited his worship from their enemies. They considered Wat Phu highly sacred and continually modified and extended the building. Nearly all the kings of Chenla were Shivaites, and the lords of Angkor were mostly followers of Shiva too, with the result that the temple regularly received donations and privileges until the fall of Angkor.

Despite its sad state of neglect, Wat Phu is a highly evocative place. Although it is pre-Angkor, its final layout is attributable to Suryavarman II. The complex is distributed along the sides of the hill in an east-west axial direction, including the reservoir, which measures 650 by 1,970 feet, and stretches for nearly one mile. The reservoir was built by Divakarapandita, an eminent Brahman who crowned no less than three kings: Jayavarman VI, Dharanindravarman I, and Suryavarman II, during whose reign he excavated the baray. Beyond it there is a 820-foot-long avenue, once lined with pillars, nagas, and lustral basins. At the end of the avenue there are two "palaces," one made of laterite and the other of sandstone, originally roofed with tiles. From here a ramp, again lined with pillars and flanked by the ruins of a gallery with a library on the left, leads to a terrace and then continues towards a platform with the remains of six brick terraces. After crossing yet another platform with two prasats and climbing seven laterite steps, one reaches the shrine level.

The main temple, which was renovated by Suryavarman, is preceded by a portico with three entrances and gives onto a mandapa with a nave and two aisles. The central vault is supported by two rows of pillars and the lateral half-vaults rest on the outer walls. An antechamber leads to the rectangular cell, where a group of modern Buddhist statues demonstrate the conversion of the ancient Hindu site. Today there is a small Buddhist monastery for followers of the Enlightened One.

To the south of the shrine there is a spring which helped to accentuate the sacredness of the spot. Its waters were channeled and used to sprinkle the linga in the cell. The lustral waters were then conveyed through the somasutra into a basin for use by worshippers. The small brick prasat next to the spring is one of the oldest Khmer temples, as demonstrated by a seventh-century stela found here.

*284 top  The pediments had triangular or arched uprights, with differently designed corners (volutes in the first case and many-headed nagas in the second), as shown in this detail from Preah Vihear.*

*284 bottom left  The door surrounded by colonettes and architraves, together with the double polylobate pediment on pillars, formed a miniature prasat in Khmer architecture, as at Preah Vihear.*

*284 bottom right  When the only entrance was dictated by the lie of the land, as at Preah Vihear, access ramps, guarded by lions, become a crucial architectural feature.*

Another mountain sacred to the god Shiva, and an equally evocative spot, is **Preah Vihear** in Sisaket province, which is more easily accessible from neighboring Thailand than from Angkor. The spectacular temple stands at a height of 1,720 feet on a triangular promontory 500 feet long and 525 feet wide that juts out southwards about halfway along the Dangrek mountain chain. As already mentioned, this natural barrier which encloses the Cambodian plain was crossed by a number of roads that led to Phimai, Wat Phu, and Preah Vihear.

The building seems to have been started in 893 by Yashovarman I, who built a temple in honor of Shiva Shikhareshvara (lord of the summit). Subsequent kings, especially Suryavarman II and his spiritual adviser Divakarapandita, renovated the older buildings and added new ones.

The temple, like Wat Phu, has an axial layout but in this case from south to north, which was essential in view of its position on the mountain. The ascent route is 2,625 feet long, passing through five gopuras connected to one another by staircases and avenues in a procession that evokes the ascent of Mount Meru. A first staircase 256 feet long, once flanked by lions, has 162 steps cut directly into the rock and leads to a platform 100 feet wide lined with nagas. The fifth gopura, a cross-shaped structure which once had a tiled wooden roof and still bears evident traces of red paint which may have been gilded, leads to a second avenue.

The route continues for another 890 feet between two rows of 65 pillars in the shape of stylized lotus buds, passing a reservoir on the left, to the fourth gopura, which is reached via a short but steep flight of steps. A bas-relief showing the "churning of the sea of milk" decorates its south tympanum. Another avenue, 500 feet long with 35 pillars, leads to the third gopura, the largest in the complex, which was originally roofed with bricks on a wooden framework as opposed to earthenware tiles. Alongside it there are two rectangular environments with inscriptions dated 1026 containing galleries and elongated halls, known as "palaces." Their façades act as the wings of the gopuras, creating a scenic front 330 feet wide.

284-285 *This aerial photo shows the position and layout of Preah Vihear: the third* gopura *with the two "palaces" at its sides can be seen in the background, and the double enclosure of the main temple with two lateral shrines in the foreground.*

| PREAH VIHEAR | | | |
|---|---|---|---|
| **A** | RAMPS | **H** | BASIN |
| **B** | GOPURA | **I** | FIRST COURTYARD |
| **C** | AVENUES LINED WITH PILLARS | **J** | MANDAPA WITH PORTICO |
| **D** | "PALACES" | **K** | CELL WITH VESTIBULE |
| **E** | SECOND COURTYARD | **L** | FALSE GOPURA |
| **F** | HYPOSTYLE ROOM | **M** | SECONDARY TEMPLES |
| **G** | "LIBRARIES" | | |

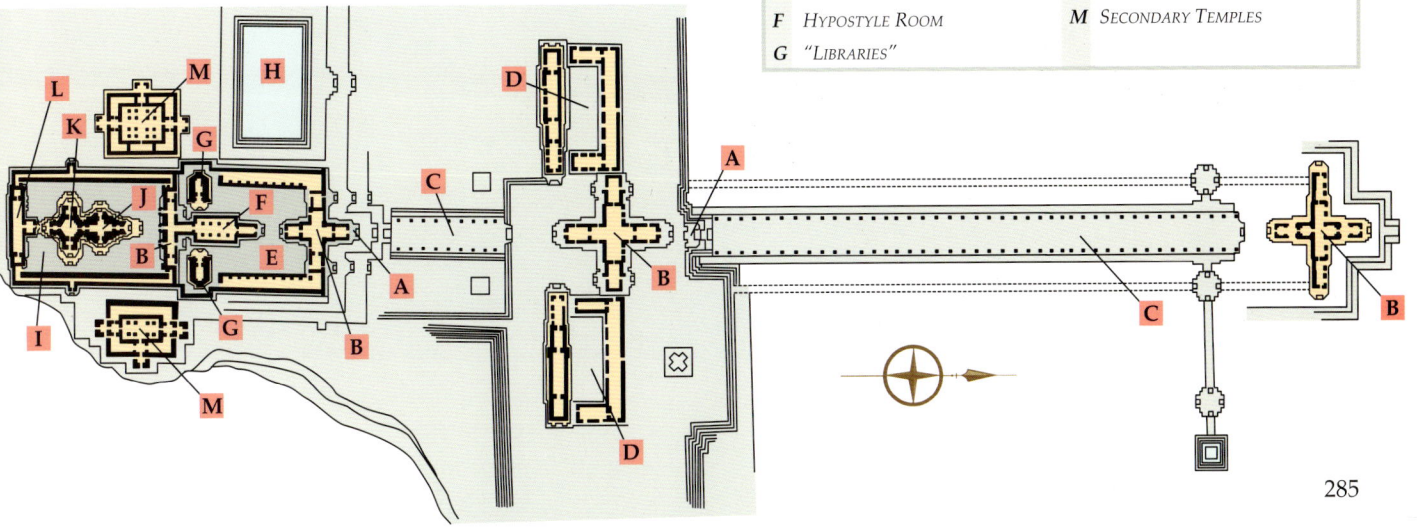

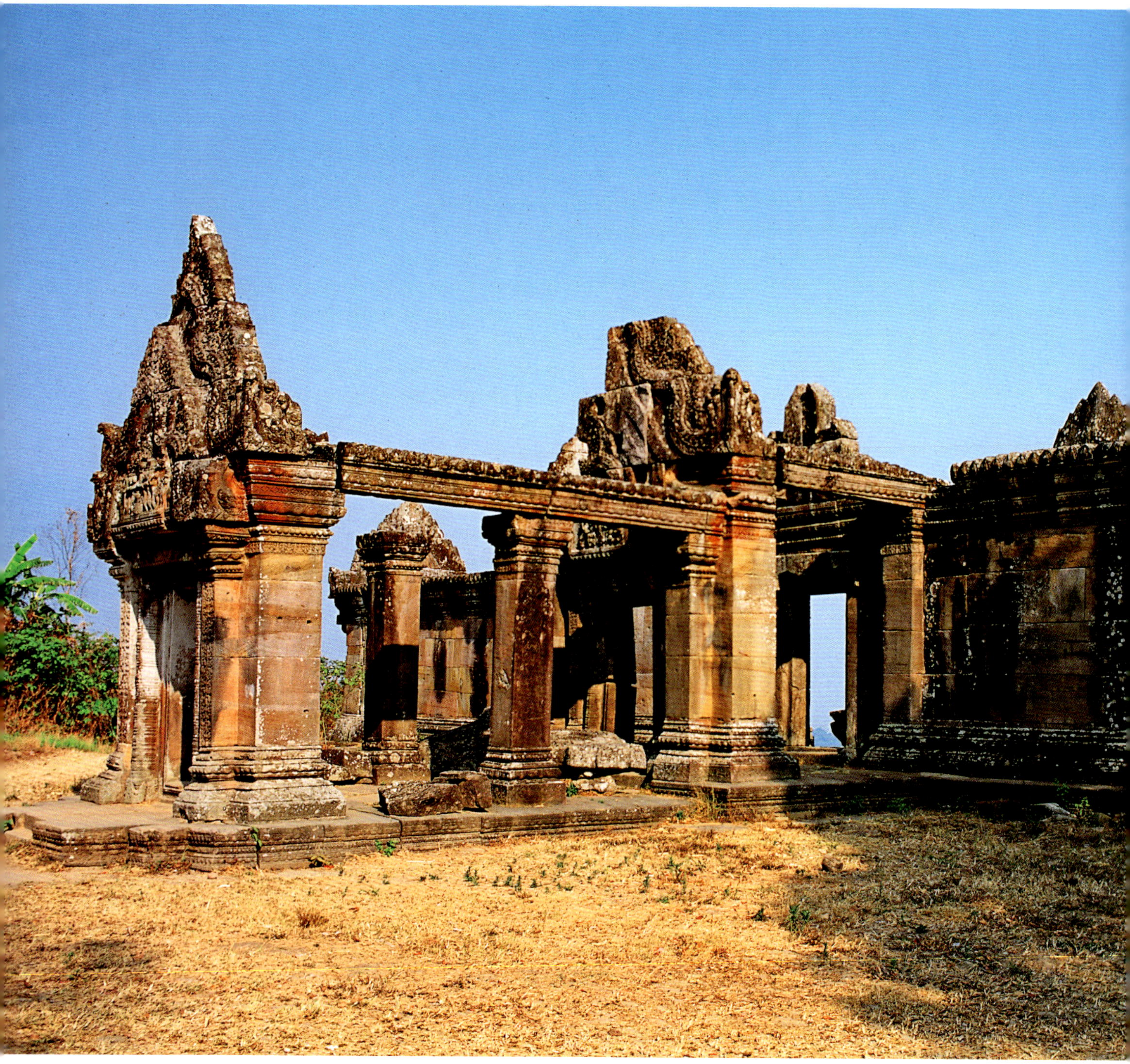

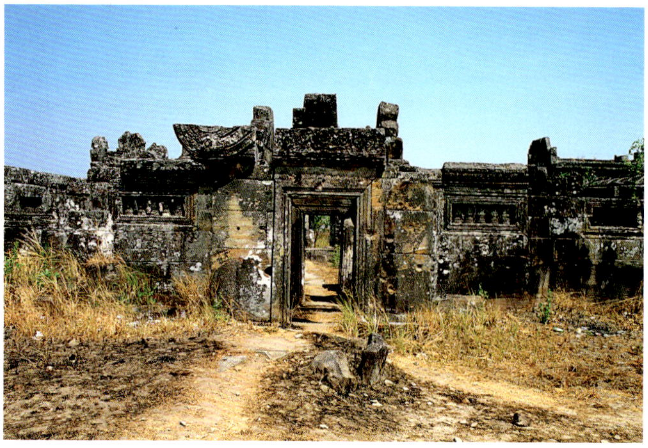

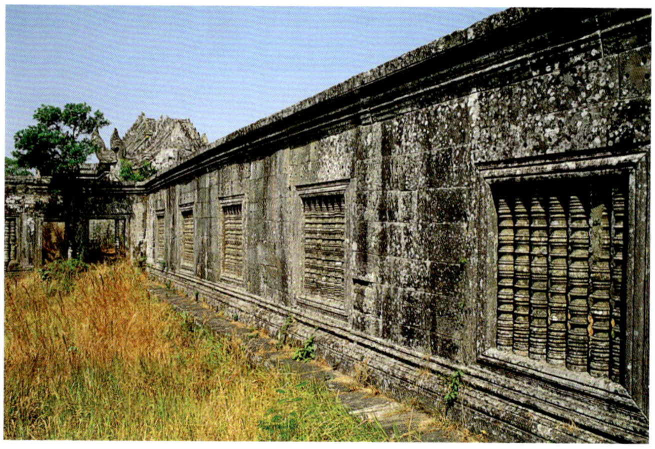

*287 center and bottom The first galleries apart from Phimeanakas to be entirely vaulted with sandstone appeared here at Preah Vihear in the early eleventh century, and are very narrow. The vault rests on a solid wall on the outside and on a wall with openings on the inside; the width of the part that spans the void is less than the width of the supports. The visible intrados has been carefully leveled.*

A short avenue which passes between two seven-headed nagas and is lined by ten pillars leads to the second gopura, again cross-shaped, with porticoes, which leads into the second courtyard. The courtyard is surrounded by a pillared gallery and contains the ruins of a hypostyle room with a triple corridor and two magnificent libraries with false aisles on either side. The north portico of the hypostyle room connects it to the access gopura of the first enclosure, a highly elongated pavilion that occupies the entire north façade of the perimeter gallery. The gallery is in excellent condition. It has a blind wall to the outside and windows on the inside and originally had a tiled roof. The main temple consists of a portico, a cross-shaped mandapa, a vestibule, and a cell with porticoes.

The roof, which has sadly collapsed, must have been more than 66 feet high. What seems to be the south gopura behind the temple actually is not, as it has a single entrance giving onto the courtyard. It may have been a retiring room or a ceremonial chamber. A door about halfway along the west gallery leads into the first enclosure, which offers a magnificent view over the Cambodian plain. On a clear day you can see Mount Kulen, over 60 miles away as the crow flies. Angkor is 25 miles further south.

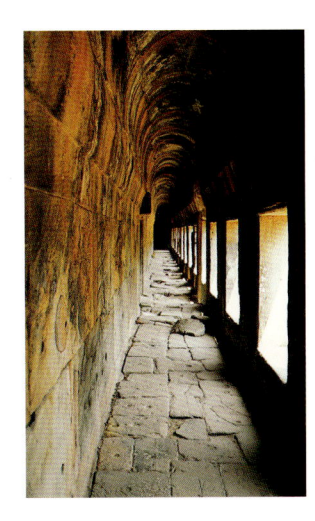

*286-287 The fifth gopura of Preah Vihear shows traces of red paint made from hematite, a ferrous mineral still used in present-day temples. The decoration used nowadays includes details highlighted in gold, which suggests that gold may also have been used in the past.*

*286 bottom left and right What are known as "palaces" actually consist of four long rooms with a blind wall and a windowed wall, surrounding an inner space.*

*287 top The triangular pediments of the gopuras, which emphasize the ends of the uprights at Preah Vihear, were designed to support the wooden trusses of the pitched roof, while polylobate pediments form the ends of the false stone vault.*

287

*289 The gargoyle portraying Kala (time) in the tympanum of the fifth* gopura *is also Rahu, the demon of the eclipse that swallows the moon. Its feral features are easily confused with those of the* simhamukha *(lion face). However, the symbol is also a* kirtimukha *(face of glory), which celebrates temporal power.*

## Preah Vihear: The Dwellings of Shiva

*288 top  In the series of entrances that demonstrate the accurate alignment of the buildings, the unusual upper part of the second door stands out, as the tympanum is inserted into a grid structure that reproduces those of wooden houses.*

*288 center  The outer tympanum of the fourth* gopura *depicts the famous scene of the "churning of the sea of milk" in which gods and demons extracted ambrosia, using the serpent Vasuki coiled around the Mandara (cosmic mountain). The mountain is portrayed here as a pillar emerging from a vessel symbolizing the sea, which in turn rests on a turtle, the incarnation of the god Vishnu, shown clinging to the pillar.*

*288 bottom  The staircases of the reservoirs (one on the left of the access avenue, between the fifth and fourth* gopura, *and the other on the right of the second courtyard) imitate* ghats, *the steps that lead down to rivers in India.*

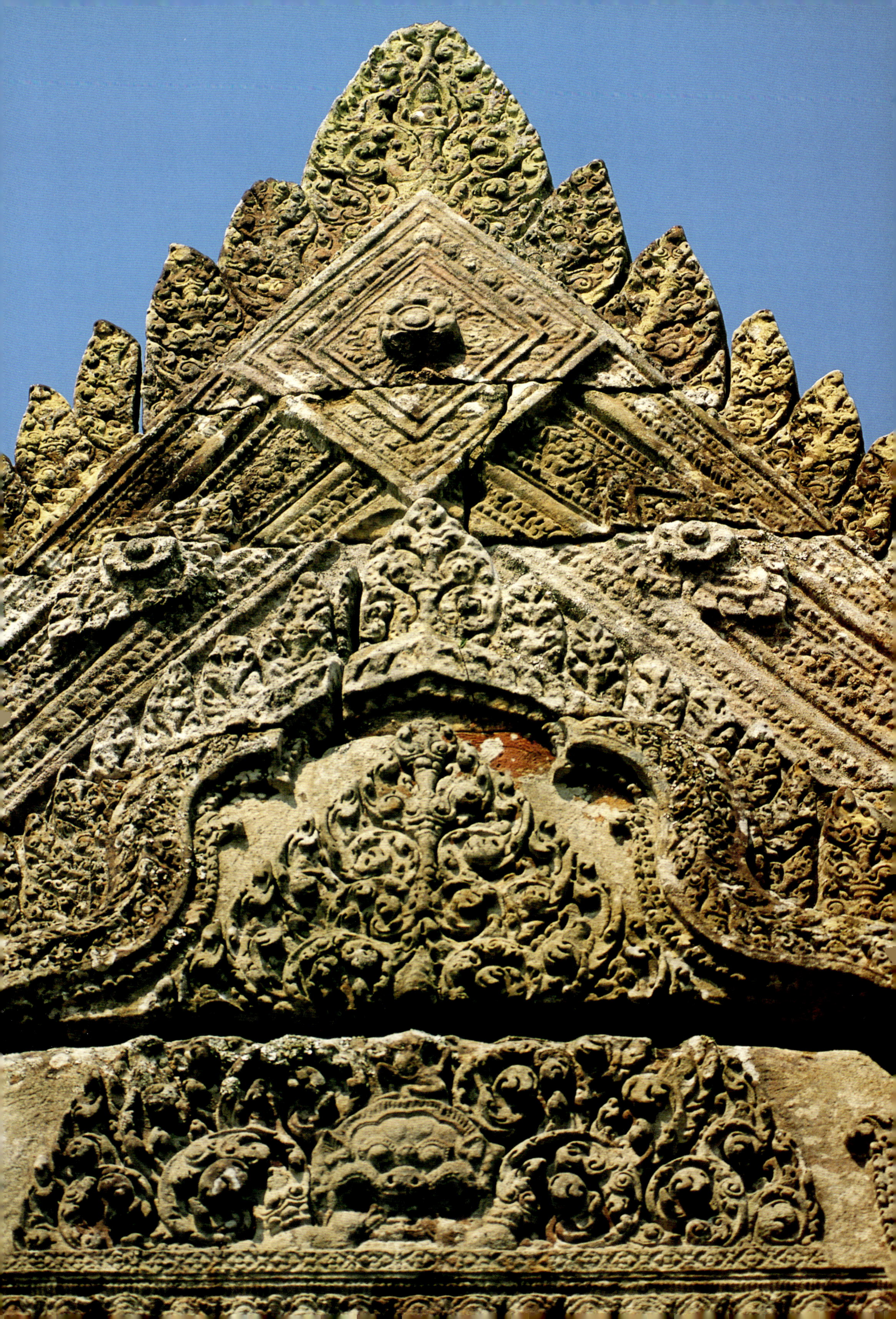

# AUTHORS

**Marilia Albanese** graduated in Sanskrit and Indology at the Department of Classical Literature at the Catholic University in Milan. She is the Director of the Lombardy Section of the Italian Institute for Africa and the Orient at the University of Milan, and the Education Coordinator at the Civic School of Oriental Cultures and Languages in Milan. As a teacher of Indian culture, she gives introductory courses to the Hindu and Buddhist religious worlds at the International Theological Seminary in Monza, which is affiliated with the Pontificia Università Urbaniana. Since the end of the 1970's, she has been in charge of teaching Indian culture at a number of training schools for yoga teachers, a subject on which she has published several books. To deepen her knowledge of Indian art and its profound significance, she has traveled to Indochina and, above all, to Cambodia, where she studied the Khmer civilization in relation to Hindu symbolism. As a freelance journalist, she is heavily involved in conferences and she is the author of articles, essays, and books. For White Star Publishers, she has contributed to the following volumes: Splendors of the *Lost Civilizations* (1998), *The Great Treasures: The Goldsmith's Art from Ancient Egypt to the 20th Century* (1998), *The World's Greatest Royal Palaces* (1999), and *The Dwellings of Eternity* (2000). For the same publisher, she has also written and published Northern India: *Guide to the Archaeological Sites* (1999), *Ancient India: from the Origins to the 13th Century AD* (2001), *Siddhartha: The Prince Who Became Buddha* (2008), and *Archaeology from above* (2010).

# GLOSSARY

(Unless otherwise specified, all the terms in this glossary are in Sanskrit)

*abhayamudra*: gesture of reassurance

*abhisheka*: anointment of the king by Brahmans

*achar*: from the Sanskrit *acarya*, meaning spiritual master

*amrita*: ambrosia, the nectar of immortality, or supreme knowledge

*ankusha*: elephant goad

*antarala*: vestibule

*antaravasaka*: ankle-length cloth worn wound around the waist

*apsaras*: celestial nymph

*Arak*: (Khmer) spirits of illness

*ardhamandapa*: half pavilion, portico

*arhat*: venerable monk of Hinayana Buddhism

*ashrama*: hermitage

*asura*: demon

*atman*: soul

*avatara*: divine descent to earth

*axis mundi*: (Latin) axis of the world

*azadirachta indica*: (Latin) nim

*baray*: (Khmer) reservoir

*bhaktimarga*: the path of salvation

*bindu*: instant

*Bixa orellana*: (Latin) annatto tree, a tropical plant from the Bixaceae family

*bnam*: (ancient Khmer) mountain

*bodhi*: illumination

*bodhisattva*: he whose essence is *bodhi*

*Brahman*: Absolute

*brahmana*: Brahmans, member of the first Hindu caste, the caste of priests

*Buddharaja*: Buddha-king

*budh*: become aware

*candravamsha*: the Moon Dynasty, descended from Krishna, incarnation of the god Vishnu

*chakra*: wheel, circle, sharp ring, the weapon of Vishnu

*chakravartin*: universal sovereign, "lord of the wheel", i.e. lord of order

*danava*: antigods

*darshana*: vision of the Sacred and, by extension, a philosophical system

*Devaraja*: god-king

*deva*: power of light, god

*devata*: deity

*devi*: goddess

*dharma*: in the Hindu world, *dharma* is the cosmic order that governs the phenomena of the universe and the moral law that inspires mankind; in the Buddhist world, it is the doctrine preached by Buddha

*dharmakaya*: according to Mahayana Buddhism, one of the bodies of Buddha, that of the Doctrine

*dhoti*: traditional Indian garment

*dhyanamudra*: gesture of meditation

*dvarapala*: gatekeeper

*eidolon*: image

*enceinte de domaine*: (French) royal enclosure, a French term given to the outermost enclosure of temples

*gandharva*: celestial beings

*garbhagriha*: embryo room, womb, temple cell

*garuda*: a creature that was part man, part bird, the mount of Vishnu

*genius loci*: (Latin) tutelary deity of a place

*ghanta*: bell

*ghi*: clarified butter

*gopura*: monumental structure above the entrances of temple enclosures

*grama*: village

*guru*: spiritual master

*hamsa*: goose with striped head or swan-goose, the mount of Brahma

*hotar*: performer of ritual sacrifices

*impluvium*: (Latin) courtyard where rainwater was collected

*Ishvara*: Lord

*jagat*: universe

*jatamukuta*: tall topknot worn by ascetics

*jaya*: victory

*kalasha*: bowl of water, finial and ornamental motif

*Kamrateng*: (ancient Khmer) Lord

*kamvujakshara*: writing of the descendants of Kambu

*karman*: deed, the cause and effect of actions that binds man to the *samsara*

*kaustubha*: the gem worn on Vishnu's breast

*Khmorch chhav*: (Khmer) the "raw dead," those who come to a bad end

*khnum*: (ancient Khmer) people devoted to the service of religious foundations

*kshatriya*: warriors, belonging to the second Hindu caste

*kudu*: small horseshoe-shaped arches

*kundalini*: divine potential latent in man, symbolized by a serpent goddess

*linga*: phallic symbol, the symbol of the god Shiva

*loka*: paradise-world

*luoma*: (Khmer) an unknown fiber used for fabrics

*mahayuga*: great cosmic cycle

*makara*: legendary sea monster

*mala*: garland, rosary

*mandala*: symbolic, esoteric pattern that reflects the order of the cosmos and the mind

*mandapa*: pavillion

*maya*: illusion, cosmic relativity

*men*: (Khmer) canopy beneath which the sovereign was cremated

*menhir*: funerary stone

*moksha*: release from the cycle of rebirths

*mudra*: physical gestures

*mukhashala*: front room, portico

*mukuta*: miter

*murti*: image of deity

*Naga*: legendary beings which were part cobra

*nagara*: capital city

*Nagaraja*: King of the Naga

*nagari*: Sanskrit alphabet from northern India

*Nagini*: the Naga's female companion

*narasimha*: lion-man, the avatar of the god Vishnu

*navagraha*: the nine planets of Hindu tradition, namely the Sun, Moon, Mars, Mercury, Jupiter, Venus, Saturn, Rahu (demon of the eclipse), and Ketu (personification of the node of the moon or the comets)

*neak ta*: (Khmer) spirit

*neak-ta-moha-reach*: (Khmer) great king of the spirits

*nirmanakaya*: according to Mahayana Buddhism one of the bodies of Buddha, the fictitious body

*nirvana*: ineffable state of extinction of existence

*pada*: residential quarters in the traditional Hindu city grid

*pallava*: relates to the Pallava Dynasty, kings of southern India

*pancashula*: five-pointed metal finial

*parijata*: tree that grants wishes

*parvat*: mountain

*phnom*: (Khmer) mountain

*pradakshina*: rite of perambulation keeping the venerated object on one's right *prajna*: intuitive wisdom or perfect knowledge

*prakriti*: primordial matter, nature

*praman*: province

*prang*: Thai term for *prasat*

*prasat*: temple

*prasavya*: funeral rite performed with left-hand perambulation

*prashasti*: panegyric written in ornate prose and verse

*pre rup*: (Khmer) body-turning

*purohita*: spiritual master and adviser to the sovereign

*raja*: king

*rajakumara*: crown prince

*rajapurohita*: royal chaplain

*rajasuya*: royal anointment

*rajavihara*: royal monastery

*rajya*: royalty

*rakshasa*: demon

*sambhogakaya*: according to Mahayana Buddhism one of the bodies of Buddha, the enjoyment body

*samjak*: (ancient Khmer) unknown military rank

*samrit*: alloy of precious metals

*samsara*: return to life in a different form

*sangama*: confluence

*saptaloka*: the seven heavens of the Hindu gods

*shloka*: verses of four octosyllables

*shunya*: empty

*shunyata*: emptiness

*skanda*: the combination of material and mental factors that constitute the human being

*snanadroni*: round base of the *linga*, terminating in a spout, the symbol of the female Origin

*somasutra*: evacuation channel for ablutions

*sruk*: (ancient Khmer) village

*stupa*: mound erected above the cremated ashes of Buddha and the most celebrated monks; reliquary

*suryavamsha*: the Sun Dynasty, descended from Rama, another incarnation of the god Vishnu

*thnôt*: (Khmer) *Borasso flabelliforme* or palmyra

*torana*: access portal

*trance*: state of sensory isolation in which paranormal phenomena occur

*tribhanga*: S-shaped triple bend of the body

*Trimurti*: the triple form taken on by the Absolute as emanator, preserver, and destroyer of the cosmos in the figures of Brahma, Vishnu, and Shiva.

*trishula*: three-pointed metal finial

*upaya*: the right way, namely compassion, which allows *prajna* to be achieved

*ushnisha*: Buddha's cranial protuberance

*uttarasanga*: cloak

*vahana*: vehicle or mount of the gods

*vajra*: thunderbolt, diamond scepter, symbol of the unchanging awareness of truth

*varaha*: boar

*varman*: breastplate, protection

*varna*: color, caste

*vastupurushamandala*: grid formed by squares which constitutes the plan of the temple

*vimana*: flying palace, chariot

*vishaya*: province

*vitarkamudra*: teaching gesture

*vrah guru*: (Khmer + Sanskrit) holy spiritual master

*wat*: (Thai) monastery

*yaksha*: tree spirit

*yantra*: esoteric diagram

*yuga*: cosmic era

*yuvaraja*: crown prince.

# INDEX

*Note: d = caption*
*nn = dedicated chapter*

## A

Abu Zayd Hasan, 31
Adhyapura, 26, 28, 29, 30
Agni, 68, 77
Airavata, 132c, 184c
Ak Yum, 29, 30, 32, 158
Akshobhya, 90
Amarendrapura, 32, 93, 154
Amitabha, 86c, 90
Amoghasiddhi, 90
Ananta, 36c, 38, 118, 175, 193c, 275
Anavatapta, 247
Ang Chan, 28, 213
Ang Chumnik, 26
Angkor, 11, 12, 20, 30, 31, **32-34**, 36c, 38, 38c, 41, 43, 44, 46, 47, 48, 55, **56-60**, 72, 93, 97, 98c, 102, 103, 104, 129, 143c, 147c, 148, 150, 153, 154, 163, 165, 166, 171, 172, 179, 182, 191, **195-199**, 200, 208, 213, **249-271**, 272, 277, 277c, 280c, 281, 283, 284, 287
Angkor Borei, 50, 84c, 121c, 126
Angkor Thom, 12c, 20, 42c, 45, 56, 59c, 124c, 134, 148, **227-247**, 265, **272-281**
Angkor Wat, 8c, 12c, 18c, 41, 47, 55, 56, 57c, 61c, 71, 71c, 72c, 76, 76c, 78, 78c, 88c, 92c, 97, 97c, 98c, 101c, 114c, 116, 117c, 123c, 133, 143, 143c, 144, 144c, 148, 148c, 180, 195, 196, 198, **200-223**, 249, 255, 271c, 279, 280c, 281
Aninditapura, 30, 32, 35
Annam, 28, 41, 44, 47, 55
Annamites, 47
Antonio da Magdalena, 56
Ansaraja, 47
Apsaras, 79
Aram Rong Chen, 158
Aravindhahrada, 38
Arjuna, 259
Arya, 75, 77
Ashvatthaman, 25
Ashvin, 20
Auberlet, 58
Avalokiteshvara, 27c, 30c, 83c, 86
Aymonier, Etienne, 20, 58
Ayodhya, 77
Ayuthya, 48, 55
Ayutthaya, 48

## B

Ba Phnom, 26
Bakheng, 162c, 164, 165c
Bakong, 32, 55, 103, 129, 138, 142, 154, 158, 159c, 160, 160c
Baksey Chamrong, temple, 35, 55, 142c, 165, 165c, 167, 181
Baladitya, 30
Balaha, 247c
Balarama, 184c
Bali, 35, 166
Bana, 213
Bangkok National museum, 81c, 279, 279c
Banteay Chmar, 43, 55, 148
Banteay Chmar, temple, 41, 247, **249-271**
Banteay Kdei, 32, 45, 55, 90c, 247, 251, 260, 261c, 262c
Banteay Prei Nokor, 32
Banteay Samré, 55, 142c, 195, 196, 197, 197c
Banteay Srei, temple, 35, 35c, 55, 59, 67c, 69c, 75c, 92, 106c, 132, 132c, 136c, 139c, 142, 144c, 148, **182-194**
Baphuon, 38, 41c, 55, 175, 175c
Barthe, Auguste, 20
Basak Romduol, 41c
Bassak, 24c
Bastian, Adolf, 56
Bat Chum, 35, 55, 168
Battambang, 43
Bayon, 12, 12c, 20, 38c, 45, 46, 46c, 48c, 55, 58, 59c, 67c, 71c, 98, 98c, 101c, 104, 105c, 107c, 108, 108c, 109c, 111, 111c, 113c, 115, 117c, 119c, 123c, 124c, 134, 134c, 138c, 142c, 147c, 148, 237, 238c, 243c, 247, 253c, 254c, 256c, 261c, 262c, 263c, 265c, 267c, 271, 271c, 280c, 281
Beng Mealea, 55, 148, **195-199**, 238, 249, 270
Bengala, Gulf of, 24
Bergaigne, Abel, 20
Bhadravarman, 28
Bhadreshvara, 66, 281
Bhagavati, 35
Bhaishajyaguru, 81c, 252
Bharata Rahu, 41
Bhattacharya, 94
Bhavapura, 29, 31, 35, 50, 150
Bhavavarman, 29, 150, 153
Bhavavarman II, 29, 30
Bhima, 106c
Binh Dinh, 28, 41
Blanche, Charles, 58
Blanche, Gabriel, 58
Boromaraja II, 48
Bosch, F.D.K., 35, 216
Bouillevaux, Charles Emile, 56
Brah Bishnukar, 201
Brah Bishnulok, 200
Brahma, 23c, 24, 65, 65c, 66, 67c, 68, 123, 127, 136, 165, 193c, 242, 252, 271
Brahmaloka, 35
Briggs, Lawrence Palmer, 29, 31, 41

Brihaspati, 164
British Museum, 113c
Buddha, 8c, 11c, 23c, 27c, 30c, 42c, 44c, 45c, 46, 47, 48c, 56, 58, 81, 81c, 82, 83, 83c, 84, 84c, 86, 86c, 88, 88c, 89, 89c, 90, 97, 113c, 117c, 119c, 121c, 132c, 133, 134c, 220, 234, 237, 247, 247c, 251, 252, 255c, 258, 259, 259c, 260, 279, 279c, 281
Buddhaghosha, 200
Buriram, 272
Burma, 23, 35, 55
Burmese, 44

## C

Cambodia, 11, 20, 23, 28, 29, 47, 50, 56, 57, 58, 59, 72, 95, 109c, 126, 139c, 165, 201, 270
Cham, 28, 38, 41, 43, 55, 98, 98c, 101c, 234c, 236c, 265, 283
Champa, 25, 26, 28, 29, 35, 41, 43, 47, 55, 70, 113, 283
Champassak, 28, 283
Chantaburi, 29, 165
Chao Phraya, 281
Chau Say Tevoca, 55, 195, 197
Chenla, 20, 23, **28-31**, 50, 102, 148, 150, 171, 277, 283
Chevreul, 56
China, 20, 26, 28, 31, 41, 47, 57, 113
Chinese, 47
Chok Gargyal, 148, 179, 198
Citrasena, 28, 29, 150
Claudel, Paul, 58
Cochin China, 28
Coèdes, Georges, 20, 58, 244, 283
Commaille, Jean, 58

## D

Da Nang, 28
Daguan, Zhou, 11, 20, 44, 47, 70, 72, 97, 100, 101, 104, 107, 110, 113, 117, 144, 174, 201, 242, 283
Dai Viet, 38, 41
Dangrek, Mounts, 35, 148, 247, 265, 272, 284
de Carné, Louis, 57
de Lajonquière, Lunet, 58
Delaporte, Louis, 57, 57c, 59c, 147c, 198
Delhi, 18c, 28, 75, 214
Devi, 31c, 67c, 113c, 127, 165c
Dhanvantari, 79
Dharanindradevi, 157
Dharanindravarman I, 41, 43, 55, 256, 283
Dharanindravarman II, 41, 55

Dharma, 280c
Dhritarashtra, 76
Diego do Couto, 56
Divakarabhatta, 35
Divakarapandita, 38, 41, 221, 283, 284
Doudart de Lagrée, Ernest, 57
Draupadi, 76
Dravida, 77
Durga, 31c, 66, 127, 127c
Duryodhana, 107c
Dvaravati, 23c, 27c, 38, 44, 113c

## F

Fa Ngun, 47
Fan Shih-man, 26
Ferguson, James, 57
Filliozat, J., 164
Finot, Louis, 20
Fournereau, Lucien, 57, 143c
France, 57
Freeman, Michael, 275
French, 184c
Funan, 20, **23-27**, 28, 29, 31, 50, 95, 97, 102
Funanese, 26

## G

Ganesh, 25c, 68, 68c
Garnier, Francis, 57
Garuda, 35c, 67c, 68, 103c, 129c, 140, 154c, 157, 166, 166c, 180
Glaize, Maurice, 58, 158
Goloubeff, Victor, 58
Govardhana, 121
Grahi, 35, 41, 44
Groslier, George, 58, 72
Groslier, Bernard-Philippe, 48, 58, 59, 160, 164, 194c, 266, 277c
Guimet Museum, 8c, 11c, 23c, 30c, 35c, 38c, 44c, 45c, 48c, 58, 62c, 65c, 67c, 69c, 84c, 89c, 90c, 94c, 98c, 113c, 114c, 121c, 123c, 124c, 129c, 130c, 134c, 140c
Gupta, 24

## H

Hanoi, 47
Hanuman, 68, 69c, 76, 77, 78c
Harideva, 44
Harihara, 8c, 29, 29c, 66, 94c, 121c, 123, 126, 127
Hariharalaya, 32, 55, 93, 142, 148, 154, 158, 160, 163, 182
Haripunjaya, 41, 44, 55
Haripura, 35
Harshavarman I, 35, 55, 165, 165c, 166, 179, 182
Harshavarman II, 35, 55, 166, 171

Harshavarman III, 32, 41, 43, 55
Hastinapura, 75
Hayagriva, 69c
Hevajra, 90, 90c, 119c
Hill of Clouds, 28
Himalayas, 24, 95, 247
Hinayana, 55
Hiranya, 274
Hiranyadama, 32, 93
Hiranyakashipu, 190c
Hsien, 47
Hun t'ien, 25
Hyang Pavitra, 35

## I

India, 11, 20, 23, 24, 25, 26, 35, 50, 56, 62, 66, 75, 77, 81, 84c, 89, 93, 109, 117c, 121, 136c, 153, 154, 247
Indochina, 11, 47, 56, 57c, 89, 102, 103
Indochinese Museum, 57
Indonesia, 58
Indra, 32, 59c, 140, 154, 165, 168, 184c, 201
Indradevi, 32, 43
Indrakumara, 41, 47
Indralakshmi, 35
Indraprashtha, 28, 75
Indrapura, 32, 93, 154
Indratataka, 32, 55, 154, 154c, 160
Indravarman, 32, 55, 265
Indravarman I, 55, 129, 154, 154c, 157, 158, 160, 160c
Indravarman II, 47, 55
Indravarman IV, 41, 43, 55
Indreshvara, 160c
Ishana, 29, 150
Ishanapura, 29, 31, 50, 148, 150, 150c, 153, 153c
Ishanavarman, 20, 29, 30, 50, 150
Ishanavarman II, 35, 55
Ishvaraloka, 32

## J

Jacques, Claude, 30, 41, 43, 208, 210, 220, 221
Jahnavi, 35
Janapada, 32
Java, 20, 31, 32, 35, 44, 47, 50, 55, 102
Jaya Harivarman I, 41
Jaya Indravarman IV, 41
Jaya Mangalartha, 45
Jaya Parmeshvara IV, 47
Jayadevi, 30, 31, 35, 50, 171
Jayakirtideva, 255c
Jayamangalarthadeva, 255c
Jayarajacudamani, 43
Jayarajadevi, 43, 46c, 92c

Jayashri, 45, 47
Jayatataka, 45, 244
Jayavarman I, 30, 31, 32, 50
Jayavarman II, 32, 35, 36, 55, 93, 102, 142, 154, 157, 167, 265
Jayavarman III, 32, 55, 154
Jayavarman IV, 35, 55, 148, 171, 179, 181
Jayavarman V, 35, 55, 92, 172, 182
Jayavarman VI, 38, 41, 55, 277, 283
Jayavarman VII, 12, 12c, 41, 42c, 43, 44, 44c, 45, 46, 46c, 47, 48, 55, 59c, 62, 81, 83c, 90, 92c, 97, 110, 134, 143, 147c, 148, 234, 235c, 237, 238, 242, 242c, 244, 246, 247, **249-271**, 272, 273, 279, 279c
Jayavarman VIII, 47, 55
Jayavarman IX, 47
Jayaviravarman, 172
Jayendranagari, 35, 55, 172
Jayendrapandita, 38
Jetavana, 56
Joubert, Eugène, 57
Jupiter, 136, 164

## K

Kab Choeng, 272
Kabandha, 78
Kailasa, 154, 182c
Kala, 140, 157, 288c
Kali, 66
Kaliya, 141c
Kalkin, 69c
Kambu, 35, 97
Kambu Svayambhuva, 20, 28
Kambuja, 28, 31, 32, 35, 36, 38, 41, 43, 47, 50, 55, 66, 81, 82, 83c, 84, 88, 93, 126, 148, 153c, 154, 179c, 180, 181, 272
Kambujadesha, 28, 200
Kambujarajalakshmi, 28
Kamvau, 38
Kapilavastu, 81
Kaundinya, 25, 50, 97
Kaundinya, Jayavarman, 26
Kaurava, 18c, 75, 76, 106c, 214
Kavindrarimathana, 167, 168, 169c, 260
Kbal Spean, 193, 193c
Kern, Hendrik, 20
Ket Mealea, 201
Ketu, 136
Ketumala, 201
Khautara, 28
Khleang, 35c, 55, 172
Khmer, 8c, 11, 20, 21, **28-31**, 38, 41, 42c, 47, 48, 50, 55, 61c, 62, 68, 71, 72, 75, 76, 78, 98c, 101c, 104, 109, 113c, 117, 136c, 141,

292

144c, 148, 154, 164, 166, 175c, 176, 190c, 234, 236c, 275, 280c, 283
Khon Kaen, 28
Klong Chakrai, 277c
Koh Ker, 33c, 35, 55, 90c, 129, 130, 130c, 142, 142c, 148, 166, **179-181**, 182
Koh Krieng, 31c
Kok Thlok, 28, 201
Kompong Cham, 32
Kompong Preah, 50, 126, 127
Kompong Svay, 38c, 44c, 48c, 55, 148, 195, 247, **249-271**
Kompong Thom, 29, 41, 50, 126, 148, 150, 195, 198, 251, 270, 271c
Korat, 44, 47, 55
Kratié, 28, 31
Krishna, 26, 66, 76, 97, 141c, 184c, 213
Krishna Govardhana, 121
Krus Preah Aram Rong Chen, 154, 158
Kublai Khan, 21, 47
Kulen, 124c
Kulen, Mount, 55, 287
Kundalini, 88, 89
Kunti, 76
Kurukshetra, 18c, 75, 76, 98c, 214, 215c
Kuti, 32

L

Lakshmana, 76
Lakshmi, 46c, 66, 68, 78, 166, 166c, 193c
Lamphun, 41
Lanka, 75c, 76, 76c, 77, 78c
Lanka, battle of, 12c, 213, 216c
Lan Xang, 47
Lao Theung, 283c
Laos, 11, 28, 29, 36, 44, 47, 50, 55, 56, 57, 110, 148, 165
Lavo, 36, 41, 44, 47, 281
Ligor, 35
Lingaparvata, 283
Liu-yeh, 25
Lobpuri, 36, 41, 316, 280, 281
Lokapala, 136
Lokeshvara, 44c, 45, 46, 59, 83c, 86, 86c, 90, 97, 113c, 134, 134c, 143, 147c, 237, 238, 247, 247c, 256, 260, 261c, 263c, 265, 265c, 266, 267c, 271, 271c, 281
Lolei, 32, 55, 101, 102, 154, 154c, 160
London, 113c
Loti, Pierre, 58, 147c
Lou Pan, 201

Lovek, 213
Luang Phabang, 47
Lumbini, 81

M

Magadha, 56
Mahaballipuram, 24
Mahaparamasaugata, 47
Mahayana, 143, 277, 279c
Mahendraparvata, 32, 94, 154
Mahendrapura, 32, 93, 154
Mahendravarman, 29
Maheshvara, 26
Mahidharapura, 38, 41, 55, 277
Mahipativarman, 31, 32
Mahisha, 31c, 127c
Maitreya, 31c, 86
Malacca, 35
Malays, 31, 50
Malaysia, 44, 47, 55
Malraux, André, 58, 184c
Malyang, 43
Mandara, monte, 79, 288c
Mangalartha, 47, 55
Manu, 94
Marchal, Henri, 58, 59, 184c
Marica, 78
Mars, 136, 168
Mebon, 35, 36c, 38, 94, 118, 168, 169, 175
Mekong, 23, 28, 30, 31, 32, 38, 41, 50, 57, 102
Menam, 23, 23c, 27c, 28, 38, 44, 50, 55, 102
Mera, 28, 35, 97
Mercury, 136, 154
Meru, Mount, 11, 95, 136, 142, 143, 158, 160, 164, 165, 184, 202c, 221, 244, 251, 284
Mi-son, 25
Moon, 136, 160
Mo-tan, 26
Mohini, 79
Mon, 27c, 41, 47, 280c, 281
Mouhot, Henri, 56
Mucilinda, 48c, 83c, 88, 88c, 89, 119c, 133, 234, 279c, 281
Mun, 28, 32, 50, 265, 277, 281
Mus, Paul, 89, 237
My Son, 28

N

Naga, 26, 48c
Nagaraja, 26, 28
Nagarajayashri, 256
Nagasena, 26
Nagini, 97
Nakhon Si Thammarat, 35
Nalanda, 89
Nan Chao, 31, 44, 47

Nandin, 20c, 24c, 68, 118, 153, 156c, 157, 170
Narapativiravarman, 35
Narasimha, 190c
Narendradevi, 157
Narendraditya, 274
Nataraja, 274c
Neak Pean, 45, 55, 246, 247, 247c
Nepal, 81
Nha-trang, 28, 35
Nicobare, Islands, 24
Nilakantha, 79
Nirvanapada, 38
Norodom, 28
Norottama, 35
Nripaditya, 30
Nripatindravarman, 30, 32, 41

O

O Klok, 103
Oc-èo, 26, 50
Orissa, 23, 24

P

Pagan, 41, 55
Pala, 24
Pallava, 20, 24
Pandava, 18c, 75, 76, 106c, 214
Pandu, 76
Panduranga, 28, 38, 41, 43
Paramakaivalyapada, 41
Paramanishkalapada, 41
Paramaraja, 48
Paramaraja II, 55
Paramarudraloka, 35
Paramasaugata, 47
Paramashivaloka, 32, 35
Paramashivapada, 35
Paramavishnuloka, 41, 97, 200
Parameshvara, 32, 55, 157, 167
Parameshvarapada, 35, 47
Paris, 8c, 11c, 23c, 30c, 57, 58, 62c, 143c
Parmentier, Henri, 58
Parvati, 25c, 66, 68, 140c, 169c, 175c, 182c, 190c
Pha Bang, 47
Phan Rang, 28, 38, 43
Phimai, 55, 110, 148, **272-281**, 284
Phimai, temple, 41, 175c
Phimeanakas, 35, 38, 55, 106, 143, 174, 240, 285
Phnom Bakheng, 32, 50c, 58, 162c, 163, 165
Phnom Bayang, 32, 55
Phnom Bok, 32, 55, 62c, 65c, 129c
Phnom Chisor, 8c, 36, 55, 174
Phnom Da, 8c, 26, 50, 126, 127c
Phnom Krom, 32, 55
Phnom Kulen, 32, 55, 93, 154, 158, 196, 198

Phnom Penh, 59, 174, 246c, 256
Phnom Penh, Archaeological Museum or National Museum, 8c, 20c, 24c, 25c, 27c, 29c, 30c, 31c, 35c, 36c, 41c, 42c, 44c, 46c, 58, 67c, 68c, 69c, 77c, 81c, 84c, 88c, 103c, 119c, 121c, 123c, 127c, 129c, 130c, 132c, 136c, 139c, 141c, 175
Phnom Rung, 55, 165, 270, 273
Phnom Ta Kream, 30c
Phu Kao, 283
Popel, 114c
Prahlada, 190c
Prana, 35
Pranavatman, 35
Prajna, 89
Prajnaparamita, 46, 83, 89, 92, 252, 255c, 260, 281
Prang, 179c, 181
Prang Brahmadat, 279c
Prang Hin Daeng, 277c
Prang Khaek, 281
Prang Noi, 274c, 275
Prasat Andet, 50, 126, 127
Prasat Kraham, 180, 180c
Prasat Kravan, 55, 166, 166c, 167c
Prasat Pen Chang, 141c
Prasat Phnom Rung, 274, 274c
Prasat Sralao, 103c
Prasat Suor Prat, 55, 242, 242c
Prasat Thom, 130, 142c, 179, 180, 182
Pre Rup, 35, 55, 170, 171c
Preah Damrei, 269
Preah Khan, 38c, 41, 44, 44c, 45, 48c, 55, 142, 148, 195, 198, 244, 247, 250, 256, 256c, 259, 259c, 260, 265c, 270, 271c
Preah Ko, 32, 46c, 55, 103, 129c, 154, 154c, 156c, 157, 160, 184
Preah Pithu, 55, 140c, 194c, 196
Preah Stung, 271, 271c
Preah Thkol, 270
Preah Thong, 28
Preah Vihar, 35, 38, 55, 148, **282-289**
Prei Kmeng, 50, 126, 127
Prei Mounts, 55, 103, 154
Prei Veng, 26, 31
Prithivindradevi, 157
Prithivindravarman, 157
Prithivindreshvara, 157
Przyluski, J., 216
Purandarapura, 30
Pursat, 126
Pushkarashka, 30, 31, 50

R

Rach Gia, 26, 50
Rahal, 35, 179

Rahu, 136, 288c
Rajendra, 168
Rajendrabhadreshvara, 35, 171
Rajendravarman I, 31, 50, 94, 130, 165, 166, 167, 170, 171, 171c, 172, 175c, 182, 260, 281
Rajendravarman II, 35, 55
Rajendreshvara, 35, 168
Rama, 12c, 28, 50c, 66, 68, 69c, 75c, 76, 76c, 77, 78, 78c, 97, 213
Rama Kamheng, 47
Ramadhipati, 48
Ratnasambhava, 90
Ravana, 75c, 76c, 77, 78c, 182c
Roluos, 32, 102, 103, 142, 148, 154, 160, 184
Rome, 26
Rudraloka, 35
Rudravarman, 26, 28, 50, 157
Rudreshvara, 157

**S**

Sadashivapada, 38
Sadesha, 66
Saluen, 35
Sam Yod, 278c, 279
Sambor, 31, 38, 50
Sambor Prei Kuk, 29, 31, 31c, 35, 50, 126, 127, 127c, 148, 150, 153
Samré, 196
Samrong Sen, 21
Sangrama, 38
Saptadevakula, 35, 36, 38
Sarasvati, 66, 68
Saturn, 136
Satyavati, 76
Sdok Kak Thom, stele of, 32, 38, 93, 94
Seidenfaden, Erik, 58
Shailendra, 31, 102
Shaka, 20, 32
Shakya, 81
Shambhupura, 36, 38, 50
Shambuvarman, 31, 50
Shankarapandita, 38
Shantanu, 76
Shindravarman, 47
Shiva, 8c, 20c, 23c, 24, 24c, 25c, 26, 28, 29, 29c, 30, 31c, 32, 35, 35c, 41c, 45, 55, 62c, 66, 67c, 68, 68c, 79, 81c, 90c, 93, 94, 94c, 95, 101, 113c, 118, 123, 127, 136, 140c, 148, 150, 153, 154, 156c, 160, 164, 165, 165c, 166, 168, 169c, 170, 175c, 180, 181, 182c, 188, 213, 259, 272, 274, 274c, 275, **282-289**
Shiva Bhadreshvara, 171
Shivakaivalya, 32, 35, 36, 38, 92, 93

Shivaloka, 30, 35
Shivapura, 30
Shivashrama, 32
Shivasoma, 32
Shreshthapura, 28, 50, 283
Shreshthavarman, 28
Shri, 66
Shri Lanka, 200
Shridharadevapura, 259
Shrindrajayavarman, 47, 55
Shrindravarman, 20, 55
Shrivijaya, 31
Shrutavarman, 28, 50
Siam, 56, 57
Siam, Gulf of, 23, 29, 35, 50, 55, 102
Siamese, 98, 214
Siddhartha Gautama, 81, 86, 89c, 121c
Siem Reap, 32, 41, 103, 110, 163, 167, 201
Silvi Antonini, Chiara, 94
Simhadatta, 30
Simhavira, 29, 30
Sisaket, 284
Sisophon, 32, 265
Sita, 75c, 76, 77, 78
Skanda, 168
Soma, 26, 50, 97
Spean Praptos, 110
Srah Srang, 8c, 45, 55, 72, 168, 260, 261c
Stern, Philippe, 58, 94, 136, 254c, 255
Stierlin Henri, 154, 181, 208
Stung Sen, 150
Subhadra, 41
Sugriva, 50c, 78, 78c
Sukhothai, 47, 48, 55
Sukshmavindu, 32
Sulayman, 31
Sumatra, 31
Sumeru, 154
Sun, 136, 160
Surabhi, 79
Surin, 272
Surpanaka, 76
Suryagiri, 174
Suryaparvata, 174
Suryavarmadeva, 43
Suryavarman, 35, 35c, 36, 38, 41, 55, 115, 132, 172c, 174, 175, 175c, 270, 281
Suryavarman II, 41, 55, 72c, 92c, 97, 103, 194c, 195, 196, 198, 200, 200c, 209, 213, 214, 216, 217, 221c, 265, 270, 274, 277, 283, 284
Syam, 47
Sydney, 119c

**T**

Ta Keo, 35, 55, 141, 142c, 172, 172c
Ta Muen Thom, 272, 273
Ta Muen Toch, 273
Ta Nei, 45, 55
Ta Som, 45, 55, 247, 256, 260, 261c
Ta Prohm, 45, 55, 247, 248c, 250c, 251, 251c, 252, 252c, 253c, 254, 254c, 255, 255c, 259, 260
Tambralinga, 35, 38, 44, 47
Tara, 90, 92c
Tataka, 78
Thai, 31, 47, 55, 266, 280c
Thailand, 11, 28, 29, 32, 36, 38, 41, 47, 48, 55, 57, 110, 265c, 272c, 279, 280c, 284
Thanesar, 75
Thommanon, 55, 194c, 195, 196
Thomson, John, 57
Thorel, Clovis, 57
Tibet, 82, 102
Tilaka, 41
Timur Khan, 20, 47, 55
Tonlé Sap, 21, 28, 41, 43, 50, 102, 236c
Tribhuvanadityavarman, 55
Tuol Kamnap, 31c
Tuol Kuhea, 118
Tuol Neak Ta Bak Ka, 20c
Tuol Pheak Kin, 25c
Tuol Ta Hoy, 27c
Trapang Phong, 29c
Trailokyanatha, 167c
Tribhuvanaditya, 259
Tribhuvanadityavarman, 41, 179, 188
Tribhuvanavarmeshvara, 259
Trocadero, 57
Trouvé, Georges Alexandre, 58
Tumburu, 66, 93
Tvashtar, 160c

**U**

Ubon, 32, 55
Udayadityavarman I, 35, 55
Udayadityavarman II, 36c, 38, 55, 103, 132, 175, 176c, 272
Udayana, 35
Umamaheshvara, 67c

**V**

Vagishvari Bhagavati, 41
Vairocana, 90
Vajrapani, 90
Valin, 78
Valmiki, 76
Vamana, 166
van Stein-Callenfels, 58

Vanara, 78c
Varuna, 68, 213
Vasuki, 79, 136, 288c
Venus, 136
Vidyanandana, 43
Vientiane, 44
Vietnam, 25, 26, 28, 38, 50
Vietnamese, 98
Vijaya, 28, 41, 43, 47
Vijayendralakshmi, 41
Vimayapura, 277
Viradha, 78
Viravarman, 28
Vishnu, 8c, 12c, 23c, 24, 26, 28, 29, 29c, 32, 35c, 36c, 38, 38c, 62c, 66, 67c, 68, 69c, 72, 75c, 76, 77c, 78, 79, 94c, 97, 101, 103c, 107, 117, 118, 118c, 121, 123, 123c, 124c, 126, 127, 127c, 129, 129c, 136, 140, 154, 157, 160, 165, 166, 166c, 167c, 175, 180, 188, 190c, 193c, 196, 199, 200, 208, 213, 216, 220, 259, 275, 288c
Vishnukumara, 182
Vishnuloka, 32
Vishvakarman, 201
Vishvarupa, 171
Vrah Vishnuloka, 200
Vrindavan, 184c
Vyadhapura, 26, 31, 32, 50
Vyasa, 62, 75, 76

**W**

Wat Baset, 38, 50c
Wat Ek, 38
Wat Mahatat, 280c, 281
Wat Na Phra Men, 81c
Wat Phu, 28, 55, 110, 148, 165, **282-289**

**Y**

Yajnavaraha, 55
Yama, 72c, 214, 216, 244
Yamuna, 141c
Yangtse Kiang, 47
Yashodhara, 32
Yashodharapura, 32, 35, 36, 41, 43, 55, 103, 148, 162c, 163, 165, 166, 171, 172, 174, 175, 179, 201, 208, 209
Yashodharatataka, 32, 103, 163
Yashodhareshvara, 32, 163
Yashovarman I, 31, 32, 35, 55, 103, 154c, 160, 162c, 163, 165, 165c, 284
Yashovarman II, 41, 55, 196, 259
Yajnavaraha, 35, 35c, 92, **182-194**
Yogishvarapandita, 36, 172c
Yunnan, 31, 44, 47

# BIBLIOGRAPHY

*A l'ombre d'Angkor. Le Cambodge années vingt*, Musée Albert Khan, Paris 1992

*Angkor et dix siècles d'art khmer*, Catalogue de l'exposition à la Galerie Nationale du Grand Palais, Réunion des Musées Nationaux, Paris January/May 1997

*Angkor: L'art khmer au Cambodge et en Thailande*, in "Dossiers Histoire et Archeologie", March 1988, Dijon

Auboyer J.: *Les Arts de l'Inde et des pays indianisés. Les neuf muses*, PUF, Paris, 1968

Béguin G: *L'Inde et le monde indianisé*, "Réunion des Musées Nationaux", Paris, 1992

Boisselier J.: *Tendances de l'art khmer*, Musée Guimet, Paris, 1956

Boisselier J.: *La statuaire khmere et son èvolution*, Pub. de l' EFEO, vol. XXXVII, 2 tomes, Saigon, 1955

Boisselier J.: *Le Cambodge*, in "Manuel d'archéologie d'Extrême Orient, Asie du sud-est, Tome I", Picard et C., Paris 1966

Briggs L. P.: *The Ancient Khmer Empire*, White Lotus, Bangkok, 1999

Chandler D. P.: *A History of Cambodia*, Westview Press, Boulder, Colorado, 1983

Chou Ta-Kuau: *The Customs of Cambodia*, The Siam Society, Bangkok, 1992

Coedès G.: *Un grand roi du Cambodge: Jayavarman VII*, Phnom Penh, 1935

Coedès G.: *Les Etats hindouisés d'Indochine et d'Indonésie*, Boccard, Paris,1964

Coedès G.: *Inscriptions du Cambodge*, 8 volumes, EFEO, Hanoi et Paris, 1937-1966

Coedès G.: *Pour mieux comprendre Angkor*, ed. A. Maisonneuve, Paris, 1947

Coedès G.: *Angkor, an introduction*, Oxford University Press, London, 1963

Comaille J.: *Guide aux Ruines d'Angkor*, ed. Hachette, Paris, 1912

(de) Coral-Rémusat G.: *L'art khmer. Les grandes ètapes de son èvolution*, Vanoest Editions d'art et d'histoire, Paris, 1951

Dagens B.: *Angkor. La foresta di pietra*, ed. Electa/Gallimard, Trieste 1995

Dauphin-Meunier A.: *Histoire du Cambodge*, PUF., Paris, 1968

Dumarçay J.: *Phnom Bakheng. Etude architecturale du temple*, EFEO, Paris, 1971

Dupont P.: *La statuaire préangkorienne*, Artibus Asiae, Ascona, 1955

Filliozat J.: *Le symbolisme du monument du Phnom Bakheng*, in BEFEO, XLIV, 1954

Finot L., Goloubew V., Coedès G.: *Le temple d'Içvarapura (Banteay Srei)*, EFEO, Paris, 1926

Finot L., Goloubew V., Coedès G.: *Le temple d'Angkor Vat*, EFEO, Paris, 1927-1933

Frédéric L.: *La Vie quotidienne dans la péninsule indochinoise à l'époque d'Angkor (800-1300)*, ed. Hachette, Biarritz, 1981

Freeman M.: *Khmer temples in Thailand and Laos*, River Books Guide, Bangkok, 1996

Garnier P., Nafilyan G.: *L'art khmer en situation de réserve*, Editions Européennes Marseille, 1997

Giteau M.: *Histoire de Cambodge*, Didier, Paris, 1957

Giteau M.: *Histoire d'Angkor*, Que sais-je?, Paris, 1974

Giteau M.: *I Khmer. Sculture khmer e la civiltà d'Angkor*, Silvana, Milan 1965

Glaize M.: *Le guide d'Angkor: les monuments du groupe d'Angkor*, Maisonneuve, Paris, 1963

Groslier B. P.: *Introduction to the Ceramic Wares of Angkor*, in "Khmer Ceramics 9th-14th Century", Southeast Asian Ceramic Society, Singapour, 1981.

Groslier B. P.: *Angkor. Hommes et pierres*, Arthaud, Paris,1968.

Groslier B. P.: *Archéologie d'un empire agricole. La cité idraulique angkorienne*, in "Le Grand Atlas Universalis de l'archéologie", 1985

Groslier B. P.: *Indocina*, in "Il Marcopolo", Il Saggiatore, Milan 1961

Guillon E.: *Cham Art*, River Books, Bangkok 2001

Istituto per la cooperazione allo sviluppo (a cura): *Cambogia. Terra dell'acqua e del riso*, Alessandria 1993

Jacques C.: *Angkor*, Bordas, Paris, 1990.

Jacques C., Freeman M.: *Angkor, cité khmer*, River Books Guide, Bangkok, 2000

Le Bonheur A.: *Cambodge, Angkor, temples en péril*, Herscher, Paris, 1989.

Le Bonheur A.: *Art khmer*, RMN, "Petits guides des grands musées" n. 60, Paris, 1986

Leclère A.: *Cambodge. Contes, legendes & Jataka*, Centre de Documentation et de recherche sur la civilisation khmere, Paris 1984

Lunet de Lajonquière: *Inventaire descriptif des monuments du Cambodge*, EFEO vol. IV, VIII et IX, Leroux, Paris, 1902-1911

MacDonald M.: *Angkor and the khmers*, Oxford University Press, 1990.

Malleret L.: *L'archeologie du delta du Mékong*, EFEO, XLIII, 4 vol., Paris, 1959-1963

Malleret L.: *Pour comprendre la statuaire bouddique et brahmanique en Indochine*, Portail, Saigon, 1942

Marchal H.: *Nouveau Guide d'Angkor*, Phnom Penh, 1961

Marchal H.: *Les Temples d'Angkor*, Guillot, Paris, 1955

Mazzeo D. e Silvi Antonini C.: *Civiltà khmer*, in "Le grandi civiltà", Mondadori, Milan 1972

Mus P.: "*Les symbolisme à Angkor Thom: le grand miracle du Bayon*", in Comptes rendus de l'Académie des Inscriptions et Belles Lettres, 1936

Nafilyan G.: *Angkor Vat. Description grafique du temple*, EFEO, Paris, 1969

Parmentier H.: *Angkor*, Portail, Saigon, 1950

Pichard P.: *Pimay. Etude architecturale du temple*, EFEO, Paris, 1976

Rooney D.: *Khmer Ceramics*, Oxford University Press, Kuala Lumpur, 1984

Roveda V.: *Khmer Mythology. Secrets of Angkor*, River Books, Bangkok, 1997

Sahai S.: *Les istitutions politiques et l'organisation administrative du Cambodge ancien (VI-XIII sec.)*, EFEO, LXXV, Paris, 1970

Stern P.: *Les monuments du style khmer du Bayon et Jayavarman VII*, Paris, 1965

Stern P.: *Le Bayon d'Angkor et l'évolution de l'art khmer*, Annales du musée, Bibl. de vulgarisation, t. 47, Librairie orientaliste P. Geuthner, Paris, 1927

Stierlin H.: *Angkor*, Architecture Universelle, Office du Livre, Fribourg, 1970

Stierlin H.: *Le monde d'Angkor*, Princesse, Paris, 1979

Thierry S.: *Les Khmer*, Le Seuil, Paris, 1964

Vann Molyvann: *Les cités khmer anciennes*, Toyota Foundation, Phnom Penh, 1999

Zéphir T.: *Khmer. Lost empire of Cambodia*, Thames and Hudson, Londra 1998

Zimmer H.: *The art of Indian Asia*, 2 vol., Bollingen Series XXXIX, Bollingen Foundation, New York, 1960.

# PHOTOGRAPHIC CREDITS

All the pictures are by Livio Bourbon/Archivio White Star, except for the following:

*Beginning*
page 3 **Erich Lessing**
pages 4-5 **Michael Freeman**
pages 6-7 **Michael Freeman**
page 8 **Luca Tettoni Photography**

*Preface*
page 10 **RMN/Richard Lambert**

*The History of Kambuja*
page 21 **Luca Tettoni Photography**
page 22 **Collezione Privata**

*Funan and the Mountain Kings*
pages 23 and 50 right **Erich Lessing/Contrasto**
page 24 **Erich Lessing/Contrasto**
page 25 top **Luca Tettoni Photography**
page 25 bottom **Erich Lessing/Contrasto**
page 26 **Luca Tettoni Photography**
page 27 **RMN/John Goldings**

*Chenla and the Advent of the Khmer*
pages 29 and 50 right **Luca Tettoni Photography**
page 30 left **RMN/John Goldings**
page 30 right **RMN/John Goldings**
page 31 left **Luca Tettoni Photography**
page 31 right **RMN/John Goldings**

*Angkor, Plain of Capitals*
page 33 **Collezione Privata**
pages 34 left and 55 left **Erich Lessing/Contrasto**
page 34 right **RMN/Richard Lambert**

*An ever-expanding Empire*
page 36-37 **Erich Lessing/Contrasto**
pages 38 and 55 center **RMN/John Goldings**
page 39 **Erich Lessing/Contrasto**
page 40 **Luca Tettoni Photography**

*Buddha, the Supreme lord*
page 42 **RMN/John Goldings**
page 43 **RMN/John Goldings**
page 44 left **Erich Lessing/Contrasto**
page 44 right and 55 right **Erich Lessing/Contrasto**
page 45 **RMN**
page 46 **Luca Tettoni Photography**
page 48-49 **RMN/Richard lambert**
page 51-54 **Erich Lessing/Contrasto**

*The Rediscovery of Angkor*
page 56-57 **Archivio White Star**
page 58 **Archivio White Star**
page 58-59 **Archivio White Star**

*The Religious World*
page 62 **Collezione Privata**
page 63 **RMN/Thierry Ollivier**
page 64-65 **RMN/Thierry Ollivier**
page 66 left **RMN/Thierry Ollivier**
page 66 right **RMN/John Goldings**
page 67 **RMN/John Goldings**
page 68 left **RMN/John Goldings**
page 68 right **Erich Lessing/Contrasto**
page 69 **RMN/John Goldings**
page 70 **Michael Freeman**
page 71 **Michael Freeman**
page 72 **Michael Freeman**
page 73 **Michael Freeman**

*The Great Myths*
page 74-75 **Michael Freeman**
page 77 **Erich Lessing/Contrasto**

*The Paths of the Enlighened One*
page 80 **Michael Freeman**
page 81 **Luca Tettoni Photography**
page 82 **Luca Tettoni Photography**
page 83 **Luca Tettoni Photography**
page 84 **RMN/John Goldings**
page 85 **Michael Freeman**
page 86 **Luca Tettoni Photography**
page 87 **Luca Tettoni Photography**
page 88 **Erich Lessing/Contrasto**
page 89 **RMN/John Goldings**
page 90 **RMN/John Goldings**
page 91 **RMN/John Goldings**

*The King and Society*
page 92 **RMN/Michel Urtado**
page 92-93 **RMN/Michel Urtado**
page 94 **RMN/John Goldings**
page 95 **RMN/John Goldings**
page 96-97 **Michael Freeman**
page 98-99 bottom **RMN/Richard Lambert**

*The Hydraulic City*
page 102-103 **RMN/John Goldings**

*Everyday Life*
page 105 left **Luca Tettoni Photography**
page 105 right **Luca Tettoni Photography**
page 106 **RMN/John Goldings**
page 109 **Luca Tettoni Photography**

*Clothing*
page 112 left **The British Museum**
page 112 right **Collezione Privata**

page 113 **Collezione Privata**
page 114 **RMN/John Goldings**
page 117 left **Renzo freschi Oriental Art**
page 117 right **Renzo freschi Oriental Art**

*Sculpture*
page 118 **Michael Freeman**
page 119 left **John Eskenazi**
page 119 right **Erich Lessing/Contrasto**
page 120 **RMN/John Goldings**
page 121 **RMN/Richard Lambert**
page 122 **RMN/Michel Urtado**
page 123 **Luca Tettoni Photography**
page 124 **RMN/Thierry Ollivier**
page 125 **Luca Tettoni Photography**
page 126 **RMN/John Goldings**
page 127 **Luca Tettoni Photography**
page 128 **Erich Lessing/Contrasto**
page 129 left **RMN/Thierry Ollivier**
page 129 right **RMN/John Goldings**
page 130 left **RMN/Michel Urtado**
page 130 right **Renzo Freschi Oriental Art**
page 131 **RMN/John Goldings**
page 132 bottom **RMN/John Goldings**
page 134 top **RMN/John Goldings**
page 134 bottom **RMN/John Goldings**

*Celestial Dwellings*
page 135 **Michael Freemann**
page 136 left **Michael Freemann**
page 137 right **Erich Lessing/Contrasto**
page 138 **RMN/John Goldings**
page 139 left **Erich Lessing/Contrasto**
page 139 right **Erich Lessing/Contrasto**
page 140 top **RMN/Michel Urtado**
page 140 bottom **Renzo freschi Oriental Art**
page 140-141 **Erich Lessing/Contrasto**
page 142-143 **Ecole Nazionale Superieure des beaux arts, Paris**

*Archaeological Itineraries Contents*
page 147 **Archivio White Star**

*Angkor: the Mountain Temples of Yashodharapura*
page 162 right **Michael Freeman**
page 167 center right **Luca Tettoni Photography**

*Angkor Vat: the Stable of the Celestial Oxen*

page 200 **Luca Tettoni Photography**
page 202 **Michael Freeman**
page 203-206 **Luca Tettoni Photography**
page 207 **Michael Freeman**
page 210-211 **Michael Freeman**
page 220 top **Erich Lessing/Contrasto**
page 220-221 **Michael Freeman**

*Angkor Thom: the City Protected by the Gods*
page 226-227 **Luca Tettoni Photography**
page 230 **Steve McCurry/Magnum/Contrasto**
page 232-233 **Luca Tettoni Photography**
page 244 **Luca Tettoni Photography**
page 245 bottom **Luca Tettoni Photography**

*From Angkor Thom to Phimai, Stages on the Royal Route*
page 272 top **Michael Freeman**
page 272 center left **Michael Freeman**
page 272 center right **Michael Freeman**
page 272-273 **Michael Freeman**
page 274 top **Michael Freeman**
page 274 center **Michael Freeman**
page 274-275 **Michael Freeman**
page 280 top **Erich Lessing/Contrasto**
page 281 top **Michael Freeman**

*Vat Phu and Preah Vihear: the Dwellings of Shiva*
page 283 top **Michael Freeman**
page 283 center **Michael Freeman**

Map page 16-17 by **Elisabetta Ferrero/Archivio White Star**

Temple maps by **Angelo Colombo/Archivio White Star**

**Cover**
Khmer sculpture of Hari Hara, Phnom-Da style, 6th century AD.
© *Alfredo Dagli Orti/The Art Archive/Corbis*

**Back Cover**
Face representing Lokeshvara, tower of the Bayon temple built by Jayavarman VII.
© *Livio Bourbon/Archivio White Star*